WOMEN, THEIR LIVES, AND THE LAW

This collection of essays honours Rosemary Auchmuty, Professor of Law at the University of Reading, UK. She has fostered the study of women's legal careers and, more politically, advanced progress on gender and equality issues including same-sex marriage and property law. Her research promotes the case of feminist legal history as a way of revealing the place of women and challenging dominant historical narratives that cast them aside.

Just as Rosemary's work does, the book seeks to end the marginalisation and exclusion of women in the legal world, by including them. The book begins fittingly with a discussion of Miss Bebb, the woman whose biography Auchmuty deployed to push feminist legal history into the mainstream. It turns then to a discussion of women known and unknown and their struggles within the legal profession, offering within those chapters a critical appraisal of the role of history and biography as a methodology. From there it moves to consider feminist perspectives and critiques of the dominant structures of private law. This is followed by chapters that explore those who educate the legal profession within the academy. The chapters, and the collection as a whole, examine areas of law that have a deep significance for women's lives.

Women, Their Lives, and the Law

Essays in Honour of Rosemary Auchmuty

Edited by
Victoria Barnes
Nora Honkala
and
Sally Wheeler

•HART•
OXFORD • LONDON • NEW YORK • NEW DELHI • SYDNEY

HART PUBLISHING

Bloomsbury Publishing Plc

Kemp House, Chawley Park, Cumnor Hill, Oxford, OX2 9PH, UK

1385 Broadway, New York, NY 10018, USA

29 Earlsfort Terrace, Dublin 2, Ireland

First published in Great Britain 2023

A catalogue record for this book is available from the British Library.

A catalogue record for this book is available from the Library of Congress.

Library of Congress Control Number: 2023943768

ISBN: HB: 978-1-50996-208-2
ePDF: 978-1-50996-210-5
ePub: 978-1-50996-209-9

Typeset by Compuscript Ltd, Shannon

PREFACE

Books written as a *Festschrift* are a distinct type of literature. In the German tradition, from which the scholarship originates, a *Festschrift* is given to an eminent scholar as a birthday present. It is an edited collection with chapters written by scholars over the age of 30. Authors are usually former students, now proficient and well-known in their field, colleagues or close friends of the scholar being celebrated. The model has been taken up across the common law world. Rather than being seen as the 'graveyard' of scholarship, *Festschriften* (or sometimes *festschrifts*) are viewed as vibrant places where cutting edge research by seasoned legal scholars appears. This *Festschrift* is no different.

Rosemary Auchmuty is an academic lawyer, who turned 70 in 2020, with an esteemed body of scholarship and a set of professional accolades. She is worthy of such recognition and celebration. She is – and has been since 2007 – a Professor in the School of Law at the University of Reading, UK. Her scholarly career is prolific: she has researched a broad range of subjects from a range of interdisciplinary and international perspectives, due to her transnational background. Above all, Rosemary is an educationalist, who has sought to build, enhance and help in improving the training of others. In this guise, she has also mentored individuals and led initiatives in teaching and education, both locally and nationally. Aside from her extensive activities in teaching and learning, Rosemary took on prestigious roles to oversee the development of legal scholarship, including sitting as a member of the national sub-panel for Law in the 2014 REF. Since then, she has continued to share her knowledge of the process providing many training sessions in both Reading and universities elsewhere in the UK.

In terms of an 'official' biography, Rosemary was born in 1950 and grew up in Newcastle, a port city in New South Wales, Australia. She began her academic career in Australia, by training as a historian. Her PhD, undertaken at Australian National University and supervised by Manning Clark, was in history; it focused on spinsters in Victorian Britain. Rosemary drew upon on issues surrounding marriage, womanhood and employment and has written widely covering women's studies as well as children's literature. In particular, Rosemary was interested in girls' school stories and she has written three books on this subject: *Australia's Daughters* (Sydney: Methuen, 1978), *A World of Girls: The Appeal of the Girls' School Story* (London: The Women's Press, 1992, 2nd edn 2004) and *A World of Women: growing up in the girls' school story* (London: The Women's Press, 1999, 2nd edn 2008). She also co-edited the 2-volume *Encyclopaedia of School Stories* (Aldershot: Ashgate, 2000) and has written several entries for the *Oxford Encyclopedia of Children's Literature* (2006). Her work has also contributed to the world of theatre on several occasions. In 2015, for example, she provided the programme note for a musical called *Crush!*, which was based loosely on the school-story tradition.

She turned to law and legal studies as her education focus later in her academic career, when she moved to the UK. It was in the UK that Rosemary's research began to focus explicitly on law. She was able to combine her knowledge of women's history and interest in education with property law. She is a pioneer of women's legal studies and feminist legal studies in higher education. She has written numerous articles on feminist approaches to property law, marriage, sexuality and legal history, and contributed several entries to the the *Oxford Dictionary of National Biography* (2004).

Rosemary's work on the legal biography of Gwyneth Bebb,[1] a woman who campaigned to open the legal profession to women in the UK, is possibly her seminal work. Although that label should properly be applied by her rather than us, *Miss Bebb* is, in our view, the contribution that pushed legal feminist biography as a methodology into the mainstream of legal research. It inspired a play featuring a cast of West End performers and retired judges including Lady Hale; it was performed in London, Birmingham, as well as by Reading staff and students at University of Reading.[2] This scholarship adds to her efforts to uncover the lost lives of the first women lawyers[3] and law students.[4] Her edited collection *Great Debates in Gender and Law*[5] was the first (and so far only) textbook that pushed gender into all facets of the law curriculum. More recently, she has begun promoting the cause of Feminist Legal History[6] as a way of revealing the place of women and challenging and revising dominant historical narratives that cast them aside. She co-edited *Women's Legal Landmarks: Celebrating the History of Women and Law in the UK and Ireland* with Erika Rackley.[7] Through this project, Rosemary and Erika brought together around 100 feminist academics, historians, activists and legal practitioners to investigate key legal landmarks and to commemorate the centenary of women's admission into the legal profession. With her work on the recent edited collection *Gender and Careers in the Legal Academy*,[8] Rosemary

[1] R Auchmuty, 'Men Behaving Badly: An analysis of undue influence cases"(2002) 11 *Social and Legal Studies* 257–82.

[2] 'The Disappearance of Miss Bebb, by Alex Giles' (The Kalisher Trust), available at www.thekalishertrust.org/theatre-events/past-productions/disappearance-miss-bebb-alex-giles.

[3] R Auchmuty: 'Recovering lost lives: researching women in legal history' (2015) 42(1) *Journal of Law and Society* 34–52.

[4] R Auchmuty, 'Early women law students at Cambridge and Oxford' (2008) 29(1) *Journal of Legal History* 63–97.

[5] R Auchmuty (ed), *Great debates in gender and law* (Red Globe Press, 2018).

[6] E Rackley and R Auchmuty, 'The case for feminist legal history' (2020) 40 *Oxford Journal of Legal Studies* 878–904, and R Auchmuty and E Rackley, 'Feminist legal biography: a model for all legal life stories' (2020) 41 *Journal of Legal History* 186–211.

[7] E Rackley and R Auchmuty, *Women's Legal Landmarks: Celebrating the History of Women and Law in the UK and Ireland* (Hart, 2018).

[8] U Schultz, G Shaw, M Thornton and R Auchmuty (eds), *Gender and Careers in the Legal Academy* (Hart, 2021).

remains committed to fostering the study of women's academic careers and, more politically, in advancing progress on gender and equality issues.

This book speaks directly to those aims. Those honoured by *Festschriften*, and celebrated by this scholarship, are those at the top of their profession. They are, by the very nature of this scholarship, insiders, who fit within the existing dominant social group. One notes, rather quickly, a dearth of women, who are recognised in this body of literature. This lack of recognition reflects the few numbers of women at the top of the legal academy, but it also serves to perpetuate existing trends. This project does not hold Rosemary up as a role model or heroine, but it seeks to end the marginalisation and exclusion of women in the legal world by including them, where appropriate, in this body of scholarship.

We held a workshop for contributors at Warwick University on 19 and 20 July 2022 jointly funded by the generosity of the Australian National University and the Max Planck Institute. There we discussed our chapters and exchanged ideas. We were pleased to have Rosemary there to listen to colleagues, and each also shared their individual stories of how Rosemary had been a mentor to them in their careers or how Rosemary and her work had made an impact on them. People had vivid memories of how Rosemary had assisted them whether through her advice or providing opportunities for professional experiences and it was clear how for each contributor Rosemary and her work holds a special place in their professional lives.

This collection brings together a group of early career and very well-established scholars each of whom has their own meaningful relationship with Rosemary. Descriptions of many of these relationships feature in the volume's chapters leading to successive retellings of Rosemary's life and the influence of her scholarship, proving as if we needed it to, that returning to original sources and contexts provides a richer picture than relying on 'official' accounts. Each of the chapters in this book tell a little more about those personal experiences in the authors' own words, sometimes at the beginning of the chapters and sometimes weaved within the chapters. Our contributors are drawn exclusively from law schools but a broad spectrum of law scholars and all the contributors would see themselves writing in the socio-legal or 'law and' tradition.[9] The chapters themselves are organised according to three main themes found in Rosemary's work: (1) Legal Biographies, (2) Feminist Approaches to Contract, Property and Equity Law, and (3) Legal Education and Legal Profession.

[9] S Wheeler, 'Socio-Legal Studies in 2020' (2020) 47 *Journal of Law and Society* 209–26.

TABLE OF CONTENTS

CONTRIBUTORS

Dr Victoria Barnes is Reader of Commercial Law at Queen's University Belfast.

Judith Bourne is Professor of English Law at St Mary's University, Twickenham.

Susan B Boyd, F.R.S.C. is Professor Emerita at the Peter A. Allard School of Law, University of British Columbia.

Dr Marie Burton is a Senior Research Fellow at the Centre for Socio-Legal Studies, Oxford University. Marie is a former Law Centre solicitor and senior policy analyst.

Fiona Cownie FAcSS, FRSA, PFHEA is Senior Associate Research Fellow, Institute of Advanced Legal Studies, University of London.

Dr Caroline Derry is Senior Lecturer in Law at the Open University.

Alison Diduck is Professor of Law at UCL, London.

Dr Nora Honkala is a Lecturer in Law at University of Reading.

Rosemary Hunter KC (Hon), FAcSS is Professor of Law and Socio-Legal Studies and Head of the Law School at the University of Kent.

Felicity Kaganas is Professor of Law at Brunel Law School, Brunel University, London.

Linda Mulcahy is the Statutory Chair of Socio-Legal Studies, Oxford University and the Director of the Centre for Socio-Legal Studies. She is a Visiting professor at ANU College of Law.

Dr Harriet Samuels is Reader in Law at Westminster Law School, University of Westminster.

Ulrike Schultz is a Retired Senior Academic, FernUniversität in Hagen, Germany.

Dr Sharon Thompson is Reader in Law at Cardiff University and is a Fellow of the Royal Historical Society.

Lisa Webley is Professor of Law at the University of Birmingham. She holds a Chair in Legal Education and Research.

Sally Wheeler OBE, MRIA, FAcSS is Deputy Vice Chancellor (International and Corporate) at the Australian National University. She holds the Chair of Law, Business and Society in the ANU College of Law.

Claire FL Young is Professor Emerita at the Peter A. Allard School of Law, University of British Columbia.

1

The Recovery of a Rising Star: Miss Bebb – Broken Biography

JUDITH BOURNE

Introduction

Many Law students consider Property Law the bane of their undergraduate life, but they were not taught by Rosemary Auchmuty – as I was. Those lectures, given in a dreary basement underneath High Holborn, educated me in Land Law and Equity and Trusts Law and opened my eyes to the sex inequality considered 'normal' in both the law and my everyday life. She founded my feminism; that feminism has shaped my life and informed my teaching and learning ever since.

Most significantly for me, Rosemary (and Graham Robson) gave me my first academic job as a part-time lecturer in Land Law at the University of Westminster. This was perhaps the lowest and most hopeless time of my life because I was fighting a sex discrimination case in the industrial tribunal; I would go on to win the sexual harassment part of the case, but lose on my right to wear a trouser suit in the workplace. I felt unemployable (no smoke without fire etc), but Rosemary quite literally 'dusted me down' and put me back on my feet; she not only believed in me, but she trusted me and set me on the path, not just of recovery, but of what has been an extremely rewarding career for the past 26 years. When I began my litigation, it was a mission for justice and principle, but it was an appalling experience, a nasty and destructive process: *I* was on trial, not my harasser. The tactics used by my former employer were, and still are, fairly typical, attempting to portray me as deviant (sexually and morally) and unsuitable for the workplace. Rosemary dissected forensically what was happening in my case from a feminist perspective. She called out the sexist stereotypes and championed my cause. Life would have been very difficult without her support. Any vote of thanks I write here will be insufficient to express my gratitude to her.

Fifteen years later, whilst I was writing my thesis on Helena Normanton,[1] Rosemary published her article on Gwyneth Bebb.[2] This was a defining moment in the study and recording of feminist legal history biography in England – it went 'mainstream'. Rosemary cemented both feminist biography in legal academia and its importance.[3] Prior to her article, legal biography was either confined to recording the lives of male lawyers, or to women's history studies. Rosemary's work placed at the forefront the importance of understanding the past in order to explain the present and was seminal to the legal profession's equality debate of the 2010s:

> [T]he formal entry of women ushered in a prolonged reaction of institutional sexism and discrimination that have still not been wholly eradicated.[4]

In Rosemary's article, Bebb was transformed from a footnote in history into a relevant, contextualised life.[5] Rosemary rediscovered Bebb, a forgotten woman in the archives, and alongside her the lives of other long overlooked first women lawyers. This article thrust into life the struggle for women's entry to the profession and challenged traditional historiography that characterised the Sex Disqualification (Removal) Act as a kindness bestowed on women in thanks for their war effort.

Rosemary's article was indeed ground-breaking, but it – and most subsequent work on first women lawyers (and suffrage) – failed to acknowledge (and celebrate) the role of 'sympathetic' men in this history.[6] Without supportive men, the struggle to enter the legal profession would have taken much longer to realise, or perhaps would not have been achieved. This chapter will explore and cognise the part of the men in this history whom Rosemary mentioned in passing in her article, and it will examine why they have been ignored.

[1] For a brief summary of Normanton's life see: J Workman, 'Normanton, Helena Florence (1882–1957), Barrister and Feminist Campaigner' in *Oxford Dictionary of National Biography* (hereafter DNB) (DNB, 2004); for a fuller history see J Bourne, *Helena Normanton and the Opening of the Bar to Women* (Hook Waterside Press, 2016).

[2] R Auchmuty, 'Whatever Happened to Miss Bebb? *Bebb v The Law Society* and Women's Legal History' (2011) 31 *Legal Studies* 199.

[3] R Auchmuty, 'Recovering Lost Lives: Researching Women in Legal History' (2015) 42 *Journal of Law and Society* 34 and R Auchmuty and E Rackley, 'Feminist Legal Biography: A Model for All Legal Life Stories' (2020) 41 *Journal of Legal History* 186.

[4] Auchmuty (n 2) 2.

[5] Other authors have also attempted to contextualise women's lives, for example see: F Cownie, *Legal Academics: Culture and Identities* (Hart 2004) and F Cownie, 'The United Kingdom's First Woman Law Professor: An Archerian Analysis' (2015) 42 *Journal of Law and Society* 127.

[6] As commented on by A John 'Between Cause and the Courts: The Curious Case of Cecil Chapman' in C Eustance, J Ryan and L Ugolini (eds), *Suffrage Reader, Charting Directions in British Suffrage History* (Bloomsbury, 2000) 145.

'Whatever Happened to Miss Bebb? *Bebb v The Law Society* and Women's Legal History'[7]

Rosemary's article examined the lack of or little attention given to Bebb's campaign to open the solicitors' profession to women in 1914.[8] It shone a spotlight on Bebb's life in order to examine and contextualise the struggle women had experienced in trying to qualify as lawyers in the early 1900s and before. The article concluded that Bebb's disappearance from history was due partly to the circumstances of her life (she died before she was called to the Bar), but mainly to:

> [T]he tendency of institutional histories, if they acknowledge women's contribution at all, to present it as a simple (though discontinuous) tale of progress, thereby masking continuing prejudice and inequality.[9]

The rediscovery of the life story of Bebb – a woman who had disappeared from history – Rosemary argued, provided role models for students[10] and challenged the 'dehumanised objectivity' central to lawyers' training.

For this article, Rosemary had successfully pieced together Bebb's biography, beginning with her childhood in Oxford,[11] her later schooling in London and university life in Oxford at St Hugh's Hall, through to her trial and subsequent death.[12] In the process, Rosemary researched Oxford life during that period, for example, how women's colleges did not have their own tutors, but rather the students having to negotiate with selected men's colleges for the use of theirs and what Bebb's study of Jurisprudence would have involved. This resurrected Bebb from a lifeless reference to a living woman. Although Jurisprudence was unprecedently popular at that time for men, Bebb was only the seventh woman to embark on such a degree. Moreover, Rosemary concluded that, while the Law was a lucrative occupation for men, it did not have a career path for women, as they were barred from entering the legal profession. Thus, for women who needed to work after graduation, there was little point to this degree. However, Rosemary produced evidence that Bebb had read Law in order to qualify and therefore prove opponents of women's entry to the legal profession wrong.[13] This was at a time when women were feeling optimistic because many feminist victories had been won in the closing decade of the nineteenth century and women were on the cusp of winning

[7] Auchmuty (n 2).

[8] For a report of Bebb's trial: *Bebb v The Law Society* [1914] 1 Ch 286; and for a summary of the campaign see: J Bourne, 'Gwyneth Bebb: The Past Explaining the Present' (*Law Society Gazette* 29 April 2019) www.lawgazette.co.uk/gwyneth-bebb-the-past-explaining-the-present/5070047.article.

[9] Auchmuty (n 2).

[10] For an exploration of role models, see C Derry, 'Ethel Bright Ashford: More or Less than a Role Model' (2000) 129 *Women's History Review* 615. See also Derry, this volume.

[11] Auchmuty (n 2) 201.

[12] ibid 202.

[13] ibid 204.

the vote.[14] Bebb passed her Law finals in 1911 with a first-class honours, the first woman at Oxford to achieve this, and began working as an investigating officer for the Board of Trade. This work was quasi-legal – she prosecuted employers in the sweated trades.[15]

The final part of Rosemary's article concentrates on 'what happened to Miss Bebb'. Pregnant with her second child, Bebb had suffered from placenta praevia, as a result of which she had a serious haemorrhage before the birth. The baby died, and Bebb experienced a post-partum haemorrhage, anaemia, thrombosis of the pelvic veins and a cardiac arrest, resulting in her death two months later on 9 October 1921.[16]

Rosemary concludes that Bebb disappeared for three reasons: her marriage and name change; her early death; and the conventions of legal scholarship and institutional histories. She acknowledges the problems of writing a history where the sources are 'patchy and elusive'.[17] But, the real issue, she argued, was that women were marginalised then and still are now. Traditional narratives paint institutions in the best possible light with feminist agency denied. However, Rosemary portrayed Bebb as both a symbol and instigator of change in that she not only achieved a personal but a political goal as well.

The main part of Rosemary's article is in retelling Bebb's case and her work to open up the solicitors' profession to women. Rosemary notes sympathetic (and often influential) men who assisted in the legal challenge to give women access to the legal profession: namely, Edward Bell, Lord Wolmer, Lord Robert Cecil and Jack Hills MP. Like Bebb, the role of these men has been underexplored, and they have not yet found their place in this history. Thus, by shining a spotlight on Bebb, we can lose the bigger picture. There is a broader story to be told – one of networks and connections,[18] ones that involve supportive men. The men were not always hostile or bystanders, and there is much to be done to put their lives and activity in this respect into context. This chapter fills this gap in the literature prompted by Rosemary's initial findings. It builds upon that work and does much to acknowledge men's involvement with the movement and provide a fuller account than has hitherto existed. Their work here was important. Indeed, the struggle of women to enter the legal profession would have taken much longer to realise without the help and support of men. In the final paragraph of her article, Rosemary speaks about 'the political tactics adopted by feminist legal reformers including alliances with

[14] ibid 211.

[15] 'Sweated trades' were industries that demanded long working hours, poor working conditions and low pay, mostly reliant on women workers. It is possible that she may have met Jack Hills MP during this work, as he was a leading figure in the National Anti-Sweating League and in 1908 brought forward a Private Members' bill on 'sweating' which anticipated the Liberal Government's Trade Boards Act of 1909. See E Green, 'Hills, John Waller (1867–1938), Politician and Angler' (DNB, 2004). Auchmuty does not make this connection.

[16] Auchmuty (n 2) 227–28.

[17] ibid 229.

[18] M Lobban and I Williams (eds), *Networks and Connections in Legal History* (CUP, 2020).

sympathetic men'.[19] This chapter adds to, and embellishes upon, Rosemary's final remark about the role of 'sympathetic' men in this history. In doing so, this chapter answers the question: who were these men?

Who were these Supportive Men, and What was Their Role?

Male Support During the Court of First Instance Trial

The *Bebb* trial was held on 1 July 1913 in the High Court, Royal Courts of Justice, the Strand, Central London. The presiding judge was Joyce J,[20] a man who had previously sat with other distinguished judges, in supposed objectivity, at Bertha Cave's House of Lords appeal against Gray's Inn's refusal to admit her in 1903.[21] Three other notable men were present in that courtroom to support Bebb: Edward Bell, Lord Buckmaster and Mr Withers. The least known about is Withers, Bebb's instructing solicitor.[22] Baptised at St John's Church, Yealand Conyers, in 1866, and educated at Cambridge University,[23] he became a partner in the London law firm, Withers Benson Birkett and Davies.[24] Given that solicitor Bell had proposed a motion to the Law Society in 1912 that it should accept women and abjectly failed,[25] the acceptance of Bebb's case was against established thinking and probably not recommended for career enhancement.

In the *Bebb* trial, Edward Bell gave evidence that he would accept Bebb as an articled clerk. It is unclear what motivated him to make that proposal to the Law Society in 1912 to admit women, or to offer Bebb a route to qualification, but it was certainly in the spirit of the suffragette conviction: 'deeds, not words'. He had joined his father's firm in 1893, Carter and Bell, Idol Lane, Cheapside.[26] Like Withers, little is known about him apart from some notable cases and bare professional facts. His short obituary in the *Solicitors Journal* states that he was admitted to the Roll of Solicitors in 1887 and died in 1944, aged 78.[27] One of his clients,

[19] Auchmuty (n 2) 230.

[20] H Hanbury and H Mooney, 'Joyce, Sir Matthew Ingle (1839–1930)' (DNB, 2004).

[21] Transcript held in the Middle Temple archives: MT3/MEM.

[22] 1854–1916: 'Obituary' in *The Planner, Journal of the Royal Town Planning Institute* Vol 2 (Royal Town Planning Institute, 1916) 179.

[23] ibid and J Venn (ed), *Alumni Cantabrigienses, A Biographical List of All Known Students, Graduates and Holders of Office at the University of Cambridge, from the Earliest Times to 1900* (CUP, 2011) 272.

[24] G Rycroft, 'A Forgotten Figure in the Garden City Movement' *Lancaster Guardian* (30 August 2015).

[25] Auchmuty (n 2) 212.

[26] See (1893) 28 *The Law Journal* 598. His father was Edward S Bell, and the firm was located at 6 Idol Lane, Eastcheap, London.

[27] See (1944) 88 *Solicitors Journal* 149.

Lord Douglas ('Bosie'),[28] commented that the firm had two names, when in fact Bell was the only partner.[29] However, this was because Bell was in fact the only surviving partner.[30] Described as an 'incorruptible solicitor', a tall, formidable man, with a strong face, and an expert in Common Law,[31] he seemed to attract notoriety. Besides his involvement in *Bebb*, he acted for Bosie, the lover of Oscar Wilde, when no other lawyer would. According to Bosie, Bell appreciated the 'Douglas fighting blood and spirit' and was willing to go on a 'fishing expedition', that is, requesting police files in the hope that something relevant would be found.[32] However, one defendant, on the opposite side to Bell, Horatio Bottomley,[33] sulkily described Bell's firm as the 'shady lawyers of Idol Lane', an interesting comment from a man who was convicted of fraud and subsequently had to resign as a Member of Parliament (MP) from the House of Commons. Even from this scant information we have the impression of Bell as a 'liberal', if not radical man, committed to justice and human rights.

The final notable supporting man in the *Bebb* trial (although there were presumably others) was Buckmaster,[34] Bebb's King's Counsel, a Lincoln's Inn Bencher and later Lord Chancellor.[35] Despite Bebb's co-plaintiff Lucy Nettlefold's exclamation of 'Ugh' at one of the KC's representations in the trial, Buckmaster was committed to opening the legal profession to women. This is demonstrated by his introduction of two bills to Parliament: the 1917 Solicitors' (Qualification of Women) bill[36] and, again in February 1919, the Barristers' and Solicitors' (Qualification of Women) bill. Both were supported by the women's movement.[37]

Buckmaster had won a junior studentship in mathematics at Christ Church, Oxford, in 1879. He was called to the Bar (Inner Temple) in 1894, joined the Midland circuit and developed a lucrative chancery practice which enabled him to take silk in 1902, the same year in which he joined Lincoln's Inn, where he came a Bencher in 1910 and Treasurer in 1934.

[28] G Cevasco, 'Douglas, Lord Alfred Bruce (1870–1945), Poet and Biographer' (DNB, 2004).

[29] L Lee, *Oscar's Ghost: The Battle for Oscar Wilde's Legacy* (Stroud Amberley, 2017).

[30] H Houston, *The Real Horatio Bottomley* (Hurst & Blackett, 1923) 142.

[31] A Hyman, *The Rise and Fall of Horatio Bottomley, The Biography of a Swindler* (Cassell, 1972) 97.

[32] Lee, *Oscar's Ghost* (n 29).

[33] Horatio Bottomley, a Member of the House of Commons, was convicted at the Old Bailey on 1 August 1922 of fraud and sentenced to seven years' penal servitude, see HC Deb 1 August 1922, vol 157, col 1286. hansard.parliament.uk/commons/1922-08-01/debates/28239328-d53e-4678-a874-5ee8142c8d1f/MrHoratioBottomleyExpelledTheHouse.

[34] W Goodhart, 'Buckmaster, Stanley Owen, First Viscount Buckmaster (1861–1934) Lord Chancellor' (DNB, 2004).

[35] May 1915–December 1916, Liberal, under Asquith's coalition Government.

[36] See 'Women and Law' *The International Suffrage News* (1 May 1917) 117, which noted that the bill passed the House of Lords without division. See also A Lentin, *The Last Political Law Lord, Lord Sumner (1859–1934)* (Cambridge Scholars Publishers, 2008) 60–80, 71, in which barrister, judge and Balliol College alumna, Lord Sumner gave his maiden speech in support of this bill. A Lentin, 'John Andrew, Viscount Sumner (1859–1934), Barrister and Judge' (DNB, 2004).

[37] Barristers and Solicitors (Qualification Of Women) Bill, HL Deb 26 February 1919, vol 33.

Buckmaster held contrary views to the establishment, which wanted to prevent women from entering the legal profession. Men such as Lord Halsbury, Lord Finlay and Lord Loreburn (all Lord Chancellors at some point) had argued that women should stay within the private sphere (ie the home) and that their admittance would threaten men's livelihoods.[38] Why did Buckmaster hold such opposite views? Answers to this may lie in his family circumstances. Buckmaster was from a non-traditional background: his father, John Buckmaster, began his working life as an agricultural labourer, at the tender age of 10, and later became a joiner. He advocated for law reform as a platform speaker against the Corn Laws.[39] Later qualifying as a teacher, John finally became a professor of chemistry. This social mobility enabled his son to excel and demonstrates the importance of a diverse profession in challenging traditional thinking, but it also highlights the transformative power of education. Buckmaster's background gave him a different perspective, one that was particularly helpful to women's position. He supported women both in public and in private – for example, his eldest daughter was Margaret Dighton Pollock, a social reformer and Labour Party activist. In 1924 she started a contraceptive clinic to assist women in controlling their reproductive rights. Her father attempted to support this initiative by introducing a bill for married women to acquire contraception funded by their local authority, however, like his bills to allow women to enter the legal profession, this too failed.[40]

'Failed' Legislators

Bebb's litigation was part of a wider movement to open the legal profession to women. Buckmaster was not the only supportive politician of this movement. There were others like Wolmer, Hills, Spoor and Cecil, all of whom attempted to introduce legislation that would allow women to enter the legal profession.

In 1912 Wolmer[41] introduced a Private Members' bill to admit women to the solicitors' profession, the Legal Profession (Admission of Women) Bill 1912.[42] Its purpose was clear: 'To enable Women to become barristers, solicitors, or Parliamentary agents.'[43] It was supported by Jack Hills MP,[44]

[38] Lentin, *The Last Political Law Lord* (n 36) 79.

[39] Goodhart (n 34).

[40] L Pollard, *Margery Spring Rice: Pioneer of Women's Health in the Early Twentieth Century* (Cambridge Open Book Publishers, 2020).

[41] M Foot, 'Palmer, Roundell Cecil, Third Earl of Selborne (1887–1971), Politician' (DNB, 2004).

[42] Legal Profession (Admission Of Women) Bill, HC Deb 9 July 1913, vol 55. hansard.parliament.uk/commons/1913-07-09/debates/0ae0830a-da37-48b9-b874-8c66cc473b91/LegalProfession(AdmissionOfWomen)Bill.

[43] HC Deb 10 April 1913, vol 51. hansard.parliament.uk/Commons/1913-04-10/debates/48ca4675-f69a-4a94-bd33-9914868f4f6c/LegalProfession(AdmissionOfWomen)Bill; and next debated HC Deb 9 July 1913, vol 55, col 426. hansard.parliament.uk/commons/1913-07-09/debates/0ae0830a-da37-48b9-b874-8c66cc473b91/LegalProfession(AdmissionOfWomen)Bill.

[44] Green (n 15).

Lord Cecil,[45] and also Charles Roberts, Murray Macdonald, and Sir Brynmor Jones. At the debate on 9 July 1913, Wolmer asked the then Prime Minister, Lord Asquith, whether his attention has been drawn to the decision in the case of *Bebb*, and whether he would grant facilities for the passage of the Legal Profession (Admission of Women) Bill? Asquith replied:

> I have seen the reports in the Press of this case. I fear I do not see my way to give facilities from Government time for the Bill referred to in the latter part of the question.[46]

It was no surprise when this bill was defeated.

Wolmer was Lord Wolmer, 3rd Earl of Selborne,[47] educated at Winchester College and University College, Oxford. He entered Parliament in 1910 for the Conservatives, and would go on to hold a host of ministerial positions. Unlike Buckmaster, he came from a political dynasty, his mother was Lady (Beatrix) Maud Gascoyne-Cecil,[48] the founder, and reputable face, of the Conservative and Unionist Women's Franchise Association (UWFA). Established in 1908, the UWFA fostered the women's movement within the Conservative Party. Lobbying, she spoke around the country promoting suffrage, invoking Disraeli, Northcote, WH Smith, and Salisbury, who had all called for the vote for women. Wolmer's father supported and assisted his wife with her feminist endeavours,[49] and his paternal grandfather had called for household suffrage and demanded a wider franchise.[50] Wolmer's paternal aunt was Laura Palmer, later Lady Laura Elizabeth Ridding,[51] who established the National Union of Women Workers in 1895 alongside Louise Creighton[52] and Emily Janes.[53] Wolmer, therefore had a sterling feminist pedigree.

Wolmer's 1912 bill was supported by Jack Hills MP, a First World War British Army Major, who had been educated at Eton, and then Balliol College, Oxford. He was described as someone 'whom British suffragists rank as one of their most faithful friends'.[54] By his marriage in 1897 to Stella Duckworth, he became half-step brother-in-law to Virginia Woolf and Vanessa Bell. Stated as a progressive voice

[45] M Ceadel, 'Cecil, (Edgar Algernon) Robert Gascoyne- [known as Lord Robert Cecil], Viscount Cecil of Chelwood (1864–1958), Politician and Peace Campaigner' (DNB, 2004).

[46] HC Deb 9 July 1913, vol 55, col 426. hansard.parliament.uk/commons/1913-07-09/debates/0ae0830a-da37-48b9-b874-8c66cc473b91/LegalProfession(AdmissionOfWomen)Bill.

[47] Foot (n 41).

[48] M Pugh, 'Palmer, (Beatrix) Maud [née Lady (Beatrix) Maud Gascoyne-Cecil], countess of Selborne (1858–1950), Suffragist and Political Wife' (DNB, 2004).

[49] D Boyce, 'Palmer, William Waldegrave, Second Earl of Selborne (1859–1942), Politician' (DNB, 2004).

[50] D Steele, 'Palmer, Roundell, First Earl of Selborne (1812–1895), Lord Chancellor' (DNB, 2004).

[51] S Kelly, 'Ridding [née Palmer], Lady Laura Elizabeth (1849–1939), Suffragist and Philanthropist' (DNB, 2004).

[52] J Covert, 'Creighton [née von Glehn], Louise Hume (1850–1936), Social Activist and Writer of Popular History and Biography' (DNB, 2004).

[53] S Kelly, 'Janes, Emily (1846–1928), Women's Welfare Activist' (DNB, 2004).

[54] *The International Woman Suffrage News* 'Celebration Dinner at the House of Commons' (April 1920) 103.

in the Woolf family,[55] on his wife's death, Hill redirected Duckworth's marriage settlement of £100 per annum each to Woolf and Bell,[56] although Woolf expressed her dislike of him.[57] As an MP, he used his position to lobby for a legal profession that was open to women.

Also supporting the Legal Profession (Admission of Women) Bill 1912 was Benjamin Spoor.[58] Like Buckmaster, Spoor's father had come from humble beginnings (he was an ironmonger, plumber and gas fitter)[59] and an active campaigner (in this case for the Liberal Party and Methodist church).[60] As his father before him, Spoor trained as a plumber and a Methodist preacher. His oratorical skills were used in his political life as a member of the Independent Labour Party.[61] Spoor was a pacifist, but had fought in Salonika in the First World War.[62] In 1918 he became an MP for his home town of Bishop Auckland for the Labour Party.[63] He was also a supporter of the women's movement.[64]

On 21 March 1919, Spoor introduced the Women's Emancipation Bill on behalf of the Labour Party as part of its 1918 party manifesto. It was an extremely broad bill, which proposed the enfranchisement of all women aged 21–30, that women be allowed to sit and to vote in the House of Lords, that all professional and judicial posts be opened to women and, finally, that women MPs be allowed to hold ministerial positions. Strongly supported by Labour mining-community MPs, it successfully passed all stages in the House of Commons but was defeated on 22 July when the Government introduced its own Bill, the Sex Disqualification (Removal) bill into the House of Lords.[65]

Lord Cecil[66] was another supporter of Wolmer's 1912 bill. Like Wolmer, Cecil was from a political family. Educated at Eton and University College, Oxford, he was called to the Bar in 1887 (Inner Temple), took silk in 1900 and became

[55] A Fernald, *The Oxford Handbook of Virginia Woolf* (OUP, 2021) 426.

[56] V Glendenning, *Leonard Woolf: A Biography* (New York Free Press, 2006) 175.

[57] V Woolf, *Diary of Virginia Woolf*, A Olivier Bell and A McNeillie (eds) (Hogarth Press, 1977–1984) vol I, 170.

[58] M Johnson, 'Spoor, Benjamin Charles [Ben] (1878–1928), Politician' (DNB, 2004). Spoor had connections to Holford Knight and Helena Normanton through the journal *India*. Spoor and Knight met Gandhi at Nagpur in 1920 to discuss the publication of which Helena Normanton was editor and dissolved it, as suggested by Normanton. She saw it as a symbol of co-operation by a country that was using non-co-operation as a tool for liberation. Gandhi agreed. Normanton saw Spoor as a co-operationist, and she maintained that he was the reason for her resigning her editorship: see NS Vinodh, *A Forgotten Ambassador in Cairo: The Life and Times of Syud Hossain* (S & S Publishers, 2020) 22.

[59] Johnson (n 58).

[60] ibid.

[61] ibid.

[62] ibid. Salonika is now Thessaloniki.

[63] ibid.

[64] J Vellacot, *From Liberal to Labour with Women's Suffrage: The Story of Catherine Marshall*, 2nd edn (McGill-Queen's Press, 2016) 328.

[65] M Takayanagi, 'Sacred Year or Broken Reed? The Sex Disqualification (Removal) Act 1919' (2020) 29 *Women's History Review* 563.

[66] Ceadel (n 45).

a Conservative MP in 1906.[67] Cecil was the son of former Prime Minister, Lord Salisbury, and had represented Bebb in her Court of Appeal case. He gave the penultimate speech for the Women's Emancipation bill. In doing so, he destroyed all arguments against the bill, mocked the Government's position and set out clearly the issues that the bill attempted to address.[68] Of course, he was unsuccessful, and the Sex Disqualification (Removal) Bill became law instead.

Sex Disqualification (Removal) Act 1919

We will see in the next section that many supportive men attended the celebration dinners after the Sex Disqualification (Removal) bill received Royal Assent on 23 December 1919.[69] This was the government bill that destroyed the Women's Emancipation bill, the bill of choice for the women's movement,[70] and finally opened the legal profession to women. Helena Normanton, like Bebb, a pioneer of the campaign to open the legal profession to women, insisted that this bill was written in her presence during a meeting with Claud Schuster[71] to persuade her from litigating against the Inns of Court (who had rejected her appeal against their refusal to admit her as a student member of Middle Temple).[72] There is no evidence to support this in the parliamentary archives,[73] although there is a mysterious letter from Schuster to Normanton, inviting her to a meeting (at which she maintained the bill was written) in February 1919.[74] Regardless of the truth in Normanton's assertions, it was clear that she had substantial help from Schuster in drafting her appeal against the Middle Temple's rejection of her initial application.[75] He also gave her specific directions as to whom she should serve these appeal papers on.[76]

Schuster was educated at Winchester College and New College, Oxford.[77] He was called to the Bar (Inner Temple) in 1895, but needed to earn a secure living, so entered the Civil Service in 1899.[78] In 1915, he took office as clerk of the crown

[67] ibid.
[68] Takayanagi (n 65) 568.
[69] ibid.
[70] ibid.
[71] A Napier and M Pottle, 'Schuster, Claud, Baron Schuster (1869–1956), Civil Servant' (DNB, 2004).
[72] 28 October 1952, letter from Helena Normanton to Ian Jacob Jackson, Director General of the BBC, WL: 7HLN/08, in which she wrote that the purpose of the meeting was to prevent her bringing litigation. The Government requested that she withdraw her appeal since they were introducing the Sex Disqualification (Removal) Bill. She said that she had evidence of the negotiations in writing and had kept a copy, though none survives in her archives.
[73] Indeed, Takayanagi states that various drafts of this bill had been made in the Lord Chancellor's Office: Takayanagi (n 65) 569.
[74] Letter from Schuster to Normanton, 11 February 1919, WL: HLN/A/03.
[75] Bourne (n 1) 72.
[76] ibid 73.
[77] Napier and Pottle (n 71).
[78] ibid.

in chancery and permanent secretary in the Lord Chancellor's Office, having been chosen by the then Lord Chancellor, Lord Haldane. However, by the time he took up office the Lord Chancellor had been replaced by Lord Birkenhead.[79] It has always been difficult to understand why Normanton did not litigate against the Inns of Court, especially given the decision in the 1911 case of *Dyson v Attorney General*.[80] The only sensible conclusion, based on letters from Schuster in Normanton's archives, suggests that Schuster was both an ally and supporter of this campaign to open the legal profession to women and had helped and supported Normanton and her campaign to achieve this goal.

Dinners to Celebrate the Sex Disqualification (Removal) Act 1919

There were many dinners to celebrate women's victory in finally being able to formally enter the professions. We will concentrate on two: the Women's Freedom League (WFL) dinner on 19 January 1920 at the New Minerva Club[81] and the celebration dinner at the House of Commons on 8 March 1920. The guest lists provide us with the names of male invitees, and we can use this to contextualise the work of these men in this campaign.

Women's Freedom League Dinner[82]

Fifty people sat down to dinner, and amongst them were two significant men: Holford Knight KC[83] and Wells Thatcher.[84] Wells Thatcher was a barrister at 5 Essex Court, Lincoln's Inn.[85] He gave a speech that night and had provided a

[79] J Campbell, 'Smith, Frederick Edwin, First Earl of Birkenhead (1872–1930), Lawyer and Politician' (DNB, online edn). www.oxforddnb.com/view/10.1093/ref:odnb/9780198614128.001.0001/odnb-9780198614128-e-36137.

[80] *Dyson v The Attorney General* (1911) 1 KB 410.

[81] 28 Brunswick Square, London, WC1. This was a residential club founded in 1920 by the Women's Freedom League. Prior to this the League had run a cafe at its headquarters in Holborn, which provided lunches and lectures. The lease on the club was purchased by Dr Elizabeth Knight and maintained by her until her death in 1933. Membership was open to both men and women who had sympathy with progressive thought. It was to become the rallying point for the extension of the franchise movement, therefore it attracted suffrage sympathisers. It also provided vegetarian food which maintained a link between vegetarianism and the suffrage movement. The club closed in 1962. For a more detailed account, see E Crawford, *The Women's Suffrage Movement in Britain and Ireland: A Regional Survey* (Routledge, 2006) 125.

[82] Reported in *The Vote* (20 February 1920).

[83] George Wilfred Holford Knight (1877–1936), barrister and labour MP for Nottingham South 1931–1935, author of *Oxford Dictionary of National Biography* (OUP, 2013).

[84] Normanton's pupil master.

[85] British Phonebooks 1880–1984, 862.

reference for Normanton's application to the Middle Temple in 1918.[86] It is unclear whether he gave Normanton a pupillage, but there is evidence that he put her touch with possible sympathetic pupil masters.[87] Also with him that night was Holford Knight.[88]

Like Thatcher, Knight had also supplied Normanton with a reference for her Middle Temple application, but he was far more involved in the campaign than just merely supplying a reference. Educated at the University of London, and then called to the Bar at the Middle Temple, he practised at the Central Criminal Court from 1911 to 1930, and then served as Recorder of West Ham from 1930 to 1937.[89] At the annual meeting of the Bar in 1913, he proposed a motion to admit women, which was rejected by a majority.[90] Again, in January 1917, he proposed a motion to the Bar Council to allow the admission of women which this time was defeated by a majority of 178 to just 22. Holford Knight wrote regularly in the press demanding women's entry. He was frustrated that England lagged behind other modern states and argued that women were already undertaking a range of employments due to economic necessity.[91]

Celebration Dinner at the House of Commons 8 March 1920

A second celebration dinner was held at the House of Commons.[92] The dinner was organised by the Committee to Obtain the Opening of the Legal Profession to Women and was hosted by Mrs Ray Strachey and Jack Hills MP as chair. Amongst the guests were many notable men (some of whom we have met before): Lord Chief Justice, Lord Reading; the Solicitor General, Sir Ernest Pollock;[93] the Attorney General, Sir Gordon Hewart;[94] Viscount Haldane;[95] the President of the Law Society, Thomas Liddle; the President of the Divorce Court, Sir Henry Duke;[96] Cecil Chapman, representing the London Magistrates;[97] and Mr Withers.

[86] WL: 7HLN/A/01.
[87] WL:7HLN/A/17.
[88] Knight (n 83) and K Gidart, D Howell and N Kirk, *Dictionary of Labour Biography*, vol 11 (Palgrave MacMillan, 2016) 166–70.
[89] M Stenton and S Lees, *Who's Who of British Members of Parliament* vol III (Harvester Press, 1979) 200. He became an MP in 1929 for Nottingham South, serving one term.
[90] P Polden, 'Portia's Progress: Women at the Bar in England, 1919–1939' (2005) *International Journal of the Legal Profession* 293, 317; and *Law Times*, 1912–1913, 317.
[91] *The Contemporary Review* (569) May 1913: WL: 7HLN/A/03 loose items from scrapbook 2 of 2.
[92] Reported 9 March 1920 in both the *Evening News* and *Evening Mail*.
[93] F Wrottesley, rev A Samuels, 'Pollock, Ernest Murray, First Viscount Hanworth (1861–1936)' (DNB, 2004).
[94] R Stevens, 'Hewart, Gordon, First Viscount Hewart (1870–1943)' (DNB, 2004).
[95] HCG Matthew, 'Haldane, Richard Burdon, Viscount Haldane (1856–1928)' (DNB, 2004).
[96] Sankey, rev HCG Matthew, 'Duke, Henry Edward, First Baron Merrivale (1855–1939)' (DNB, 2004).
[97] *Scotsman* (9 March 1929).

Questionable Male Guests

However, there were also some questionable male guests, not necessarily known for their feminist support, but an invitation was necessary presumably to foster a collegiate profession: male lawyers were going to have to work with women lawyers from then on. The guest of honour was the Lord Chancellor, Lord Birkenhead,[98] a man who was 'notorious for his personal antagonism to women's causes'.[99] Although he had given government support for the Women's Emancipation bill and the Barristers and Solicitors (Qualification of Women) bill,[100] he later 'killed off' and 'systematically rubbished' the Women's Emancipation bill.[101] As Attorney General, he had 'bitterly opposed women's suffrage', but then had to navigate the Representation of the People bill in 1918.[102] He perhaps would not have been Strachey's choice as guest of honour?

Birkenhead was educated at both University College, Liverpool (where he spent four terms), and Wadham College, Oxford, in 1891, before joining Gray's Inn and setting up in practice on the northern circuit.[103] He took silk in 1908 and by 1910 was earning more than £10,000 per annum.[104] During his career, he appeared for Horatio Bottomley, who had described Bell so disparagingly (and Bell, of course, was instructing solicitor for the other side);[105] he successfully defended Ethel le Neve; and he also defended Arthur Ransome's biography of Oscar Wilde against Lord Alfred Douglas's, again with Bell on the other side.[106]

However, at the dinner he was charming. He congratulated Millicent Fawcett upon the success of her life's work and said that she 'was entitled to regard herself as driving in a victorious chariot over her victims'.[107] He spoke of the great ability that he had seen in the female clerks in the law courts and how he had tried to persuade his daughter that the law was the career for her, but she wanted to be a movie star.[108] After dinner Bebb (now Thomson) proposed the toast to the Bar of England and Wales.[109] Birkenhead responded, stating that he had always supported women entering the professions.[110]

Lord Birkenhead's speech was echoed by Lord Reading,[111] the man who had in 1912 prosecuted Emmeline Pankhurst for conspiracy to commit criminal injury

[98] Campbell (n 79).
[99] Takayanagi (n 65) 568.
[100] ibid 566.
[101] ibid 568.
[102] ibid 569.
[103] Campbell (n 79).
[104] ibid.
[105] ibid.
[106] ibid.
[107] Takayanagi ' (n 65) 569.
[108] ibid.
[109] *Manchester Guardian* (9 March 1920).
[110] Takayanagi (n 65) 569.
[111] A Lentin, 'Isaacs, Rufus Daniel, First Marquess of Reading (1860–1935), Politician and Judge' (DNB, 2004). He had led the prosecution case in the infamous *R v Seddon* 1912 fly paper poison case.

and damage, although he now apparently favoured votes for women. Reading was admitted as a student to the Middle Temple in 1885, had ambitiously set up in chambers on his own, 1 Garden Court, Temple, and made a huge success of his practice. He spoke at the dinner of his anticipation of the time when women would plead in his court.

Also in attendance at the dinner was the Solicitor General, Sir Ernest Pollock,[112] educated at Eton College, he matriculated at Trinity College, Cambridge, in 1863, and was called to the bar by Lincoln's Inn in 1871.[113] He devoted himself to the study of the law as an essayist, professor and editor. Pollock supported Hills' symbolic amendment to the Sex Disqualification (Removal) bill by introducing the word, 'A person shall not be disqualified by sex or *marriage*', but only because he said that the proviso would allow discretion in certain areas (ie, the civil service and teaching).[114] When Samuel Hoare introduced another proviso to the bill, which was supported by the women's movement, Pollock opposed it. In answer to Hills' assertion that without the amendment women would rather have no legislation at all, Pollock retorted: 'I cannot believe that women could be so unreasonable.'[115]

With Pollock that night was the Attorney General, Gordon Hewart, first Viscount Hewart.[116] Educated at Manchester Grammar School and University College, Oxford, he was called to the Bar (Inner Temple) in 1902, joined the northern circuit, took silk in 1912, and in 1913 was elected Liberal member of parliament for Leicester.[117] In 1916 he became solicitor-general (and was knighted).[118] He was not respected as a judge, being considered rude to counsel in court, and to his fellow judges out of court.[119] Schuster wrote a warning letter to the then Conservative Lord Chancellor, Lord Hailsham, about Hewart's behaviour.[120] It appears that Hewart was a friend of neither men or women lawyers.

'Unquestionable Male Guests'

Also attending that night were male feminist activists. Samuel Garrett was one such guest.[121] Strachey noted Garrett's role:

> Entry to the legal profession had been one of the objects of the feminist societies for many years, and a special committee, with Mr Samuel Garrett as its chairman, had existed for the purpose of securing this reform.[122]

[112] R Cosgrove, 'Pollock, Sir Frederick, Third Baronet (1845–1937), Jurist' (DNB, 2004).
[113] ibid.
[114] Takayanagi (n 65) 571.
[115] ibid 572.
[116] Stevens (n 94).
[117] ibid.
[118] ibid.
[119] ibid.
[120] ibid.
[121] Venn (n 23) 19.
[122] R Strachey, *The Cause* (Virago, 1928) 235.

Educated at Rugby School and St John's College, Cambridge, Garrett had been President of the Law Society from 1917–18.[123] Garrett had pristine feminist credentials: one sister was the esteemed physician Elizabeth Garrett Anderson, friend of Emily Davies, the founder of Girton College, Cambridge, for women. Garrett Anderson was an active member of the Langham Place circle, a group associated with the Society for Promoting the Employment of Women.[124] He was also brother-in-law to Henry Fawcett, husband of another his sisters, Millicent.[125] She needs no explanation, save that she was leader of the constitutional campaign for women's suffrage.[126] Another of his sisters was Agnes Garrett, also committed to the opening of the professions to women,[127] and with her cousin to Rhoda Garrett became an interior designer.[128]

Garrett had been a vital member of the women's movement, and previously, on 28 March 1919, at a special general meeting of the Law Society Council, held 'as a matter of urgency' to consider the implications of the Barristers and Solicitors (Qualification of Women) Bill, he had moved:

> That in view of the present economic and political position of women, it is in the opinion of this meeting expedient that the existing obstacles to their entry into the legal profession should be removed; and the Council is requested to report this opinion to the Lord Chancellor.[129]

Urgency was required as the Law Society needed to reform its long-standing opposition to the admission of women in the face of a looming change in the law. After seven speeches in favour, and just two against, the resolution was carried by 50 votes to 33.[130]

The dinner would not have been complete without the attendance of Cecil Chapman, a London Magistrate.[131] Educated at Tonbridge School and the University of Oxford, he was called to the Bar at the Inner Temple in 1878.[132] His story has been extensively written about by Angela John.[133] After practising law on the South Eastern Circuit, he became a Justice of the Peace for Surrey and a Conservative County Councillor for Chelsea.[134] He was an advocate for women's

[123] ibid.
[124] ibid.
[125] J Howarth, 'Fawcett, Dame Millicent Garrett [née Millicent Garrett] (1847–1929), Leader of the Constitutional Women's Suffrage Movement and Author' (DNB, 2004).
[126] R Symonds, *Inside the Citadel, Men and the Emancipation of Women 1850–1920* (Palgrave Macmillan, 1999) 170.
[127] S Kelly, 'Garrett, Agnes (1845–1935), Interior Designer and Suffragist' (DNB, 2004).
[128] ibid.
[129] 'As a Matter of Urgency' (*Law Society Gazette*, 28 March 2019). www.lawgazette.co.uk/obiter/as-a-matter-of-urgency/5069787.article.
[130] ibid.
[131] 'CECIL CHAPMAN, 86, EX-LONDON JURIST; Noted Justice and Champion of Poor Became an Author' *New York Times* (24 June 1938) 19.
[132] ibid.
[133] John (n 6) 145.
[134] C Chapman, *The Poor Man's Court of Justice: Twenty-Five Years as a Metropolitan Magistrate* (Hodder & Stoughton, 1925).

suffrage,[135] and at one time, was chair of the Men's League for Women's Suffrage (MLWS), until his employers, the Home Office, forced him to stand down.[136] There were 950 members of the MLWS, and 300 of those were lawyers. In 1911 he took part in a Women's Social and Political Union debate and was complained about by Arnold Ward, son of Mrs Humphrey Ward,[137] the well-known President of the Women's National Anti-Suffrage League. Chapman was forced to apologise, stating that he did not expect the event to be so large! John described him as paradoxical, a man who dispensed justice, but also was a potential law breaker as he supported suffrage.[138]

Conclusion

Before the enactment of the Sex Disqualification (Removal) Act 1919 women were resolutely obstructed from entering the legal profession by the male establishment. To even begin the process of qualification pre-1919, it was prescribed that the candidate had to be male. This prescription was justified by reliance on *The Mirror of Justices*, a medieval treatise, written by an unknown man, which stated that the law would not suffer women to be attorneys, nor infants of serfs.[139] It was used (by powerful men) to deny Bertha Cave membership of Gray's Inn, to refuse Normanton membership of the Middle Temple[140] and to prevent Bebb from sitting the Law Society exams.[141] Essentially, it was used to discriminate against women in order to prevent competition from women; the institutions were terrified of change as change meant competition to an already struggling profession. To include women also meant to include all men and thus was a threat to livelihoods, and political and legal dominance.

1873 saw the first recorded network of women demanding entry to the legal profession, some 50 years before women were finally admitted.[142] Entry was denied until male MPs and male lawyers used their power to open the profession to women, either by lobbying the two branches of the profession (as we saw by Bell, Knight and Garrett) or by presentation of bills to Parliament (as presented by Hills, Spoor, Wolmer and Buckmaster). Men, and men alone, were in control

[135] 'DISTURBANCES: Speech of Mr Cecil Chapman, Metropolitan Magistrate, in Favour of Women's Suffrage' Speech held in the National Archives, HO 45/10645/209446.

[136] ibid.

[137] J Sutherland, 'Ward [née Arnold], Mary Augusta [known as Mrs Humphry Ward] (1851–1920), Novelist, Philanthropist, and Political Lobbyist' (DNB, 2004).

[138] John (n 6) 145.

[139] WJ Whittaker and FW Maitland (eds), *The Mirror of Justices* (Selden Society, 1893) 88. *The Mirror of Justices* was relied on by the legal writer Sir William Blackstone for his argument regarding the doctrine of coverture, W Blackstone, *The Commentaries of the Law of England* 4 vols, WR Prest, DSS Lemmings, TP Gallanis and R Paley (eds), (OUP, 2016) vol 1, 294–95.

[140] See the papers of the refusal by the Inns of Court Parliament 30 January 1919, WL: 7HLN/A/01.

[141] [1914] 1 Ch 286, 293–94.

[142] Bourne (n 8) 79.

of the discriminatory method of admittance to the professions, but it was also men who challenged and pushed the establishment to finally admit women; they gave voice and used political and institutional power to achieve women's demands. These men acted for women, they challenged the status quo and require recognition. As Johns said: '[t]he marked presence of lawyers active in male support groups advocating women's suffrage is an under-researched area'.[143] Her comment equally applies to male support groups advocating women's admittance to the legal profession. Not all men supported sex discrimination or the segregation of the public sphere.

This recognition of supportive men does not deny the agency of women. It does not mean that women did not struggle, sacrifice, face numerous disappointments and suffer economically. Nor does it mean that women did not organise themselves into powerful pressure groups and exert a legally limited autonomy to demand an end to discrimination. It simply means that women needed men to open the door of a closed profession for them on their behalf because men controlled the established institutions that women aspired to join. To ignore this is to tell an incomplete history. The complete story needs to be told – the opening of the legal profession was a joint achievement by women and men.

The danger is that, if we speak of men's role in this history, we deny the agency of women. We continue to mute women's voices as history had done until articles such as Rosemary's. There is also a danger that we perpetuate Blackstone's depiction of women as 'infant', dependent on men and in need of male support to achieve or exist at all. How then do we speak of men's role in this history without denying the agency of women? We do this by thrusting women into the limelight as Rosemary did in her article, but we also record and represent men's role.

[143] John (n 6) 145.

2

Women Jurists Under the Swastika

ULRIKE SCHULTZ

Prologue

I first met Rosemary Auchmuty at a meeting of the Research Committee on Sociology of Law (RCSL[1]) in the International Sociological Association in the 1990s, probably in Antwerp in 1997 in a session on women's rights. At the time few colleagues attended and only female colleagues. Women's rights and gender issues had not yet moved into the mainstream. It was for a long time considered to be a marginal topic for blue stockings, although due to the influence of colleagues from the United States, it had already been one of the main topics of the big international socio-legal meeting in Amsterdam in 1991. Change happened in the past 20 years and meanwhile not just one but several sessions on women rights and gender issues are on the agenda of socio-legal meetings. It is no longer an exclusionary female subject, but still few male colleagues turn up.

Meanwhile I cannot count how many times we have met at RCSL and LSA,[2] at workshops of the International Institute for the Sociology of Law in Onati/Spain,[3] special working group meetings, particularly of the RCSL working group on Legal Professions[4] which Rosemary has headed as my successor for four years from 2014–18. I have always admired her sharp mind and clear reasoning and I have benefitted from her solidarity and support.

She has contributed to the international comparative project on Gender and Careers in the Legal Academy which I launched in 2011. For the edited collection[5] which came out in 2021, together with Jennifer Temkin she submitted a chapter

[1] Research Committee 12 of the International Sociological association. For details see rcsl.hypotheses.org/.

[2] The American Law and Society Association, www.lawandsociety.org/.

[3] See www.iisj.net/.

[4] See rcsl.iscte.pt/rcsl_wg_professions.htm.

[5] U Schultz, G Shaw, M Thornton and R Auchmuty (eds), *Gender and Careers in the Legal Academy* (Hart, 2021).

entitled 'The Road to Olive Stone' on the first woman lecturer in law at the London School of Economics (LSE) for the section on Feminism in the Legal Academy, and when I needed support in the editing process she unselfishly helped, truly enhancing the quality of the collection.

Rosemary is a lawyer and historian, hence why I chose a historical subject for this contribution. I am essentially a black letter lawyer who tries to work socio-legally. In my work on women's rights and gender in the legal profession I had by necessity to include historical perspectives. For my German book on gender and careers in the legal academy in Germany,[6] I had finally written a big chapter on the first and early women law professors. By coincidence I was asked some time ago to deal with a particular phase of German legal history, the situation of women lawyers during the Nazi era. Our Justice Academy in Northrhine-Westfalia, where I teach frequently,[7] has set up a research unit on the Judiciary in the National Socialism in 1989,[8] and after finding out that they had neglected the situation of women judges I was asked to give a presentation on the subject. This gives me the opportunity to devote an overview of the results of my work on women lawyers in the dark years of my country to Rosemary.

The Beginnings

A Brief Account of When and How Women were Allowed to Enter the Legal Profession

The history of women in the legal profession in Germany is brief – in Germany and worldwide.[9] Women were ascribed gender characteristics, being thought too emotional to be able to judge objectively and too soft for the hard legal work. The

[6] U Schultz, A Böning, I Peppmeier, and S Schröder, *De jure und de facto: Professorinnen in der Rechtswissenschaft. Geschlecht und Wissenschaftskarriere im Recht* (Nomos, 2018).

[7] On decision making, communication and mediation, didactics of teaching law, legal profession etc.

[8] Although the Americans had carried out thorough re-education and democratization programmes after the war in Western Germany, and although in many fields there was a lot of dealing with the past, the Ministries of Justice and the law courts only started late to analyse their files and dig deeper into the National Socialist injustice in the justice system. It was a taboo to think that there were unjust jurists in the justice system. They were hesitant to put their house in order as too many former Nazis had returned to the judiciary after the war. There were rope teams, but also a lack of enough educated legal staff. Other federal states joined in with this memory work much later. Work on the biographies of our early judges of the Federal Constitutional Court has only started recently. 'The Federal Constitutional Court, the highest German court, was said to be unencumbered, that there were no National Socialist continuities, as was the case with other courts and authorities: This myth has lasted a long time.' See www.deutschlandfunkkultur.de/wiltraut-rupp-von-bruenneck-von-der-ns-juristin-zur-bundesverfassungsrichterin-100.html.

[9] For a comprehensive overview, see U Schultz, 'Introduction: Gender and Careers in the Legal Academy: Overview and Synthesis' in Schultz, Shaw, Thornton and Auchmuty (n 5) 6.

political scientist and Prussian politician Heinrich von Treitschke stated in his lectures on politics in 1897: 'Authority is masculine, that is a sentence which is actually self-evident. Of all human talents, none is so far removed from women as the sense of justice. Almost all women learn what law is only through their husbands. [...] In the state it is necessary to act rationally and without regard to the person. Only the man is capable of both.'[10] Another obstacle was that women did not learn Latin[11] in their women's lyceum which was a prerequisite for being admitted to law faculties in countries with a Roman law-based legal system. Zürich was the first university in the German speaking world to accept women in legal studies in 1878. The story of the first one, Emilie Kempin-Spyri, is well documented.[12] Anna Mackenroth became in 1898 the first woman in Switzerland to pass the bar exam.[13] Anita Augspurg was the first German woman who took her legal doctorate there in 1897.[14] In Germany, women were gradually offered the possibility to attend legal lectures between 1900 and 1909 but were not allowed to take part in the legal state examinations. They completed their studies with the doctoral examination. They were not allowed to sit the first legal examination (*Referendarexamen*) which, however, was and is only the first step on the way to practise law and were not allowed to use the title *Referendar*. These half-qualified women lawyers took on very different legal activities, were active in women's legal advice centres, took on auxiliary jobs in lawyers' offices and in business, worked as teachers at social schools, as journalists, in welfare or other private or public social associations and taught law to women and in girls' school.[15] 'In many cases, they worked in three or four of the aforementioned occupations side by side and still earned barely enough to live on.'[16]

After the end of the first World War the German emperor had to abdicate, the *Kaiserreich* came to an end, and a republican order was constituted. The social democrats got the majority in the National Assembly who had on their agenda equal rights for men and women. In the so-called Weimar Constitution

[10] H von Treitschke, *Politik. Vorlesungen*. 1897–1898, 2 volumes (Hirzel, 1911–13) 252.

[11] Until the 1970s many faculties still demanded the 'Large Latinum' equalling the successful completion of at least five years of Latin at school and for a doctorate a Digest exegesis (*Digestenexegese*, an analysis of a text from the '*corpus iuris civilis*', law books of emperor Justinian from the sixth century) had to be completed in addition to writing the thesis.

[12] The first one was Emilie Kempin-Spyri, who has been called 'the first female lawyer in Europe'. See kempinspyri-derfilm.ch/. See also E Hasler, *Die Wachsflügelfrau*, 13th edn (Nagel & Kimche, 1991) and Virgina G Drachman, *Sisters in Law: Women Lawyers in Modern American History* (Harvard University Press, 1998) 123–126).

[13] M Röwekamp, *Juristinnen – Lexikon zu Leben und Werk* (Nomos, 2005) 228.

[14] See jurios.de/2021/08/31/drei-historische-juristinnen-die-in-deutschland-rechtsgeschichte-schrieben-teil-1/ She was a lesbian and part of the radical wing of the first women's movement.

[15] Many of us feminist jurists continue this tradition, see U Schultz, 'Knowledge and Opinion About Law – The importance of Law Related Education' in H Hyden, D Nelken, R Cotterell and U Schultz (eds), *Combining the Legal and the Social in Sociology of Law. Anthology in Memory of Reza Banakar* (Bloomsbury, 2023) 161–72.

[16] The female Minister of Justice Brigitte Zypries in her opening address for the German Women Lawyers Association's exhibition 'Jewish Women Lawyers' (see n 73).

women got the same civic rights as men, which meant mainly the suffrage, a prerequisite for practice as a judge. According to Article 128(1) of the Weimar Reich Constitution, all citizens without distinction were to be admitted to public office in accordance with the law and according to their qualifications and performance. Paragraph 2 provided, 'All exceptional provisions against female civil servants shall be abolished.' In 1919 more states of the new democracy therefore allowed women to sit the first state examination and to gradually take part in the preparatory legal service leading to the second state examination – formally and informally. But women still had to fight for their rights. At that time, voices rose against overcrowding in the legal profession, and women were also seen as undesirable competition.

Only after pressure from the women delegates in the new Parliament assisted by women from the German Women Jurists Association, which had been founded by the first few women in law in 1914,[17] a special 'Law on the Admission of Women to Offices and Professions in the Administration of Justice' was passed in 1922, which gave women the right to be admitted to the judiciary and advocacy. We have just celebrated 100 years of women in the legal profession. The first woman lawyer was Maria Otto in Munich in December 1922 via special permission as she did not fulfil the formal requirements for admission.[18] She had not gone through the second phase of legal education, the practical training in the various legal occupations in the so-called *Referendarzeit* which is organised by the appeal courts and in which the young lawyers hold the status of a civil servant. After this they have to pass a second qualifying examination (*Assessorexamen*) which is organised by the state Ministries of Justice. It is worth mentioning that up to the present day the structure of legal education in Germany has remained the same.[19]

[17] Deutscher Juristinnenverein, founded in 1914 by Margarete Berent, Margarete Meseritz (Margarete Muehsam-Edelheim), Marie Munk and Marie Raschke, 31.4 per cent of the women in the Juristinnenverein were Jewish. It was dissolved in 1933, and after the war a Deutscher Juristinnenbund was refounded in 1948.

[18] S Jörn-Schellenberg 'Die erste Anwältin: Maria Ottos Weg in die Anwaltschaft' (*Anwaltsblatt online*, 24 May 2022) anwaltsblatt.anwaltverein.de/de/anwaeltinnen-anwaelte/anwaltspraxis/maria-ottos-weg-in-die-anwaltschaft; W Clemens, 'Die ersten Rechtsanwältinnen in München' in M Anwaltverein (ed), *12 Jahrzehnte Münchener Anwaltverein. Festschrift* (Deutscher Anwaltverlag, 2000) 19–25.

[19] German lawyers study law for at least four years at law faculties in universities, followed by a first legal examination which is organised and held at the appeal courts of the ordinary jurisdiction. They then have to go through practical training in the judiciary, prosecution, civil service and the legal profession, also organised by the appeal courts, leading to a second state examination organised by the appeal courts and the Ministries of Justice. This is the German civil service model of the system of justice. For details see U Schultz, 'Legal Education in Germany – an ever (never?) ending story of resistance to change' (*RED, Revista de Educación y Derecho* n. 4, 2011) 1–24, revistes.ub.edu/index.php/RED and M Kilian and U Schultz, 'Germany. Resistance and Reactions to Demands of Modernisation' in R Abel, H Sommerlad, O Hammerslev and U Schultz (eds), *Lawyers in 21st Century Societies*, vol. 1 (Hart, 2020) 209–33.

The 1920s

The number of those taking advantage of this newly gained entitlement remained, however, miniscule.[20] The patriarchal family law that had come into force in the civil code (BGB) in 1900, and economic stringency caused by the high reparations Germany had to pay after the war resulting in hyperinflation,[21] combined with the imminent world economic crisis, created a hostile environment for women's career ambitions. In 1921, in its function as guardian of the constitution, the *Reichsgericht* had announced the unconstitutionality of a celibacy clause that had applied to female civil servants until then.[22] Only unmarried women could become civil servants. However, Article 128(2) was undermined just two years later: The Personnel Reduction Ordinance of 27 October 1923 authorised the Reich government to dismiss female civil servants at any time at the end of the month if they were married or had a child out of wedlock.[23]

The first female German judge was Maria Johanna Hagemeyer (1896–1991 in Bonn). She passed her second state examination in October 1924, then worked as an assistant in the Prussian Ministry of Justice. In May 1927 she became the first woman in Prussia to be appointed as a court assessor and then got a permanent position in 1928 as a judge in Bonn. After her, Gertrud Cichorius in Chemnitz, Gertrud May in Leipzig, Else Samulon in Berlin, and Elisabeth Krumme in Essen were appointed as judges in 1929, followed in 1930 by Marie Hurtig in Chemnitz, Marie Munk in Berlin, and Hedwig Brann-Frank in Frankfurt.[24]

In terms of numbers, therefore, there remained very few women working in law. This is also shown by the development of the number of female law students: in 1914, 51 women studied law out of a total of 9,003 law students. This corresponded to 0.6 per cent of law students and 1.4 per cent of women at German universities. In 1917, 74 women were studying law, and by 1919, 450 (2.6 per cent) out of a total of 17,224 law students.[25] In 1933, the number of women studying law

[20] U Schultz, 'The Status of Women Lawyers in Germany' in U Schultz and G Shaw (eds), *Women in the World's Legal Professions* (Hart, 2003) 271–91; Schultz et al (n 6) 69.

[21] When the Germans defaulted to pay the reparations which they had been forced to pay under the Versailles Treaties, the French and Belgians occupied the Ruhr district in 1923 which led to sabotage and uprising, the so-called Ruhr-crisis and in consequence to hyperinflation.

[22] G Kling, 'Die rechtliche Konstruktion des "weiblichen Beamten". Frauen im öffentlichen Dienst des Großherzogtums Baden im 19. und frühen 20. Jahrhundert' in U Gerhard (ed), *Frauen in der Geschichte des Rechts* (Beck, 1999) 600–16, 612 (with further references).

[23] K Plett, 'The Loss of Early Women Lawyers from Collective Memory in Germany: A Memoir of Magdalene Schoch' in S Karstedt (ed), *Legal Institutions and Collective Memories. Criminology and Policing* (Hart, 2009) 353–70; Schultz et al (n 6) 77.

[24] M Röwekamp, 'Women's Admission to the Legal Profession in Germany between 1900 and 1933' in E Schandevyl (ed), *Women in Law and Lawmaking in Nineteenth and Twentieth-Century Europe* (Routledge, 2016) 91.

[25] Plett (n 23) 358.

was also around 400 to 500 (2–3 per cent of law students) whereas 6 per cent of students at German universities were women.[26]

In 1930, there were 74 women – 66 of them as court assessors in non-permanent positions – in the judicial service out of a total of over 10,000 judges.[27] By 1933, there were 23 female judges with permanent positions.[28] The overall proportion of women in the judiciary was 0.3 per cent. 252 of the 18,766 (1.3 per cent) admitted lawyers were women.[29] There is no evidence of female public prosecutors. Prosecution was considered to be a hard job for tough men,[30] and there are no statistical data on the first women lawyers in other functions, for example in other positions in the civil service.

The situation of women in legal academia was still more difficult than in the judiciary and the legal profession.[31] By 1933 some women had part-time positions as assistants at chairs in law faculties. To get a call for a chair they did not only need the state examinations and the dissertation (*Promotion*), but also the second big book, the habilitation. The first to submit an application for habilitation had been the aforementioned Emilie Kempin-Spyri in Zürich in 1888, but it was unanimously rejected by the academic senate.[32]

The habilitation as a selection criterion had been enforced in the nineteenth century. It was regarded as the 'guarantor of the world standing of German science'.[33] The Prussian government had asked universities in a circular letter at the beginning of the twentieth century 'whether it is at all compatible with the present constitution and the interests of the universities to admit women to academic careers'. The law faculty of the University of Göttingen thought 'that the armed academic youth could not be trained by women as teachers and educators to men'.[34] After the Weimar Constitution came into force in 1919 with its new equality rights, the exclusion of women from academic careers was no longer legally tenable. In 1920, even before the 'Law on the Admission of Women to Offices and Professions in the Administration of Justice', a decree of the Ministry of Science gave women in Prussia the possibility of habilitation and thus access to a university teaching career.[35] 'However, the requirements for women who

[26] S Bajohr and K Rödiger-Bajohr, 'Die Diskriminierung der Juristin in Deutschland bis 1945' (1980) 13(1) *Kritische Justiz* 41, 44.

[27] D Juristinnenbund (ed), *Juristinnen in Deutschland. Eine Dokumentation (1900–1984)* (Nomos, 1984) 14.

[28] Röwekamp (n 24) 91.

[29] M Röwekamp, *Die ersten deutschen Juristinnen: Eine Geschichte ihrer Professionalisierung und Emanzipation (1900–1945)* Böhlau, 2011) 459; Bajohr and Rödiger-Bajohr (n 26) 45; F Ostler, *Die deutschen Rechtsanwälte 1871–1971* (Juristischer Verlag W. Ellinghaus, 1971) 174.

[30] Until the 1970s, prosecutors were seen as 'blood hounds of the nation', an image which did not fit women.

[31] Schultz et al (n 6).

[32] It took almost 100 years before another woman, Beatrice Weber-Dürler could do her habilitation in Zürich in 1983, she got a chair in 1986. Schultz et al (n 6) 20.

[33] Röwekamp (n 29) 507 with further references.

[34] Röwekamp (n 29) 508.

[35] E Boedeker and M Meyer-Plath, *50 Jahre Habilitation in Deutschland* (Otto Schwartz, 1974) 5; F Misselwitz, *Marie Luise Hilger. Zum Leben und Wirken einer Arbeitsrechtlerin im 20. Jahrhundert*

wanted to habilitate were higher than for their male colleagues. [...] From the beginning, hardly any women dared to advance into the tradition-rich law faculties, for it was foreseeable that the lawyers thought even less than other faculties about admitting female colleagues into their ranks.'[36] Else Koffka was the first woman in Germany to receive a teaching position at the University of Rostock in the summer semester of 1931, then assistant judgeships in Berlin, then in 1931 a full position as an assistant with a temporary teaching assignment for criminal law exercises. This provoked indignation. An anonymous letter was received by the Ministry of Justice: 'Feminine justice! It is positively scandalous that a female assessor has been appointed. Students must involuntarily get the idea that all male assessors are inferior, for there are many thousands more of them than female ones.'[37]

The first woman who got the habilitation with the formal *venia legendi* was Magdalene Schoch in 1932 who had since 1920 been an assistant for Albrecht Mendelssohn-Bartholdy at the University of Hamburg, a grandson of the famous composer. She was specialised in international, English and American Law and legal comparison, and as such was also a division manager at the Institute of Foreign Relations which was cofounded by Mendelssohn-Bartholdy in the wake of the Paris Peace Conference. However, she never got a chair in Germany. Her life is meanwhile well documented.[38] No other female jurist got the habilitation until the end of the war and none a chair. Gerda Krüger had applied for the habilitation in 1937, in the historical faculty, but did not get it as it was considered to be too legal, and she was only granted it finally at the law faculty of Göttingen in 1946 after the Second World War. She then could only use the title and finally got the *venia legendi* after a 10-year legal dispute going as far as an Administrative Court of Appeal in 1962 as a restitution measure.[39]

Thus, in a 1929 account of 'the female lawyer', it was stated, 'The path of women lawyers has often been described as a path of suffering, and rightly so. No profession had to be fought for by women as this one.'[40] Even the brief biographies of the first female lawyers that can be found on the Internet show their manifold problems, which led to frequent changes of profession:

(Nomos, 2016) 323. The decision was taken after a petition by Edith Stein, see Plett (n 23) 358 with further references.

[36] 'The prerequisite was that their admission was justified by extraordinary scientific importance. In the humanities and law, this was a criterion that always made rejection possible, because here the assessment of performance is more subjective than in the more strictly measured natural sciences or medicine.' Röwekamp (n 29) 511.

[37] Röwekamp (n 29) 187.

[38] R Nicolaysen, 'Für Recht und Gerechtigkeit über das couragierte Leben der Juristin Magdalene Schoch (1897–1987)' (2006) *Zeitschrift des Vereins für Hamburgische Geschichte, Band 92* 113–43; Plett (n 23).

[39] Schultz et al (n 6) 83 with further references. A brief account of her life is now documented in Wikipedia under her name.

[40] M von Erffa and I Richarz-Simons, 'Der weibliche Rechtsanwalt' in J Magnus (ed), *Die Rechtsanwaltschaft* (W Moeser, 1929) 471–85, 472.

One example is the already mentioned Marie Munk, (1885 in Berlin – 1978 in Cambridge/Massachusetts/USA) who studied law from 1907, obtained her doctorate in Heidelberg in 1911, then – because access to the legal profession was still closed – worked as an assistant in a law firm and for a legal advice centre for women, and taught law at the Munich Municipal Women's School, worked for the German Red Cross and the National Women's Service during the war, passed her first law exam in January 1920 with a grade of 'good', then worked as a legal assistant in a mineral oil supply company before she was able to enter the hard-won preparatory service. In January 1924, she was the first woman in Prussia to pass the assessor's examination. She became an advisor to the Prussian Minister of Justice, but was dismissed a few months later due to the desolate budget situation. In 1924, she was one of the first women in Germany to be admitted as a lawyer, and in 1929 she was appointed judge in Berlin, dismissed in 1933 because of non-Aryan descent. In 1936 she emigrated to the USA, took on various teaching and research tasks, passed the Bar Exam in 1943, probably as the first German lawyer to do so, was admitted to the bar in 1944, but did not find a position in a law firm, took on various activities again and [maybe] taught at Harvard from 1953.[41]

The fact that women can do legal work just as well as men is most beautifully demonstrated by the certificate, received during her training period at the criminal court, by Clara Daus, another Jewish woman, the first female trainee lawyer in Hamburg. It is dated 27 January 1923. In it she is confirmed:

> Distinguished in personal interaction by her modest and really womanly demeanour, in official matters by objectivity and clarity, she has met all the expectations directed towards the first female legal trainee in the most pleasant and favourable way. Her perceptiveness and diligence, even in small matters such as taking minutes, distinguish her from most of her male predecessors; in addition, she has good knowledge and an obvious desire to expand it and her life experiences at every opportunity. The time of her work at the Schöffengericht (local court) X [in Hamburg] was therefore also full of stimulation for me as a training judge.[42]

The doubts expressed in the previous decades about the aptitude of women for jurisprudence were thus disproved, but were not dispelled, and women continued to encounter reservations for decades to come. But what was worse: the first women lawyers who had often fought hard for their law degrees, their two state examinations and their legal careers in Germany at an even older age, lost it all again a few years later.

[41] O Cordes, *Marie Munk (1885–1978) Leben und Werk* (Böhlau, 2015); M Röwekamp, *Marie Munk. Rechtsanwältin – Richterin – Rechtsreformerin* (Hentrich & Hentrich Verlag, 2014); M Röwekamp, 'Margarete Berent (1887–1965) und Marie Munk (1885–1978). Pionierinnen im Kampf um gleiche Rechte für Frauen' in *Kritische Justiz.* Sonderheft Streitbare JuristInnen (2016) 72–107. Cordes has also set up a website on her project on Munk: www.cordes-munk.de/.

[42] See www.stolpersteine-hamburg.de/index.php?MAIN_ID=7. The second part translated by the author from the original document can be found here: www.personalbeurteilung.de/soziale_erwnschtheit.html.

In 1929 the world was struck by the black Friday which led to the great depression with enormously high unemployment that, in addition to the antisemitism which had pervaded Europe in the past decades, helped to prepare the ground for the Nazi regime. The NSDAP was founded in 1920 in Munich, Hitler became party chairman in 1921, and in the following decade the NSDAP gained ground.

The Situation of Jews in German Legal Life Before 1933

German Jews[43] were overwhelmingly urban and education-oriented and in the course of the nineteenth century in the Jewish middle class girls were increasingly given the opportunity of a higher education.[44] Law had been a preferred subject for Jews, as historically they had been excluded from many occupations and professions and in the religious tradition the study of the Torah and interpretation of its rules was deeply ingrained.[45] Therefore lawyers of Jewish descent were overrepresented in the legal field. 'While Jews accounted for 0.9 per cent of the population of the German Reich,[46] the percentage of Jewish students in 1930 at German universities was 4.3 per cent (with great difference among the universities: while the figure was 10.7 per cent for Berlin, it was 0.5 only for Münster)'.[47] In 1929/30, Jewish women accounted for 7.1 per cent of female students, but for 15.8 per cent of female law students.

In 1930 4,394 (22 per cent) of about 19,500 admitted Anwälte – in the Prussian part of Germany 29 per cent[48] – were of Jewish descent and in Berlin 60 per cent of the admitted lawyers had at least one Jewish grandparent (so-called 'quarterjews').[49]

Among the first female lawyers, the proportion of Jewish women or women of Jewish origin was very high. In 1929/30, Jewish women accounted for 7.1 per cent of female students overall, but 15.8 per cent of female law students. In comparison, the overall Jewish share of the population in the German Reich was not even one

[43] If I use the term 'Jews' in this contribution, it includes Jewish jurists or jurists of Jewish origin/descent/faith, all those who were persecuted by the Nazi regime as Jewish. The Nazis did not distinguish between those who professed the Jewish religion or those without religious affiliation or converted to Christianity or other religions. For them, it was a matter of the blood.

[44] See www.bpb.de/themen/zeit-kulturgeschichte/juedischesleben/336170/geschlechterrollen-im-deutschen-judentum/. See also D Juristinnenbund (ed), *Juristinnen in Deutschland. Die Zeit von 1900 bis 1998* (Nomos, 1998) 29; H Häntzschel and H Bußmann (eds), *Bedrohlich, Gescheit – Ein Jahrhundert Frauen und Wissenschaft in Bayern* (Beck, 1997) 108.

[45] This is what German Jewish jurists have given me as a reason.

[46] 502,799 people, 144,000 of them in Berlin, 3.8 per cent of the population there. About 65 million people in total lived in the German Reich. Most of the 6 million Jews killed in the Holocaust were from Poland, Ukraine, the Baltic countries, Russia and Belarus, Hungary, Czechia and Romania.

[47] R Zimmermann, 'Was Heimat hieß, nun heißt es Hölle' in J Beatson and R Zimmermann (eds), *Jurists Uprooted. German-speaking Émigré Lawyers in Twentieth-century Britain* (Oxford University Press, 2004) 1–72.

[48] 3370 of the 11,674 lawyers.

[49] I Müller, *Furchtbare Juristen. Die unbewältigte Vergangenheit unserer Justiz* (München, 1987) 67.

per cent. The proportion of Jewish women among female lawyers was estimated at about 25 per cent.

'By the end of the Weimar Republik in 1933, Jews and persons of Jewish descent contributed very significantly to German university life: The overall percentage of Jewish academics and Jewish students far outnumbered that of Jewish Germans in general. 34 (=26%) of the 132 law professors were of Jewish descent.'[50] As Zimmermann writes in the book on *Jews Uprooted*, about German Emigré Jurists to England: 'The most enduring influence on German legal culture, however, was that exercised by legal academics who were Jewish or of Jewish descent. Their relative importance within the academic community may be gauged, for instance, by looking at the Festschrift organised by the German law faculties on the occasion of the fiftieth anniversary of the Reichsgericht. [...] Sixteen of the seventy-one contributors, that is 23 per cent, were of Jewish descent'.[51] Of course all of them were men.

1933–1945

On 30 January 1933, Hitler was nominated chancellor, and in the following weeks, which were marked by National Socialist terror, President Hindenburg restricted political and democratic rights by means of emergency decrees whereby the fundamental rights were de facto suspended. The so-called Enabling Act, passed by a two-thirds majority of the new Reichstag on 23 March 1933, abrogated the Reichstag's sole right to legislate, as established in the Weimar Constitution, and the Nazi-dominated government itself could enact laws. This was the way into the subsequent transformation of the parliamentary democracy of the Weimar Republic and its constitution into a centralist dictatorship operating according to the National Socialist Führer principle. The antisemitism was soon taken to extremes in a perfidious manner by the National Socialists.

The Nazis fast changed the legal situation for women and women lawyers and immediately enacted laws against Jews. Female Jewish jurists had therefore the double burden of being women and Jews, and if they were active for left wing parties even a triple burden.

The Expulsion of Women Jurists from the Legal Profession/Occupations

The celibacy clause for female civil servants had already been reintroduced in 1932. Women as a whole were forced out of working life under the pretext of 'double

[50] Zimmermann (n 47) 16.
[51] Zimmermann (n 47) 21.

earning'. In 1933, for example, marriage loans were paid out to husbands – on condition that the future wife, who had been employed before the marriage, gave up her paid work. A provision was added to the Reich Civil Service Law in 1933 that female civil servants could not be appointed for life until they reached the age of 35; for male civil servants, this was possible from the age of 27.[52] Beginning in 1934, overall female enrolment in universities was limited to 10 per cent.[53]

> The role of women under National Socialism was reduced to motherhood, which was continually glorified as an ideological ideal. In the propaganda of the Third Reich, women's only reason for existence appeared to be to give birth as caring and loving mothers to the future generation of the German, 'Aryan' race and to raise them according to National Socialist sentiments.[54]

Hitler said at the Reich Party Congress of the NSDAP in Nuremberg on 8 September 1934, '[T]he word of women's emancipation is a word invented only by the Jewish intellect. We do not feel it right when woman invades the world of man, but we feel it natural when these two worlds remain separated.' The 'predetermined gender order' should remain intact.[55]

The Nazis paid homage to a cult of masculinity. The ideal German man corresponded to the image of the Nordic race and was strong, able bodied and healthy.[56]

By decree of 29 June 1933, Justice Minister Kerrl ordered the establishment of a so-called communal camp, where trainee lawyers were grouped together by order of presentation (*Gestellungsbefehl*, a military term calling men to up the army) after completion of the written examinations, in order to live together in camaraderie for eight weeks until the oral examination. This, of course, excluded women. It is said that about 20,000 young lawyers have gone through this camp, among them later prominent West German politicians.[57] Kerrl's deputy, Roland Freisler, later the notorious blood judge and President of the Volksgerichtshof, demanded that the German jurist of the future be 'heroic' in contrast to the bourgeois or Marxist jurist. The training of jurists, he said, must take into account the formation of German male characters.

On 22 July 1934, under the auspices of Otto Palandt,[58] the newly appointed president of the Reich Judicial Examination Office and department head in the Reich Ministry of Justice, a new judicial training ordinance came into force. It

[52] § 1a in the Reich Civil Service Act of 31 March 1873, as amended by the Act of 30 June 1933.

[53] After remilitarisation and the beginning of the Second World War, when the number of male students decreased drastically, the percentage of women increased again and even exceeded the 50 per cent mark towards the end of the Second World War. See Plett (n 23) 360 with further references.

[54] U Schultz, 'Wie männlich ist die Juristenschaft?' in U Battis und U Schultz (eds), *Frauen im Recht* (C. F. Müller, 1990) 319–59, 325. Own translation.

[55] See www.zukunft-braucht-erinnerung.de/die-deutsche-frau-und-ihre-rolle-im-nationalsozialismus/#_ftn. Own translation.

[56] Hitler did not correspond to this in any way, and neither did the propaganda minister Goebbels.

[57] F Schmerbach, *Das 'Gemeinschaftslager Hans Kerrl' für Referendare in Jüterbog 1933–1939. Beiträge zur Rechtsgeschichte des 20. Jahrhunderts* (Mohr Siebeck, 2008).

[58] The large standard commentary on the civil code was called Palandt until December 2021 and was only then renamed Grüneberg due to increasing protests from young lawyers.

was prefaced as a guiding principle: 'The aim of the training of the jurist is to produce a servant of the law who has been thoroughly trained in his subject, who has an irreproachable character, who lives among the people and with them, and who wants to be and can be an incorruptible and unerring helper and guide in the legal shaping of their lives [...]'.[59] These quotations show that women were not meant to be trainee lawyers or part of the legal profession. On 20 December 1934, the law amending the Code of Lawyers followed, according to which women were no longer admitted as lawyers, because this would have meant an 'intrusion into the old-hallowed principle of the masculinity of the state'. Even after the new laws were passed, Palandt unequivocally stated that it was 'up to the man to uphold the law'.[60]

On the basis of a 1935 decree, women were 'in the future not to be offered employment in judicial or prosecutorial careers'. In 1936, the Reich Minister of Justice was informed by the Fuehrer's deputy: 'He [the Fuehrer] has decided that women should not be lawyers or judges. Women lawyers can therefore be used in the civil service only in the administration.'[61] That the jurist should be a man was again emphasised in the 'Ordinance on Qualification for the Judiciary, the Public Prosecutor's Office, the Notary's Office, and the Bar' of 4 January 1939, where section 5 states that law students should 'acquire an overview of the entire intellectual life of the nation', 'as must be expected of an educated German man'.[62] In 1939, nine women were still employed as judges,[63] the remaining women judges had been dispensed from their judicial duties and relegated to administrative positions. Women lawyers were mainly employed 'in positions suitable for women', in the field of welfare in the care of women and children, the NS Women's organisations, and similar.[64] Some moved up to high and influential positions in this area, which was marked as female but could give them influence beyond it.[65] Many worked in non-legal jobs. Very few were able to continue their work as lawyers in legal practice, among them Elisabeth Selbert, who had been admitted to the bar in 1934, despite great opposition. Her husband had become unemployed as a

[59] The guiding principle continues, 'To achieve this, education must take hold of the whole person, bring body and mind into good harmony, consolidate character and strengthen the will, shape the national community in the young person into an unlosable experience, provide him with a comprehensive education, and build up a solid professional skill on this basis.' See also S Wolf, *Das Jenaer Studium der Rechte im Dritten Reich. Zwischen Tradition und nationalsozialistischer Ideologie*. Rechtshistorische Reihe 442 (Peter Lang, 2013) 21, n 19. Section 46 on assessments in the Legal Education Law NRW strangely rules: 'In this context, comments are to be made on the technical and general knowledge and skills, on the practical aptitude, on the state of education and on the overall image of the personality.'

[60] H Wrobel, 'Otto Palandt zum Gedächtnis 1. 5. 1877–3. 12. 1951' (1982) 15(1) *Kritische Justiz* 1–17, 7.

[61] Juristinnenbund (n 44) 26 and appendices 25 and 26.

[62] I Staff (ed), *Justiz im Dritten Reich. Eine Dokumentation*, 2nd edn (Fischer Taschenbuch Verlag, 1978) 118.

[63] Bajohr and Rödiger-Bajohr (n 26) 49.

[64] D Juristinnenbund (ed), *Juristinnen in Deutschland. Die Zeit von 1900 bis 2003*, 4th edn (Nomos, 2003) 27.

[65] F Michl, *Wiltraut Rupp-von Brünneck (1912–1977)* (Campus, 2022) 78; Misselwitz (n 35) 133.

politically disliked person. After the war, she fought with great commitment in the Constitutional Assembly (Parlamentarischer Rat) for the principle of equal rights (Article 3(2) GG) to be incorporated into the Basic Law.[66]

During the war – despite an increasing shortage of lawyers – women were only hesitantly and cautiously appointed as deputies for lawyers. They were able to represent lawyers in their offices sporadically. But if the owner of the practice fell at the front, they were not allowed to take over the practice on their own.[67] In spite of the limited professional possibilities some women still studied law and took the two state examinations. One example is Wiltrud Rupp-von Brünneck (first examination 1939, second 1941) who has shown some closeness to Nazi ideology, worked in the Ministry of Justice during the war, after the war as judge and in the Ministry of Justice in Hesse and became the successor of Erna Scheffler, the first woman justice at the Federal Constitutional Court, in 1963.[68] In the legal academia, no other woman was habilitated, accordingly no female law professor appointed. In 1938, there were only 12 female professors of all subjects in Germany.[69]

Acts and Actions Against Jewish Jurists

Two months after the Nazi's seizing power (*Machtergreifung*), on 7 March 1933 an Act to Restore the Civil Service was passed with a special rule against Jews, the so-called Aryan paragraph (*Arierparagraph*) in section 3 paragraph 1: Non Arian civil servants (including judges and prosecutors) have to be sent into retirement.

On 1 April 1933 the boycott of Jews, their shops and services was declared. On 7 April 1933 an Act on the Admission to the Legal Profession followed which excluded Jews, even 'quarter Jews' ('lawyers of non-Aryan descent'), from further entering legal practice and 1,084 lost their admission.[70] In a 1934 Amendment to this Legal Profession Act, Jews were no longer allowed to use the title *Rechtsanwalt*. The male Jewish jurists who had fought for Germany in the First World War got however an exemption from the rules in these laws (*Frontkämpferprivileg*)[71] and could stay in the civil service and were able to continue practising their profession until 1938 but it was, however, no option for women. Of 38 Jewish women lawyers the admission was immediately revoked for 36 of them. Within a year, all but two Jewish women lawyers were banned from practising law and thus deprived of their livelihood. None of the Jewish

[66] B Böttger, *Das Recht auf Gleichheit und Differenz* (Westfälisches Dampfboot, 1990).

[67] Bajohr and Rödiger-Bajohr (n 26) 49.

[68] Michl (n 65).

[69] G-F Budde, *Frauen der Intelligenz. Akademikerinnen in der DDR. 1945 bis 1975* (Vandenhoeck und Rupprecht, 2003) 160.

[70] G Fieberg, *Catalogue for the exhibition of the German Ministry of Justice 'Im Namen des Deutschen Volkes. Justiz und Nationalsozialismus'* (Verl. Wiss. u. Politik, 1989) 77.

[71] Due to the Law for the Restoration of the Civil Service of 7.4.1933. Reichspräsident von Hindenburg (in office from 1925 till he died in 1934) had enforced these exemptions.

women jurists had been able to practise after 1938, with one exception resulting from reasons of expediency: Dr Hanna Katz who was a specialist in trademark law and secretary of the international society for World Trademark law. If she had been forced to give up her position, the British would have acquired it which would have been a loss for the German economy.[72] Some women helped their non-Jewish husbands in the back office.[73]

The Law against Overcrowding of Schools and Universities of 25 April 1933, in conjunction with an implementing decree, limited the new enrolment of Jewish students to 1.5 per cent, provided that the total number of Jewish students did not exceed 5 per cent. As a result, the proportion of male Jewish students fell from 2,698 in the summer semester of 1932 to 486 in the summer semester of 1934, and that of female Jewish students from 1,252 to 170.[74]

In the spring of 1933, the National Socialist Legal Association demanded that 'all Jews must be completely removed from any form of legal life', and thus wanted to get rid of competitors who were also hated as supporters of the Republic, committed democrats, socialists or pacifists.

As a consequence of the Reich Citizenship Act 1935 all Jewish judges, also the few female judges, and all prosecutors, were finally sent to retirement. Section 5 of an Act on Abuse of Legal Services from 13 December 1935 excluded Jews from admission even as legal advisers, ie paralegals. On 3 and 4 October 1936 more than 100 university teachers of the National Socialist Legal Association gathered for a conference 'Judaism in jurisprudence' with the aim of defining, identifying and eliminating the 'Jewish spirit' in German jurisprudence.[75] At the beginning of 1938 there were still 1,753 Jews among the 17,360 lawyers in the Reich,[76] but in September 1938 the *Frontkämpferklausel* (combatants rule) was also abolished and all Jewish lawyers had to stop practising. Only a small number got permission to work as legal advisers for Jews.[77] The Jewish women lawyers who stayed in Germany mainly worked for Jewish welfare organisations.

[72] S Ladwig-Winters, 'Lebenswege jüdischer Rechtsanwältinnen nach 1933' (*Anwaltsblatt* online, 2022) anwaltsblatt.anwaltverein.de/de/anwaeltinnen-anwaelte/portraets/lebenswege-juedischer-rechtsanwaeltinnen-nach-1933.

[73] S Ladwig-Winters, 'Verfolgung, Exil und Tod – Die Situation der jüdischen Juristinnen nach 1933' in D Juristinnenbund (ed), *Jüdische Juristinnen* (Catalogue accompanying the exhibition 'Jüdische Juristinnen und Juristinnen jüdischer Herkunft') in German and English) (Beck, 2019) 24–32, 28.

[74] Cl Huerkamp, *Bildungsbürgerinnen. Frauen im Studium und in akademischen Berufen 1900–1945* (Vandenhoek und Ruprecht, 1996) 104; also Huerkamp, 'Jüdische Akademikerinnen in Deutschland 1900–1938' (1993) 19(3) *Geschichte und Gesellschaft* 311–31. Plett (n 23) 359.

[75] S Felz, 'Das Judentum in der Rechtswissenschaft. Die deutsche Rechtswissenschaft im Kampf gegen den jüdischen Geist' Eine 'wissenschaftliche' Tagung im Oktober 1936 in Berlin in *ZNR* 2017, 87–99.

[76] G Plum, 'Wirtschaft und Erwerbsleben' in W Benz (ed), *Die Juden in Deutschland 1933–1945* (Beck 1988) 288.

[77] S Heim (ed), *Die Verfolgung und Ermordung der europäischen Juden durch das nationalsozialistische Deutschland 1933–1945 (Quellensammlung) vol 2: Deutsches Reich 1938–August 1939* (R. Oldenbourg, 2009) 18.

The progroms of November 1938 (called *Reichskristallnacht* as windows and shop windows of Jewish property were smashed) marked the transition from discrimination against German Jews from 1933 onward to their systematic expulsion and oppression. Three years later the Holocaust began, the annihilation of all Jewish life. In the following four years until the end of the Second World War six million European Jews were killed.

The Consequences

Parts of the Jewish jurists decided to emigrate after the occupational ban in 1933 and before the beginning of the war, women with their husbands and some also alone, although not all could accomplish their emigration plans, especially later in the 1930s. Some preferred to stay with family members in Germany. A total of about 500,000 people, more than 90 per cent of the Jewish as defined by the National Socialist racial laws, managed to flee the German Reich, Austria and the German-speaking part of Czechoslovakia. Many of them eventually made their way, often under adventurous circumstances, to the United States,[78] and about 150,000 to England. They were not all well received, some were interned, some deported.[79] There is no precise estimate of how many of them were jurists.

It was difficult to practise in other countries. Their German legal qualification had no value in the host countries. The legal regimes were too different, particularly the gap between common law legal thinking and continental European scholarship. They had to retrain and in many countries they needed citizenship, which can only be obtained after years. The difficult living conditions in a foreign country weighed heavily on them. They had lost or had to leave behind all their belongings. They struggled with language problems. Many – particularly of the male jurists – had learned Latin but not English at school, let alone Spanish. Many worked in low-paid unskilled jobs to finance their lives. The majority of those who managed to flee to England and retrained, studied at the London School of Economics. Some became barristers, a few solicitors. A large percentage of the Jewish women jurists who remained in Germany were systematically murdered in the Holocaust. Some survived in hiding.

The legal libraries were 'cleansed' of Jewish publications, and due to a citation ban on Jewish authors, an important part of legal scholarship was no longer received and thus became invisible. It cannot be measured what German jurisprudence has

[78] EC Stiefel, 'Die deutsche juristische Emigration in den USA' (1988) *Juristenzeitung* 421–26.

[79] H-P Benöhr, 'Review of Jurists uprooted. German-speaking émigré lawyers in twentieth-century Britain ed. by Jack Beatson and Reinhard Zimmermann 2004' (2007) *Zeitschrift der Savigny-Stiftung für Rechtsgeschichte. Germanistische Abteilung* 124.

lost through the expulsion and extinction of the Jewish part of its jurists. It was an irreplaceable brain drain and destruction of spiritual goods.[80]

After the War

After the war, women jurists in Germany initially often became 'stopgap' replacements for men who had been killed in the war or were prisoners of war, or who had not received a '*Persilschein*' and could no longer work in the civil service because of their National Socialist past. The few women jurists there were, could again be admitted to the bar and were hired primarily out of historical demographic necessity in the judiciary and administration, though often only for temporary and lower-paying positions than men.[81] When more men became available again, women usually had to leave or were left sitting in the entry grades, and men leapfrogged them in their careers. Male judges continued their careers almost seamlessly.[82]

Although a woman was appointed to each of the federal courts when they were founded, these proportions did not change for a long time, and women made only slow inroads into promotion positions at courts of first and second instance. As late as 1950, the provisional version of the civil service law still contained the so-called celibacy clause, according to which women could be dismissed for marrying because they would then be economically secure. After the abolition of the celibacy clause, in the restorative atmosphere of the Adenauer era, in which a conservative image of the family prevailed, the discussions about double incomes resumed.

Only a few of the emigrated women jurists remigrated. It is depressing that former Jewish women lawyers had problems obtaining reparations or restitution after the war.[83] Erna Proskauer, who wanted to become a judge in the early 1930s and had been appointed as an assistant judge until 1933, litigated for years after the war to be reinstated in the judicial service. In the final instance, she lost. It was decided that her appointment as a judge on a permanent position would have been denied even if she had not been dismissed at the time, since female lawyers secured by their husbands would not have been admitted to the bench due to the celibacy clause.[84] The abovementioned Else Koffka also did not get a chance to work as a judge, when Berlin lawyers were temporarily appointed to a judgeship after 1946 to fill the shortage of judges – despite her discrimination during the National Socialist era.

[80] S Höpel, 'Die Säuberung der deutschen Rechtswissenschaft – Ausmaß und Dimensionen der Vertreibung nach 1933' (1993) 26(4) *Kritische Justiz* 438–60.

[81] Schultz (n 54) 316 with further references.

[82] This is impressively described in the fact-based novel: U Krechel, *Landgericht* (Jung und Jung, 2012).

[83] Juristinnenbund (n 64) 28. The few emigrated men who resumed their office as judges in Germany met former Nazis in the judiciary who might be favoured with regard to promotions. This was difficult for them to bear. See also Krechel (n 82).

[84] E Proskauer, *Wege und Umwege. Erinnerungen einer Berliner Rechtsanwältin* edited and afterword by S Berghahn and C Wickert (Fischer, 1996).

Gertrud Schubart-Fikentscher[85] was the first German woman who got her habilitation after the war in 1946 and a chair in Leipzig in the newly founded GDR; in West Germany, it took until 1965 till Anne-Eva Brauneck got a chair. Magdalene Schoch, the first woman with a habilitation in Germany, a pupil of Mendelssohn-Bartholdy, herself a non-Jew, had been an opponent of the regime. She refused to give the Hitler salute and refused requests to stop naming Jewish authors in publications. When she was pressured to join the NSDAP in 1937, she resigned her position and emigrated to the United States. From 1946 to 1966, Magdalene Schoch worked as an expert in international and foreign law in leading positions in the US Department of Justice and as a lawyer in Washington, at last admitted to the US Supreme Court. She was initially refused restitution in Germany after the war as it was claimed that she had voluntarily asked to be released, another decision based on legal formalities which today meets with disbelief and incomprehension, knowing that former Nazis were reinstated.[86]

Biographies

Sources

How do we know and what do we know in detail about the early women jurists and amongst them the Jewish women who were affected in their lives and professional opportunities by National Socialism? In the 1970s, the life, work and role of Jewish jurists, the national socialist injustice in law and the judiciary were increasingly researched. Meanwhile the German and foreign literature on lawyers of Jewish origin, can no longer be surveyed. But most of it is written by men on men, for example Beatson/Zimmermann's 2004 edited volume is one such example.[87] Göppinger has collected more than 500 brief portraits of Jewish lawyers,[88] although there have been some thousands. Only 22 women are included.[89] Breunung/Walter deal in their first publication of their extended research project on emigrated lawyers with 24 male jurists.[90]

[85] R Fikentscher, *Liebe Arbeit Einsamkeit. Wilhelm Schubart, Papyrologe. Gertrud Schubart-Fikentscher, Rechtshistorikerin. Ein Gelehrtenpaar in zwei Diktaturen* (Mitteldeutscher Verlag, 2014).

[86] Nicolaysen (n 38); Plett (n 23).

[87] Beatson and Zimmermann (n 47).

[88] H Göppinger, *Juristen jüdischer Abstammung im 'Dritten Reich'*, 2nd edn (Beck, 1990) (1st edn *Die Verfolgung der Juristen jüdischer Abstammung durch den Nationalsozialismus*, 1963).

[89] Also the book 'Zwischen Recht und Unrecht. Lebensläufe deutscher Juristen' edited by the Ministry of Justice NRW portraits only men – with one exception after 1945: Hilde Benjamin, the notorious female Minister of Justice in GDR.

[90] L Breunung and M Walther, *Die Emigration deutscher Rechtswissenschaftler ab 1933/ Westeuropäische Staaten, Türkei, Palästina/Israel, lateinamerikanische Staaten, Südafrikanische Union* (De Gruyter Saur, 2012).

In the 1980s the second wave women's movement set itself the goal of working out the history of important women to make women and their achievements visible. They collected the available information, did interviews, went to archives, published articles and thus also the history of Jewish women jurists was gradually documented.

Marion Röwekamp has compiled an encyclopedia on women jurists, their life and work with 150 portraits of early women jurists which includes a number of portraits of female Jewish lawyers.[91] Oda Cordes has dealt with the 'First German Women Lawyers and Their Demands for Reform in the Weimar Republic'.[92] Simone Ladwig-Winters has documented more biographies of Jewish women jurists and has dealt with their life and work, their minority experiences and female discrimination in detail.[93] In 2019 the Deutscher Juristinnenbund launched an exhibition on 'Jewish Women Lawyers and Women Lawyers of Jewish Origin' 'which portrays 17 women who represent many other Jewish women lawyers or women lawyers of the first generation of women lawyers who were persecuted by the National Socialists as Jewish'.[94] A press release for the exhibition states: These 'women lawyers have played an important role in the development of the legal profession in Germany. Their biographies show what Jewish life in Germany was like – and could be like today – what part Jewish women lawyers played in the emergence of the field of social work, and what part in the struggle of women for equal rights in the Weimar Republic. The history of women lawyers is not only a professional history, but also a history of democracy and a part of German Jewish history.'[95]

Meanwhile several detailed biographies have been published, for example Röwekamp and Cordes on Munk,[96] Misselwitz on Hilger,[97] Hansen on Scheffler,[98] and Michl on Rupp-von Brünneck.[99] Many of the jurists have a biographical entry in Wikipedia[100] and the Jewish women jurists also appear in the Jewish Women's Archive and the Central Data Bank Yad Vashem.[101]

[91] Röwekamp (n 13).

[92] O Cordes, *Frauen als Wegbereiter des Rechts: Die ersten deutschen Juristinnen und ihre Reformforderungen in der Weimarer Republik* (Diplomica, 2012).

[93] S Ladwig-Winters, *Das Ende eines Aufbruchs – jüdische Juristinnen und Juristinnen jüdischer Herkunft nach 1933: Minderheitenerfahrung und weibliche Diskriminierung* (Verlag Bundesanzeiger, 2016).

[94] D Juristinnenbund (ed), *Jüdische Juristinnen* (Beck, 2019) (Catalogue accompanying the exhibition 'Jüdische Juristinnen und Juristinnen jüdischer Herkunft') in German and English.

[95] Press release 5 March 2020 'djb opens exhibition "Jewish Women Lawyers"' in Berlin.

[96] See n 41 above.

[97] Boedeker and Meyer-Plath (n 35), see also U Schultz, 'Marie Luise Hilgers – Zum Leben und Werk einer Arbeitsrechtlerin im 20. Jahrhundert. Rezension des gleichnamigen Buches von Frederike Misselwitz' (2016) 4 *djbZ* 185–87.

[98] M Hansen, *Erna Scheffler (1893–1983). Erste Richterin am Bundesverfassungsgericht und Wegbereiterin einer geschlechtergerechten Gesellschaft* (Mohr Siebeck, 2019).

[99] Michl (n 65).

[100] And eg in www.digitales-deutsches-frauenarchiv.de/.

[101] Jewish Women's Archive, see jwa.org/, Central Data Bank Yadvashem, see yvng.yadvashem.org, see also *Gedenkbuch Opfer der Verfolgung der Juden unter der nationalsozialistischen Gewaltherrschaft*

Brief Summaries of Some Jewish Women Jurists' Biographies

In the following, some brief biographical notes of some of the female lawyers of Jewish origin are listed, which exemplify their difficult career path and the multi-faceted stories of Jewish women in the Third Reich, their problems and sufferings. They can, however, not represent the entire spectrum of oppression and persecution and are far from doing justice to all of them.

Jewish women lawyers

Death by suicide

Clara Israel[102] (1876 Spandau–1942 Berlin)

1929 first female magistrate, from 1933 Jewish home care association

Suicide by poisoning due to threat of deportation

Dr Lucy Nelly Liefmann (1884 Frankfurt–1942 Frankfurt)

1918 first woman with a promotion in law in Frankfurt

Welfare work, training of volunteer nurses for the poor and orphans in Frankfurt

1933 dismissed as a Jew and Social Democrat[103]

Killed in Concentration Camps

Clara Daus[104] 1899 Hamburg–1942 KZ Ausschwitz

1926 second examination, lawyer in Hamburg administration at the welfare office (1926–1927), youth welfare office (1927–1931) and the finance deputation (1931–1933)

After 1933 work for her family, emigration failed

Ella Kessler-Reis 1899 Stuttgart–1944 KZ Auschwitz

1932 Lawyer in Stuttgart

Since 1933 leading position at the Jewish welfare association

Elisabeth Kohn 1902 München–1941 Lithuania

Lawyer in Munich 1928, represented SPD, interests of Jewish citizens, co-founder of the red help

1933 disbarred, deported to an extermination camp in Lithuania, killed there[105]

in Deutschland 1933–1945, Bundesarchiv Koblenz (*Memorial Book Victims of the Persecution of Jews under the National Socialist Tyranny in Germany 1933–1945* at www.bundesarchiv.de/gedenkbuch/en).

[102] P Reinicke, 'Israel, Clara' in H Maier (ed), *Who is who der Sozialen Arbeit* (Lambertus, 1998) 273f.

[103] See aktuelles.uni-frankfurt.de/en/menschen/lucy-liefmann-ehrung-einer-vergessenen/.

[104] See www.stolpersteine-hamburg.de.

[105] EG Lowenthal (ed), *Bewährung im Untergang. Ein Gedenkbuch. Im Auftrag des Council of Jews from Germany, London* (DVA, 1965) 103–105.

Dr Erica Sinauer 1889 Freiburg – 8.3.1945 KZ Auschwitz (fictitious date for all those whose date of death there is not known)

1927 lawyer, also scholarly historical work

1933 work on habilitation, also historical work on Saxon law and Monumenta Germaniae Historica 1940 internment camp Gurs/France, 1942 deported to Auschwitz

1940 internment camp Gurs/France

1942 deported to Auschwitz

Emigration

Dr Margarete Berent[106] 1887 Berlin–1965 New York

1913 *Promotion* in Erlangen

1925 First admitted lawyer in Prussia, Berlin, founding member of German Academic Women's Association

1933 in Central Office for Jewish Economic Aid, and head of the department for women's issues

1939 emigration to Chile, 1941 New York, retrained

1949 lawyer in New York, 1956 to 1965 in legal department of the New York City Council

Dr Brigitte Bodenheimer, née Levy 1912 Berlin–1991 Davis/California

1934 *Promotion* in Heidelberg, emigration

1937 Washington Bachelor of Law, 1946 Associated Professor, 1951 Professor University of Utah

Dr Hedwig Sara Brann-Frank 1899 Frankfurt–1978 Chicago

1938 emigrated to Palestine, 1939 New York, retrained, 1945 lawyer in Chicago

Ruth Ehrlich, née Zucker 1907 Essen–2007 Philadelphia

1932 Rechtsreferendarin, 1934–1941 worked in Jewish Community family welfare in Berlin

1941 immigration visa USA, retrained 1958–1961, 1962 admission to Chicago bar

Dr Edith Kosterlitz née Dosmar 1904 Mönchengladbach–1994 New York

1933 excluded from second examination, emigrated to Belgium

1935–1940 working in law office, 1940–1943 active in underground

1945–1947 head of Comité Israelite des Victimes des Lois Raciales in Brüssel

1947 emigration to USA, 1948 working for UNO, later in leading positions

[106] See www.digitales-deutsches-frauenarchiv.de/akteurinnen/margarete-berent.

Remigration

Nora Platiel née Block 1896 Bochum–1979 Kassel

Could not finish school, worked as secretary during the First World War in the war relief service in Romania, then for the women's rights activist Helene Stöcker, who convinced her to finish school and she studied law. 1922 member of SPD, active in red help

1931 first female lawyer in Bochum

1933 flight to Paris, work for Comité d'assistance aux refugiés, 1940 camp Gurs, interned

1942 flight to Switzerland, work for the workers' relief society

1949 return to Kassel, judge and later presiding judge at a compensation /restitution chamber

1954–1966 member of the Hesse parliament for SPD

Dr Käthe Manasse née Loewy 1905 Berlin–1994 Hamburg

1932/33 court assessor in Berlin

1938 emigration to Palestine

1949 return to Hamburg, employee in office for reparation

1952 judge, 1962 presiding judge

Dr Martha Mosse 1984 Berlin–1977 Berlin

1920 *Promotion*, 1922 councillor in police headquarters in Berlin, 1926 promotion to regular position

1933–1943 work for the Jewish community in Berlin, 1939 at housing counselling centre for Jews

1941 participation in 'resettlement' measures for Jews despite serious misgivings

1943–1945 interned in concentration camp Theresienstadt

After the war accused of collaboration by fellow Jews, but classified as a victim of fascism

Advisor of the American Military government for the Nuremberg trials

1948–1953 Police Counsellor in Berlin

Two of those who had managed to survive in Germany

Alice Prausnitz, 1906 Mauritius–1996 Plön, half Jew

1933 second exam, commercial clerk, during war obliged to war service (*Kriegsdienstverpflichtung*)

1945 lawyer and later notary in Leipzig, opponent of the DDR system, 1949 Hamburg

1960 first female presiding judge after the war, at a compensation chamber
Women's rights activist

Dr Erna Scheffler née Friedenthal[107] 1893 Breslau–1983 London, half Jew (two Jewish grandparents),

1914 *Promotion* in Munich, second exam 1925

1925–1928 lawyer in Berlin

1928 court assessor, 1932–1933 judge in Berlin

Her later husband was not allowed to marry her due to the Racial Defilement Laws (Nuremberg laws)

Survived persecution hidden in a garden house

31 May 1945 judge in Berlin, 1948 after the currency reform judge at the administrative court in Düsseldorf

1951–1963 first female judge at the Federal Constitutional Court

Postscript: A Personal Note

The story of the emigrated German-speaking lawyers in England[108] is special to me as I encountered several of the emigrés mentioned in the book in the late 1960s and 1970s mainly when doing interviews for an empirical project on freedom of establishment for lawyers and cross border legal interchange. I mention here mainly those whose wives or close relatives were also lawyers.

The first I got to know was Clive Schmitthoff, born in 1903. When he 'left for England in 1933, he was able to read for an LLM at the London School of Economics (LSE) where his future wife Ilse Auerbach ("Twinkie") was also a student. She too had been qualified as a German lawyer, and had practised as an advocate in Frankfurt am Main.'[109] He organised summer courses on English and Comparative Law and European Law at the City of London College/later City of London Polytechnic. I attended them in 1968 and 1971. Clive Schmitthoff and his wife gave receptions for the students of the summer courses, and this is how I met her, a friendly old lady, very supportive of her husband.

I also went to see Rudolf Graupner, who retrained as a solicitor, in London, whose half-Jewish sister-in-law Hildegard Jacobi, Dr. iur. and lawyer in Cologne, became a lecturer in international relations in London after the war. Murad Ferid, his friend from pre-war times who taught international law and comparison of law in Munich had given me a letter of recommendation for him.

Frederic Mann received me in his solicitor's office for an interview, but soon told me that I was not doing serious jurisprudence with my research and that it

[107] See n 98 above.
[108] Beatson and Zimmermann (n 47).
[109] JA Adams, 'Clive Schmitthoff (1903–1990)' in Beatson and Zimmermann (n 47) 367–80.

had no scholarly value. Eleonore Ehrlich, Francis Mann's wife, had been one of the few and early law faculty assistants and also one of the first women to become a doctor of law in Germany in 1930 (383 f.) 'After her emigration to Britain she qualified as a solicitor, and handed cases for the poor in a practice [...] a precursor of the later neighbourhood law centres.'[110] I also interviewed amongst others Ernst J Cohn, a barrister and a friendly old scholar whose articles on comparison of law had impressed me.

There was a whole Jewish legal emigré community in London. Some invited me to lunches, and they asked me a lot about life in Germany. They had all retrained in law and become solicitors. These were very friendly encounters, although I was an offspring of the country where so many injustices had happened to them and where they had lived in danger. Most of them had lost family members in concentration camps. Some had also got a second admission in Germany which had become possible due to restitution rules after the war and did not require a second office in Germany. They worked partly in German and in English law. I met many more of the emigrated Jews at the regular meetings of the German-British Lawyers' Association. This is how Margot Hoare née Blaut, who was born in Frankfurt in 1917, but had qualified in England, a barrister at Middle Temple, became my friend. She died in 1982.

[110] J Beatson, 'Aliens, Enemy Aliens, and Friendly Enemy Aliens. Britain as a Home for Emigré and Refugee Lawyers' in Beatson and Zimmermann (n 47) 73–104, 84.

3

Beyond Firsts: Feminist Biography and Early Women Barristers

CAROLINE DERRY

Introduction

A consistent theme running through Rosemary Auchmuty's publications on the history of women in law schools and the legal profession is the need for a nuanced, feminist approach which eschews straightforward narratives of progress. Through her ground-breaking exploration of the life of Gwyneth Bebb, a pioneering law student who challenged women's exclusion from the legal profession, Auchmuty has argued that the 'great lives' model of biography, focused upon a single and singular individual, is ill-suited to exploring the systemic effects of gender upon women's engagement with the law.[1] The failings of the earlier model, which suffered only a slow and incomplete death over the course of the last century and lingers on in legal biography,[2] have important political as well as historiographical consequences: 'to reveal women's legal history too clearly would be to uncover the many mechanisms by which men have retained power for themselves in law and to give the lie to the vaunted equality of opportunity for men and women'.[3] Auchmuty is at the forefront of feminist historians who are working to uncover precisely that.

The development of feminist methods and methodologies to do this work is, of course, an ongoing process. This chapter examines a persistent survivor of the 'great lives' approaches still apparent in recent celebrations of early women

[1] R Auchmuty, 'Whatever Happened to Miss Bebb? Bebb v The Law Society and Women's Legal History' (2010) 31 *Legal Studies* 199; R Auchmuty, 'Researching Women in Legal History: The Case of Miss Bebb' (2014) 14 *Legal Information Management* 19; R Auchmuty and E Rackley, 'Feminist Legal Biography: A Model for All Legal Life Stories' (2020) 41 *Journal of Legal History* 186.

[2] Auchmuty and Rackley (n 1) 191; and see V Barnes, C MacMillan and S Vogenauer, 'On Legal Biography' (2020) 41 *The Journal of Legal History* 115. However, for the disruptive potential of legal biography, see C Smith, 'The Disruptive Power of Legal Biography: The Life of Lord Phillimore – Churchman and Judge' (2020) 41 *Journal of Legal History* 164.

[3] R Auchmuty, 'Recovering Lost Lives: Researching Women in Legal History' (2015) 42 *Journal of Law and Society* 34.

lawyers: a focus upon 'firsts'.[4] Through considering several pioneers in England and Wales, including Olive Clapham (first women to pass Bar Finals examinations) and Monica Geikie Cobb (first woman briefed to appear in court), it will explore why the status of 'first' has been given such importance. It will consider the benefits and limitations of framing women's roles and achievements in this way, particularly from a feminist perspective, and the implications for our understanding of today's profession. It does so by considering what effects this specific temporalisation of women's experiences produces, not only upon our interpretations of the past but also upon the ways they interact with our present and 'conceivable futures'.[5]

Olive Clapham and Monica Geikie Cobb

In considering women's entry to the Bar of England and Wales, it is not simple to identify *the* first.[6] The initial step towards qualification was joining one of London's four Inns of Court, all of which had excluded women until 1919. The first woman admitted to an Inn of Court was Helena Normanton.[7] There were then two steps usually taken more or less simultaneously: passing a series of examinations culminating in the Bar Finals and keeping 12 dining terms (eating several dinners each term) at one's Inn. The first woman to pass the Bar Finals examinations was Olive Clapham, widely but erroneously reported in the contemporary press as the 'first woman barrister'.[8] When examinations and dining were both completed, the final step was the ceremony of being called to the Bar by one's Inn: the point at which one became a qualified barrister. The first woman called to the Bar of England and Wales, in May 1922, was Ivy Williams, who chose to continue her academic career and never practised.[9] Normanton was the first woman called to the Bar who intended to practise, but that is a very fine distinction as she was one of nine women called on the same night. (They were all a year behind the first woman barristers in the UK, however: Frances Kyle and Averil Deverell had been called to

[4] Auchmuty's own work refers to 'early', rather than 'first', women law students: R Auchmuty, 'Early Women Law Students at Cambridge and Oxford' (2008) 29 *Journal of Legal History* 63.

[5] E Grosz, 'Histories of a Feminist Future' (2000) 25 *Signs: Journal of Women in Culture and Society* 1017.

[6] See U Schultz, 'Introduction: Gender and Careers in the Legal Academy: Overview and Synthesis' in U Schultz et al (eds), *Gender and Careers in the Legal Academy* (Hart, 2021) 1, especially Table 1 (which nonetheless simplifies 'first' to the date of admission).

[7] J Bourne, 'First Woman to Be Admitted to an Inn of Court, Helena Normanton, 1919' in E Rackley and R Auchmuty (eds), *Women's Legal Landmarks: Celebrating the History of Women and Law in the UK and Ireland* (Hart, 2018) 147.

[8] 'The First Woman Barrister' *The Times* (London, 26 May 1921) 10; 'The First Woman Barrister' *The Scotsman* (Edinburgh, 27 May 1921) 5; 'Yorkshire Distinction' *Leeds Mercury* (27 May 1921) 12.

[9] H Fox, 'Williams, Ivy (1877–1966)' in D Cannadine (ed), *Oxford Dictionary of National Biography*, (DNB, 2020); C Morris, 'Dr Ivy Williams: Inside yet Outside' (June 2020) 29(4) *Women's History Review* 583–614.

the Dublin and Belfast bars in 1921.)[10] The first woman briefed to appear in court in England and Wales was Monica Geikie Cobb, who simultaneously became the first woman to prosecute a criminal case, the first woman to appear in a jury trial, and the first woman to win her case.[11] There followed a series of first women appearing in various specific courts, but soon there would be a barren period as the early women barristers met persistent systemic barriers to further progression. They had to wait until after the Second World War for the first women King's Counsel and judges.[12]

This chapter explores the biographies of two of that plethora of early women barristers who could be described as firsts: Olive Clapham and Monica Geikie Cobb. Both were admitted to Middle Temple within weeks of the Bar being opened to women by the Sex Disqualification (Removal) Act 1919. It had received Royal Assent on 23 December and, as soon as Middle Temple reopened after the Christmas holidays, Monica Geikie Cobb was admitted on 2 January 1920;[13] Olive Clapham followed a fortnight later, on 17 January.[14] They had now formally begun their path to qualification.

It was an unlikely path for Clapham. She was a Roman Catholic, working-class Yorkshirewoman born in Wakefield in 1898. After her father, a printer and compositor, died when she was not quite five years old, she, her two older brothers, and her mother had gone to live with his sister and brother-in-law in Kingston-upon-Hull.[15] Marian MacKenzie, professionally known as Madame Clapham, was a famous couturier whose clientele included minor royalty. Her husband Alexander was her business manager, and Clapham's mother became her housekeeper, looking after the young women employees who both lived and worked on the premises. Madame Clapham was known as a demanding employer, but also one capable of real generosity.[16] She certainly treated her niece and nephews well: while she was a Christian Scientist, they were educated in leading Catholic schools and Clapham also studied piano.[17] After Clapham completed her schooling at the French Convent School in Hull, she continued her education as an Oxford University 'home student' (that is, one not a member of a college) while

[10] L Goldthorpe, 'First Woman to Practise as a Barrister in Ireland and the (Then) United Kingdom, Averil Deverell, 1921' in Rackley and Auchmuty (n 7) 175.

[11] GE Gates (ed), *The Woman's Year Book 1923–1924* (NUSEC, 1924) 42; C Derry, 'Cobb, Monica Mary Geikie (1891–1946)' (DNB, 2018).

[12] L Lammasniemi, 'First Woman to Hold Regular Judicial Office in England and Wales, Rose Heilbron, 1964' in Rackley and Auchmuty (n 7) 257.

[13] HAC Sturgess, Register of Admissions to the Honourable Society of the Middle Temple (Butterworth & Co, 1949) 842.

[14] ibid 844.

[15] Birth certificate of Olive Catherine Clapham; National Probate Calendar (Index of Wills and Administrations), 1858–1966, 1903, 72; 'Hull's Lady Barrister' *Hull Daily Mail* (27 May 1921) 3; C Derry, 'Clapham, Olive Catherine [Married Name Miles] (1898–1973)' (DNB, 2018).

[16] *Hull Daily Mail* (n 15); 'College of Music Concert', *Hull Daily Mail* (7 December 1914) 3; J Tyler and C Parsons, *Madame Clapham: Hull's Celebrated Dressmaker* (Kingston Upon Hull City Museums and Art Galleries, 1999).

[17] *Hull Daily Mail* (n 15).

residing at St Frideswide's hostel for Catholic women students.[18] After studying English for a year, she changed to Jurisprudence and graduated in that subject in 1919. She went on immediately to study the postgraduate Bachelor of Common Laws, which had opened formally to women only a year earlier.[19] Three women, including Cornelia Sorabji and Ivy Williams, had received special permission to study it before 1918.[20] Clapham's final year saw the university return to something like its pre-war state after the rigours of the First World War, and also saw women admitted to degrees. Clapham was thus among the first women to graduate from Oxford. However, she must have had limited opportunity to enjoy the pleasures of peacetime since she was already studying for her Bar Finals examinations, which she passed in May 1921.[21]

Monica Geikie Cobb was seven years older than Clapham and came from a more typically professional background.[22] Her father was a leading, if notorious, Church of England clergyman and her elder brother would become a well-known Harley Street doctor.[23] The Reverend Geikie Cobb not only championed divorce reform but also supported women's rights and would speak at suffragette leader Emmeline Pankhurst's funeral in 1928.[24] Cobb studied at the University of London which, unlike Oxford, had awarded degrees to women since 1878:[25] first at Queen's College (a 'junior department' of King's College, London) and then at University College, London. She graduated with a BA in Philosophy in 1914, then returned to the university in 1918, taking her LLB Law and graduating with third-class honours in 1921.[26] She combined her study with employment as Joint Secretary for the Professional Classes War Relief Council which aimed to provide practical assistance to members of the professional classes suffering 'distress … due to the War'.[27] Cobb received an MBE for that work and continued to be involved in the Society long after it reinvented itself as a peacetime organisation, the Professional Classes Aid Council.[28] Meanwhile, she was working towards qualification as a barrister and, although she passed her Bar Finals later than Clapham, she would

[18] ibid.

[19] 'St Anne's', *Combined Register: 1878–1920*, Oxford, 2020, archives of the Association for the Education of Women in Oxford, Bodleian Library. www.firstwomenatoxford.ox.ac.uk/files/students1878to1920-allcollegesfinalxlsx-0.

[20] Auchmuty (n 4) 88.

[21] *The Times* (n 8) 10.

[22] Derry (n 11).

[23] 'Obituary: The Rev Dr WF Geikie Cobb' *The Times* (London, 15 December 1941) 6; 'Obituary: Dr I Geikie Cobb' *The Times* (London, 18 August 1953) 8.

[24] J Purvis, *Emmeline Pankhurst: A Biography* (Routledge, 2003) 353; 'The Passing of a Great Spirit' (1928) *British Journal of Nursing* 182.

[25] University of London, 'Leading Women 1868–2018' *History of the University of London* (2018) www.london.ac.uk/about-us/history-university-london/leading-women-1868-2018#.

[26] University of London Graduate List, 1836–1926, 354; University College London Archives, 'COBB, Monica Mary Geikie'.

[27] Professional Classes War Relief Council, London, 1914, 3.

[28] 'Professional Classes Aid Council' *The Times* (London, July 1939).

be among the first cohort of women would-be practitioners called to the Bar in November 1922.[29]

Within a fortnight of call, on 1 December 1922, Cobb was briefed to prosecute a case of bigamy at the Birmingham Assizes. The defendant, bricklayer Thomas Fallow, was convicted of bigamously marrying Ada Howell while his first wife Sarah Ann was still alive. He was found guilty and sentenced to six months' hard labour.[30] The press reports were as impressed by the 'trim and neat' prosecutor's 'perfectly fitting silver horse-hair wig and black gown' as by her 'brevity': '[s]he confined her remarks to essential points in the charge, every one of which she drove home with clarity and force'.[31]

Firsts in Time

What were contemporaries doing when they described women as 'firsts'? And crucially, what do we do when we repeat or reapply that description today? The label of 'first' imposes a particular temporality upon its subject: they are frozen in an instant, the moment at which they are the 'first' to do something. That fragmentation of time separates them from their pasts and broader presents; it suggests a completeness to the act which allows difficult histories and potential futures to be ignored. This endless rebirth of the subject is a key mechanism in producing the (masculine) liberal subject who, thus shorn of context and history, is able to act rationally and autonomously, unencumbered by relational responsibilities or systemic oppression. It is a function of linear time, the dominant construction of time in European cultures and which pervades the law. Linear time is understood as a straight line or arrow moving from the past, through the present, to the future. It is measurable and thus divisible into discrete periods, episodes or events. Linear time may seem natural, an observable scientific fact, but is culturally produced and serves specific political functions. Emily Grabham has described this process as 'brewing': temporalities are 'not either "natural" or "social" but always both, brewed through changing relationships of humans and material forms'.[32] The understandings of time thus created are a collection of intertwined temporalities with 'world-making capacities'.[33]

What, then, are the world-making functions performed by the designation of women as 'firsts'? This chapter suggests that it performs several temporal tasks: to isolate the subject in time, to render her singular, to emphasise that she is untimely, to hide the difference in tempo between the speed of her achievements

[29] 'Calls to the Bar', *Solicitor's Journal and Weekly Reporter* (No 67) (25 November 1922) 115.
[30] 'Woman Barrister Secures a Conviction' *The Scotsman* (Edinburgh, 2 December 1922) 8.
[31] 'Women Lawyers' *Aberdeen Press and Journal* (4 December 1922) 3.
[32] E Grabham, *Brewing Legal Times: Things, Forms and the Enactment of Law* (University of Toronto Press, 2016) 14.
[33] ibid 13.

and the slow pace of legal change, and to obscure the 'temporalities of precarity' in which she existed after the brief, shining moment of being 'first'.[34] However, that does not mean that the effects of identifying firsts are wholly negative. They reveal as well as obscure; indeed, they are revealing in what they obscure. They also offer times for celebration, valuable in themselves and for the effects they can produce.[35] This chapter does not, then, call for an outright abandonment of firsts but rather for a more sparing, critical use of them in both historiography and public engagement.

Isolating Times

Auchmuty has pointed out that 'a life is not always interesting in itself': without more, it can leave the reader asking, '*So what?*'[36] That the subject of a biography was the first to do something might seem to be an answer to that question. In reality, it simply raises another: *so what* that she was the first? Why is being a first given such significance? There is, of course, more than one answer to this question but, too often, firsts have been allowed particular significance for what they conceal as much as for what they reveal. In the context of women's entry into the legal profession, the 'first' as an isolated moment in linear time has specifically allowed the difficult history of exclusion to be downplayed, consigned to a less-enlightened 'past', hermetically sealed away from a progressive present. It, therefore, obscures the past in order to avoid examination of the present and the taking of difficult actions in the future. The 'bad old days' of women's exclusion are marked as having ended, meaning that further exploration of them is not required. As a consequence, the reasons why women were previously excluded, including enduring systemic obstacles and persistent discriminatory attitudes, remain conveniently unexamined.

In that light, the contemporary over-excitement of the press at Olive Clapham's pioneering success in the Bar Finals examinations begins to make sense. Having passed them, Clapham still had to complete her dining terms before she could be called to the Bar, and she had six terms (about 18 months) remaining. However, most newspapers directly misrepresented the facts. Even the *Times*, which ought to have known better since it regularly published the results of the Bar examinations, described her as 'the first woman barrister'.[37] The *Hull Daily*

[34] J Goodman, 'Afterword: Histories of Women's Higher Education, Time, and Temporalities' (2020) 56 *Paedagogica Historica* 6.

[35] I should declare my own involvement in celebrating firsts, not least through organising the *Diversities, Dilemmas and Discoveries* conference to celebrate the centenary of Clapham's Bar Finals success (Open University, May 2021). www.youtube.com/watch?v=3IDs2VABp0k&list=PLLeOSYXGYWMvJoOZJe0aWijaPa9TizrD3.

[36] Auchmuty (n 3) 43.

[37] *The Times* (n 8) 10.

Mail, devoting a longer article to its hometown success, included a detailed and accurate account of the qualification process to date but erroneously suggested that, if the Benchers allowed, she could be called immediately.[38] Only the *Sphere* recognised that Clapham might not be the first woman barrister, despite her early success.[39] Ignoring or downplaying the future challenges in progressing to qualification, and rendering invisible the even greater difficulties of establishing a practice at the Bar, the reports trapped Clapham in her instant of success. They could avoid the complexities of her path from Hull to the examination hall, and from the publication of results to qualification and her eventual departure from the profession.

Imported into our histories, the 'first' can perform a similar function: the shining moment is identified and celebrated; the often-miserable aftermath need not be addressed and, indeed, is frequently ignored. Researching Clapham's life, it was difficult to discover what happened to her between Finals and call night, as well as after her call to the Bar, since the secondary sources were silent and the primary sources scarce. In fact, she was not called until 1924 because she had moved out of London in order to work. Once called, she remained at the Bar only briefly. She nonetheless lived a rich life including many years in Ceylon (now Sri Lanka) with her husband and four children; a wartime spent in London, Yorkshire and the South Coast; and continued pursuit of her intellectual curiosity.[40] Thus her Bar Finals success was not a singular event, still less a conclusion, but one moment in a process of becoming.

Indeed, it was a moment in several such processes: Clapham's own as well as the profession's. Those processes of becoming, the former lasting decades and the latter extending beyond any single person's career or lifespan, are reduced through the characterisation of 'firsts' to single events. Yet, over a century after the major firsts of women's entry into the United Kingdom's legal professions, women are still in the same process of becoming as they seek full membership in a profession which does not yet wholly embrace them. Despite their increasing numbers, they face particular barriers throughout their careers and are disproportionately absent from the profession's highest levels: in 2020, only 32 per cent of barristers with over 15 years' experience, 28 per cent with over 20 years, 32 per cent of court judges, and 17 per cent of Queen's (now King's) Counsel were women.[41]

[38] *Hull Daily Mail* (n 15).

[39] 'Women at the Bar' *The Sphere* (London, 4 June 1921) 5.

[40] I am indebted for much of the information here to Clapham's daughter, Margaret Miles (personal communications, 2021); and see M Miles and C Derry, 'Olive Clapham' (recorded lecture) The Open University, May 2021 www.youtube.com/watch?v=3IDs2VABp0k. The record of Clapham's marriage was not easily found since she wed in Sri Lanka. That disappearance of women upon marriage, when their names change and even their given name often disappears from records, is an enduring issue for historians of women's lives.

[41] Ministry of Justice, 'Diversity of the Judiciary: Legal Professions, New Appointments and Current Post-Holders' (MoJ, 2020) 11–18.

Singular Times

The production of the endlessly reborn liberal subject slices duration, the rich and undivided flow of subjective time, into singular moments which are severed from past and future. In other words, it removes her from her context: she is the universal autonomous individual, shorn of her history and isolated from her wider relations. She is thus placed upon liberalism's imaginary 'level playing field' where she competes on equal terms. The systemic power structures which oppress her and the social relations which sustain her are hidden from view.

A focus upon Helena Normanton as the first woman admitted to an Inn of Court, for example, obscures the question of why Cobb did not join the same afternoon but had to wait until the new year. The answer is that Normanton already had a relationship with officers of Middle Temple, thanks to her earlier unsuccessful requests for admission and ongoing appeal against refusal, so the office was opened specially for her on Christmas Eve 1919.[42] Looking beyond the first woman, then, paradoxically brings her own prior struggles into view and in doing so, starts to uncover the whole history of women's efforts to enter the profession and its adamant refusal to admit them. It also throws light upon how the apparent equality which followed was, as Catherine MacKinnon has termed legal sex equality, 'designed for the exceptional individual whose biography approximates the male one'.[43] To ask, then, 'what about the *second* woman?' is to expose a history in which admission to the profession was not gifted by a kindly Parliament through the Sex Disqualification (Removal) Act 1919 but was the consequence of decades of women's campaigning, fiercely resisted by many senior lawyers.[44]

The celebration of Cobb's courtroom victory similarly obscured a difficult future in which she would encounter the problems of a pioneer woman barrister. One of these was the very fact of being a 'first'. While newspapers continued to report on women's legal firsts, many clients were understandably not eager to risk their cases coming under press scrutiny should their barrister happen to be, for example, the first woman appearing in their local court.[45] That was even assuming that they or their solicitor were willing to instruct a woman at all. Nor were the problems quick to disappear: Enid Rosser (later known by her married name Enid Rosser Locket), called five years later and writing in 1938, described the difficulties faced by women as 'enormous'.[46] There were material challenges: for example, the lack of toilets was an excuse for chambers not to accept women pupils

[42] J Bourne, *Helena Normanton and the Opening of the Bar to Women* (Waterside Press, 2016) 102–106.

[43] C MacKinnon, 'Reflections on Sex Equality under Law' (1991) 100 *Yale Law Journal* 1297.

[44] See also Auchmuty, 'Whatever Happened to Miss Bebb?' (n 1).

[45] See, eg, the lengthy report of a magistrates' court order for two dogs to be kept under control, presented as 'remarkable' because Cobb was 'the first lady advocate to appear at Oxted': '"Loving Dogs" at Felbridge Ladies' Colony' *Courier* (Oxford, March 1926). For a summary of the problem, see Enid Rosser, 'Women and the Legal Profession' *St Hugh's Chronicle* (Oxford, nd) 13.

[46] Rosser (n 45).

or tenants, as well as a constant issue when attending court (along with the lack of robing-room facilities).[47] Male colleagues could be patronising, when they were not actively hostile. At the end of her first case, Cobb 'was heartily congratulated', not a usual courtroom response.[48] Such differential treatment was not always couched in benign terms: Rosser, early in her career, received a message from a High Court judge stating, 'women in the law are matter out of place'.[49]

Early women barristers thus appeared either frozen alone in the moment of being first, or as a collective outsider class similarly frozen in the present as a sudden intrusion. A change of temporal framing, so that the 'first' was not a self-contained occasion but rather one moment in the flow of a wider social movement, can transform this history into a relational one. That was understood by activists of the time: looking forward to the prospect of the first woman barrister following Cobb's exam success, the *Woman's Leader* wrote, 'Priority of a few months is, after all, not a very important matter, but the status of women at the Bar will depend very much upon the tact and ability of the first *flight of successful women*' (emphasis added).[50]

The significance of paying attention to networks, especially where histories are sparse or suppressed, has been an enduring theme of Auchmuty's work for over three decades.[51] Her influence upon the historiography of gender in the legal profession is apparent in recent work which has moved from individualistic biographies to explore the connections between pioneering legal women.[52] Such work is not straightforward: like most research into these women's lives, it is inhibited by the loss of most women's personal papers. For some of the first cohort of women at least, that seems to have been a deliberate omission: Ethel Bright Ashford, who was also an enthusiastic amateur historian, ensured the archival preservation of records belonging to an organisation she chaired but not of her own personal or professional papers. Helena Normanton did keep her papers, now held in the Women's Library at LSE, but their tantalising glimpses of networks raise as many questions as answers. For example, Cobb wrote to her stating that she understood Normanton wished to have a separate women's table in Middle Temple. Cobb had dined with six other female students, and they were unanimous that they did not want any such action. They felt grateful for the consideration shown to

[47] See, eg, L Noakes, 'Early Women Barristers and the Negotiation of Professional and Political Identity' (2022) *Women's History Review* 8.

[48] *Aberdeen Press and Journal* (n 31). She would also be congratulated by the Chairman of the bench at Oxted magistrates' court (see n 45).

[49] Rosser (n 45).

[50] 'The First Woman Barrister?' *Woman's Leader* (London, June 1921).

[51] R Auchmuty, 'By their Friends We Shall Know Them: The Lives and Networks of Some Women in North Lambeth, 1880–1940' in Lesbian History Group (ed), *Not a Passing Phase: Reclaiming Lesbians in History 1840–1985* (The Women's Press, 1989) 77; Auchmuty, 'Researching Women in Legal History' (n 1).

[52] This is apparent both in the greater attention to wider networks in individual biographies and in group and comparative biographies, eg, L Noakes, *Chrystal MacMillan and Elsie Bowerman: First Women Barristers' Negotiation of Professional and Political Identities* (The Open University, 2021).

women students and wished to fall in with the arrangements made.[53] It is not clear that Normanton did in fact want such an arrangement – her papers reveal nothing further on the subject, although it is suggestive that Rosser described her as 'always trying to organise the women into forming a separate group from the men'[54] – but the letter shows some of the tensions within this small group of women who shared common ambitions but varied in ages and social and political backgrounds.

Viewed in social rather than singular time, these women were not only part of a community but also part of other temporal forms, not least as members of a generation. That was keenly felt by Rosser who defined herself in her unpublished memoir as 'of the newer generation of women and … therefore not a fanatical feminist'. By contrast, the 'first' women who had joined the Bar before her were 'part of history', and not only because of their historical status as firsts. They also represented an older politics, as well as a lack of professional success.[55] For example, Rosser described Elsie Bowerman (called in 1924) as 'another old Equal Pay for Equal Work campaigner … She did not achieve much but she was there constantly seen about the Courts', making 'no headway at all'.[56] Helena Normanton was 'a war horse from the Old Feminist days', 'a comic character' and 'a menace to the movement'.[57] This generation gap is all the more striking since Rosser was called only a few years later, in 1927. Of course, many women called in the earliest years were much older, having waited years or decades for the profession to admit them.[58] However, here the generation difference was not 'a linear temporal enumeration',[59] so much as a metaphor for a subjective temporal shift in women's sense of being and becoming. That insight into two generations of women emerges only when the historical tempo shifts from the singular temporalities of firsts.

Untimely Women

Firsts, then, can function as moments in time within which their subjects are not only frozen but also isolated. That does not mean that 'firsts' have no place in our history. The identification of how certain women were on certain occasions positioned by their contemporaries as firsts can serve an analytical purpose.

[53] Monica Geikie Cobb to Helena Normanton, 19 January 1920, Women's Library at LSE (London) 7HLN/A/17.

[54] E Rosser Locket, unpublished memoir: Women's Library at LSE (London), LOCKET: Papers of Enid Rosser Locket (1899–1980), quoted in K Broomfield, 'Enid Rosser Locket' (Celebrating the Centenary of Women Lawyers 2017) celebratingthecentenaryofwomenlawyers.wordpress.com/enid-rosser-locket/.

[55] Rosser did not acknowledge that some of these women, including Bowerman, remained activists foremost: see Noakes (n 47).

[56] Rosser Locket, unpublished memoir, 276–277, quoted in Noakes (n 52).

[57] Quoted in Broomfield (n 54).

[58] Bowerman was aged 35 and Normanton 40 when called.

[59] Goodman (n 34) 7.

In particular, the consequent isolation of these women by their professional peers and contemporary media emphasises their untimeliness. In the related context of women's entry into higher education, Joyce Goodman writes that in a 'future they did not control, untimeliness brought with it a newness that raised anxieties that clashed with stagnating temporalities of accepted practice along gendered lines'.[60] The very notion of a first implies something new, unprecedented, and potentially disruptive.

In a profession which, given England and Wales's common law system, was unusually focused upon precedents, 'first' was a particularly anomalous and uncomfortable status. It made itself felt in material ways: the lack of toilet and robing facilities, the uncertainty over dining arrangements. It also created a psychic atmosphere where women were intensely conscious of themselves in uneasy relation to their peers and seniors in the legal profession. The men of the profession, meanwhile, moved to contain the threat of the new: the statutory 'eruption' that admitted women was to be incorporated into the fabric of the known through 'defensive counter-reaction'.[61] This process was familiar to barristers, given the courts' propensities for minimising the potential ruptures of new legislation by integrating it into the structure of the preceding common law.[62]

The wider social disruption caused by this growing class of professional women was also contained through the construction of 'firsts' as untimely women. Reporters remained fascinated by such instances long after Monica Geikie Cobb won her first case.[63] The cumulative effect of their reports was not, however, to create a sense of collective professional engagement or of transformation of the legal profession. Instead, by casting each woman on each occasion as untimely, they pushed her out of the wider flow of time. Isolated in her singular moment of strangeness, she could not be connected with her peers but was placed under solitary scrutiny. Static and alone, she was the antithesis of a women's *movement*: it is unsurprising, then, that one continuing legacy of contemporary reporting has been the enduring perception of the interwar years as a time of fracture and stasis for the women's movement (a perception firmly countered by recent scholarship on the period).[64] Even at the end of that era, Rosser was still obliged to write of women lawyers that they 'are *beginning* to be accepted without astonishment' (emphasis added):[65] the shock of the first repeated itself for a very long time.

[60] ibid 3.

[61] E Grosz, 'Thinking the New: of Futures Yet Unthought,' (1998) 6 *Symploke* 38.

[62] See my current research on sexual consent (*Legal Temporalities of Sexual Consent* (Edinburgh University Press 2024 forthcoming), where the changes wrought by section 74 of the Sexual Offences Act 2003 have been minimised by judgments drawing upon caselaw from as far back as the nineteenth century (eg the reliance upon *R v Dee* [1884] 14 LR Ir 468 and *R v Clarence* (188) 22 QBD 23 in *R (on the application of 'Monica') v DPP and Boyling* [2018] EWHC 3508 (Admin)).

[63] See Cobb's case before Oxted magistrates (n 45).

[64] Including that produced and prompted by Auchmuty's project with Erika Rackley on women's legal landmarks, 14 of which are from that period: Rackley and Auchmuty (n 7).

[65] Rosser (n 45) 15.

Tempos

Yet these were not the only temporalities at work. The slow pace of change in the legal profession was at odds with the speed at which women advanced their educational and professional achievements. After centuries of exclusion, it took only decades for women to establish a place in higher education, confront the legal establishment on its own terrain – the Inns of Court, the civil courts, and Parliament – and achieve the changes in law which allowed them to qualify. These networks of women together constructed changing times in which their advance upon the Bar benefited women not only as lawyers but also as clients and as activists. The speed with which they pursued change is apparent in Olive Clapham's fast route to qualification and Monica Geikie Cobb's near-immediate progression from Call to courtroom. The temporalities of forward movement were both cooperative and competitive: these women's desire to move ahead of their peers as well as the constraints which had been imposed upon them is apparent, but there is also evidence of mutual support.

By contrast, the masculine profession sought to achieve stasis. Many of its members wanted not to move into a 'feminised' future, but to hold onto the wholly masculine past. Their temporal goal was in direct conflict with that of the pioneering women; but the profession had the force of privilege, patriarchy and vested interests behind it. While that was not enough to wholly resist the momentum of women's advance, it was certainly enough to significantly slow it. Having been admitted to the profession, women found multiple forms of resistance to their continuing progress within it. From the provision of facilities to the availability of work, to advancement to King's Counsel and the judiciary, they were forced to slow their own tempo to a crawling speed.

Some women, unsurprisingly, concluded that adopting this new tempo was the only route to success. They attempted to heed advice given to male barristers to 'play the game' until 'the great brotherhood of the Bar … eventually welcome his intrusion as inevitable'.[66] Rosser's memoir asserted her own adoption of this code and the need for 'fitting in with the traditions of the profession'.[67] Nonetheless, those traditions explicitly stretched back before the admission of women, thus implicitly excluding them, rendering them anomalous, and supporting the masculine profession's continued resistance to them. Women barristers' tempo was thus slowed still further. Experience was gained only gradually since briefs were slow to arrive: as Ashford explained in 1927, '[s]he did not hold out any very glowing prospects that after eating the required number of dinners, passing some examinations, and paying the fees, there were many women who were making a large, or even a subsistence living out of their practices'.[68] Formal recognition was slower still: the

[66] Sir Ernest Wild, quoted in N Alden Franz, *English Women Enter the Professions* (Cincinnati, Ohio, privately published 1965) 269.

[67] Quoted in Noakes (n 47) 8.

[68] Portia, 'House and Home', *Hull Daily Mail* (22 December 1927) 10.

first full-time woman judge, for example, was not appointed until 1962.[69] While the tempo did increase in subsequent decades, it is striking that Lady Hale was still able to achieve a string of significant firsts in the twenty-first century including first woman Lord of Appeal in Ordinary (House of Lords judge) in 2004 and first woman President of the Supreme Court in 2017. Those changes of pace, too often obscured by the relative rapidity of the prominent early 'firsts', is a potent reminder that 'it has certainly not been a steady uphill climb nor, crucially, an inevitable one, and things are not perfect yet'.[70]

Precarious Times

Despite the impressive tempo of the first women barristers' initial advance, some of the most potent temporalities thereafter were 'the discontinuous and fragmented temporalities of precarity'.[71] These were to some extent built into the profession which Clapham and Cobb entered. Barristers were (and most remain) simultaneously self-employed and obliged to find a tenancy in a set of chambers. Qualification was therefore only one step in the process of building a legal career, which would depend upon being able to attract instructions from solicitors on a case-by-case basis. That in turn involved a web of relationships including those with solicitors themselves, with clients who could make their own preferences known to the solicitor they employed, and crucially with chambers clerks who were responsible for the distribution of work to their barristers. Men as well as women entering the profession faced challenges in establishing a practice, but for women these were considerably greater. Sexism was systemic and endemic; almost all solicitors and all barristers' clerks were men;[72] and a sexist reluctance by any one of the parties (client, solicitor or clerk) to instruct a woman barrister would ensure that she was not briefed. Class structures and the financial burdens of qualifying and supporting oneself while building a practice compounded these issues: as Rosser advised, it was a profession either for 'those who can afford it and have patience' or for those 'lucky enough to possess sympathetic relatives or friends already in the profession'.[73]

The consequences, and the extent to which precarity did indeed impose a 'discontinuous and fragmented' temporality upon women's careers at the Bar, are apparent in the experiences of Olive Clapham. This talented and driven young woman was able to become the first woman to pass her Bar Finals, having studied for them at the same time as for a demanding postgraduate degree at

[69] This was the appointment of Elizabeth Lane as a County Court judge.
[70] Auchmuty (n 3) 51.
[71] Goodman (n 34) 6.
[72] The first women solicitors in England and Wales, like the first women barristers, qualified in 1922 and their numbers were very small.
[73] Rosser (n 45) 14–15.

the University of Oxford. However, she then moved to Cambridge to work for a tutorial college, probably through financial necessity. In consequence, she was not able to complete her dining terms at her Inn of Court in London as quickly as many of her peers. She finally qualified in 1924, two years after the first women's cohort. It is unclear how far she was able to practise at the Bar before leaving permanently the following year in order to move to Sri Lanka and marry.

Monica Geikie Cobb was from a more conventional background for a barrister, and her family home was in London. She was, therefore, spared many class and economic disadvantages – indeed, it is likely her father's contacts helped her to secure briefs – but she was not immune from precarity's discontinuous temporalities.[74] In January 1925 she registered for a doctorate in law at University College London, which was never completed. Her registration suggests that she was looking at an alternative future in academia, and indeed her career in practice may have been saved by a quasi-legal appointment which reduced her reliance upon attracting briefs. In March 1926, she was appointed deputy chairman (*sic*) of London's Court of Referees, a tribunal of mostly lay members created under the Unemployment Insurance Act 1920.[75] Chairmen were the legally qualified members of these courts, earning a fee of 2½ guineas a sitting; by 1928, Cobb was the only woman in the role, although she did receive the same fee as her male colleagues.[76] Despite having to shift much of her time into activity outside the Bar, Cobb was probably the most successful of the first cohort of women barristers in terms of maintaining a practice. Nonetheless, success was relative: as a woman barrister, she remained subject to the fragmented temporalities of precarity.

It is important to note that such precarious times did not only affect the financial security of women barristers. The lack of a stable and continuous career tempo also had profound consequences upon their professional identities. As Laura Noakes commented, the earliest women barristers had to negotiate a complex 'relationship between assimilation and transgressing norms' which meant 'their career strategies remained in constant flux'.[77] This complicated entwining of tempos and rhythms, fundamental to their experience and still significant in the profession today, emerges from attention to these pioneering women – but only if we develop our research beyond the singular moment of the 'first'.

[74] An obituary of solicitor Sir George Fowler noted that he was both 'the first in [Bedford Row] to brief a woman barrister' and, as 'the legal champion of women's rights' had often shared a platform with Cobb's father, 'the clerical champion of women's rights in London': 'Our London Letter: Woman's Champion' *Nottingham Journal* (21 October 1937) 6.

[75] 'Woman Barrister's Post' *Daily Mail* (March 1926).

[76] Sir A Steel-Maitland, 'Oral Answers to Questions' in HC Deb 14 November 1928, vol 222, cols 879–80.

[77] Noakes (n 47) 11.

Celebrating Firsts

Studies on 'first women' can offer a productive entry point from which to explore more extensive histories. They can also serve a practical purpose: generating anniversaries and highlighting human stories as a starting point for wider commemorations and explorations. We can use singular 'firsts' to draw people into the extensive histories that lie behind them. The centenaries of the Sex Disqualification (Removal) Act 1919, Olive Clapham's exam success in 1921, and the first women called to the Bar of England and Wales in 1922 have prompted a rise in popular and academic interest in the subject (of which this chapter is an example) with events and initiatives directed towards a wide range of audiences.[78] The celebration of firsts, then, has value even when viewed through a critical lens.

The use of firsts in this way is not, however, without difficulties. It does not offer a clear route to sustaining the momentum it generates, meaning it provides a starting point rather than an enduring approach. The audience for our work may drift away if we do not actively continue to engage them: after all, they have 'done' the centenary now. We also need to engage critically with our own research directions, so that we are creating sustainable scholarship and resources. How do we continue to deepen and extend research into a subject such as women in the legal profession, despite the temptation to look for the next anniversary to celebrate? Inevitably, some of those enthusiastic about the centenaries of the first women lawyers have moved on to other projects; nonetheless, collective foundations have been laid. Auchmuty and Rackley's work on feminist biography is a key reference point in considering how best to build upon them.[79]

Even while anniversaries are attracting attention, the commemorative approach risks diverting attention towards specific achievements of 'exceptional' women rather than encouraging an understanding of the importance of collective efforts and persistence. It promotes the tempting but problematic framing of these women as 'role models', two-dimensional exemplars, rather than the flawed, complex, endearing and frustrating people they – much like today's students who seek to follow them into the legal profession – really were.[80] That is not to say that paying attention to 'firsts' may not offer other possibilities. Their expanded biographies do show both their location in time and place and that they moved through their

[78] Examples available online include academic conferences, lectures and publications (eg *Diversity, Dilemmas and Discoveries* (n 35); 'Women in Law' exhibition and podcasts, Inner Temple Library, 2019 www.innertemple.org.uk/women-in-law/); resources for general audiences (eg 'Digital Museum', First 100 Years, first100years.org.uk/digital-museum/biographies/; C Derry and C Howells, 'Biography of the First Female Judges' (OpenLearn 2019) www.open.edu/openlearn/society-politics-law/law/biography-the-first-female-judges and articles in the solicitors' professional journal: 'Centenary', *Law Society Gazette*, www.lawgazette.co.uk/people/women-in-the-law.

[79] See, eg, Auchmuty and Rackley (n 1).

[80] ibid 204–208; C Derry, 'Ethel Bright Ashford: More and Less than a Role Model' (2020) 29 *Women's History Review* 615.

time in varied and variously significant ways. In particular, attention to the first *cohort* of would-be practitioners called to the Bar in November 1922 has allowed for consideration of the connections and relations between them; although since the primary unifying point is that singular moment, the Call Night, it does not altogether escape the challenges considered here.

Conclusion

A number of early women barristers have been described as various kinds of 'firsts'. This is a temporal labelling, which can shed light upon key facets of their experiences. It highlights their disproportionate visibility at their moment of entry to the profession; it encapsulates the fragmentation of their experience so that one moment of 'success' could be isolated, allowing the profession and wider system to congratulate themselves upon their progressiveness. For historians, it can be a helpful tool in attracting initial attention from audiences, who may then be directed to more nuanced and relational histories. Anniversaries may be rooted in linear time but, as Grosz concedes, they are 'as good an excuse as any for engaging in reflections on the past and speculations about the future'.[81]

Nonetheless, the practical and analytical advantages of identifying 'firsts' must not be allowed to distract us from the complexities of feminist biographies, particularly our subjects' wider networks and the need to contextualise their experiences in the broader social structures of the period. We must be particularly careful not to replicate past shortcomings. This requires awareness of the negative functions which 'firsts' could serve for their contemporaries: marking them as untimely, isolated individuals frozen in singular moments of time. The past and present are not neatly separated, as linear time would suggest, but are woven together; we cannot therefore be too quick to assume that 'our' use of firsts is different from and better than our predecessors'. We must think carefully about the various temporalities at play, and about which we use and how. We need to be alert to the different times constituting and constituted by women barristers' professional lives: the faster tempos with which they moved into the profession, the slow, halting and precarious pace at which they progressed thereafter. We should be attentive to the relational nature of those temporalities, including material relations (forms pre-printed with 'Mr', buildings with no facilities for women, wigs and gowns which obscured gender differences) as well as interpersonal relations (with each other, established male colleagues, and wider familial, activist and social networks).

Our role as historians is to situate these women within complex and multiple temporalities. We must pay attention to how those were constructed through

[81] E Grosz, 'Histories of a Feminist Future' (2000) 25 *Signs* 1017.

the women's relations with the world in which they campaigned, learned, lived and worked. Those temporalities were not the singular moments of the classic liberal subject but enduring and variegated. Nor did they end 100 years ago, since as historians we are endlessly rewriting their histories in ways shaped by and shaping our presents and futures. The ways in which we analyse and address them thus continue to matter, since 'not only are we writing the event, we are positively reinscribing it, producing it anew, writing it as an opening up to a life that is not exhausted in its pastness'.[82] The temporal relationship between historian and subject is not linear.[83]

Now that so many centenaries have passed, we have little choice but to move beyond 'firsts', and we should be glad to do so. The effort is worthwhile because, as Auchmuty reminds us, 'the struggle is the same, and this makes women's legal biography very much a dialogue between past and present'.[84] First women are a valuable starting point for that dialogue, but it is vital that we continue to expand the conversation. In that process, we are creating fresh timescapes which produce richer histories and thereby open new possibilities for conceivable futures.

[82] ibid 1020.
[83] EH Carr famously characterised it as 'an unending dialogue between the present and the past': EH Carr, *What Is History?* (Penguin, 1961).
[84] Auchmuty (n 3) 49.

4

Anna van Zwanenberg – A Life History[1]

ANONYMOUS

Introduction

This is a biographical life history of my Mother, Anna van Zwanenberg. I think that gives me the right to refer to her as 'Anna', but I do so with some diffidence because, as is noted, we do not commonly refer to our male subjects by their first names.[2] I am writing it because her life is the kind of lost life about which Rosemary Auchmuty and colleagues have been able to write so vividly. I am doing so with some anxiety because her story is also my story – pretty obviously – and exposes me to the charges of selectivity, subjectivity, bias (none of which particularly bother me), as well as to a reflexive account of my own class and the effect it has had on my career progression (which does). The other preoccupying anxiety is whether this chapter is 'academic' work. I deal with these issues in the opening substantive section in which I discuss positionality and method.

At the conference where the papers in this collection were presented, my paper did not mention that I was discussing my mother (although certain attendees were aware) until the end. At the time, that device (rhetorical or otherwise) was used to enable me to contain my emotion and, unusually, I read my paper. However, in reflecting on Auchmuty's oeuvre, and the feminist traditions within which it stands, I have come to realise that was a mistake.[3] Here, it is upfront.

[1] I am grateful to Rosemary Auchmuty for her detailed comments on this chapter and incitement to write this life history. Its weaknesses are entirely mine despite Rosemary's encouragement, however. I also wish to thank Victoria Barnes for the sensitive editing process and enormous assistance in contextualising this study.

[2] R Auchmuty and E Rackley, 'Feminist Legal Biography: A Model for All Legal Life Stories' (2020) 4 *Journal of Legal History* 186, 208. Accordingly, I refer to the key men in this story by their first names, and academics by their surnames as is convention. My father, on the other hand, I refer to as such. This is, of course, not the way I would have referred to him. This style also acts as a device to preserve his anonymity.

[3] See eg R Auchmuty, 'Early Women Law Students at Cambridge and Oxford' (2008) 29 *Journal of Legal History* 63; R Auchmuty, 'Recovering Lost Lives: Researching Women In Legal History' (2015) 42 *Journal of Law and Society* 34.

In this version, I place my Mother, and my relationship with her, centre stage. She died when I was four years old. Nobody particularly spoke about her during my life – certainly not my Father, Anna's husband. Accordingly, rather like Gwyneth Bebb,[4] her life is a 'lost life' reconstructed here by me for the purposes of this collection because of one important fact: she was a barrister in the 1960s.

She was not a pioneer, and I think that this is important because history is made not just by the firsts and the landmarks but by the forgotten. I write about her lost life because she has been forgotten and her memory extends solely now to a few. In historical terms, she is a nobody because she has been forgotten and bypassed. Simon quotes a saying of a famous Rabbi that 'forgetting leads to exile; remembering leads to redemption'.[5]

However, as Auchmuty and colleagues have noted, those firsts, and the reforms augmented around them, did not lead to an abandonment of discrimination, nor inclusion.[6] The story I want to tell is of struggle, as an insider/outsider, of being exceptional/unexceptional; but also of joy and fun. Originally, I had presented Anna's story as *unexceptional*, as the story of a nobody (albeit one who could have been somebody), but one participant questioned my use of this term, rightly.[7] They have made me think about the ways in which these dichotomies have internally operated, not to diminish Anna's achievements, but to remember how context constructs us and our research objects. As Auchmuty has written, 'no scholar need apologize for focusing on women; the problem is, rather, the paucity of information about those legal pioneers, for whom records have not been kept precisely because their lives were deemed unimportant'.[8] In the context of this chapter, that comment is prescient as I discuss how Anna's time as a Bristol law academic was subsequently deemed unimportant in a story about the first 50 years of the school. I return to these dichotomies in my conclusion.

Anna is not one of the great and the good (perhaps because her life was cut short in 1970), and she is not one about whom a magnificent and loving history can be written, like Rose Heilbron.[9] It is, certainly, a story about the life of a woman in law, and, as her friend (my 'aunt') Janet put it, somewhat wistfully as we said goodbye after a lovely morning spent together, 'she was very much a girl in a man's world'. Janet did not mean this as a feminist statement per se, but as a statement of fact (she had earlier described Anna as a 'man's woman'); as with so many statements of fact, however, they have their own truths which we read into them.

[4] On whom, see in particular R Auchmuty, 'Whatever Happened to Miss Bebb? *Bebb v The Law Society* and Women's Legal History' (2011) 31 *Legal Studies* 199.

[5] R Simon, *The Touch of the Past: Remembrance, Learning and Ethics* (Palgrave, 2005) 1.

[6] See eg R Auchmuty and J Temkin, 'The Road to Olive Stone' in U Schultz, G Shaw, M Thornton and R Auchmuty (eds), *Gender and Careers in the Legal Academy*, Onati International Series in Law and Society (Hart, 2021); C Wells, 'Working out Women in Law Schools' (2001) 21 *Legal Studies*116; S Thompson, *Quiet Revolutionaries: The Married Women's Association and Family Law* (Hart, 2022).

[7] See Derry, ch 3, this volume, on role models and firsts. See also C Derry, 'Ethel Bright Ashford: More and Less than a Role Model' (2020) 29 *Women's History Review* 615.

[8] Auchmuty, 'Recovering Lost Lives' (n 3) 34–35.

[9] H Heilbron, *Rose QC – The Remarkable Story of Rose Heilbron: Trailblazer and Legal Icon* (Hart, 2019).

Anna's story is one about silence – silences during her life, after her life, and about whom we do not talk. In the important rush to write about the great and the good, we should not forget about people like Anna because it is in those silences that we find the crevices of power/knowledge, hegemony and professional resistance. I address Anna's story in the second section, seeking to explain absences by reference to other social and economic materials. I address what is known about her legal life (not much, as it happens), and weave that in with what I know of her personal life (not much, as it happens). This material is constructed from fragments of knowledge over many years, piecing things together that perhaps might not fit. This chapter is a melding of the academic and the personal. Most of the information here is gleaned from conversations of a personal nature with family members and friends. This information should not be academised. I have also had assistance from the archivists at Gray's and Lincoln's Inns, for which I am grateful. This is fragmented knowledge, memories of lost documents, and discussions over lengthy periods.

In a way, what follows is not as intended when I conceived the idea for this chapter. I suspect that the editors imagined that, when asked, I would want to write about Auchmuty's contribution to property law, specifically equity. Auchmuty's published work has been particularly influential on identifying equity's hidden assumptions about women and the home,[10] and it is no exaggeration to say that it revolutionised the way in which I approached land law in the classroom, breaking the shackles of a heavily doctrinal land law module. But Auchmuty has also written about women's legal history and legal biography,[11] and she encouraged me to tell this story. And although I have chosen to write a legal biography, this chapter is also a property law story, partly because Anna practised as a property lawyer (or its derided cousin, landlord and tenant), and partly because I seek to capture in my account the same kinds of sensibilities as Auchmuty captured in her discussions about the family home about women's labour and its value.[12]

Images

As Mulcahy says:

> For those doing archival work there may be many images to be found and used to construct revisionist histories of socio-legal subjects who were not considered important enough to be asked to leave a trace on the written records of the state.[13]

[10] See, in particular, R Auchmuty, 'Unfair Shares for Women: The Rhetoric of Equality and the Reality of Inequality' in H Lim and A Bottomley (eds), *Feminist Perspectives on Land Law* (Routledge Cavendish Glasshouse, 2007).

[11] Auchmuty and Rackley (n 2).

[12] This is especially apparent in her teaching ethos. See R Auchmuty, 'Using Feminist Judgments in the Property Law Classroom' (2012) 46 *The Law Teacher* 227.

[13] L Mulcahy, 'Eyes of the Law: A Visual Turn in Socio-Legal Studies?' (2017) 44 (Supp) *Journal of Law and Society* 111, 121.

I begin with two images, which I hope enable the reader to visualise Anna, and provide graphic context for what follows because they represent how Anna chose to be seen and represented. I do so, following Moran, by 'understanding [them] as three dimensional objects and accounting for the importance of a wide array of social and cultural factors that influence their production, circulation, and consumption. All impact on their capacity to generate meaning'.[14]

Figure 1 Oil painting of Anna by Ottilie Tolansky

Figure 2 Photograph from which Tolansky painted Anna's portrait

Image 1 is a photograph of an oil painting of my Mother by Ottilie Tolansky, a Jewish émigré from Germany in 1933. She was a local artist, who lived close to us in Richmond, Surrey, on the borders of London. My memory is that I was told that the Tolanskys and our family were friends, but I cannot verify that; more likely, the Tolansky family were my father's patients.[15] I am vaguely aware that my father never liked this picture. The photograph itself has faded, and is crudely symbolic also of my memory. However, this picture was the one which hung in an area off our hallway by a staircase in our home, surrounded by Chancery Law Reports. It was where, growing up, we watched TV and played. It hung over us, but was never discussed, and attention was never drawn to it nor to those curious dusty books of no interest to a child or teenage boy. It was a presence to which over the

[14] L Moran, 'Researching the Visual Culture of Law and Legal Institutions: Some Reflections on Methodology' (2022) 48 (Supp) *Journal of Law and Society* 44, 50.

[15] My father was a local GP in Richmond.

years I became immune. Thinking about it in this way enables me to recognise in my research the way in which signs and things which themselves are silent speak through their translation at different moments. Ignored for so long, they can become mediators spontaneously.

Image 1 was painted after Anna's death, at my father's request, I suppose. Image 2 was the photograph from which Tolansky painted her picture. This highly stylised, managed image was probably taken in the mid-1960s, perhaps shortly after she married my father. I am not sure what it conveys to you, the reader, but, to me, it conveys a sense of warmth, fun, and kindness (that smile!). However, there is something else to me. It is a portrait of a Jewish woman in the orthodox tradition, wearing dark clothes and, tellingly, a wig. Our family were, at least until her death, 'relatively' orthodox, if there is such a thing, but this is as likely to be a matter of manufactured memory.[16]

The other telling sign is what is absent – there is no sense in which Anna is anything other than a (rather beautiful) woman in this photograph. Artefacts, such as portraits, communicate identities and culture.[17] The photograph de-professionalised her, fitting her into the tradition of the apparently professionless wife.[18] Now I am thinking about it, I have never seen a photograph of Anna in her professional regalia. There must have been a photograph of her 'gowned up', at least at her call to the bar, but that image is not what has been preserved. Rather, the beautiful Jewish woman with the kind smile is what remains. This is the meaning that posterity wanted to generate, or was actively conserved, about Anna.

Methods

In this section, I address my method. Anna's life, as will be obvious by now, was not the carefully and intentionally preserved life like that of Rose Heilbron. There was nobody employed to maintain cuttings of achievements.[19] To my knowledge, Anna never gave public talks. There are no references to her as counsel in Westlaw or LexisNexis. For me, as a socio-legal researcher with a passing interest in property, there are certain things that are part of my trade – recognising social and political context for a study, the contingency of 'facts' and 'truths', as well as their suppression; the problem of objectivity and neutrality. As Auchmuty has pithily put it, 'our "facts" are not always true, as published accounts may be wrong, and

[16] Memory is not always a perfect resource. See V Barnes, 'Interrogating the Self-Told Narrative: Lord Lindley's Autobiography, His Life and His Legal Biography' (2020) 41 *Journal of Legal History* 143.

[17] R Hurdley, 'Dismantling Mantelpieces: Narrating Identities and Materializing Culture in the Home' (2006) 40(4) *Sociology* 717–33.

[18] The trend now is to personalise the professional photographs. See V Barnes and L Newton, 'Visualizing Organizational Identity: The History of a Capitalist Enterprise' (2018) 13 *Management and Organizational History* 24.

[19] Heilbron (n 9) 104–07.

our conjectures may not be founded in "fact"'.[20] While Anna's story is also my story, I simply cannot comprehend what life was like for her – all I can do is my best with the limited evidence available to me, my own partial assessment of that evidence, and hypothesise.[21]

That is even more true in this case, because the facts are my facts and the truths are those which make me up. It is a result of this that I have written this chapter in the first person – this is my story after all – to emphasise the subjectivities it contains. I willingly fall into the pitfall identified by Auchmuty and Rackley of historical inaccuracy in as much as I have written this based on my and others' memories. It is a faithful representation and interpretation of those memories – in this respect, accurate – but one can expect those memories to be inaccurate, and to be made up. They are valid and reliable as far as I know, but I also know that how we construct what we say, and translate that into documents, can also be self-serving.[22] As Sarat put it,

> My community expects that when I make observations or interpret those observations what I represent has as close a relationship to what I saw or heard as is possible given the inexorable interconnectedness of sub jects and objects, the unstable character of the multiple meaning systems in which I am trapped, and the limits imposed by my biography and my biases, by language and by history. The ultimate arbiter of what counts as a close connection is not, however, the objects seen or the voices heard; it is the research community itself.[23]

Accordingly, issues of selectivity, subjectivity, and bias are not negatives in this chapter, but something to be cherished as 'doing my best' to represent and interpret.

Where I have felt less comfortable, however, has been in confronting my own positionality. In his important intervention on positionality in socio-legal studies, Massoud has argued that there are costs to the turn to positionality in socio-legal studies, most particularly to marginalised academics likely to heed the call.[24] I cannot claim to be a marginalised academic, as a white, male, straight university academic of some seniority; although the socio-legal approach and the subjects about which I write have historically been marginalised in law schools. But, as Anna's story is also a middle class story, that is my story. And I must own the privilege which my own history has offered me. It enables me to write as I do, with the confidence and speed that I do. It has facilitated my career progression, as much as being told how brilliant Anna was.

Massoud argues that positionality comes at a price:

[20] Auchmuty, 'Recovering Lost Lives' (n 3) 42.
[21] Auchmuty and Rackley (n 2) 208.
[22] See R Freeman, 'Learning by Meeting' (2008) 2 *Critical Policy Analysis* 1.
[23] A Sarat, 'Off to Meet the Wizard: Beyond Validity and Reliability in the Search for a Post-Empiricist Sociology of Law' (1993) 15 *Law and Social Inquiry* 155, 161.
[24] MF Massoud, 'The Price of Positionality: Assessing the Benefits and Burdens of Self-Identification in Research Methods' (2022) 49 (Supp) *Journal of Law and Society* 64, 66.

> When an author consciously blurs the boundaries between the personal and the professional by inserting their experiences into their scholarly work, they open up themselves – not only their ideas – to criticism and harm. That harm may include the devaluation of the scholarly content of the work because, for example, it is therefore presumed not to meet social science standards of neutrality or objectivity. Positionality also requires emotional labour. In some cases, scholars communicate painful memories to their research subjects, reviewers, and readers. Doing so may cause discomfort or exhaustion. At the extreme, researchers who have experienced physical or psychological trauma may retraumatize themselves by retelling their suffering.[25]

I have minimised here the emotional nature of Anna's story to me – not because I am seeking some sort of objectivity (in which I do not believe anyway), but because it is *her story*. Since reading Massoud's article, I have wondered about whether this chapter can claim to be 'academic', or, as we now must see it, whether it has sufficient originality, significance and rigour.[26]

I now address how this study was constructed. I engaged in correspondence with my aunt, Janet,[27] and uncle, Roger. Roger is a couple of years younger than Anna would have been, and they were relatively close siblings. Anna and Roger were born before the Second World War. Janet was much younger, having been born after the war. She and her younger brother were their mother's favourites, according to Anna's friend. I corresponded with my father's sister-in-law, Jennifer, with whom Anna and my father were close. I also met with Anna's lifelong friend, a different Janet, who took us in on days when my father was working after Anna's death. In the sunshine of a July morning, we met in her garden in Richmond, her house redolent of so many childhood memories, and talked about her memories of Anna and her career. I was explicit about asking what Auchmuty describes as the 'woman question'.[28] What was it like for Anna to be a woman, and a Jew, in these places.

Anna's work associates are deceased. However, by chance after his death, I came across a file retained by my father. It was a file which contained details of the criminal court cases which occurred as a result of the car accident in which Anna died. It was a file which was difficult to read, but contained a letter from a Victor Wellings,[29] who said that he had been Anna's pupil master. Parts of it are reproduced in the next section of this chapter. It is a key artefact in that it is the only documentary evidence about Anna's career at the bar. I recognise that reducing such matters to

[25] ibid.

[26] REF 2021, *Panel Criteria and Working Methods* (2019), Part 3, ref.ac.uk/media/1450/ref-2019_02-panel-criteria-and-working-methods.pdf.

[27] There are two Aunt Janets – Anna's sister; and Anna's friend whom we also knew as an aunt.

[28] Auchmuty, 'Recovering Lost Lives' (n 3) 43.

[29] Victor went to Reading School, and then on to Oxford where his studies were cut short by the war. Following distinguished service in the War, he joined Gray's Inn in November 1946, and was called to the bar on 26 January 1949. His reference from the Rector of Exeter College said that he had been a 'satisfactory student and, had the war not intervened, he would probably have obtained a Second Class in the Honours School of Jurisprudence'. His recreations were listed as golf and fishing – he had golf in common with Anna (card note, supplied by librarian).

writing are as much about the author as they are about the subject; and present the author in the way in which the author wishes to be presented. Inscription into a document is 'a conduit or corridor, something through which other things (power, meaning) flow'.[30] It is, in other words, a complex set of translations in which there is also an important omission or silence – any reference to Anna's gender.

Victor seems to have been a mentor to Anna, and following the actors (female or male, in this case) is part of the trade.[31] In this process, after a period of finding nothing, I have been assisted by colleagues at the Bar, and weave Victor's history into this tale. I should say, though, that what I found out did not conform to what I expected – I had expected to find somebody who was a champion of women's access to the Bar, but what I found suggested something rather more complicated. Indeed, what I found did not necessarily contradict that expectation, but cast Victor in a different light in terms of his reputation at the Bar.

One of the benefits of writing a biography as a child of the subject is that I can weave the personal with the legal. To the extent to which I am able, I address how Anna managed her career and family. There must have been domestic challenges. Anna's life was different from that of Rose Heilbron, in that Anna's husband was developing a self-employed medical practice as a GP, which required him to be on call, and I cannot say that he was 'supportive' nor that he helped with the housework or children.[32]

There is another important fact about the van Zwanenberg family. Although Anna's parents were particularly conventional, and embraced both convention and conservatism, the same could not be said of their children, grandchildren, and subsequent generations. Roger, who was privately educated at his father's former school, took a doctorate in developmental studies and, in the 1960s, was part of the band of UK academics (including those who have had such a great influence on law schools since) who went to Dar es Salaam as an academic. He was involved with radical publishing houses.[33] Janet trained as a social worker and remains a radical in her field. Another sibling, with whom I have lost touch, has reputedly been involved with right wing groups. Where Anna sat politically is unknown to me.

Anna – A Life History

Early Life and University

Anna was the first child of two middle class parents, Jack and Rosemary. Earlier generations had been Jewish refugees at different times. Jack was a Lloyds broker,

[30] R Freeman and L Maybin, 'Documents, Practices and Policy' (2011) 7 *Evidence and Policy* 158, 165.

[31] As Auchmuty and Rackley put it, women's legal history is also an important part of men's: Auchmuty and Rackley (n 2) 198.

[32] ibid 202–03.

[33] See R Kuper, 'A History of Pluto Press: 50 Years of Radical Publishing' (Pluto Press, nd) www.plutobooks.com/blog/history-pluto-press-fifty-years-radical-publishing/.

and Rosemary a homemaker. They were comparatively well-off. The surname – van Zwanenberg – was a Dutch concoction, as with so many Jewish surnames. Jack and Rosemary had been born Jewish but sought, as I see it, to syncretise with their Christian community. This made them a kind of cultural curiosity. Nobody could have called Jack and Rosemary 'easy' people and the kindest thing that might be said about them was that they were products of their time. They had a love of golf which they instilled also in Anna, who regularly played with them, and competitively in father and daughter matches.

Anna was privately educated at boarding school (where she met her friend, Janet). Roger wrote to me about the family's discovery, when she was 16, that 'She suddenly got 10 O levels to the surprise of everyone'. From then on, Roger wrote, Jack, with whom she was particularly close at that time, directed her future: 'which University to go, which law department. Jack had nil experience of higher education and felt it was largely a waste of time … Common sense was all a man required'.

Anna did attend University – Southampton University law school – in the 1950s. It may have been selected by Jack because it was one of the only University law schools with a female academic on staff, Antonia Gerard.[34] As it happened, I studied law there in the late 1980s, and was in the same hall of residence as Anna. Highfield Hall was in the traditional hall of residence modelled on Oxbridge.

At one time, that law school had a large leather-bound book which contained details of students, like a school report. The entry for Anna said that she wrote particularly well, but that was probably a product of her privileged education. It told of promise but little else. In fact, Anna could claim a women's landmark in that she became the first female Fulbright scholar,[35] and she went to Yale to study for an LLM. The LLM on which she studied was specifically developed for future leaders, and appears to have made Anna an international lawyer. It was at Yale that Anna met and befriended Bob and Dorothy Summers – Bob becoming one of the great jurisprudence scholars of his generation – and they talked of her sunny disposition.

On 1 February 1955, at about the same time as she started at Southampton, she was admitted to Lincoln's Inn. The librarian at Lincoln's Inn told me that Anna was called to the bar 16 June 1959 by the Treasurer, Sir Charles Harman (the head of the Inn for that year) having been proposed by Sir Lynn Ungoed-Thomas, a member of the Inn's governing body, known as benchers (see Figure 3 below). Ungoed-Thomas was a former Labour MP, who had been involved with the creation of the European Convention of Human Rights.[36] He was, in other words, an eminent proposer in every way. I have been told that Anna was the top scholar in her year,[37] but that may not be accurate. Either way, it appears she was a prodigious scholar.

[34] Auchmuty and Temkin (n 6) 447.
[35] This may be a family myth. I decided not to check it because family myths should be preserved.
[36] See Lynn Ungoed-Thomas, Wikipedia, en.wikipedia.org/wiki/Lynn_Ungoed-Thomas.
[37] See n 35.

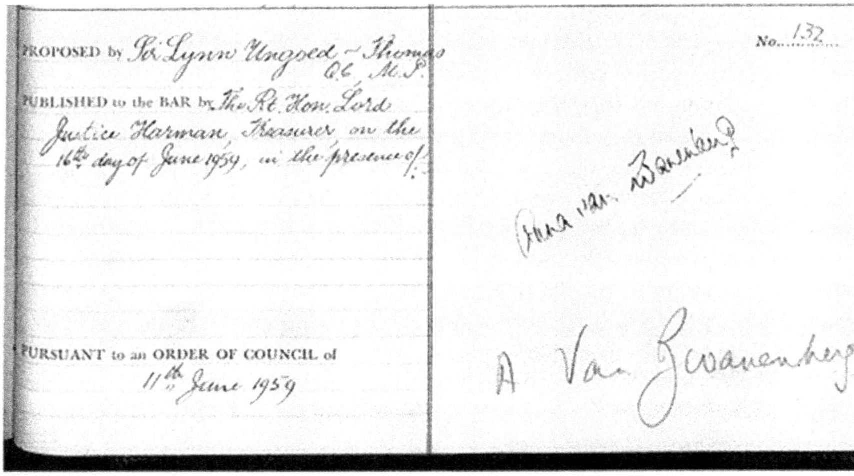

Figure 3 The record of Anna's proposal by Sir Lynn Ungoed-Thomas

Source: Lincoln's Inn records, supplied by librarian.

Professional Life – Academia

Despite her evident academic success, like so many female legal scholars of the time, she was unable to obtain pupillage. The alternative for someone with that academic talent was to become an academic. Reading the scholarship that has been produced about the women professors and academics, what struck me was how they appeared to wish to become academics.[38] In Anna's case, this was coerced choice. Her chosen profession would not have her, seemingly because she was a woman. This seems to be part of the untold history of at least some female academics, particularly legal academics, during this period. As McGlynn notes, there is a 'paucity of data concerning *women* in law schools', and the 1966 survey of law schools omitted gender.[39] Anna was, almost certainly, an outstanding applicant for a law academic post, given her credentials from Yale.[40]

As an academic, she returned to Southampton for a year, went to The Hague for a few years, came to Bristol for a year, and moved to Liverpool law school for a period as well. We know that Southampton and Liverpool already had at least one woman law academic at the time. However, at Bristol law faculty in 1960–61, Anna was the first female member of staff during a period of expansion from 1954.

[38] Auchmuty and Temkin (n 6); F Cownie, *Legal Academics: Cultures and Identities* (Hart, 2004).

[39] C McGlynn, 'Women, Representation and the Legal Academy' (1999) 19 *Legal Studies* 68, 71; J Wilson, 'A Survey of Legal Education in the UK' (1966–67) 9 *Journal of the Society of Public Teachers of Law* 1.

[40] Auchmuty and Temkin (n 6).

The first year undergraduate intake in 1960 was 149, of which there were 30 women. In their history of the first 50 years of the Bristol law faculty, Borkowski and Thomas do not note Anna's first at all, merely remarking that Anna was one of the newcomers to join the Faculty staff during this period, some of them only for a short time'.[41] The men in the Faculty of that period are given plenty of space, with their mythology implanted on its pages. Discussion of the teaching is focused on the men, their approaches (which would be regarded as problematic by today's standards), and the fact that all lecture attendees wore gowns.

However, the fact that Anna was the first woman member of academic staff in the law school – which only appeared to me when I looked at the list of all the academic staff from 1933–83[42] – goes unmentioned by Borkowski and Thomas. Perhaps it is because Anna was at Bristol only for a year; but Eileen Young, who arrived for two years in 1961, has her subsequent career mentioned, albeit briefly.[43] The book is largely a history of men, but Anna's arrival must have been a significant moment in the life of the law faculty, as the proportion of women law students grew. It seems that, although she was a permanent member of staff wherever she went, she was always on short-term contracts. Tenure was not for her, but perhaps that also suited her as she was continually seeking pupillage during this period.

Although it is likely that she taught across a range of subjects as staff had to do in a law school in those days, she published on subjects of international law. In October 1961, in a still cited 33-page paper in the *International and Comparative Law Quarterly*, she dealt with the subject of interference with merchant vessels in peacetime, a subject which had 'provoked more political than legal furore'. She published two book reviews in that Journal in 1963, neither of which pulled their punches, commenting about a 'misleading analogy' in one, and that the other was 'little more than a manual of quotations from the major authorities'.

Anna's friend Janet remembers spending Summer vacations with Anna warmly. What also seems to have been the case is that Anna was a risk-taker. They would drive off in Anna's drophead MGB around Europe for long periods, having fun. And it is that element of Anna which is, perhaps, most important to remember. It does not necessarily square with one's vision of a woman academic and aspiring barrister in the 1950s and 1960s, but I suspect that says something about me looking back on this period. What we have is a middle class, white aspiring woman academic and barrister, seeking to forge both a career as well as having the maximum amount of enjoyment with her friends. That is as much as I know about this period.

It must have been during this period that Anna conducted her sittings (or dinners) at her Inn, Lincoln's Inn.[44] Anna's friend, Janet, told me that she had

[41] JA Borkowski and HG Thomas, *The Bristol Law Faculty – The First Fifty Years* (University of Bristol, 1984) 48.

[42] ibid.

[43] ibid 61.

[44] How little I knew of Anna's life, and the faultlines in my own memory, is exemplified by the fact that, when I joined the Bar in 2005, I joined Middle Temple in part because I was under the impression it had been Anna's inn.

accompanied Anna to those dinners at Lincoln's Inn (which enabled her to be called to the bar); she had done so because the student always had to bring a person of the same sex to those dinners. Janet remarked on the fact that, in her memory, Anna and she were the only women at those dinners, and that Anna was very much a 'man's woman'. The impression from Janet was of a woman who was at home in male company; but, again, although those dinners are supposed to be training opportunities (perhaps more so then than now), there was silence about that part of it. As Janet put it, 'it was quite fun and interesting. They were chatty. We ate our meal and then we left. … I don't remember the food being that good. And the judges sat on a [higher bit] and the students sat underneath' (laughter).

There is another significant fact about this period. Anna was a serial engagee. That is to say, she was engaged to a variety of different men serially – 'she always had a fiancé', as Janet put it. None of them were regarded by Rosemary as what she called suitable, although Janet spoke fondly about an airline pilot fiancé. I had always found this an amusing curiosity about Anna – she loved to, and was quick to, fall in love. She must have had a brilliant time, and a full social life with plenty of intrigue.

However, in writing this, and thinking about Anna's life in this context, I see it slightly differently – that we have a clever, attractive woman who may well have used those engagements for three different complimentary and intersecting purposes. First, they would have acted to ward off unwanted attention so that 'she wouldn't get pestered'. Secondly, they operated to distance her from Jack and Rosemary. There were signs of fracture, certainly from Anna's 21st birthday, between her and Jack, with whom she had been close. Thirdly, there is the state of what Oakley describes as 'structural ambivalence', in which there were contradictions between alternatives of equal legitimacy.[45] On the one hand, Anna was striving to fulfil her obvious intellectual potential; on the other hand, she was seeking out the wife role; although perhaps the better way of looking at this complexity is performatively. Did Anna intend to marry any of these men? That is unclear – Rosemary told a story about having to go to New York to rescue Anna from one of them (but the idea of 'rescue' was never expanded upon).

Professional Life – Barrister

Then, after some considerable time, in 1963, it appears that Anna was accepted for pupillage, and became pupil to Victor Wellings. She lived just off Ebury Street in central London in a flat, which she bought in 1962 or 1963. We know something about this period from the remarkable letter sent by Victor to my father after Anna's death, in which he sought to correct certain impressions which had

[45] A Oakley, *Housewife: High Value–Low Cost* (Penguin, 1974) 81–82.

developed about Anna. It was apparently being said after her death that Anna was effectively a part-timer, and somebody whose career at the bar was a matter of play for her, to which she had no particular commitment. This is particularly telling, I think, in terms of the way in which the Bar might have thought about an aspirational middle class woman barrister, who also had a family. Victor wrote about Anna's pupillage in these terms:

> Altogether I have had four pupils. All of them were able and gifted, and Anna's ability and gifts were at least the equal of any of the others. She was certainly the most industrious of them.

Victor himself is something of an enigma. He must have been progressive – in terms of the Bar – because he took on a female pupil who, it seems, had been unsuccessful in obtaining pupillage for at least four years. This was not a question of whether or not Anna could afford a pupillage and the struggles of life as an early career barrister – she could have done. Nor was it the case that she lacked the academic credentials. There can only be one reason why she struggled to obtain pupillage: she was a woman. This was a period when there were only about 100 or so women at the Bar, who were restricted in their social activities.[46] Victor was also something of a contrarian, who upset his leader in one case by seeking to disavow certain submissions by his leader.[47]

Accordingly, it speaks volumes about Victor that he took Anna on as a pupil at that time. It also demonstrates something quite remarkable about Anna. It seems that, during her academic career, she was developing a strong interest in international law. However, Victor was a landlord and tenant specialist, in a Chancery set. Anna followed Victor's specialism. Victor himself became co-editor of the practitioner's landlord and tenant bible, *Woodfall*, for the editions in 1963 and 1968, and subsequently lead editor. To me, this demonstrates Anna's intellectual adroitness and ability to shift subject track, something unthinkable today. However, we should also remember that, just as academics taught across numerous subjects, it was considered entirely normal practice for lawyers to have command of the range of legal subjects.

In 1963, Anna also met my father, a GP, who was a little older than her. It was a whirlwind affair – Janet, who fixed them up for a round of golf when Jack pulled out, left the country for a few months only (to take Greyhound buses across the US – '99 days for $99') and had to return early for the wedding. My father, an orthodox Jew, insisted that Anna convert to Judaism, which she did (leading to Jack and Rosemary effectively disowning her). In terms of the chronology of events, what we have is a woman who recently became married, was converting

[46] H Heilbron, 'Women at the Bar: A Historical Perspective' (31 May 2013) *Counsel*, www.counselmagazine.co.uk/articles/women-the-bar-historical-perspective.

[47] See *Horford Investments Ltd v Lambert* [1976] Ch 39 – the law reports detail about submissions corresponds with this assertion. I am grateful to Justin Bates and Andrew Arden KC for eliciting this information.

to Judaism, and about to, or actually conducting pupillage. Victor does not talk or hint at either status in his letter. I can find no discussion of Anna's treatment at the Bar as a Jew. She wore a wig, as we have seen, as an orthodox Jew, at least for the photograph. I doubt that she wore the wig at the Bar because, as Janet inferred, her relationship with Judaism was part of her relationship with my father. But, Janet also suggested that her conversion was more a matter of form than substance, to please my father's parents. Nobody could provide any information to me about Anna's identity as a Jewish woman at the Bar. The trail that I expected to hear about anti-semitism must rest there but is one which should be picked up given the history of Jewish women and the Bar.

Anna gave birth to her first son shortly after her pupillage ended. There were nannies and a nurse, together with other support on hand to facilitate Anna's return to practice. However, in that first Christmas, her friend Janet moved in to assist Anna with the newborn baby because Anna had no appreciation of how to look after the baby – Janet and Anna were 'looking after a baby between us' (as Janet recounted to me). My father, it appears, was unhelpful because his practice had taken off. He had become GP to the Beatles. That Christmas Eve, Janet recalls, my father announced that he had invited Ringo Starr, his wife, Maureen, and George Hamilton and others for supper on Christmas day. Apparently, they 'just sat. They weren't exactly scintillating company'. Janet remembers that she made turkey sandwiches, and they brought a record signed by them all.

The Lincoln's Inn librarian told me that their records indicated that Anna practised from chambers at 4 Kings Bench Walk, Temple (1965–67). This must have meant that she moved chambers after pupillage. Quite why that happened is not known to me, especially given Victor's evident admiration for her ability. Perhaps it was a result of having a child. During this period, I was born on a Friday. Whether myth or anecdote, I cannot say, but I was always led to believe that Anna returned to chambers on the Monday. In his letter, Victor wrote that, after she joined that set, 'I kept in touch with her and I remember her anxiety at that time because in those chambers she was not getting enough work'. Perhaps, the crime of having a child was regarded as inimical to self-employed practice at the Bar. This part of the letter suggests that Victor saw himself as a practice mentor to Anna, who was practising in the same field as he was. In my experience, such mentorship is not unusual between former pupils and pupil masters, but, in this context, it would suggest a continuing relationship of care and support.

At Victor's instigation, Anna joined Gray's Inn Chambers, Gray's Inn (1967–71), which is now known as 4–5 Gray's Inn Square. In October 1967, Anna applied to become an *ad eundem* member of Gray's Inn, and was admitted as such. Such a member becomes entitled to use the library and the facilities of the Inn.

The head of chambers was, at that time, Douglas Frank. His obituary in *The Times* states that '[h]aving led a move from the Temple to Gray's Inn, he triggered a period of prosperity that transformed a small, undistinguished set into one of the country's largest and most successful chambers'.[48] Victor wrote in his letter to my father that this set was 'very expensive' and 'since the burden of the expenses of chambers is borne by members in proportions directly related to their earnings any member not intending to practice seriously or whose practice is unsuccessful is soon told politely to go'.[49] This was meant as a put down to those who had suggested Anna's practice was merely a pastime. He noted that all her solicitors praised her work, and

> She was developing a substantial practice of her own in my own field (the law of landlord and tenant). Not only had she given me excellent and major assistance in the preparation of some of my own books but she had become an editor in her own right. She had published three books of value to the profession. I have no doubt that had she lived she would ultimately have taken silk and would have had reasonable expectations of appointment to the Bench.[50]

Of the three books, the only one which I can find is that she was the editor of the 10th edition of Volume 3: Permanent Supplement to Sir Robert Megarry's *Rent Acts*, regarded as the leading text in that specific field. It should be remembered that this was a time when struggles over landlord and tenant were capable of bringing down governments – the Rent Act 1965 was emergency legislation following the election of Harold Wilson in 1964 as a result of the Profumo scandal which linked in to rented housing as a result of the connection with Perec Rachman.[51] This Act was of a new and radical design. It swept away the control and decontrol of rents, providing for their regulation within a new system. It was these sweeping changes, described in brilliant detail in David Nelken's classic text, *The Limits of the Legal Process: A Study of Landlords, Law and Crime*,[52] with which Anna's edition was concerned.

Her preface notes the consolidation of provisions in the Rent Act 1968, but laments the fact that the Act of 1968 does not contain 'the whole of the relevant law',[53] referring to other key interventions by the Labour government of the Leasehold Reform Act 1967, Matrimonial Homes Act 1967, Caravan Sites Act 1968 among others. All of these were included in this volume alongside her textual annotations. In masterful understatement, Anna wrote that the whole of the law on the subject had been included to July 1970, and that 'nobody could pretend [the law] to be simple'.[54]

[48] *The Times* (London, 9 December 2004).
[49] Private letter held by the author, from the file maintained by my father.
[50] At the time, there were two women judges, so this was a bold and unusual prediction.
[51] The detail and significance of this legislation is covered in D Cowan, *Housing Law and Policy* (CUP, 2011) ch 3.
[52] D Nelken, *The Limits of the Legal Process: A Study of Landlords, Law and Crime*, (Academic Press, 1983).
[53] A van Zwanenberg, 'Preface', *Megarry's Rent Acts*, 1st Permanent Supplement (Stevens & Sons, 1970).
[54] ibid.

On 14 September 1970, Anna and my father were involved in a car accident in Edinburgh, following which Anna died of her injuries.

Concluding Discussion

And that is all that is known. After what was always (and still is) known as 'the accident', Anna was simply never spoken of again, other than the odd indiscretion. I cannot say why that happened, perhaps the pain, perhaps other factors; but, Anna was simply airbrushed from family history. She might, as Victor Wellings have suggested, have been one of the pioneer female QCs and judge, but the point of this chapter is that she wasn't.

Those are the barest 'facts' about her legal life. They suggest a potentially eminent, opinionated academic scholar, who was seeking a career in practice. There is little to tell about her life as a woman barrister or academic, and the struggles of temporary contracts and seeking pupillage. In my discussions with Anna's family and friends, one of the notable things I heard was silence about her professional life.

It appears she simply did not talk about it at all *domestically*. There must have been struggles and disappointments – in obtaining academic employment and pupillage, with her clerks, and with colleagues at the Bar (as suggested by her period at 4 King's Bench Walk, at least in Victor's telling). There are snippets of memories. Janet remembers Anna always having 'her nose' in the Chancery Law Reports. Neither Jennifer nor Roger, nor either of the Janets could remember Anna talking about her work, at all. And, as Janet (Anna's friend) said, it would have been interesting to hear about that work. Anna helped Roger find direction, and her sister, Janet, with a room while she was training.

It is this silence on which I wish to reflect in the closing paragraphs and I do so in the context of the literatures with which I am familiar. I recognise both the poignancy and the power of that repressive silence. Oakley's near contemporaneous, brilliant work alerts us to the cultural position that higher education and the professions were stereotyped as masculine – 'it is the "career" which is particularly equated with masculinity'[55] – and '"masculine" behaviour on the part of women is frequently the subject of social ridicule'.[56] Oakley further points out that, 'to call a man "ambitious" is to complement him, to call a woman "ambitious" may be to insult her. Ambition itself is a masculine attribute'.[57]

Nevertheless, reflecting on Anna's career as an academic and at the Bar, it is clear to me that she was ambitious and that she was a professional woman. Her stamina and strength to maintain those careers, and the desire to join the Bar,

[55] Oakley (n 45) 88.
[56] ibid 85.
[57] ibid.

suggest that she suffered numerous setbacks during those careers mainly because of her sex. There could be no doubt, as Victor wrote, about her 'industriousness', nor, indeed, her intellectual credentials.

Yet those careers were not the subject of domestic discussion or confession as we might do today. Anna appears to have adopted, and adapted, a more traditional gender role domestically, a privileged middle class one to be sure. That role division, or splintering or bifurcation, meant that the confessions she made were to Victor, *professionally*.[58] These were not discussions or comments that she made to her family members. It may have been difficult to confess the lack of work at the bar because it may have appeared as a failure. This dividing practice between home and work is emphasised by the images of Anna presented above and that photographic recording, as Susan Sontag puts it, is always a means of control and gives control over the thing photographed.[59] In each sphere of her life, perhaps, she was emphasising the living discursive power of repression and oppression, the 'polymorphous techniques of power'.[60]

Returning to my original framing of Anna as 'unexceptional', and the dichotomy of exceptional/unexceptional, I am reminded of Baroness Hale's observation that exceptionality is an outcome and not a guide.[61] Her life was 'not considered important enough to be asked to leave a trace on the written records of the state', as Linda Mulcahy put it.[62] In the sense in which Ann Oakley describes the Housewife of the period, Anna's life was unexceptional. It conformed to those norms.[63] In that sense, Anna was not the exception – she was a professional woman subject to the same everyday discriminations that women both then and now still endure. She took precautions, warding off unwanted attention through her serial engagements, for example. On the other hand, as my discussion of her career demonstrates, and the apparently firm dividing line between home and career, she was exceptional. I see that exceptionality/unexceptionality as deriving from her insider/outsider status, which she appears to have carefully preserved. As a woman, she was an outsider. Yet, she was comfortable around men and they appeared to be comfortable with her, too. She had a good career at the bar and, in doing so, hid the aspects that made her an outsider. The silence about her Jewishness (and internal conflicts about that) is notable.[64]

[58] To be fair, I simply do not know whether she discussed these issues with my father. That was part of the great silence.

[59] S Sontag, *On Photography* (Penguin, 1977) 156–67.

[60] M Foucault, *The History of Sexuality*, vol 1 (Vintage Books, 1980).

[61] *Manchester CC v Pinnock* [2010] UKSC 45, [51]. See also Bourne, ch 1, this volume, and CA MacKinnon, *Feminism Unmodified: Discourses on Life and Law* (Harvard University Press, 1987) ch 5.

[62] Mulcahy (n 13).

[63] For more on the importance of class and socialisation, see the chapters by Derry (ch 3) and Bourne (ch 1) in this volume.

[64] For more on this point, see D Sugarman, 'Hart Interviewed: HLA Hart in Conversation with David Sugarman' (2005) 32 *Journal of Law and Society* 267; N Lacey, *A Life of HLA Hart: The Nightmare and the Noble Dream*, 1st edn (OUP, 2006); D Herman, *An Unfortunate Coincidence: Jews, Jewishness, and*

My penultimate reflection is a personal one. It was Rosemary Auchmuty who suggested to me that the above might be of interest more broadly. However, I began writing it as catharsis. I cannot say that has been achieved. Anybody who knows me may be struck, as I have been, by the coincidental crossovers between Anna and my life. I am insufficiently deterministic nor psychoanalytic to see this as anything other than spontaneous connections.

However, what I hope is that, if you have read this chapter, it will tell you something about women's legal history as Erika Rackley and Rosemary Auchmuty have argued it should be told.[65] It is not neutral; it is not objective; it is both personal and political.

English Law (OUP, 2011); DM Seymour, 'English Law and the Dilemmas of Assimilation' (2012) 21 *Social and Legal Studies* 567.

[65] E Rackley and R Auchmuty (eds), *Women's Legal Landmarks: Celebrating the History of Women and Law in the UK and Ireland* (Hart, 2018).

5

Gender, Feminism and Unsung Workers: The Early Years of the Law Centres Movement 1970–1980

MARIE BURTON AND LINDA MULCAHY

Introduction

This chapter examines the early history of the Law Centres movement in England, Wales and Northern Ireland. More specifically, it considers the role that women played in shaping the way that Law Centres worked and the work they did. The discussion draws on a four-year project funded by the Arts and Humanities Research Council which is being conducted by the authors in partnership with the British Library, the Law Centres Network and Queen's University Belfast.[1] The Enhancing Democratic Habits project aims to produce an in-depth account of activist lawyering in Law Centres from the 1970s to the present day. It has two key goals: to produce an oral history sound archive and a national collection of Law Centre reports, both of which will be deposited at the British Library on an open access basis. In this contribution to the celebration of Rosemary Auchmuty's life and work we use data collected during the first phase of the research to ask a series of questions that are relevant to her body of work on feminist legal history. We address three main questions. How can uncelebrated women be found? What roles did women play in Law Centres? And what impact did they have?

Several of the themes which emerge from the first stage of the Enhancing Democratic Habits project reflect ideas that have emerged from Rosemary's work on women's history and the methodologies associated with marginalised legal lives.[2]

[1] AHRC grant AH/T007710/1. In the course of the project, we will conduct five case studies which focus on particular Law Centres. Anna Bryson and Kieran McEvoy will take the lead in conducting the Northern Ireland case study.

[2] R Auchmuty, 'Early Women Law Students at Cambridge and Oxford' (2008) 29 *Journal of Legal History* 63; R Auchmuty, (2011) 'Whatever Happened to Miss Bebb? *Bebb v The Law Society* and Women's Legal History' (2011) 31 *Legal Studies* 199; R Auchmuty, 'Recovering Lost Lives: Researching Women in Legal History' (2015) 42 *Journal of Law and Society* 34.

Firstly, she has argued that feminist legal history remains largely undeveloped in the United Kingdom (UK).[3] We argue that Law Centres' role in foregrounding the problems faced by women forms a relatively unexplored part of the history of radical lawyering and the history of women's liberation more generally.[4]

Secondly, Rosemary has urged historians to adopt a broad definition of legal biography which moves beyond those women who qualified as lawyers to include those engaged in legal work.[5] This has a particular resonance for Law Centres, where community workers often worked alongside lawyers in identifying legal problems and appropriate responses to them. Thirdly, her work has emphasised the need to set subjects in a wider context than the world of law. This has been made possible in the Enhancing Democratic Habits project because of the use of the life-story method which focuses on capturing holistic accounts of lives that include details of family life, education, political beliefs and outside-of-work activities. Finally, Rosemary's work with Erica Rackley encourages us to avoid the siren call of anecdote and myth when delving into personal and community histories.[6] As will become clear, this is an issue which has dogged earlier histories of the Law Centre movement which, we argue, have failed to recognise the particular contribution made in their 'origin' stories by women workers. We argue that looking at the Law Centres movement from a feminist perspective provides an excellent opportunity to add nuance to existing 'canonical' accounts of its early years. These accounts have tended to focus on the achievements of a relatively small group of men and rarely mention gender except when talking about women as clients or the women's groups that were represented on the management committees of Law Centres.[7]

This chapter involves an analysis of 10 long interviews with Law Centre 'pioneers' and a discourse analysis of 25 annual reports produced in the first 10 years of their history.[8] Oral history and life stories have been identified as

[3] R Auchmuty, 'Early Women Law Students' (n 2); R Auchmuty, 'Spinsters and Trade Unions in Victorian Britain' (1975) *Labour History* 109–22; E Rackley and R Auchmuty (eds), *Women's Legal Landmarks: Celebrating the History of Women and Law in the UK and Ireland* (Hart, 2018).

[4] See, for instance, M Jolly, *Sisterhood and After: An Oral History of the UK Women's Liberation Movement, 1968–Present* (OUP, 2019). It is noticeable that despite the importance of legal reform to second-wave feminists, there is only one lawyer in the Sisterhood and After project www.bl.uk/sisterhood. See also M Stephens, *Community Law Centres: An Appraisal* (Avebury, 1990); A Byles and P Morris, *Unmet Need: The Case of the Neighbourhood Law Centre* (Routledge, 1977).

[5] Auchmuty, 'Recovering Lost Lives' (n 2). See, for instance, her discussion of Lilian Orme in Auchmuty, 'Spinsters and Trade Unions' (n 3). In this context see also F Batlan, 'The Birth of Legal Aid: Gender Ideologies, Women, and the Bar in New York City, 1863–1910' (2010) 28(4) *Law and History Review* 931–71.

[6] E Rackley and R Auchmuty, 'The Case for Feminist Legal History' (2020) 40 *Oxford Journal of Legal Studies* 878.

[7] See, for instance, C Grace and P Lefevre, 'Draining the Swamp' (1985) 7 *Law and Policy* 97; FH Zemans and A Thomas, 'Can Community Clinics Survive? A Comparative Study of Law Centres in Australia, Ontario and England' in F Regan et al (eds), *The Transformation of Legal Aid* (OUP, 1999); R Smith, 'Clinics in a Cold Climate: Community Law Centres in England and Wales' (1997) 35 *Osgoode Hall Law Journal* 895.

[8] Our thanks go to Max Zahnd who worked as a postdoctoral fellow for the first year of the project and assisted in developing a coding framework for the reports on which this analysis loosely draws.

particularly appropriate to feminist and radical engagements with history.[9] As an extended form of oral history interview, the life-story method gives the interviewer scope to explore the broader context of an interviewee's life including family background, education, motivations, personal interests, activities and political affiliations. Life-story interviews also tend to be much longer than other forms of interview, lasting up to 12 hours and taking place over several sessions. In common with other oral histories, the focus has traditionally been on recording the 'unheard voice'.

In the sections which follow, we seek to explore three key issues which disrupt existing accounts of English Law Centres. In the first section we describe our attempts to bring the stories of the women who helped to establish Law Centres to the fore. We then consider the roles that women played in Law Centres with particular reference to the opportunities offered to them and the day-to-day working of collectives. In the final section of the chapter, we consider how women began to change the work undertaken by Law Centres and the broader network of female activists that women in Law Centres collaborated with across organisations. In doing so, we draw attention to the manner in which women began to influence the activities of Law Centres and the ways in which structural inequalities were perceived. In presenting the voices of those involved in the early years of the movement we draw on interviews with female workers, but also on the accounts provided by the men who worked alongside them in their efforts to realise systemic change for impoverished communities.[10] The picture we paint is one of radical activists giving voice to and responding to the subordination of women in broader society and within their own networks. The women we interviewed might identify as radical, socialist or liberal feminists.[11] What is fascinating about their accounts is the way in which they render visible the emergence of second-wave feminism and the ways in which it began to take root within progressive politics.

[9] See Jolly (n 4); M Jolly, P Russell and R Cohen, 'Sisterhood and After: Individualism, Ethics and an Oral History of the Women's Liberation Movement' (2012) 11 *Social Movement Studies* 211. But see also J Scanlon, 'Challenging the Imbalances of Power in Feminist Oral History: Developing a Take-and-give Methodology' (1993) 16 *Women's Studies International Forum* 639; S Gluck, 'Has Feminist Oral History Lost its Radical/Subversive Edge?' (2011) 39 *Oral History* 63; K Fobear, 'Do You Understand? Unsettling Interpretative Authority in Feminist Oral History' (2016) 10 *Journal of Feminist Scholarship* 61; M Jolly and L Huibo, 'Hearing Her: Comparing Feminist Oral History in the UK and China' (2019) 45 *The Oral History Review* 48.

[10] R Auchmuty and E Rackley, 'Feminist Legal Biography: A Model for all Legal Life Stories' (2020) 41 *Journal of Legal History* 186. They argue that feminist legal biography is not just about uncovering the lost lives of women but the relationship between the sexes. They anticipate that biographies of men require consideration of the ways in which men maintained their dominant position in law and society. In this chapter we outline a number of ways in which men have also contributed to the liberation of women.

[11] On the issue of origin stories and how different types of feminist emerged, see Jolly (n 4); P Bartley, *Women's Activism in Twentieth Century Britain: Making a Difference across the Political Spectrum* (Palgrave, 2022).

Finding Women and Rethinking the Concept of 'Pioneer'

The first year of the Enhancing Democratic Habits project has been dedicated to conducting a series of life-story interviews with early Law Centre activists involved in the setting up of the first 10 Law Centres.[12] This is a group we originally referred to in our grant proposal as 'the pioneers'. It soon became apparent that the very idea of a 'pioneer' was more problematic than originally anticipated, not least because this characterisation tends to isolate the individual rather than viewing their work in the broader context of the group or movement.[13] Our initial review of work in the field found that a familiar group of men tended to be discussed in the literature on the early years of Law Centres. Examples of those regularly referred to include Michael Zander, who has been credited with initiating the debate about setting up Law Centres,[14] or Tony Gifford, the co-founder of North Kensington Neighbourhood Law Centre. Amongst this group, Peter Kandler, the first Law Centre solicitor at the first UK Law Centre, has variously been described as 'the driving force'[15] of 'his' Law Centre[16] or a rock-n-roll lawyer.[17] To some extent the story of Peter Kandler's many achievements has become a foundational story of the movement which continues to be told.[18] Important though the contributions of these men have been to the field, the authors were aware of the danger of this project reinforcing the 'great man' approach to legal history.[19] Indeed, the iconic photograph of North Kensington Law Centre reproduced at Figure 1 remains of interest to feminist historians because of the four women pictured about whom so little has been written.

[12] 13 in England and Wales, and two in Northern Ireland.

[13] Auchmuty and Rackley (n 10).

[14] Stephens (n 4).

[15] O Boycott, '"We are the A&E of Law": The First UK Law Centre for Poor People Turns 50' *The Guardian* (London, 28 July 2020) www.theguardian.com/society/2020/jul/28/we-are-the-ae-of-law-the-first-uk-law-centre-for-poor-people-turns-50.

[16] K Schuyt, K Groenendijk and B Sloot, 'Access to the Legal System and Legal Services Research' in B Blegvad, C Campbell and C Schuyt (eds), *European Yearbook in Law and Sociology* (Springer, 1977) 98.

[17] T Kingsley, 'Meet the "Rock n Roll" Lawyers of Kensington who Started in an Old Butcher's Shop' *West London News* (London, 11 June 2020) www.mylondon.news/news/west-london-news/meet-rock-n-roll-lawyers-18395890.

[18] See eg M Prescott, '50 Years of the NKLC' (2020) *Socialist Lawyer* 48; O Subhedar, 'From a Butcher's Shop to the Tory Cuts' (2018) *Socialist Lawyer* 19; P Kandler, 'North Kensington Law Centre: Reflections 40 Years On' (2010) *Socialist Lawyer* 29; Byles and Morris (n 4 above). See also A Gifford, 'The Founding of the North Kensington Law Centre' (North Kensington Law Centre, nd) nklc.org.uk/the-founding-of-the-north-kensington-law-centre. When discussing its own history, North Kensington Law Centre's website focuses on Peter Kandler, Tony Gifford and James Saunders along with six other male members of the organising committee. Of the two women who are mentioned one is Pansy Jeffrey, the head of the local Citizen Advice Bureau and the other is Kate Gifford, identified as the pregnant wife of Tony who assisted by writing letters to funders.

[19] Auchmuty and Rackley (n 10).

Figure 1 Photograph taken outside North Kensington Neighbourhood Law Centre[20]

Our point is not to disparage the incredibly important work that men did in contributing to the establishment of Law Centres and improving the lives of women, men and families. Our argument is merely that the time has come for the particular contribution and perspective of women to be researched, understood and celebrated.

At first sight, the focus of the existing literature on men might appear justified when discussed in the context of the legal profession of the early 1970s. When Law Centres were set up, just under 3 per cent of solicitors with practising certificates were women.[21] By way of contrast, our analysis of early Law Centre reports (1970–1980) shows that women made up approximately half of all Law Centre staff, playing the role of community workers and administrative staff, as well as solicitors.[22] The role of community workers is particularly important in the present context as many were recognised as having a much more in-depth knowledge and

[20] An original of this photograph is held by the Law Centres Network.

[21] '75 Years of Women Solicitors' (*BBC News*, 19 December 1997) news.bbc.co.uk/1/hi/uk/40448.stm.

[22] It has been difficult to identify the exact roles that women played in Law Centres as their job titles are often not included in annual reports. The authors surmise that this reflects the collective spirit of many Law Centres and formal recognition that no job was more important than another.

experience of the problems of the poor than many solicitors of the time.[23] Female community workers remain critical to our sample because of the fact that they were women in law rather than women lawyers.

Our interest in untold stories of women's legal activists has prompted us to search out the details of those who have been marginalised in the histories produced to date. Tracking down the women involved in the first 10 years of the movement is not without its problems. Many Law Centre reports from the period have not survived, and finding up-to-date contact details for those we are able to identify can be difficult in a search that goes back 50 years. We have, however, actively sought out references to women workers, volunteers or management committee members in our analysis of annual reports and other archives and encouraged male and female interviewees to talk about the women they worked alongside.[24] We have also extended our sample frame beyond the traditional notion of a pioneer as a person at the very beginning of an initiative and increased the relevant time period to the first 10 years of the movement. This gave us the flexibility to include more women in the sample of interviewees. This has not solved all of our problems in identifying uncelebrated women. Trails peter out and women from the early years have sometimes changed their names upon marriage. We have also discovered that those who were not lawyers, or who did not become lawyers, have been more reticent about recording life-story interviews on the basis that they do not consider their stories important enough.

Despite these setbacks it has been possible to unearth a range of new and interesting data about women in Law Centres. It soon became clear once interviews commenced that an extensive range of women are known and remembered within activist networks. Four excellent examples of interviewees can be given,[25] starting with Pamela Ditton who was the second solicitor and first ever female Law Centre solicitor in an English Law Centre. She was appointed just six months after North Kensington Neighbourhood Law Centre opened and developed a huge breadth of experience, going on to be one of the first workers at another Law Centre in Islington. Despite her absence in existing histories of UK Law Centres, Pamela has also gone on to do 'great things' at the Central Australian Aboriginal Legal Aid Service.[26] Jane Hickman, who worked as a lawyer at North Kensington Neighbourhood Law Centre and Balham Neighbourhood Law Centre in the 1970s, went on to act for the women at Greenham Common Peace Camp in the early 1980s, representing them in the UK courts and in their case against

[23] P Leask, 'Law Centres in England and Wales' (1985) 7 *Law and Policy* 61. It seems that other community workers were radical young graduates keen to advocate for the disadvantaged. During the 1960s, students started taking a more avid interest in campaigns for social change: see R Smith, *Justice: Redressing the Balance* (Legal Action Group, 1997).

[24] The relative invisibility of women was compounded when we turned our attention to seeking out women of colour.

[25] We have the express consent of all four women to include their names in this paper.

[26] J Faine, *Lawyers in the Alice: Aboriginals and Whitefellas' Law* (Federation Press, 1993).

United States President Ronald Reagan.[27] With Ben Rose, she subsequently set up her own firm which became one of the leading criminal defence and human rights firms in the country. In 2007, Jane was also appointed by the Lord Chancellor's Department as a Commissioner at the Legal Services Commission.[28] Angela Mason, who began her Law Centre career as a community worker at Camden Community Law Centre in 1973, trained as an articled clerk in the late 1970s at Battersea Law Centre and practised as a qualified solicitor at West Hampstead Law Centre in the early 1980s. Later, in 1992, Angela was to become the Director of Stonewall, where she led a number of successful gay rights campaigns, including campaigns in favour of the lowering of the age of consent for gay men, against the ban on gays in the military, and in support of gay adoption and civil partnerships. From 2003 to 2007 she was the head of the Government Equalities Office and received a CBE for her 'services to homosexual rights' in 2007.[29]

Other women who continued to work at the coalface have also made a mark. Included in this group are women such as Wendy Pettifer who began her career as a community worker at Manchester Law Centre. She later qualified as a solicitor and, after working in private practice and at the College of Law, she became the senior housing solicitor at Hackney Community Law Centre in 2009.[30] Even after her retirement, Wendy remains a committed activist and campaigner: in 2016 and 2017 she worked as a volunteer lawyer at the Calais Jungle.[31] As the project develops we hope to reveal many more accounts of the women, including women who never qualified as lawyers, who fuelled the early Law Centres.[32] Women such as Baroness Martha Otito Osamor and Baroness Margaret Prosser, whose fascinating histories we are currently exploring.

The Involvement of Women in the Early Years of Law Centres

Accounts of the lives of individual female legal activists remain important to our project but run the risk of isolating the individual at the expense of the collective.

[27] For a history of the Greenham Common protest, see E Woodcraft, 'Greenham Common Women's Peace Camp 1981–2000' in Rackley and Auchmuty, *Women's Legal Landmarks* (n 3).

[28] See 15 September 2016 statement on the Hickman & Rose website, 'Hickman & Rose Founding Partner Retires' www.hickmanandrose.co.uk/hickman-and-rose-founding-partner-retires/.

[29] L Ward and T Branigan, 'Level's Best' *The Guardian* (London, 14 November 2007) www.theguardian.com/society/2007/nov/14/guardiansocietysupplement.equality.

[30] Hackney Community Law Centre, 'Wendy Pettifer retires from HCLC' (24 June 2016) www.hclc.org.uk/2016/04/wendy-pettifer-retires-from-hclc/.

[31] Wendy Pettifer, 'About the Author' www.lovelines.net/about/.

[32] Some women in this category such as the politician Harriet Harman have already come to the attention of the public and list their involvement in Law Centres in their personal profiles: See further 'About Harriet' www.harrietharman.org/about_harriet.

This tension has been recognised by other feminists[33] as raising a series of ethical issues about whether we can understand movements through an accumulation of individual narratives. It has been persuasively argued that individual interviews also serve to engender a political understanding of the personal,[34] but tensions still ensue in selecting who to talk to and determining who can represent a movement that is ideologically defined as communal. The issue of the group versus the individual is especially important when researching early Law Centres, many of which came to operate as collectives.[35] This way of working involved an active decision by workers to remove the sorts of hierarchical structures associated with class and gender differentials in broader society. In a review of the first 10 years of operation, North Kensington Neighbourhood Law Centre explained:

> Just as the centre's relationship to its surrounding community has evolved toward a model of democratic control, so too has its internal organisation as a workplace. Although differences in experience and prior training were always recognised, the goal became gradually to share responsibility and to conduct in-service training to ensure that knowledge is pooled.[36]

Receptionist and secretarial roles were phased out in some centres in which 'self-servicing' became the norm.[37] These collective structures were often accompanied by pay parity which benefited non-legally qualified staff, who, at the time, were more likely to be women.[38] Finally, decisions about case work, campaigns, appointments and the organisation of the office involved everyone coming to a consensus rather than managers imposing decisions.

It is important to note that these equalising measures, aimed at levelling out the hierarchy between lawyers and community workers, managers and administrators, attracted criticism from the communities in which early Law Centres were based.[39] Local residents and some Law Centre workers expressed concerns that administrative and secretarial roles offered opportunities for employment for local women who lacked the expertise and experience required to compete for the diverse professional roles in Law Centres.[40]

The dynamics of collective working, and its benefits and limitations, are rarely examined in any depth in the existing literature on UK Law Centres[41] or the

[33] Jolly et al (n 9).

[34] ibid.

[35] The idea of the collective became less feasible in subsequent decades.

[36] North Kensington Law Centre, 'The First Ten Years, 1970–1980' (North Kensington Law Centre, 1980) 16.

[37] Leask (n 23); C Robinson, T Chakraborty and C Dabezies, *18 Years: Coming of Age, 1970–1988* (North Kensington Law Centre, 1988).

[38] See, for instance, North Kensington Law Centre (n 36). Subsequently, low pay for solicitors in the sector was raised as an issue in terms of the recruitment and retention of experienced solicitors: Leask (n 23). By this point, far more women were working as qualified lawyers in Law Centres.

[39] Leask (n 23) 71–72.

[40] ibid; M Prosser and G Watts, *Your Seat is at the End: My Story* (Feather Duster Publications, 2010).

[41] See, for instance, Byles and Morris (n 4); Stephens (n 4).

annual reports of Law Centres themselves, meaning that we have had to rely on interview data to produce insights into the everyday experiences of the collective from both women and men. It was argued in interviews that the shift away from traditional workplace dynamics often aided the personal development of the women concerned. In the words of one female Law Centre worker:

> [T]he way Law Centres were organised did facilitate women being involved and taking, having space to take a more active role than they would have done in a very formal hierarchical setting, where they would have just acted as legal secretaries or receptionists. (Interviewee 8, Female)[42]

And a male worker from another Centre argued that playing a more active role could also encourage activism:

> I could see when the collective was formed that in fact, after they got over their initial nerves, certain of the women who'd been secretaries really blossomed in terms of their personality and doing case work and helping people. It really encouraged them to take part and be an activist. (Interviewee 1, Male)

The overwhelming demand for services often meant that those with less formal qualifications were encouraged to increase their skills. By way of example, in a review of the first five years of operation, Camden Community Law Centre reflected on its recognition that receptionists needed to be provided with in-house training to enable them to move beyond merely greeting people to taking full statements, giving basic advice and signposting people to services – and even to visiting people in remand homes and prisons.[43] Law Centres also provided broader opportunities for solicitors. One interviewee described how her increasing interest in employment law led to her becoming the shop steward at the Law Centre and her appointment as a delegate to the local Trades Council. By the mid-1970s, she was the convenor of the local Trades Council Equal Opportunities Sub Committee and became involved in actively seeking out local situations in which women were being underpaid for work of equivalent value to that of men.

New opportunities for women to develop as caseworkers or community workers and, in a number of cases, to become legally qualified were clearly prospects which would not ordinarily have been available to them in the more traditional setting of private practice. However, the lack of a formal hierarchical structure did not mean there was no structure or hierarchy. For some workers, power relations

[42] There is some indication that the people recruited into these roles were sometimes graduates attracted by the radical potential of the Law Centre. Walter Merricks, for example, qualified as a solicitor in 1970, but he is listed as the reception worker in North Kensington Neighbourhood Law Centre, 'Annual Report, 1972' (North Kensington Neighbourhood Law Centre 1972). In 1973, he became the first Director of Camden Community Law Centre (see further J Rayner, 'Class Warrior' *Law Society Gazette* (London, 3 June 2019) www.lawgazette.co.uk/people/class-warrior/5070436.article). He is also listed as 'Solicitor (Director)' in Camden Community Law Centre, 'Half-Yearly Report, 1973' (Camden Community Law Centre, 1973).

[43] Camden Community Law Centre, 'Annual Report and Five Year Review, 1977–78' (Camden Community Law Centre, 1978).

transformed into something more informal and opaque.[44] In the words of one female worker:

> I personally felt that the structurelessness opened up a different sort of power structure. But it wasn't really that different, in that the most dominant people, usually the white males, still retained the power, whilst kind of pretending that they didn't. (Interviewee 4, Female)

For this worker, the lack of structure led to a situation where time was wasted, particularly in meetings:

> But it did evolve into a really tortuous complex decision-making process, whereby sometimes we would spend, I don't know, about half a day if not a whole day just talking about the politics of the Law Centre, the contradictions between state funding and wanting to facilitate people's power or whatever, to enhance the growth of the community to make their own decisions.

The possible inefficiencies of collective working arose in other interviews as well.

Nevertheless, interviewees were often supportive of collective organisation, possibly due to their left-wing political values. Responses sometimes suggested that it was not so much a lack of structure that was a problem, but the longstanding influence of broader societal expectations about how women should behave and be. By way of example, several male interviewees noted that female administrative staff were often reluctant to be involved in collective decision making. In the words of one:

> we had the staff meetings – everyone together and you'd alternate the chair. Well it was pretty obvious that some of the support workers didn't like that. And in retrospect you say, 'But we insisted on it.' Well who is the 'we'? Who is making the decision? The majority, but they were the minority. So there's the element of coercion, isn't there? And I don't know, you're doing it for what you think are the best of motives, but if they're sort of shit scared of having to go into the meeting, it's not really very helpful. (Interviewee 7, Male)

Despite these limitations, Law Centres were often remembered as comfortable places for feminists and lesbians to work at a time when they were commonly met with discrimination and hostility in wider society.[45] Manchester Law Centre is worthy of note as a pioneer in this field, publishing a Gay Rights book called *The Law and Sexuality* in 1977. An interviewee reflected on how the Law Centre was a place where she was able to openly express her sexuality:

> Being a lesbian was something as well. I mean, that was, it wasn't just acceptable in Law Centres, it was, you know, it was a badge of pride. Nobody dared say anything … Which

[44] C Landry et al, *What a Way to Run a Railroad: An Analysis of Radical Failure* (Comedia Publishing, 1985).

[45] See further R Auchmuty, S Jeffreys and E Miller, 'Lesbian History and Gay Studies: Keeping a Feminist Perspective' (1992) 1 *Women's History Review* 89; R Auchmuty, 'The Rhetoric of Equality and the Problem of Heterosexuality' in L Mulcahy and S Wheeler (eds), *Feminist Perspectives on Contract Law* (Routledge-Cavendish, 2005).

> was lovely, because there was a lot of prejudice otherwise out in society. So it was a safe haven. (Interviewee 2, Female)

Attention has often been drawn to the important part that working with other activists who were comfortable with challenging traditional ways of doing things played out in creating less stereotypical ways of working. As the same interviewee explained:

> I just couldn't imagine being in a traditional law firm with all of that – you would have had to wear a skirt and a suit and stockings, as it was, suspenders and stockings every day, high heels, lipstick ... And if Law Centres hadn't been there, I just think what the hell would have happened to me? (Interviewee 2, Female)

These accounts provide a clear sense of the ways in which the progressive politics of Law Centres allowed traditional hierarchies to be broken down and a more diverse range of voices to engage in decision making. But what impact did this have on decisions about the type of work undertaken by Law Centres? Did the type of work that was prioritised demonstrate equal respect for the rights of women and their unmet legal needs?

How Did Feminist Values Impact on the Sort of Work that Was Done?

The work undertaken by Law Centres was determined by reference to their aspirations, the formal constraints placed upon them and pragmatic concerns about their level of resourcing. Alongside other advice centres and activists, early Law Centres aspired to play a central role in addressing unmet legal need and filling in the gaps left by other solicitors. In the early 1970s, areas of unmet legal need where legal aid was not available, or where it was routinely refused in the Magistrates' Court, included proceedings before Rent Tribunals, Rent Assessment Committees, Social Security Tribunals and Industrial Tribunals; all of which adjudicated on issues which primarily affected poor people.[46] Law Centres also aspired to serve the poor in other ways. Rather than focusing solely on case work, as private solicitors firms did, they were commonly driven by a desire to have an impact on the systemic issues that caused or exacerbated poverty and discrimination.[47] For these reasons, Law Centres demonstrated a keen interest in campaigning for change and educating local communities. By way of example, Benwell Community Law Project chose

[46] North Kensington Neighbourhood Law Centre, 'Annual Report, 1971' (North Kensington Neighbourhood Law Centre, 1971).

[47] Stephens (n 4). The case work they did nonetheless remained an important part of their work and often allowed workers to identify recurring problems in the neighbourhood that could form the basis of a campaign: see Hackney Advice Bureau and Law Centre, 'Annual Report, 1976–1977' (Hackney Advice Bureau and Law Centre, 1977).

to tackle the need for systemic change through close collaboration with working class organisations such as trade unions.[48] This approach was facilitated in the early years of the movement by the fact that Law Centres were supported by government grants and charitable donations rather than being reliant on legal aid, which only funded specified clients.

Constraints were, however, imposed on Law Centres' work. At the time, the Law Society rules prohibited solicitors from advertising, fee-sharing and cost-cutting. Law Centres needed to do all three: they had to advertise their services to the local community; their fee-sharing arrangements fell outside of the normal partnership model; and, by providing free legal services, they were undercutting other solicitors. Thus, in order to provide free legal services, Law Centres needed a Law Society waiver of their breach of these rules. In the early years of their development, their case work activities were not restricted by the Law Society as long as Law Centres were seen as responding to unmet need. However, as the number of Centres grew, so did fears within the profession that Law Centres were competing with private practice for clients. As a direct result of these fears, the Law Society sought to use conditions attached to the grant of the waiver to limit the areas of law in which they could work. Despite the claim by Law Centres that their work increased popular awareness of legal process,[49] conflict over the grant of the Law Society waiver eventually led to a compromise whereby Law Centres were prevented from working in the areas traditionally occupied by private practice lawyers such as divorce, serious accidents, personal injury compensation claims and much adult crime.[50]

The overwhelming demand for the services offered by Law Centres from the outset also imposed constraints on what they could achieve and meant that hard decisions had to be made as to what kinds of work should be prioritised.[51] In some instances, the gender dynamics of the work being done were highly visible. The appalling misconduct and flagrant racism of the police exposed by Law Centres meant that many of them focused on criminal defence work,[52] more particularly to supporting young (often black) men, who were more likely to come into contact with the criminal justice system than were women. In other instances, the gender dynamics of Law Centre's case work were more subtle. Most Centres fell quite quickly into a portfolio which included a focus on housing, social security, employment, juvenile crime and consumer issues. Some of this work such as housing problems relating to security of tenure, harassment, disrepair, fire safety, unfair rents and illegal evictions could be viewed as impacting on men and women

[48] Benwell Community Law Project, 'Annual Report, 1975' (Benwell Community Law Project, 1975).

[49] North Kensington Law Centre (n 36); Robinson et al (n 37).

[50] M Zander, *Legal Services for the Community* (Maurice Temple Smith, 1978) 88–93; Smith (n 23).

[51] See eg North Kensington Neighbourhood Law Centre (n 46); Camden Community Law Centre (n 42); Camden Community Law Centre (n 43); Balham Neighbourhood Law Centre, 'A Case for Change: Annual Report, 1975–76' (Balham Neighbourhood Law Centre, 1976); Brent Community Law Centre, 'Annual Report, 1976' (Brent Community Law Centre, 1976).

[52] Leask (n 23).

equally and was commonly presented in this way. The fact that the traditional caregiving role of women and their relative lack of financial independence meant that women undoubtedly experienced the fear and consequences of such events more keenly was much less frequently reflected on in the early Law Centre reports analysed for this project. The note of a meeting of women Law Centre workers organised by Pam Ditton between 1973–1975 makes the point that the gendered dynamics of legal issues often went unseen by male workers:

> Most law centres have adopted a blanket exclusion of matrimonial law. We don't think that this is either fair or logical. To date the law centres have been very deeply involved with housing problems – but who has a greater housing problem than the married woman attempting to leave or get rid of her husband after a marriage has broken down, and avoid the trap of losing her children into care and not being able to get a flat without them? The problem of battered wives is a very real one – and one that the police refuse to involve themselves in. There is the problem of the cohabitation rules and its effect on social security payments – should we be fighting harder against this? And also the currently controversial immigration policy which directly discriminates against women. The legal problems of women are countless and we only raise headlines in the hope of provoking discussion.[53]

It is certainly the case that hardly any consideration was given in early annual reports to the systematic abuse suffered by women through domestic violence. Early reports are largely silent on, or do no more than make passing reference to, the need to use injunctions to protect 'people' in fear of assault or molestation in the context of 'family problems'.[54] References to battered wives, women assaulted by their 'men friends' and 'family problems' now seem out of step with contemporary discourse around the topic and suggest the ways in which these problems were isolated from recognition of larger structural inequalities in society. The limited response of Law Centres may, in part, be a reflection of the fact that a small, but growing, number of private practice solicitors had now started to do this work. What is significant, however, is that, unlike other areas of work in which case work examples frequently prompted a strategic or policy response, cases involving emergency injunctions were not seen as being worthy of broader campaigns or educational initiatives:

> But we didn't have feminist politics in the Law Centre. You know, that, there was no institutional recognition in Law Centres of, of the oppression of women as such. And the work that was done on domestic violence was done because there was a legal need, not because there was a perception that there was a political position there. (Interviewee 2, Female)

The significance of the neglect of domestic violence as a systemic issue went beyond the discussions of Law Centre priorities. It also gave rise to problems at case level

[53] 'Women in Law Centres': this document was given to our collection by Pam Ditton and dates from between 1973–1975. This quotation is taken from page 5 of the unnumbered document.

[54] See, for instance, North Kensington Neighbourhood Law Centre (n 42).

when conflict arose between defending male perpetrators of abuse, protecting the wider community against brutality and being a feminist lawyer. As one of our female interviewees explained:

> I do remember very, very traumatically, one of the [criminal defence] cases was a GBH where a man had stabbed his girlfriend through and through with a sword. And my job was to get him bail. (Interviewee 2, Female)

The same interviewee described how at one point she was driven by such dilemmas to write a paper on why the Law Centre should not continue to defend men in rape cases.[55] These attitudes towards domestic violence began to change significantly in the mid-1970s as awareness of violence as a feminist issue became more widely understood. An interviewee who worked at two different Law Centres in succession in the early 1970s, contrasted them in this regard:

> And right from the beginning … in [my second Law Centre] there was a very strong feminist approach to issues that I have no memory of back in [my first Law Centre] in, at the beginning. In [my second Law Centre] we certainly took on domestic violence issues and I remember just talking, talks within the, among the workers about the contradiction about acting in criminal cases for male perpetrators when the victim is a local woman and the dichotomy this raises. (Interviewee 10, Female)

Gendered differences in recollections of the importance of domestic violence to the work of Law Centres are evident from interviews despite the occurrence of the problem in local communities. There were instances where male interviewees made no reference to these issues when describing the initial work of a Law Centre or had little recollection of domestic violence work, apart from mentioning links with the local Women's Aid. This provided a direct contrast to the accounts of female community workers who identified their collaboration with Women's Aid as a central element of their work from the outset. A possible explanation for the lack of awareness of the broader societal context within which feminists understood violence against women and rape is the politics of the left in the 1970s. Structural Marxism was a particularly important lens through which the role of Law Centres was viewed by legal activists. This approach primarily diagnosed the ills of society as a tension between the working classes and the capitalist state, rather than as a struggle between the sexes.

While the literature on these issues in relation to Law Centres is limited, there are some useful parallels to be drawn from the extensive research on the

[55] This became less of an issue because of the constraints of the rules under which Law Centres were able to operate as not-for-profit organisations. In the early 1970s rules 1, 2 and 3 of the Solicitors Practice Rules prohibited touting, advertising, cost-cutting and sharing of profit costs. The 'Law Society waiver' allowed Law Centres to provide free legal advice but required that they did not work on adult crime cases as this would take work away from other practitioners in private practice who relied on legal aid.

Community Development Projects (CDPs) of the 1970s.[56] This formed part of a national government Urban Programme aimed at tackling poverty in disadvantaged communities. There are a number of similarities between Law Centres and CDPs. A number of early Law Centres actually emerged from CDPs, taking some of the CDP staff with them, and their working methods and desire to challenge the orthodoxy around the causes of, and solutions to, deprivation were very similar.[57] It has been argued that the predominant focus in CDPs on class-based analysis led to the marginalisation of structural issues around gender or race.[58] Further, even when CDPs engaged with women's rights, they did so in the workplace, but did not consider the position of women within the domestic sphere and the oppressions they faced there,[59] leading some to label the Marxist-based analysis of social problems in CDPs during the 1970s as 'gender-blind'.[60]

Our research on the early years of Law Centres indicates that a number suffered from similar failings. In addition to the above description of the ways in which priorities were set, this is also indicated in the ways in which annual reports discuss the problems faced by generic 'workers' or 'people'. In doing so they render invisible the fact that some problems such as low pay and poor conditions often had a disproportionate impact on women clustered in certain industries or were part of a system based on institutionalised sexism.[61] Interviews also revealed the ways in which the focus on class-based structural causes hampered the ability of Law Centres to recognise and respond to domestic abuse. As a male lawyer explained:

> [P]artly we saw it as sort of difficult to, you know, difficult to organise collectively, the [domestic violence] cases. … But maybe we shouldn't have been as complacent about the services that were available. And there was a very good firm of solicitors who set up

[56] There were 12 local Community Development Projects (CDPs). The CDPs are associated with a radical approach to community development. See eg K Popple, *Analysing Community Work: Its Theory and Practice* (Open University Press, 1995); S Banks and M Carpenter, 'Researching the Local Politics and Practices of Radical Community Development Projects in 1970s Britain' (2017) 52(2) *Community Development Journal* 226–46; J Green and A Chapman, 'The British Community Development Project: Lessons for Today' (1992) 27 *Community Development Journal* 242; M Loney, *Community Against Government: The British Community Development Project, 1968–78: A Study of Government Incompetence* (Heinemann Educational Books, 1983).

[57] J Burdett, 'Professional Accountability and Community Control in Legal Services Provision: A Study of Community Law Centres in England' (PhD thesis, London School of Economics, 2004); Loney (n 56); M Carpenter and B Kyneswood, 'From Self-Help to Class Struggle: Revisiting Coventry Community Development Project's 1970s Journey of Discovery' (2017) 52 *Community Development Journal* 247; K Popple, 'Rise and Fall of the National Community Development Projects 1968–1978: Lessons to Learn?' in R Gilchrist et al (eds), *Reflecting on the Past: Essays in the History of Community Youth Work* (Russell House Publishing, 2011); Green and Chapman (n 56); J Green, 'Action-Research in Context: Revisiting the 1970s Benwell Community Development Project' (2017) 52 *Community Development Journal* 269.

[58] Carpenter and Kyneswood (n 57); Popple (n 56); Popple (n 57).

[59] Green and Chapman (n 56); Green (n 57).

[60] Green and Chapman (n 56) 254; Popple (n 56) 37.

[61] See, for instance, Lambeth Community Law Centre, 'Annual Report, 1978–79' (Lambeth Community Law Centre, 1979); Brent Community Law Centre, 'Annual Report, 1979' (Brent Community Law Centre, 1979).

> specifically to do that kind of work very near the beginning of the Law Centre in [local area]. And I think we thought, 'Well that work is appropriate for … you know, the Legal Aid system kind of works with that.' And gave it less priority. (Interviewee 3, Male)

In common with several Law Centres, this interviewee explained that their Law Centre identified domestic violence as being managed elsewhere, therefore choosing to support the work of the local Women's Aid at an organisational level, rather than prioritising working directly with women suffering domestic violence in order to try and improve the law or the legal response to the problems they faced.

It seems unlikely that the shifts in attitude which occurred from the mid-1970s onwards would have occurred without women being given the opportunity to engage in debates about the issue within Law Centres. As one of our male interviewees acknowledged:

> But I didn't think in terms of domestic violence till I was educated by people like [female solicitor, Interviewee 2]. And that will go for practically every lawyer I can think of. We didn't think in those terms. That women were being brutalised. And we didn't think in general terms. And I didn't know that it was so widespread either; I didn't have any idea, until the publicity by women's movements and by women's refuges and so on about what was happening. I had no idea it was that widespread. So if we did get a domestic violence case, you know, as far as we were concerned it was just an occasional one. (Interviewee 1)

These reflections by a male activist many years after Law Centres were first established demonstrate how far debate has evolved within society generally, and within radical networks in particular. This is not to say that the failure to recognise violence against women is a problem that has gone away.[62] What it does do is suggest the difference that giving women space to raise these concerns in a collective environment can make *within* movements. In the section which follows we delve deeper into the resources that women drew upon in making their fellow activists aware of the gendered nature of violence.

Beyond Law Centres: A Broader Sense of Community

Movements rarely operate in a vacuum, rather they are frequently engaged in cause coalitions or radical friendships which animate or amplify cross-movement activism.[63] Indeed. Rosemary herself has commented that:

[62] See, for instance, LF Fitzgerald, 'Still the Last Great Open Secret: Sexual Harassment as Systemic Trauma' (2017) 18 *Journal of Trauma and Dissociation* 483; EA Jane, 'Systemic Misogyny Exposed: Translating Rapeglish from the Manosphere with a Random Rape Threat Generator' (2018) 21 *International Journal of Cultural Studies* 661.

[63] On this point see D Kelliher, 'Striking Solidarity: Friendship and the 1984–5 Miners' Strike' (History Workshop, 17 June 2020) www.historyworkshop.org.uk/friendship-solidarity-and-the-1984-5-miners-strike/.

> Your paper brought back lots of memories of my feminist activist days. We were all aware of North Ken Law Centre, probably because lots of lesbian separatists lived in North Ken so we knew people there, and … some came to my Lesbian History Group. (Rosemary Auchmuty, personal correspondence with authors)

The influence that community groups had on Law Centres varied considerably over time, but a bottom-up approach to engaging with the local community has been a defining feature of Law Centres from their inception. This is often reflected in the inclusion of the word 'community' or 'neighbourhood' in the names that Law Centres adopted. Community groups frequently campaigned for the establishment of a Law Centre and were routinely represented on Law Centre management committees once established. North Kensington Neighbourhood Law Centre reported in 1974, for instance, that it had 27 community groups on its advisory council with meetings with them taking place once a month.[64]

This demonstrates that connections with the local community were clearly important to the ethos and values of Law Centres. Law Centres also encouraged disgruntled residents to set up their own community groups and gave legal advice to them, for example about issues relating to their leases, applications for charitable status and the drafting of constitutions. In some instances Law Centre workers also sat on the boards of the local community groups.[65] Umbrella groups consisting of all the advice-giving agencies in a borough were even established in the interests of sharing resources and maximising service delivery options.[66]

This sense of being rooted in communities beyond a particular Law Centre is especially relevant to the story of the ways in which feminists found voice in Law Centres, and more particularly how domestic violence came to be understood. The lack of structure, referred to as a negative aspect of collectives in early sections of this chapter, emerges as a positive in this context. For some personnel, the fluid and open structure of Law Centres gave female workers the freedom to decide for themselves the issues they would tackle and their methods of doing so. For several of the women interviewed, their work in the Law Centre provided an extension of the feminist activism they had undertaken elsewhere or the other feminist networks they were already involved with. Feminist networks are particularly evident in the links that formed between women in Law Centres and the emerging network of women's refuges. As one interviewee explained:

> Well, we set up, oh yeah I got involved in women's aid and set up the … , so I got a group together around the Law Centre set, and we worked up to set up what was only the

[64] North Kensington Neighbourhood Law Centre, 'Annual Report, 1974' (North Kensington Neighbourhood Law Centre, 1974).

[65] Brent Community Law Centre (n 51); Brent Community Law Centre, 'Annual Report, 1978' (Brent Community Law Centre, 1978); Paddington Neighbourhood Advice Bureau and Law Centre, 'Annual Report, 1973–4' (Paddington Neighbourhood Advice Bureau and Law Centre, 1974).

[66] Balham Neighbourhood Law Centre (n 51); Vauxhall Community Law Centre, 'Annual Report, 1974–75' (Vauxhall Community Law Centre, 1975).

> second women's refuge in the country, so that was quite a good thing. (Interviewee 8, Female)

Another interviewee described how, before joining a Law Centre, her growing awareness of women's rights and women's oppression, meant that she and others had established and helped to run a women's refuge on a voluntary basis. In the absence of any guidance about what she should do as a community worker at the Law Centre she went on to work for, she simply continued to focus on domestic violence because it was an area in which she was already active:

> So we were all, not exactly floundering but they were doing case work and my job was as a community worker so obviously I didn't have to do case work. But nobody gave me any guidance as to what I should be doing, so obviously I just developed the things that I [was] involved in. (Interviewee 4, Female)

Significantly, Women's Aid, which set up refuges for victims of domestic violence, was emerging at the same time as Law Centres were first being established. The National Women's Aid Federation was formed in 1974 bringing together nearly 40 independent refuge services as a national network and enabling women and children experiencing violence and fear in the home to travel across the country to a place of safety.[67] Several interviewees drew attention to the connections they formed with their local refuge.

Furthermore, our analysis of Law Centre annual reports in the latter part of the 1970s shows a growing awareness of deep-seated issues around domestic violence and the problems that women then faced in seeking help. Manchester Law Centre seems to have been particularly active in this regard, working closely with Women's Aid groups to get information out to women about their rights. In turn, this generated an upturn of case work involving domestic violence which the Manchester Law Centre characterised as a form of sexual discrimination. It also worked with an Asian Women's refuge group in the hope of understanding the particular isolation and oppression of Asian women.[68] In addition, Manchester Law Centre published a series of handbooks on women's social security rights, women's rights on relationship breakdown and housing and a booklet on how to get an injunction in cases of domestic violence. This proved very popular and had run to a third edition by 1978. A feminist activist who was involved in at least one of these publications explained that over 40 years later this remains an initiative which she continues to be proud of:

> [I]t was the first project ever. And I was amazed because it just sold out really quickly and all these women from other Law Centres, and most of the Law Centres were in London, were ringing me up and they wanted more copies and, yeah, it was a really was a great success so that was, you know, very gratifying. (Interviewee 4, Female)

[67] See Women's Aid, 'Our History' www.womensaid.org.uk/about-us/history.

[68] Manchester Law Centre, 'Annual Report, 1977–78' (Manchester Law Centre, 1978); Manchester Law Centre, 'Annual Report, 1978–79' (Manchester Law Centre, 1979).

Around the same time, North Kensington Neighbourhood Law Centre also began to give more prominence to the issue of domestic violence in its annual reports. In part this was prompted by the increasing demand for injunctions following the Domestic Violence Act 1977. It also appears to have been motivated by growing recognition of the need for a local refuge for battered women and their children which female workers at the Law Centre were instrumental in setting up.[69] Increasing reference is also made in the reports of other Law Centres to working with Women's Aid,[70] and it is also noticeable that Women's Aid groups gradually began to be represented on the management committees of Law Centres.[71]

Another legal issue that particularly affected women and came to have increasing importance for Law Centres during the 1970s was care proceedings within public family law. At that time, there was no legal aid for parents in care proceedings, meaning that it constituted a category of unmet legal need which private practitioners had no financial incentive to address. As the 1970s progressed, a growing number of annual reports show this as a developing area of work.

In 1975, attempts were made to establish a women's Law Centre to deal with the generic issues being experienced by female clients across Law Centres. A meeting called to discuss women's issues attracted women from across the Law Centres movement and a number of feminist barristers. A working group was established, but after driving the initiative for a year, the group was unable to obtain funding. From the perspective of our interviewee, not only did the group have insufficient geographic focus to garner the support of a local authority, it was also evident that the Lord Chancellor's Department did not see a women's Law Centre as a priority. Rather than giving up entirely, the working group focused on what was possible and instead its members set up Rights of Women, to provide a legal resource for women suffering, or at risk of suffering, violence and abuse. Rights of Women was initially entirely run by volunteers, but, at the time of writing, it is a well-established 'women's legal rights organisation' with a particular focus on tackling violence against women and girls. It has a core paid staff group of 14 and numerous volunteer lawyers who provide telephone advice to women.[72]

As the 1970s progressed, Law Centres became instrumental in expanding the forms of support available to women. In some Law Centres, this included lawyers and community workers assisting women with obtaining domestic violence injunctions or referring them to local legal aid firms to act on their behalf.[73]

[69] North Kensington Neighbourhood Law Centre, 'Annual Report, 1978' (North Kensington Neighbourhood Law Centre, 1978).

[70] Balham Neighbourhood Law Centre, 'Inside Story: Annual Report, 1974–75' (Balham Neighbourhood Law Centre, 1975); Balham Neighbourhood Law Centre (n 51).

[71] See Manchester Law Centre, 'Annual Report, 1977–78' (n 68); Manchester Law Centre, 'Annual Report, 1978–79' (n 68); North Kensington Neighbourhood Law Centre (n 69); Camden Community Law Centre (n 42).

[72] Rights of Women, 'Helping Women Through the Law' www.rightsofwomen.org.uk/about-us/what-do-we-do/helping-women-through-the-law.

[73] An interviewee described self-help initiatives that were tried and failed because women were usually too scared of their abusers to represent themselves in court.

By the late 1970s Paddington Advice and Law Centre was reporting that the demand for help from large numbers of women subjected to domestic violence but also attempting to manage housing, money, welfare benefit and child support problems was something that they 'could not, and should not, ignore'.[74] In this way, Law Centres played an important role in raising awareness of the issue of domestic violence and opening up new forms of work to the profession. In the words of one interviewee:

> Because I think what Law Centres did was they opened the door to people to access legal aid because before hardly anybody did; people didn't know they could get legal aid for things, people didn't challenge their landlords or their employers or their violent husbands. And I really think that was a pivotal role for Law Centres in the 70s was opening that door. And then other lawyers thought, 'Oh yes, we can make money out of legal aid, we can do this', you know, we can, we can professionalise this and that's what happened. (Interviewee 4, Female)

The passing of the Employment Protection Act 1975, the Social Security Pensions Act 1975, and the Sex Discrimination Act 1975 galvanised Law Centres to encourage women to mount cases under this new legislation[75] and to raise awareness of the new rights for female workers amongst trade unions,[76] predominantly female workforces and in schools.[77] An example of this sort of activity was that North Kensington Neighbourhood Law Centre received a grant from the Commission for Racial Equality and the Equal Opportunities Commission to undertake research on structure, pay and conditions in the hotel and catering industry.[78]

The change in attitudes and growing recognition of the emergence of second-wave feminism in the first decade of the Law Centres movement received symbolic recognition when Manchester Law Centre set up a dedicated Women's Rights team in 1978. By 1980 they had devoted 13 pages of their 54-page annual report to the subject of women's rights, support for setting up a rape crisis counselling service, working with local women's and prostitute's rights groups, ongoing assistance to the Women's Aid centre and plans to devote more time to work on financial dependence.[79] Looking beyond the sort of class-based structural inequality favoured by prominent pioneers, they asserted their belief that women's rights had to be understood within the broader context of the women's movement:

[74] Paddington Advice and Law Centre, 'Annual Report, 1978–80' (Paddington Advice and Law Centre, 1980) 8.

[75] Camden Community Law Centre (n 42).

[76] Brent Community Law Centre (n 51).

[77] Camden Community Law Centre (n 42); Brent Community Law Centre, 'Annual Report, 1978' (n 65); Manchester Law Centre, 'Annual Report, 1977–78' (n 68). For a history of the Sex Discrimination Act, see A Morris, 'Sex Discrimination Act 1975' in Rackley and Auchmuty (n 3).

[78] North Kensington Law Centre (n 36).

[79] Manchester Law Centre, 'Annual Report, 1979–80' (Manchester Law Centre, 1980). For a history of women's refuges and rape crisis centres, see F Kaganas, 'First Women's Refuge 1971' and A Diduck, 'First Rape Crisis Centre 1976' in E Rackley and R Auchmuty (ed), *Women's Legal Landmarks: Celebrating Feminist Legal History* (Hart, 2018).

> One thing we are agreed upon is that women's rights and the women's liberation movement should be closely linked. This might seem obvious but in America women's rights have become big business which lines the pockets of professionals who have no connection with the women's movement … To try to avoid this split between women's rights and the women's movement we want to work with existing women's group acting as a resource to enable them to achieve their aims to help women start new groups around areas of particular concern.[80]

Significantly, the new team at Manchester recognised that their decision to work within the women's movement meant that the issues they prioritised might not always be strictly legal, but might touch upon forms of inequality and injustice not covered by law. Examples of the type of work meant by this are given in the following year's annual report: an educational course on women and health and a campaign regarding the setting-up of a Well Women Clinic in Levenshulme.[81] It was recognised that these activities were outside the usual remit of the Law Centre, but health was considered an important issue for women in the area. The above summary shows the broad scope that Law Centres were able to encompass through their work at the time.

Conclusion

Seeking out women involved in the nascent Law Centres movement can add considerable nuance to existing histories of progressive political movements and the role that feminists have played in creating and sustaining them. What we have striven to show is the important, and largely untold, story of how women, feminists and in time men within Law Centres were successful in transforming debates about gender within their own networks and beyond. The progressive politics of Law Centres meant that some forms of structural disadvantage, most notably that suffered by young black men, were identified from the inception of the movement, but their radicalism did not extend in the early years to an appreciation of the structural disadvantage routinely experienced by women. It took the hard and often uncomfortable work of women, supported by their connections with other feminist networks, to bring the woman question to the fore. As more women joined Law Centres, they became increasingly influential in them, and the particular legal problems faced by women and their unmet legal needs became more visible. This is a story we will continue to unravel in subsequent publications. For present purposes, we do not intend simply to offer a progressive account of history in which we end by reflecting on how the lot of women has improved. In some ways, contemporary practices and attitudes, such as those currently reflected in statistics about gender-based

[80] Manchester Law Centre, 'Annual Report, 1978–79' (n 68) 14.
[81] ibid.

violence, racial discrimination and misogyny within the police force or figures relating to the prosecution of rape, are depressingly similar to those faced by women in the 1970s. What this reveals to us is that the struggle goes on. This is a theme that, sadly, it seems we are likely to revisit many times in the course of this project.

6

Rosemary Auchmuty – Doing Feminist Legal Biography

FIONA COWNIE*

Introduction

Anyone familiar with the publications of Professor Rosemary Auchmuty cannot fail to notice the extent to which her professional identity is rooted in her intellectual background both as a historian and as a lawyer, together with her commitment to feminism. This chapter explores the way in which her research and teaching has fused together her interests in law, feminism and history, and how, as she has continued to develop her professional identity, they have led to her recent contributions to the developing field of feminist legal biography. In this chapter, those three themes are used to frame a contextual analysis of Rosemary's ideas, demonstrating her development as an academic, and shining a light on the forces and ideas that influenced her.

At the start of her academic career, in the early 1970s, it is significant that Rosemary Auchmuty chose to study history at the Australian National University (ANU). The ANU history department at that time was fortunate to benefit from the influence of Charles Manning Clark, a charismatic character, who 'had famously built a department out of talented teachers and historians'.[1] Clark was an eminent academic, best known for his six-volume history of Australia, which reflected his eclectic and interdisciplinary approach.[2] Rosemary's father, himself an academic historian, was much more traditional in approach. She explained that her 'father was an old-style historian and for him, as for most historians, history was the story

* The author would like to thank Dr Susan Bartie and the editors of this book for their comments on a previous draft of this chapter. (All errors remain the responsibility of the author.)

[1] R Fraser, 'Beginnings – Some Reflections on the ANU Historical Journal 1964–70' (2019) II(3) *ANU Historical Journal* 3.

[2] M McKenna, 'Clark, Charles Manning (1915–1991)' (2019) 19 *Australian Dictionary of Biography* adb.anu.edu.au/biography/clark-charles-manning-225.

of public events and public figures – politics, war and great men'.[3] Rosemary's father had concerns about her proposed supervisor:

> [my father] had once reviewed a book by Manning Clark rather critically and Manning fell out with him, and my father was worried that he would also take against me. This did not happen. Manning never taught me, but I evidently got on good terms with him in my undergraduate years as he chose to supervise my PhD …[4]

Looking back on her experience recently, Rosemary notes, with the benefit of hindsight, how different the history department at ANU was in its approach to the subject compared to more traditional departments. While '[s]ocial history was in its infancy, and women's history did not exist', at ANU the students studied the civil rights movement in America, and Pacific history (regarded by traditional historians, including Rosemary's father, as 'not history at all, but current affairs and anthropology respectively').[5] In her final year Rosemary was able to take 'Literature and History' as her special subject, writing about Virginia Woolf, Elizabeth Bowen and Rosamund Lehmann: 'The women's movement had started, and I never did "straight" history again – always social, always feminist. A door had opened and ANU swept me through it'.[6]

Rosemary's choice of PhD topic gave a clear indication of the intellectual agenda that she has pursued throughout her academic career. As a supervisor Manning Clark was prepared to give her the freedom to explore her subject using the interdisciplinary perspective that he himself favoured, and to which she had been exposed at ANU, for example by building on her undergraduate 'History and Literature' special subject and using literature as one of her sources of evidence.[7] Completed in 1975, and entitled 'Victorian Spinsters', from the very beginning of the thesis, when she made clear that the term 'spinster' is to be read not as a synonym for 'old maid', but as a term to indicate an unmarried woman of the middle (or sometimes upper) classes. Rosemary's objective was to challenge historical misconceptions about the role such women played in nineteenth century society.[8] Placing her analysis in its wider social context, she notes that single middle class Victorian women (of whom there were a large number, as compared with the number of men at the time) needed to earn their living. This fact, combined with the aspirations of a small group of educated, leisured women of the upper middle class, led to a process of emancipation, given impetus by a movement which, though it did not call itself feminist, aimed to open up a greater choice of career for women.[9] In Auchmuty's view, this movement not only led to the increased

[3] R Auchmuty, 'The Past is Another Truth' (2019) II(1) *ANU Historical Journal* 35.
[4] ibid.
[5] ibid.
[6] ibid.
[7] In her final undergraduate (honours) year, Rosemary took a course on 'Literature and History'; see ibid. The use of literature to inform a historical analysis is discussed in R Auchmuty, *Victorian Spinsters* PhD Thesis (Australian National University, 1975) 14–17.
[8] Auchmuty (n 7).
[9] ibid 7.

emancipation of women in Victorian England, but also prepared the ground for the extension of women's liberation in the twentieth century.[10] The following statement, found towards the end of the Introduction, characterises Auchmuty's approach to her subject:

> The thesis aims to show that the Victorian spinster was a not inconsiderable figure, and that she had aspirations and concerns not necessarily shared by married women. The focus is not just of women who have been remembered for their achievements, but also of the forgotten multitude of 'superfluous women'.

The reference to the 'forgotten multitude' clearly indicates the way in which the thesis addressed some of the themes which were to form a continuing feature of Rosemary's intellectual interests. Repeatedly, she was to focus on uncovering the hitherto neglected lives of women in the past, and to use her analysis to challenge stereotypes of women and emphasise their contributions to society, not as mere ornaments to the activities of men, but as independent beings, valuable in their own right.[11]

The Feminist, the Lawyer and the Historian

Three key perspectives: feminism, law and history, have informed Rosemary's work throughout her career. Looking at the ways in which they have played out as she developed her ideas is not only informative. It provides a context for the consideration of her approach to historiography which follows later in this chapter.

Rosemary has written about her commitment to feminism in many different publications. In the 1990s, she wrote two books about the girls' school stories, which she had always loved.[12] In doing so, she provided, for the first time, a feminist analysis of books, which had for long been regarded with derision by many commentators and with open contempt by literary critics.[13] But, for Rosemary, the books had a significance which were to prove much more important to her than their literary merit. They provided the source of her feminism. In *A World of Girls*, the first of these two books, she has no difficulty in making links between the stories she enjoyed so much and the ideals of the women's movement with its emphasis on positive role-models and discussion of the benefits of single-sex education. She became part of this community on her arrival in London in 1978.

[10] ibid 13.

[11] See eg R Auchmuty, 'Spinsters and Trade Unions in Victorian Britain' (1975) 29 *Labour History: Women at Work* 109; R Auchmuty, 'Early Women Law Students at Cambridge and Oxford' (2008) 29(1) *Journal of Legal History* 63; R Auchmuty, 'Whatever Happened to Miss Bebb – *Bebb v The Law Society* and Women's Legal History' (2011) 31(2) *Legal Studies* 199–230; E Rackley and R Auchmuty 'The Case for Feminist Legal History' (2020) 40(4) *Oxford Journal of Legal Studies* 878.

[12] The two books are: R Auchmuty, *A World of Girls* (The Women's Press, 1992) and R Auchmuty, *A World of Women: Growing up in the Girls' School Story* (The Women's Press, 1999).

[13] Auchmuty, *A World of Girls* (n 12) 9–12.

There she discovered that she was not alone: 'In conversation, friends agreed that their ideas about women's capabilities and roles had been shaped by the strong adventurous heroines of the school stories they had read in girlhood'.[14] In the second book, *A World of Women* (which focuses on the characters as they grow up and leave school), she makes the connection explicit, writing about her experience, at 11 years old, of reading the stories of Elsie J Oxenham:

> psychologically they had tremendous impact. From that point on, my life was dedicated to the pursuit of independence, for myself and for other women, in a society predicated on the notion that a woman's rightful place was dependency within marriage. Elsie Oxenham would not have called herself a feminist, but she certainly made me one.[15]

More recently, looking back on her life in London in the 1970s and 80s, she writes:

> I taught various history and women's studies classes in the then burgeoning adult education sector, and later for the Open University. The women's movement was in full swing and it was easier to put together a portfolio of part-time teaching than to try to get a full-time post in history with all the British competition. Or perhaps I just did not try, because I was enjoying myself so much being a feminist.[16]

For Rosemary Auchmuty, feminism is not just an abstract ideal; it informs the choices she has made about every aspect of her life, and that has been true since she was a small girl in Australia, avidly reading about the Chalet girls and the Abbey girls, in the books she enjoyed so much.

After doing jury service, Rosemary 'decided law looked interesting, as something to teach in Women's Studies'.[17] She read Law at the then Polytechnic of Central London as one of the first cohort of part-time Law students, graduating in 1989 with First Class Honours, and then took up a lectureship in Law in the department in which she had studied.[18] Having moved into the discipline of Law, feminism continued to inform her work as she continued her intellectual journey. Her feminism is reflected not only in terms of the research she has published, but also in terms of her teaching. In 2018 she edited *Great Debates in Gender and Law*, which highlights the relevance of gender as a tool of analysis applicable to the entire undergraduate Law curriculum. In the Introduction to that volume, Rosemary wrote:

> The book is premised on the belief that, for too long now, law teaching has proceeded on the basis that there *are* no gender perspectives in most of the curriculum – too often, if you want to 'do gender', you will be advised to take family law as an option – and teachers who would like to raise gendered concerns are not encouraged by most

[14] ibid 3.
[15] Auchmuty, *A World of Women* (n 12) 15.
[16] Auchmuty (n 3) 37.
[17] R Auchmuty, 'Email to author' (20 March 2022) private correspondence quoted with permission; on file with the author.
[18] ibid and see also Auchmuty (n 3) 38.

> available textbooks. The authors of *Great Debates in Gender and Law* would like *all* students to emerge from university recognising the importance of gender in everything they study, seeing it not a an optional 'add-on' for a few people who are interested 'in that kind of thing' but integral to law-making and the legal process, as well as their own lives.[19]

The emphasis placed on the all-pervasive relevance of gender reflects the passion with which Rosemary has pursued her feminist beliefs. It is also a perspective which is shared by other feminist legal historians; for example, writing recently in the *Virginia Law Review Online*, Paula Monopoli wrote that the absence of women's legal history from the law school curriculum:

> results in law school graduates who, when they become judges and advocates, are blind to the ways that law reifies the socio-economic subordination of women in terms of the gender pay gap, the disproportionate burden of caregiving, and the structural barriers they face in the workplace.[20]

We know that this is a view with which Rosemary Auchmuty would concur. In her article, 'Agenda for a Feminist Curriculum' she made exactly the same point, along with a series of others, building an argument for the centrality of feminism to the legal curriculum in order to change this state of affairs.[21]

Despite moving into the discipline of Law, Rosemary's identity as a historian has been of continuing importance to her intellectual journey. Reflecting on this recently, she wrote:

> I still love history first and most, but I was able to make a career in law because there was much less competition – at the Poly when I started I was the only person with a PhD and it wasn't in law. I wouldn't have been able to get into a history department in London and I am glad now …[22]

Once she was located within the academic discipline of law, Rosemary was able to develop her ideas about *legal* history and gender in the direction she wanted. We can see this very clearly in the chapter on legal history which she wrote for *Great Debates on Gender and Law.* In it, she explains the way in which using the concept of gender opens up different questions for the legal historian, enabling them to explore exactly how and why women were not mentioned in traditional legal histories.[23] She outlines three ways in which legal historians have treated women in their research: ignoring them completely; mentioning them only when absolutely necessary (eg in relation to female enfranchisement) or foregrounding gender 'and the relationship between the women trying to work under and with the law and

[19] R Auchmuty, 'Introduction' in R Auchmuty (ed), *Great Debates in Gender and Law* (Red Globe Press, 2018) xi.

[20] PA Monopoli, 'Feminist Legal History and Legal Pedagogy' 108 (2022) *Virginia Law Review Online* 91, 94.

[21] R Auchmuty, 'Agenda for a Feminist Curriculum' (2003) 23 *Legal Studies* 377, 381.

[22] Auchmuty (n 17).

[23] Rosemary Auchmuty, 'Legal History' in Auchmuty, *Great Debates* (n 19) 173.

the men fighting to keep them out'.[24] She is scathing about the way in which some (male) legal historians have in her view put forward excuses for the ways in which men behaved (for example in delaying the admission of women to the legal profession), presenting this as a matter of 'changing social attitudes' without mentioning the decades of feminist action that preceded it.[25] Instead, Rosemary signposts her readers to the third approach she identified: foregrounding gender. This not only allows the researcher to 'ask the woman question', but, she argues, it 'treats the law as a set of historical documents requiring analysis in context, and law-makers not as neutral actors applying clear and wise rules but as men engaged in a power struggle with women'.[26] Rosemary goes on to discuss, with approval, Felice Batlan's history of legal aid in the United States.[27] Batlan shows how legal aid in the United States had its roots not in the first law centres, staffed by qualified male lawyers, as had previously been thought, but in associations set up by women who were themselves denied the opportunity to qualify as lawyers, but who nevertheless had the expertise to give legal advice to poorer women.[28] Later, by insisting that only 'real' lawyers could provide legal advice, men were able to take control of this female space. Batlan comments: '[t]he history of legal aid fits into a much larger pattern of men professionalizing women's work, and then using that professionalism to exclude women'.[29] This approach to legal history using detailed and rigorous research to uncover the hidden contributions of women to the law can be found in Rosemary Auchmuty's own work, where she fuses together her commitment to feminism and her intellectual interest in history with legal topics.

Building the Foundations of Feminist Legal Biography

In 2011, Rosemary published what was to become one of her best-known pieces of research, when she told the life-story of Gwyneth Bebb, who challenged the Law Society's continuing refusal to allow women to practise as solicitors.[30] The subtitle to the article, '*Bebb v The Law Society* and women's legal history' is significant, in terms of Rosemary's later focus on historiography, especially in biographical writing. In her article about Miss Bebb, we find a substantial concluding section, in which she sets out a critique of 'the conventions of legal scholarship and institutional histories'.[31] She argues that the fact that very little was known about Miss Bebb, despite the significance of the case which bore her name. This is typical of

[24] ibid 179.
[25] ibid 180.
[26] ibid 181.
[27] F Batlan, *Women and Justice for the Poor: A History of Legal Aid 1863–1945* (CUP, 2015).
[28] ibid, quoted in Auchmuty 'Legal History' (n 23) 173, 182.
[29] Batlan (n 27), quoted in Auchmuty 'Legal History' (n 23) 173, 183.
[30] Auchmuty, 'Whatever Happened to Miss Bebb?' (n 11).
[31] ibid 228.

mainstream legal history, as it tends to ignore the role of women in the events which are studied. It thus marginalising them now in the same way as they were marginalised in earlier times.[32] But it is here, as she develops this argument, that Rosemary makes a very direct criticism of traditional legal historians:

> Miss Bebb's story poses a challenge to the complacent narrative that depicts the admission of women to law as a reform handed down by a benevolent legislature to an unresisting profession at the due time. Such interpretations paint institutions in the best possible light, as responsive to social change and capable of reforming themselves from within; they excuse the grudging and belated nature of the response and, crucially, they minimise – if possible, deny – any feminist agency in bringing about reform.[33]

In the case of Miss Bebb, Rosemary argues, the complacency of legal historians involved ignoring the long campaign waged by both women and men to try to secure admission of women as solicitors, as well as failing to tease out the strategies of resistance employed by those whose privileges were under threat.[34] This is a substantial criticism of the intellectual rigour (or lack of it) demonstrated by mainstream legal historians, and it laid the foundations of a body of work on women's legal history, and in particular on feminist legal biography, which was to follow.

Some years later, in 2013, Rosemary spoke at a training workshop on legal biography held at the Institute of Advanced Legal Studies in London.[35] An article, 'Researching Women in Legal History', based on her contribution to the workshop, was later published in a special issue of *Legal Information Management*.[36] In it she draws on her experience of researching the life of Gwynneth Bebb to discuss 'how we write legal biography'.[37] Her main aim, she says, was to demonstrate the range of sources which could be used to tell the life-histories of women in the law, about whom there was often very little information in the public record. It was not only that material from these sources could add context and colour, but also without them significant aspects of a woman's life could be overlooked. This article is interesting in the context of Rosemary's work on legal biography because it offers us a window into her working methods, and thus into her view of historiography. In that regard, two issues stand out in the article. The first is the way Rosemary approached her subject. The story of Miss Bebb had been told many times before; it would have been easy just to accept those accounts. However, Rosemary went back to the primary sources (the case report and the campaign that led up to the litigation), realising, as she read them, that previous accounts had not only been 'over-simplified', but had also misrepresented even what was in the public record.[38]

[32] ibid 229.
[33] ibid 229.
[34] ibid 230.
[35] D Gee, 'Guest Editorial: Legal Biography' (2014) 14 *Legal Information Management* 15.
[36] *Legal Information Management* (2014) 14(1).
[37] R Auchmuty, 'Researching Women in Legal History: The Case of Miss Bebb' (2014) 14(1) *Legal Information Management* 19.
[38] ibid.

Re-telling with much more accuracy the history of this very well-known case reflects Rosemary's methodological concern as a historian to examine the primary sources for herself, not merely relying on previous accounts. As John Tosh observed in his seminal work, *The Pursuit of History*, 'the primary sources are not an open book, offering instant answers. They may not be what they seem to be, they may signify very much more than is immediately apparent'.[39] This was certainly true of the Bebb case, and it was not the only instance in which Rosemary's attention to her source material enabled her to demonstrate that previous research into the lives of early women lawyers contained inaccuracies. In 2008, she published an article in the *Journal of Legal History* entitled 'Early Women Law Students at Cambridge and Oxford'.[40] The article focuses on the twelve women who studied Law at Cambridge and Oxford in the years before 1900. Unlike the story of women's entry to the legal profession, their entry to legal education in England had been largely ignored.[41] In this case, the inaccuracies to which Rosemary draws attention are the references to Cornelia Sorabji as being '[t]he first woman ever to read Law at a British university'. In fact, although Sorabji was the first woman to pass the Bachelor of Law Civil Examinations (at Oxford in 1892), as Rosemary points out, she was not the first woman to *study* Law at a British university. Rosemary discovered that Sorabji was preceded by other women who studied Law at London and at Cambridge.[42] Uncovering such inaccuracies is not mere pedantry. Setting the record straight allowed Rosemary to show, in the case of Miss Bebb, the importance of her role in the campaign leading up to the litigation which bears her name, and in the case of Sorabji, to throw light on other women whose achievements had previously been overlooked These examples demonstrate the way in which Rosemary was able to draw on her two disciplines, uncovering hitherto neglected aspects of the history of these two women, both involved in the law, and using them to throw new light on an aspect of legal culture. Importantly, these articles also reveal a strong feminist perspective. Writing about the early women law students, she concludes:

> Women's success at 'masculine' studies like law not only undermined theories of female inferiority … but also made it harder for men to continue to deny women access to their professional preserves. Most importantly, university life changed and emboldened the women who were fortunate enough to experience it … [helping] to form the confident feminist pioneers who kept up their quiet crusade to enter the legal professions, and finally succeeded.[43]

It is the choice of language here which reinforces the view that this is an article informed by feminism. These women were part of a 'crusade' against male oppression

[39] J Tosh, *The Pursuit of History: Aims, Methods and New Directions in the Study of History*, 7th edn (Routledge, 2022) 103–104.

[40] Auchmuty, 'Early Women Law Students at Cambridge and Oxford' (n 11) 63.

[41] ibid 64.

[42] ibid 64.

[43] ibid 96–97.

and, as such, provide classic examples of feminist political action, even though they may not have described themselves in this way. Similarly, in concluding her article on Miss Bebb, Rosemary draws attention to the way in which Gwyneth Bebb's life raises gender issues that are still relevant today, including 'the "choices" available to men and women, the political tactics adopted by feminist legal reformers … and, most tellingly, the defensive strategies adopted by those whose privileges are under threat'.[44] Again, there is no doubt that the author of these words is writing from a feminist perspective, as Rosemary goes on to refer to the relevance of Miss Bebb's life to 'current struggles' and argues that history reminds us that 'women usually have to fight for their rights'.[45]

The other key issue that Rosemary included in her consideration of 'researching women in legal history' is one which is fundamental for biographers: the balance between 'facts' and 'conjecture'. Although Rosemary does not refer to it, this is an issue much debated in the literature.[46] Rosemary's focus is more pragmatic; having acknowledged the problem, she is more interested in guiding the work of other legal biographers in practical terms than in engaging in extensive methodological debate. In terms of working methods, she argues that the most important task is to ask the right questions, since this will lead the researcher to uncover the context of the subject's life, and thus be able to fill in, with some accuracy, the gaps in the publicly available record.[47] Throughout her work on Miss Bebb, the key question for Rosemary was 'what would it have been *like* for her?'[48] In this way, she was aiming to reconstruct Miss Bebb's life by drawing on additional research into the context of the society in which she moved – her associates, her Oxford college, her choice of giving birth in a private nursing home. This approach involves trying to ground 'conjecture' in evidence, so that the researcher can show how likely it was that their subject would have had a particular experience. In adopting this approach, Rosemary, like many biographers, is trying to maintain a balance between 'facts' and 'conjecture'. As Leon Edel famously wrote in his article, 'Biography: a manifesto':

> Biography is a work of the imagination – the imagination of form ad style and narrative. The biographer is allowed to be as imaginative as he [sic] pleases, so long as he does not imagine his facts. Saturated with fact, he may allow himself all the adventures of literary artifice, all the gratifications of story-telling – save those of make-believe.[49]

[44] Auchmuty, 'Whatever Happened to Miss Bebb?' (n 11).
[45] ibid.
[46] For an overview of the debates in twentieth-century biography, see J Walter, 'The Solace of Doubt? Biographical Method after the Short Twentieth Century' in H Renders and B de Haan (eds), *Theoretical Discussions of Biography: Approaches from History, Microhistory and Life Writing* (Brill, 2014) ch 4. See also F Cownie, 'The United Kingdom's First Woman Law Professor: An Archerian Analysis' (2015) 42(1) *Journal of Law and Society* 127, 130–33.
[47] Auchmuty (n 37).
[48] ibid, italics in original.
[49] L Edel, 'Biography: A Manifesto' (1978) 1 *Biography* 1.

Writing about this issue recently, Kiera Lindsey uses the concept of 'informed imagination' to convey a similar idea.[50] She argues that by carefully examining existing sources, however sparse they may be, it is possible to find 'recurring clues that can be used to shape how we image (sic) and construct our subjects'.[51] It is then possible to use our knowledge of the wider historical context, in conjunction with the existing sources, to enable the biographer to recreate a life that would otherwise remain obscure. In adopting this approach, Lindsey is very clear that biographers should 'resist the impulse to romance archival gaps' and is insistent that they should immerse themselves in the primary sources to ensure that any 'speculation' is informed by, and deeply embedded in, the historical record.[52] This approach chimes with Rosemary's working methods; in the case of Miss Bebb, for example, she uncovered research into the greater mortality rates of middle class women like Miss Bebb (who tended to choose to give birth in a nursing home) compared to working class women (who used public hospitals). She was then able to use this evidence to show that Miss Bebb was not just one unlucky middle class woman, but one of many 'against whom the scales were weighed in terms of both gender *and* class'.

Rosemary developed many of these ideas in a subsequent article in the *Journal of Law and Society* in 2015, 'Recovering Lost Lives: researching women in legal history'.[53] While she covers much of the same content as in her workshop presentation, this article continues to throw light on her working methods (and those which she is urging others to adopt). There is more detail, for instance, on the ways in which she asked questions about her primary source – the case report. Faced with a short report (as was the custom in the early twentieth century), containing the facts of the case, counsels' main arguments and three judgments, Rosemary pays careful attention to the material, noting that Miss Bebb was described in one of the judgments as 'a distinguished Oxford student', which suggested a future line of inquiry. She then goes on to place the case report in context, relying on research into the judiciary as part of a discussion about legal reasoning. She brings out the way in which doctrinal legal reasoning suppresses most of the human story which lies behind the litigation, although we as readers are often curious to know about these 'irrelevant' facts.[54] Rosemary points out the gendered consequences of this approach. For instance, Miss Bebb was, in the year the case was heard, an Investigating Officer for the Board of Trade, prosecuting employers, and thus carrying out exactly the sort of legal work that a qualified lawyer would do. Rosemary comments: '[t]his went unmentioned in the judgment, lest the outcome

[50] K Lindsey, '"Deliberate Freedom": Using Speculation and Imagination in Historical Biography' (2018) 50 *Text: Special Issue* 'Life Writing in Troubled Times' 1, K Douglas, D Lee Brian and K Cordell (eds).

[51] ibid 2.

[52] ibid 12.

[53] R Auchmuty, 'Recovering Lost Lives: Researching Women in Legal History' (2015) 42(1) *Journal of Law and Society* 34.

[54] ibid 38.

be too clearly revealed as senseless and contradictory'.[55] Elaborating on her insistence that 'asking the right questions' is a fundamental aspect of good practice as a biographer, in this article Rosemary focuses on 'asking the woman question'. Whether researching a male or female figure

> you must ask, does this statement, law or situation apply to both sexes, or only to men? If to both, how would their experiences of the same phenomenon be different? If only to men, where were the women?[56]

In this article, Rosemary also explicitly wants to challenge 'the myth of continuous progress'.[57] While it is true that things are easier for women than they were in Miss Bebb's day, she notes, this state of affairs has not been achieved as a result of an inexorable and inevitable march of progress. Indeed, giving that impression, she argues, completely ignores the many extended and hard-fought campaigns conducted by feminists over the decades.[58] Rosemary is critical of the fact that women's emancipation is often ascribed by traditional legal historians to 'changing social attitudes'. Her criticism takes on a polemic tone as she asks: 'Yes … attitudes have changed – but *why*? Because the men suddenly decided it would be a good idea to let women in? Or might it be because women fought a long arduous battle to convince them?'[59] Asking the woman question and countering the myth of continuous progress both reflect those three perspectives which run throughout Rosemary's work: law, gender and history, which we can now appreciate in terms of historiography, and not only in terms of the subject-matter which Rosemary chose to write about.

Auchmuty and Historiography

It is in some of her more recent work, co-authored/co-edited with Erika Rackley, that Rosemary directly addresses the issue of historiography. Co-ordinating the Women's Legal Landmark Project involved directly facing the interaction between her two academic disciplines. The aims of the project included providing 'a way into an under-explored research methodology in the U.K. and Ireland' (which was a reference to the 'niche' status of legal history in those jurisdictions) and embedding 'women's legal history in legal scholarship and mainstream knowledge'.[60] To achieve these aims, the editors wanted to harness 'the subject-specific discipline expertise and disciplinary knowledge of both lawyers and historians, to ensure

[55] ibid 39.
[56] ibid 43–44.
[57] ibid 51.
[58] ibid 51.
[59] ibid 51.
[60] R Auchmuty and E Rackley, 'The Women's Legal Landmarks Project: Celebrating 100 Years of Women in the Law in the UK and Ireland' (2016) 16(1) *Legal Information Management* 30.

the accurate interpretation of complex legal provisions in their correct historical context'.[61] This was to be achieved through a project involving over 100 'landmarks' and nearly that many individual contributors. The interdisciplinary nature of the project put historiography in the spotlight, since it demanded that all the contributors had (or acquired) at least some expertise in a discipline in which the majority of them did not usually work. A failure in historiography (understood as the craft of historical research) would have completely undermined the academic credibility of the project.

Emphasising the need to locate the law and legal actors in their appropriate historical, social, political and economic context, Auchmuty and Rackley point to the challenge this presented for some of the legal scholars who contributed to the Landmarks Project, finding that many of them 'were taken aback when they discovered how much historical writing had already been done on the issues relevant to their Landmark event or life'.[62] It is unsurprising, given the interdisciplinary nature of the project, that the editors and their contributors came up against the long-acknowledged challenge of doing socio-legal research. As Anthony Bradney put it, law, from this perspective, is 'a parasitic discipline'.[63] The consequence is that socio-legal scholars need to immerse themselves not only in the literature of another discipline (and maybe more than one), but also in the methodology and culture of the other discipline. This is very challenging, and if not done with real rigour and attention, can result in poor-quality socio-legal research. The problem was well recognised when I interviewed legal academics in 2004. As one of them put it:

> I also think there's a problem with the fact that law borders on other areas … at this conference there was one paper which drew very superficially on work in political theory – the person didn't have sufficient background in the subject to use it properly, they would never survive in a political theory journal, but because it was law, and they were just dipping in ad hoc to a couple of things, people were quite impressed by the sound of these words, but if you really knew about political theory you wouldn't have been. (Lecturer, early career, female, old university)[64]

The challenges presented by feminist legal history as a form of socio-legal research were clearly understood by the editors, who arranged two methodology and training events for contributors, one on working with archival sources, and the other on the production of secondary sources in women's legal history.[65] They underlined the importance of method when they wrote in the Introduction to the book in which the landmarks were published: '[t]here is an important (though

[61] ibid.

[62] R Auchmuty and E Rackley, 'Feminist Legal Biography: A Model for All Legal Biographies'(2020) 41(2) *Journal of Legal History* 186, 192.

[63] A Bradney, 'Law as a Parasitic Discipline' (1998) 25(1) *JLS* 71.

[64] F Cownie, *Legal Academics: Culture and Identities* (Hart, 2004) 67.

[65] E Rackley and R Auchmuty, 'Women's Legal Landmarks: an Introduction' in *Women's Legal Landmarks: celebrating the history of women and the law in the U.K. and Ireland* (Hart, 2019) 3.

often unremarked) difference between doing feminist legal history and collating accounts of the lives of women lawyers and/or women in law'.[66] Feminist legal history, they emphasised, not only involves foregrounding gender and 'asking the woman question'. It also involves locating men in the stories and experiences which are uncovered (whether offering support or in opposition to women's aims) and establishing women as agents, rather than simply subjects of the law. Placing events in their social context, and 'challenging assumptions of unabated progress and liberal incrementalism' are, in their view, also important goals of feminist legal history, reflecting the fact that this is a political project, as well as an intellectual one.[67]

Rackley and Auchmuty's awareness of the importance of paying attention to historical method is reflected in two articles they wrote together, the first addressing the question of method in feminist legal history generally, and the second focusing on feminist legal biography in particular. In 'The Case for Feminist Legal History' they write: 'without a strong scholarly method, politics and purpose, there is a danger that these celebrations [of votes for women and women's entry to the legal profession] will also encourage the proliferation of well-meaning but uncritical heroine narratives replete with myths and anecdote'.[68] A key theme of the article is the distinction between 'women's legal history' and 'feminist legal history'. While acknowledging that the two are closely connected, and that sometimes the choice of nomenclature may be strategic ('women' at times being more acceptable than 'feminist'), the main thrust of the discussion is to identify and analyse the distinctive features of feminist legal history. The main argument is summed up as follows:

> Women's legal history simply adds women to the story; feminist legal history seeks to *change* it, to contest the 'assumed contours' of the past, contradict the lie of women's linear progress from oppression under the law to equality in modern times and create a more complete and more accurate account of the past' (italics in original).[69]

Rackley and Auchmuty identify six features of feminist legal history: asking the woman question; including women's stories, experiences and voices; (re)locating men; establishing women as agents, not just subjects of law and law reform; avoiding heroine narratives and challenging the tale of steady and inevitable progress. Each of these are examined in detail as they seek to illuminate the contrasting approaches of women's legal history and feminist legal history in each case.

However, it is in the article entitled 'Feminist Legal Biography: a model for *ALL* legal biographies' that we find a more detailed methodological discussion. Auchmuty and Rackley note that despite the recent proliferation of studies of legal women, 'there has been little discussion of the content, method and purpose of

[66] ibid 4.
[67] ibid 5.
[68] Rackley and Auchmuty, 'The Case for Feminist Legal History' (n 11) 879.
[69] ibid 889.

feminist legal biography'.[70] They argue that feminist legal biography does more than merely recount the subject's public achievements, which for them is the hallmark of traditional legal biographies. This, they argue, merely reinforces and justifies women's absence. Instead, feminist legal biography focuses on gender, which it regards as one of the main organising principles in society.[71] This allows feminist legal biography not only to offer more accurate legal life histories, but also 'to give both men and women a presence and a (not always comfortable) heritage that will help to explain why things were as they were and are as they are'.[72] Once we have a more accurate understanding of the past, Rackley and Auchmuty argue, 'we are better armed to move forward'.[73] Feminist legal biography which takes method seriously has a unique contribution to make to the genre of 'legal life writing'.[74]

They go on to provide some guidelines 'as to how to approach feminist legal biography'; these are based on three guiding principles: women's issues are part of legal history; the personal matters and 'heroines do not help'.[75] The inclusion of women's issues in legal biographies is a point which Rosemary has made on numerous occasions, and the argument made here, that women's role in legal life (or their absence from it) needs to be explored, together with the role of men in their marginalisation or exclusion, is familiar in her work.[76] This is a point also frequently made by other feminist legal historians, though as Auchmuty and Rackley themselves point out, there is much more discussion of this issue in the North American literature than in the UK.[77] In terms of dealing with the personal lives of biographical subjects, Auchmuty and Rackley argue that '[l]egal biography lags behind other biographical forms in its reluctance to embrace the relationship between the private persona and the public performance'.[78] They are also critical of the way in which, in biographies of women, while the private life may be mentioned, the approach is often simplistic (was she married? Did she have children?) and tends to reinforce the idea that women are identified with the private sphere.[79] On the contrary, they argue, reference to the private sphere should be used to raise the question of 'how she managed to combine career and family … in a context which has always discouraged this'.[80] The principle that 'heroines do not help' is an argument against any tendency to portray a female subject as 'heroine' or 'role model'. The problem with heroine narratives, it is argued, is

[70] Auchmuty and Rackley (n 62) 198.
[71] ibid 198–99.
[72] ibid 198.
[73] ibid 198.
[74] Cownie (n 46) 130–33.
[75] Auchmuty and Rackley (n 62) 200.
[76] ibid 202.
[77] See eg T Thomas and T Boisseau (eds), *Feminist Legal History: Essays on Women and Law* (NYU Press, 2011).
[78] Auchmuty and Rackley (n 62).
[79] On this, see also M Thornton and H Roberts, 'Women Judges, Private Lives: (In)visibilities in Fact and Fiction' (2017) 40(2) *University of New South Wales Law Journal* 761.
[80] Auchmuty and Rackley (n 62) 203.

that they offer an over-simplified version of women's lives, which is then used to show that women who succeed do so on men's terms. Such an account indicates that these are the 'rules' for success and thus the parameters within which anyone who wishes to emulate the biographical subject's success must contain themselves. These 'thoughtless narratives of achievement' are also likely to lead to 'disappointment, self-doubt and a sense of powerlessness' on the part of readers aspiring to follow in the footsteps of the 'heroine'.[81]

Auchmuty and Rackley conclude their article by detailing three 'pitfalls' which should be avoided by feminist legal biographers (and, by implication, *ALL* legal biographers, as the title of their article suggests, since these potential errors apply to all biographical writing, and are certainly not confined to biographers adopting a feminist approach). Firstly, over-familiarity: biographers feeling that they really 'know' their subject (which is, of course impossible). And that approach quickly leads to the second pitfall, of falling into anachronism and historical inaccuracy, whereas, Auchmuty and Rackley argue, what we should be doing as biographers is to engage in informed conjecture about our subjects' lives, based on our knowledge of the historical context and of women's position in society, gleaned from as wide a range of sources as possible.[82] The third pitfall is what Auchmuty and Rackley term 'the siren call of anecdote and myth'.[83] They acknowledge that anecdotes can add colour to a biography, but caution that it is very easy to confuse oft-repeated anecdotes with myth. Repeating an inaccurate myth, they say, can undermine the work of others who have engaged in painstaking and rigorous biographical research, which results in a more accurate picture of the subject. Such research can then be ignored by those who prefer to continue believing the myths.[84]

Conclusion

Auchmuty and Rackley conclude their article as follows:

> This article has outlined the principles of feminist legal biography and offered a justification – indeed an exhortation – for its adoption as not only a more complete and more accurate representation of what it was like for a given biographical subject but also a fairer assessment of his or her contribution to legal history.[85]

Much of what Rosemary Auchmuty has written about historiography in this and the other articles discussed in this contribution is uncontroversial. Many novice biographers will find a great deal of the practical advice which can be drawn from this body of work to be very useful. However, I would add a note of caution about

[81] ibid 206.
[82] ibid 208.
[83] ibid 209.
[84] ibid 209.
[85] ibid 210.

this last contribution in particular. It is important to remind oneself that this article is entitled 'A' model for all legal biographies, not 'THE' model, and I think it is important to keep that in mind. Hermione Lee, herself a distinguished biographer (also cited by Auchmuty and Rackley) wrote that '[t]here are no rules for biography', characterising it as 'a mixed, unstable genre, whose rules keep coming undone'.[86] While she goes on to say that there are some conventions in writing biography, it is clear that she does not think there is 'one right way' to approach biographical writing, and further, that the methods used by biographers are in a perpetual state of re-working and development. It would be unfortunate if some of Rosemary's writing about historiography gave the impression that there is only ONE way to 'do' feminist legal biography. As scholars, we need to be open to debate and to new ways of doing things. Indeed, in repeatedly criticising 'traditional legal historians', this is what Rosemary herself is suggesting. Continually re-imagining our approach to legal biography, and fully engaging with current debates outside the discipline of law, could lead to some exciting contributions to historiography. It is always important to remind ourselves, as socio-legal biographers, of the importance of real knowledge and understanding of the discipline of history and the genre of biography, so that, in terms of historiography, we 'do it right'. And engaging with the ideas of feminist legal biography are an important part of that process. But equally, we need to remain open to new ways of doing things and to nurture the intellectual space where that can happen, so that feminist legal history can achieve its political, as well as its intellectual, aims. As Rosemary herself wrote: 'in the end, to be a feminist and not to want to change things seems to me a contradiction in terms'.[87] Remaining alert and open to novel possibilities of biographical method, while ensuring we are also academically rigorous, gives feminist biographers the best chance of contributing to the changes in biographical method that Rosemary Auchmuty herself is advocating.

[86] H Lee, *Biography: A Very Short Introduction* (OUP, 2009) 18.
[87] R Auchmuty, 'Agenda for a Feminist Legal Curriculum' (2003) 23(3) *Legal Studies* 377, 385.

7

Spinsters, Goblins and Contract

SALLY WHEELER

In the Beginning

My career as an academic started some 35 years ago, in 1987, in the Law School at Brunel University. Over the course of that 35 years, I have never been asked to write a *Festrchrift* contribution before,[1] let alone thought about taking on the editing of an entire volume of contributions. *Festschrifts* apparently occur most frequently in 'hot beds' and 'outliers'.[2] I am of the view that the areas of scholarship covered in this collection – feminist legal history and biography and aspects of property, contract and equity seen through a gendered lens – fall into both of these categories.[3] Guidance was needed on the part I was required to play as an individual. On consulting the academic life-support system, otherwise known as 'google scholar', I discovered that the literature on preparing *Festschrift* contributions is not particularly illuminating as to how the task at hand should be approached. The word *Festschrift* itself apparently derives from two Indo-European word roots:[4] one from *DHES* which gives us *inter alia* the English derivatives *feast*, *festival*, and *festoon* and one from *SKRIBH*. The Latin verb, *scribere*, descends from this. Taking them together gives us the word *Festschrift*, on loan from German.[5] So if the word

[1] This might say something about me such as that I have no friends, or I am a terrible writer. I rather hope neither of these things are true.

[2] A Ender and B Wälchli, 'The Making of a Festschrift, Is It a Ritual?' in A Ender, A Leemann and B Wälchli (eds), *Methods in Contemporary Linguistics* (De Gruyter Mouton, 2012) 143, 153.

[3] See the positions within the legal academy subscribed to these subjects in R Auchmuty, 'Using Feminist Judgments in the Property Law Classroom' (2012) 46 *The Law Teacher* 227; R Auchmuty, 'Introduction' in R Auchmuty (ed), *Great Debates in Gender and the Law* (Red Globe Press, 2018); and E Rackley and R Auchmuty, 'The Case for Feminist Legal History' (2020) 40 *Oxford Journal of Legal Studies* 878.

[4] Indo-European in the context of linguistics refers to 'similarities in inflexion, word-formation and vocabulary between the Celtic, Italic, Germanic, Baltic and Slavonic languages, Greek and Albanian in Europe; and Armenian, the Iranian languages and Sanskrit and its cognates and derivatives further east': see R Crossland, 'Indo-European Origins: The Linguistic Evidence' (1957) 12 *Past and Present* 16.

[5] J Aronson, 'When I use a word … Festschrift' (*The BMJ Opinion*, 31 May 2019) blogs.bmj.com/bmj/2019/05/31/jeffrey-aronson-when-i-use-a-word-festschrift/.

itself means 'celebratory writing', how does that translate into actual practice, the words on the page?

We have moved beyond the idea that *Festschrifts* celebrate only 'men',[6] although as the introduction to this volume makes clear, there is a long way to go before we see gender equality. This comment is a shorthand way of pointing out the under-representation of women in research leadership[7] and senior management[8] roles more generally in higher education worldwide.[9] Rosemary Auchmuty has played a not insignificant role in contesting these issues within United Kingdom (UK) Law Schools and championing progress through cultural change[10] around structural problems such as working hours and workload management, questions of values and the absence of practices such as listening,[11] as have others, some of whom are included in this volume. Whilst UK Law Schools are not perfect workplaces, it is easy to forget that even these advances have not necessarily transferred to Law Schools overseas,[12] to other disciplines such as those within STEM (science, technology, engineering, mathematics)[13] and to institutions such as Business Schools.[14] There are many spaces within the academy where the gains made in UK Law Schools have yet to be realised.[15] For non-white women,[16] for women working in the Academy outside the global north[17] and for those whose identities intersect on this axis,[18] the struggle for success and then appropriate recognition of that success is much greater.

[6] G Wilkinson, 'Prepare a Festschrift' (1989) 299 *British Medical Journal* 612 citing Gerd Buchdahl: 'Festschriften are for men who have put their stamp on some branch of enquiry during a certain period of time' who himself was reviewing a volume of essays for Ernest Nagel in 'Nagel's Message' (1971) 231 *Nature* 399.

[7] L Morely, 'Troubling Intra-Actions: Gender, Neo-Liberalism and Research in the Global Academy' (2016) 31 *Journal of Education Policy* 28.

[8] V Baker, 'Women in Higher Education: Re-Imagining Leadership in the Academy in Times of Crisis' (2021) 35 *Journal of Faculty Development* 57. Whilst this is essentially an article about a possible post-COVID-19 dividend for female leaders, it does contain a very useful literature review of the research demonstrating the relative absence of women from university leadership structures. See also P O'Connor, 'Gender Imbalance in Senior Positions in Higher Education: What Is the Problem? What Can Be Done' (2019) 3 *Policy Reviews in Higher Education* 28.

[9] K Longman, 'Perspectives on Women's Higher Education Leadership from around the World' (2018) 35 *Administrative Sciences* 35.

[10] C Westoby, J Dyson, F Cowdell and T Buescher, 'What Are the Barriers and Facilitators to Success for Female Academics in UK HEIs? A Narrative Review' (2021) 33 *Gender in Education* 1033.

[11] J Harford, 'The Perspectives of Women Professors on the Professoriate: A Missing Piece in the Narrative on Gender Equality in the University' (2018) 8 *Education Science* 50.

[12] U Schultz, 'Introduction: Gender and Careers in the Legal Academy: Overview and Synthesis' in U Schultz, G Shaw, M Thornton and R Auchmuty (eds), *Gender and Careers in the Legal Academy* (Hart, 2021) 1.

[13] L Howe-Walsh and S Turnbull, 'Barriers to Women Leaders in Academia: Tales from Academia and Technology' (2016) 41 *Studies in Higher Education* 415.

[14] A Reilly, D Jones, C Vasquez and J Krisjanous, 'Confronting Gender Inequality in a Business School' (2016) 35 *Higher Education Research and Development* 1025.

[15] See the accounts contained in M Ronksley-Pavia, M Neumann, J Manakil and K Pickard-Smith (eds), *Academic Women: Voicing Narratives of Gendered Experiences* (Bloomsbury Academic, 2023).

[16] R Zambrana, *Toxic Ivory Towers* (Rutgers University Press, 2018).

[17] S J Aiston and C Fo, 'The Silence/ing of Academic Women' (2021) 33 *Gender and Education* 138.

[18] C Turner, V González and K Wong, 'Faculty Women of Color: The Critical Nexus of Race and Gender' (2011) *Journal of Diversity in Higher Education* 199.

David Schleicher,[19] now Professor of Law at Yale, also researched the appropriate style for *Festschrift* contributions. Having apparently examined numerous contributions, he alighted on a three-pronged format: a contribution should begin with praise for the subject's work, then move to an explanation of a 'problem' or 'hole' within that work which the contributor can use to emphasise the independence of their assessment of the subject, and then finally there should be a link to the identified problem/hole through the contributor's work. This link should seek to suggest that the issue identified can be improved or explained by the contributor's own work. Rather than being presumptuous on the part of the contributor, this is actually a way of identifying intellectual debts to the subject. Schleicher's explanation is very amusing – much better expressed than I have managed in my paraphrasing here. To his format, others[20] would suggest adding an account of how the contributor knows the subject and making more personal the effect that their work has had upon you, the contributor, in the context of developing your own work.[21] The qualitative research on *Festschrift* contents undertaken with editors of *Festschrifts* by Ender et al[22] suggested that a photograph of the subject was important as were anecdotes around connection. My google scholar search revealed 19,700 instances of the words *Festschrift* and *anecdote* appearing in the same piece of work.

Anecdotes, chosen well, reveal the humanity of the subject but the idea of including biographical comment and associated context would seem to go to the heart of what is required. Biography and context are particularly important in this *Festschrift* given Rosemary Auchmuty's pioneering work on using biographical and general contextual sources[23] to reconstruct and illuminate the lives of previously under-researched early women lawyers.[24] Added to this, is her call (with Erika Rackley) for the adoption of an avowedly feminist legal biography[25] as a method for historical socio-legal research. This is designed to place women on the record as the visible and essential enablers of successes documented as the experience of males only. A lens on the previously disregarded sphere of private space, to wit family life and personal life history details, for so long considered to be irrelevant to the 'hero' model of biographical subject is now considered to be fundamentally

[19] D Schleicher, 'From Here All-the-Way-Down, or How to Write a Festschrift Piece' (2013) 48 *Tulsa Law Review* 401.

[20] See A Soble, 'Fact and Value: Essays on Ethics and Metaphysics for Judith Jarvis Thomson' (2003) 4 (1/Jan) *Essays in Philosophy* 1. Soble expressed annoyance that the Festschrift he was reviewing had, in his view, insufficient biographical detail about the subject and that there were a number of contributors who established neither a social nor intellectual connection with the subject.

[21] P Clarkson and N Presmeg, *Critical Issues in Mathematics Education: Major Contributions of Alan Bishop* (Springer, 2008).

[22] Ender and Wälchli (n 2) 143.

[23] R Auchmuty, 'Recovering Lost Lives: Researching Women in Legal History' (2015) 42 *Journal of Law and Society* 34.

[24] R Auchmuty, 'Early Women Law Students at Cambridge and Oxford' (2008) 29 *Journal of Legal History* 63.

[25] R Auchmuty and E Rackley 'Feminist Legal Biography: A Model for *All* Legal Life Stories' (2020) 41 *Journal of Legal History* 186.

constitutive of the modern 'who, what and why' biography. Turning this approach to examine my relationship with Rosemary, I realise that, despite knowing (of) each other for many years through socio-legal and law and gender conferences in the UK, our deepest connection is through the Australian National University (ANU) and our experiences there, separated by the passage of 45 years or so.

Sharing Australia

It had escaped me, in conscious terms, until Rosemary visited ANU Law in September 2018 as its annually appointed Distinguished Visiting Mentor[26] that she was not only Australian but also an ANU graduate for both of her degrees. I am sure I must have known on some level that she was from Australia. However, we had never spoken about this part of her life, and she certainly did not present to me as I thought an Antipodean *emigrée* should, but rather as a sophisticated north Londoner. I was appointed Dean of the ANU College of Law in late October 2017 and moved to Canberra from the Queen's University Belfast to begin work at the ANU in January 2018. The ANU[27] and Canberra[28] are almost certainly very different from the rest of Australia, and they and Australia are certainly very different in terms of social and political culture than one might imagine either to be from a distance of 12,000 miles or so,[29] and economic policy (including in relation to higher education)[30] has different drivers and settings. These differences did not feel as though they could be weighed in positive or negative terms of one is better than the other or vice versa. They were simply too overwhelming for that. Admitting that there are differences, some of which one finds hugely challenging, is, it turns out, the first small step to reaching an equilibrium. Recognising that one's memory of pre-Australia experiences as uniformly fantastic may not be entirely accurate in an objective sense makes creating a positive environment

[26] 'Professor Rosemary Auchmuty: Distinguished Visiting Mentor' (Australian National University, nd) law.anu.edu.au/about-us/visitors-honorary-profiles/professor-rosemary-auchmuty.

[27] S Forster and M Varghese, *The Making of the Australian National University* (ANU Press, 2009).

[28] J Webb and J Williams, 'Canberra: Ideal City, Imagined City' (2015) 29 *Continuum* 490.

[29] My impressions of Australia came from a childhood spent looking at the pictures in National Geographic magazine and watching *Skippy the Kangaroo* on television. For a discussion of *Skippy* and other icons of Australian popular culture see M Gibson, 'Tchk, tchk, tchk: *Skippy the Bush Kangaroo* and the Question of Australian Seriousness' (2014) 28 *Continuum* 574.

[30] The differences include higher education funding for research, the respective income- contingent loan systems operated by the two jurisdictions, enterprise bargaining in Australia as opposed to collective bargaining in the UK, the size and segmentation of the two sectors, and the narrowness and temporal inflexibility of the traditional UK three-year degree compared with the four+ years of the Australian double degree. For an overview of Australian higher education policy with some UK comparative work, see the online commentary of A Norton, 'Higher Education Commentary from Carlton' andrewnorton.net.au/. To this should be added general peculiarities of the Australian workplace, such as a positive work–life balance and long- service leave: see S Ferris, N Parr, R Markey and T Kyng, 'Long Service Leave: Past, Present and Future' (2015) 3 *Australian Journal of Actuarial Practice* 5.

in the present an easier undertaking. During her 2018 visit at the end of my first bitterly cold Canberra winter, spent with none of my possessions as they toured the high seas in a container, Rosemary gave me the tools with which to let go of my previous academic life and recast my situation at ANU by discussing with me the very conflicting views she held about her time at ANU as an undergraduate and postgraduate. In a subsequent piece for the *ANU Historical Journal*,[31] she reflects that her

> overwhelming recollection of my years at ANU is one of misery and loneliness … In Newcastle,[32] I had a close circle of schoolfriends and a secure place in the middle class[33] of a largely working-class city. In Canberra, every other student seemed to be the offspring of a diplomat or politician.[34] They were all privately educated and frighteningly articulate. Beside them, I felt like I knew nothing, that I was nothing.[35]

Later in the same piece she reveals a recent memory triggered by the study of some ANU archival material;

> I did enjoy my studies; and now I see I enjoyed the extracurricular activities too[36] … So, subjecting my past to the historian's critical scrutiny, can I see how my days as a student historian moulded my future life? Well, they made me a good historian, if I say so myself … as I approach the end of my academic life, I realise I owe ANU much more than I thought.[37]

I regard her intervention as pivotal for me in my journey to embracing the considerable opportunities on offer at ANU and coming to terms with a life in Australia.

[31] R Auchmuty, 'The Past is Another Truth' (2019) *II ANU Historical Journal* 35 press.anu.edu.au/publications/journals/anu-historical-journal.

[32] Newcastle is the second largest city in the state of New South Wales some 60 miles north of Sydney. It is located at the mouth of the Hunter River, and its harbour is one of the largest coal export sites in the world.

[33] To enhance my understanding of this, Rosemary referred me to the biography of her father, Professor James Auchmuty CBE, a history graduate of Trinity College Dublin, an academic and the first Vice-Chancellor of the University of Newcastle from 1965–1974: K Dutton, 'Auchmuty, James Johnston (1909–1981)' (2007) 17 *Australian Dictionary of Biography* adb.anu.edu.au/biography/auchmuty-james-johnston-12155. From this I learned of the family's arrival in Australia from Egypt, Rosemary's early years living in a Nissan Hut shared with two other families and the subsequent occupation of a Housing Commission cottage 'for needy families'. Whilst rich in cultural capital, the transition to associating with those long familiar with economic, political and social capital must indeed have been disorientating. See K Dutton, *Auchmuty* (Boombana, 2000) 225, 245, 262 and 288.

[34] Founded as the National University by an Act of the Federal Parliament in 1946, by 1976 ANU was still attracting 75% of its students from the Canberra and southern New South Wales region. In this respect Australian students were following the Australian tradition of studying at the geographically most proximate university. Rosemary was both a pioneer in choosing ANU and correct in her view that the majority of students were from a Canberra-based diplomatic and public service background: see Forster and Varghese (n 27) 198.

[35] Auchmuty (n 31) 36.

[36] Rosemary submitted her ANU PhD thesis in 1975. At that time there were some 5200 undergraduates at ANU and 524 PhD students. The number of PhD students was more than double that of any other Australian University. It would have been a more vibrant graduate community than that found anywhere else in Australia, see Forster and Varghese (n 27) 200.

[37] Auchmuty (n 31) 36, 38.

As a result of this connection I have taken as my starting point for this chapter the doctoral work Rosemary undertook at ANU and the publications that come immediately from it. Fiona Cownie's contribution to this volume explains the premise of Rosemary's thesis on 'Victorian Spinsters';[38] the spinster should be seen not as a woman who having failed to find a husband is to be pitied but as woman who joyfully earned her own living. Often belonging to the upper echelons of the middle classes, these women drove through emancipation for others around divorce laws, married women's property and the acceptance of careers for women. In a journal article[39] published immediately post her PhD, Rosemary, drawing on both Victorian fiction literature and commentary, sets out the reasons, in her view, for the Victorian veneration of marriage; economic, religious, a particular view of nature, and an understanding of Protestant virtue derived from Luther and Calvin.

While she refers to the legal consequences of marriage for women in terms of their inability to own property and generally being subsumed into the identity of their husband, there is no discussion of marriage as a legal device, as a contract in essence. This is hardly surprising given that the study of law and legal academia was something that she was yet to embark upon. Later in her career she does turn to consider contract law, and then her focus is on using the doctrine of undue influence in mortgage transactions to demonstrate how legal structures fail to protect the interests of the vulnerable and instead buttress business interests and facilitate men 'behaving badly'.[40] She has viewed judicial confirmation[41] that the undue influence doctrine protects not only wives but anyone in an intimate relationship whether that relationship is heterosexual or homosexual, involving marriage or co-habitation, in critical terms as masking, in particular, the gendered power dynamic ever present in heterosexual relationships around the economic domination of men and the economic subordination of women. This determination she bases upon the numerical significance of cases that involve males misusing or misapplying the equity interests of their female partners[42] as security for further borrowing and the absence of judicial or other comment on this behaviour.[43]

What I want to do in the remainder of this chapter, in a rather *Schleicher-esque* way, is pick up some of the threads of Rosemary's work that relate to gendered power flowing through marriage and aspects of contract doctrine and broaden them out into a discussion of contract, including marriage, and the market

[38] R Auchmuty, *Victorian Spinsters* (Australian National University PhD Thesis, 1975).

[39] R Auchmuty, 'The Victorian Theory of Spinsterhood' (1976) 2 *University of Wollongong Historical Journal* 38.

[40] R Auchmuty, 'Men Behaving Badly: An Analysis of English Undue Influence Cases' (2002) 11 *Social and Legal Studies* 257.

[41] *Royal Bank of Scotland v Etridge (No 2) and Other Appeals* [2001] 4 All ER 449, 456.

[42] As she points out, all five Law Lords in *Etridge (No 2)* use the word 'husband' to describe the usual undue influencer and the word 'wife' when describing the usual victim, see R Auchmuty, 'The Rhetoric of Equality and the Problem of Heterosexuality' in L Mulcahy and S Wheeler (eds), *Feminist Perspectives on Contract Law* (Glasshouse 2005) 51, 55.

[43] ibid 57.

as both legal and social institutions. I take as my illustrative vehicle the life of Christina Rossetti and one of her poems, *Goblin Market*. The storyline of this poem features several contractual settings; from spot purchases to the most relational of contracts, marriage.[44] Despite this, it has never been analysed as a text about contract. In the second section of this chapter, I draw on some of the different meanings and interpretative stances that commentators have read into *Goblin Market*. In the final section some of its vignettes are explained as contract settings drawing on the work of Ian Macneil. Macneil's relational contract[45] may seem a strange choice as a frame because his work comes from observations of commercial exchange settings.[46] However, that aside, it offers a perspective that is based upon relationships and connections; Macneil considers all activities in which exchange is a significant factor as contract relationships including private and domestic interactions,[47] which the usual neoliberal explanation of contract as individualised exchanges[48] screens out.

Rosemary comments that Jane Austin disavowed marriage for herself but nevertheless kept with convention for her protagonists by marrying them off.[49] Rossetti's position was similar; she never married. The principal characters in *Goblin Market* are revealed to have married at the end of the poem. As an unmarried female author, Rossetti largely conducted her own commercial relationships with her volume-length publishers, Alexander Macmillan, Frederick Startridge Ellis and Roberts Bros, delegating matters to her brothers when it suited her to do so. Her letters, some of which are discussed below, show her negotiating royalty payments, illustrations and print runs.[50] These commercial niceties, these contractual arrangements, would have been outwith the experience of any of her married contemporaries. Gilbert offers an explanation for the resort to convention; for her, *Goblin Market* as a text is about an allegory of limitations; Rossetti was well aware of the freedom she enjoyed and played this out in her imagination for her characters in their adventures but ultimately cleaved to allowing their freedoms to be circumscribed by what convention would permit.[51] A different explanation reveals itself in a letter to her brother William in August 1853.[52] There she suggests

[44] See the extensive discussion of marriage as a relational contract, in I Macneil, 'Relational Contract Theory as Sociology: A Reply to Professors Lindenberg and de Vos' (1987) 143 *Journal of Institutional and Theoretical Economics* 272.

[45] I Macneil, *The New Social Contract: An Enquiry into Modern Contractual Relations* (Yale University Press, 1980).

[46] J Wightman, 'Intimate Relationships, Relational Contract Theory and the Reach of Contract' (2000) 8 *Feminist Legal Studies* 93.

[47] M Enright, 'Contract Law' in Auchmuty, *Great Debates* (n 3) 1.

[48] S Wheeler, 'Visions of Contract' (2017) 44 *Journal of Law and Society* 74.

[49] Auchmuty (n 39) 62.

[50] A Harrison (ed), *The Letters of Christina Rossetti* vol 1 (University of Virginia Press, 1997).

[51] S Gilbert and S Gubar, *The Madwoman in the Attic: The Woman Writer and the Nineteenth-Century Literary Imagination* (Yale University Press, 1997) 573ff.

[52] Harrison (n 50).

(playfully) that her story, *Nick*,[53] would be not only accepted for publication but well remunerated if it was accompanied by a portrait of her. It is not clear whether she means a self-portrait, or a portrait painted by her other brother, Dante Gabriel. In either event she seems to be suggesting that a female face will sell her work rather than her talent as an author. The idea that women are more likely to sell themselves in a commercial setting than they are to participate in economic activity in any other way is a persistent theme of Victoriana, including in *Goblin Market*.

Explaining *Goblin Market*

Goblin Market is a narrative poem by Christina Rossetti of some 570 lines published by Macmillan in 1862 as the title poem in Rossetti's first public collection of her work. The poem explores the twilight adventures over seemingly a period of months of two sisters, Laura and Lizzie, and their friend, Jeanie, at a fruit market run by Goblin 'men'. I use inverted commas for men because despite 11 references interspersed throughout Rossetti's text to Goblin men,[54] it is unlikely that they were conceived by her as possessing a particular physical form, human or not.

Laura is initially cautious about interacting with the Goblins,[55] and Lizzie endorses this caution. However, Laura then becomes curious about the Goblins and their market. Her desire is to look at the market rather than buy fruit. She approaches the market, which appears to be some distance from their home,[56] on her own without any money. When she explains her impecuniosity to the Goblins, they suggest a lock of her 'golden'[57] hair as consideration. In response Laura cuts off a lock of her hair, hands it to the Goblins and eats a considerable amount of fruit. Lizzie meets Laura on her return and reminds her of Jeanie's fate when she too ate the fruit. We do not find out who Jeanie is. We do learn that she is dead[58] but not how her death occurred. Laura wants to visit the Goblins again, but they do not return. She then starts to fade away through illness and general melancholy.

Lizzie hears the Goblins return, but Laura cannot hear them. Lizzie knows intuitively that only fruit from the Goblins can cure her sister who is wasting away before her eyes. She therefore resolves to visit the Goblins on her own. She has money and takes it with her on the visit. The Goblins encourage Lizzie to get close to them. She is very wary of them and throws her money, a 'silver penny',[59] to them in an attempt to keep them from closing in on her.

[53] *Nick* was published in 1870 by American publisher FS Ellis as part of the short story collection *Commonplace and Other Short Stories.*

[54] *Goblin Market (GM)* at lines 42, 49, 55, 70, 88, 146, 241, 274, 307, 456 and 474.

[55] ibid lines 40–45.

[56] ibid lines 216 (across a brook) and 325 (across a heath).

[57] ibid line 125.

[58] ibid lines 157 and 312.

[59] ibid line 324.

Figure 1 Laurence Housman's depiction of the Goblins as almost shape-shifters in the 1893 edition of *Goblin Market*

The Goblins want Lizzie to eat their fruit in front of them, trying to physically force her to do so. She will not do this and demands the return of her money. The Goblins squeeze fruit all over her and then throw the silver penny back to her. Lizzie returns home. Laura licks the juice of the fruit from her body and is restored to health.[60] The poem ends with Lizzie and Laura warning the children of their subsequent marriages about the dangers of interacting with the Goblins[61] and Rossetti offering an ode to sisterhood as a relationship that offers the protagonists the strongest support in good times and bad.[62]

The range of readings that have been suggested for *Goblin Market* and the potential audiences[63] offered for it stand in sharp contrast to Rossetti's own downplaying of its significance throughout her lifetime, perhaps reflecting her always modest view of her own achievement.[64] Contemporary audiences for it ranged from 'working men' introduced to it by its publisher, Alexander Macmillan, to those attending 'elocution' readings and musical recitals.[65] More recent audiences, by which I mean post-Second World War, have divided into adult sexual fantasists (for example in September 1973 *Playboy* magazine commissioned artist Kinuko Craft to provide four illustrations for its *Ribald's Classics* series[66]) and children,[67] with this division being made clearer (fortunately!) by the power of illustration and marketing methods supporting the creation of different streams of interest.[68]

Finding Religion and Sexuality in *Goblin Market*

Interpretations, using a wide variety of methodologies from discourse theory to the psychoanalytical,[69] cut across themes *inter alia* from religion, sexuality and

[60] ibid lines 492, 510 and 540–42.

[61] ibid lines 544, 545 and 552–55.

[62] ibid lines 562–67.

[63] L Kooistra, 'Visualizing the Fantastic Subject' in M Arseneau, A Harrison and L Kooistra (eds), *The Culture of Christina Rossetti* (Ohio University Press, 1999) 137. Excellent open access resources are also available at 'An Introduction to "Goblin Market"' (British Library, 15 May 2014) www.bl.uk/romantics-and-victorians/articles/an-introduction-to-goblin-market and 'Goblin Market' (Cove, June 2018) editions.covecollective.org/edition/goblin-market.

[64] Mackenzie Bell, in his near contemporary account of her life and work, quotes her brother William in correspondence to him as saying that she saw *Goblin Market* as a fairy story without any 'profound or ulterior meaning': M Bell, *Christina Rossetti: A Biographical and Critical Study* (Roberts Brothers, 1898) 231. William Rossetti repeats this claim in his own later volume of his sister's work, *The Poetical Works of Christina Georgina Rossetti* (Macmillan, 1904) 459.

[65] C Hassett, *Christina Rossetti* (University of Virginia Press, 2005) 16.

[66] L Kooistra, *Christina Rossetti and Illustration: A Publishing History* (Ohio University Press, 2002) 241–43.

[67] In a letter dated 7 March 1862 to an unknown recipient, Christina Rossetti explained that she did not consider 'children' to be the audience for her work: see Harrison, *The Letters of Christina Rossetti* vol 1 (n 50) 159, letter 157.

[68] L Kooistra, 'Modern Markets for "Goblin Market"' (1994) 32 *Victorian Poetry* 249.

[69] S Waldman, '"O Wanton Eyes Run Over": Repetition and Fantasy in Christina Rossetti' (2000) 38 *Victorian Poetry* 533 and E Golub, 'Untying Goblin Apron Strings: A Psychoanalytic Reading of "Goblin Market"' (1975) 25 *Literature and Psychology* 158.

economy to produce both singular and hybrid accounts.[70] A popular singular explanation is to cast it as a specifically Christian allegory of 'temptation, fall and redemption'[71] in dialogue with Milton to varying degrees.[72] It is notable that the most prominent piece of fruit in the frontispiece of the first edition, a woodcut by Rossetti's brother Dante Gabriel Rossetti, is an apple.

Figure 2 Frontispiece to the first edition of *Goblin Market*

[70] The most informative account of the interpretations of *Goblin Market* in terms of both a temporal and thematic analysis is A Pionke, 'The Spiritual Economy of "Goblin Market"' (2012) 52 *Studies in English Literature* 897.

[71] J McGann, 'Christina Rossetti's Poems: A New Edition and a Revaluation' (1980) 23 *Victorian Studies* 237, 247. As Pionke points though, there are precious few moments of redemption in *Goblin Market*; of seven interactions with the Goblins, only one results in redemption: Pionke (n 70) 899.

[72] K Vejvoda, 'The Fruit of Charity: Comus and Christina Rossetti's *Goblin Market*' (2000) 38 *Victorian Poetry* 555 and K Brandt, *Christina Rossetti's 'Goblin Market'* (Åbo Akademi University Press, 2006).

There are obvious overtones of the temptation and fall of Eve. This fits with Rossetti's own religious faith – much of the rest of her work is devotional prose and poetry. Building on this religious faith in the vein of more hybrid accounts, some have seen Lizzie as a female Christ[73] who saves her sister through her self-sacrifice and her example (the exhortation to Laura to 'eat me, drink me, love me' has a clear parallel with the eucharistic)[74] while others have used Rossetti's particular religious practices within the Oxford Movement[75] to see *Goblin Market* as a text about incarnational theology (the divine nature of the mystery of faith) and sacramental participation.[76] Using Rossetti's theocracy in an account that encompasses both of these religious interpretations, Rappoport[77] sees *Goblin Market* as a narrative of redemptive gift exchange. Laura's fall takes place within the economy of the market where without money she has no power. Lizzie is able to rescue Laura and ultimately redeem her through having a silver coin which she offers in an exchange which is ultimately rejected by the Goblins. Lizzie participates in the market economy but succeeds through her gift to her sister. In terms of sexuality there are readings of *Goblin Market* as a text warning that indulging in female sexual desire results in illness and death either physically or metaphorically speaking[78] (perhaps contrasted with the notion of sisterhood that Rossetti experienced during her voluntary work at the Highgate Penitentiary[79] between 1859 and 1870) and a text about sororal sexual desire.[80]

Reading Economics into *Goblin Market*

Standing apart from the readings of *Goblin Market* that place it in an essentially religious or sexuality setting are those that see it as a text grounded in an economics of exchange, as an encounter with Victorian mercantilist concerns where the 'dangerous' public space occupied by the Goblins' market is contrasted in a variety

[73] L Peterson, 'Restoring the Book: The Typological Hermeneutics of Christina Rossetti and the PRB' (1994) 32 *Victorian Poetry* 209.

[74] *GM* line 471.

[75] D D'Amico and D Kent, 'Rossetti and the Tractarians' (2006) 44 *Victorian Poetry* 93.

[76] M Arseneau, 'Incarnation and Interpretation: Christina Rossetti, the Oxford Movement, and Goblin Market' (1993) 31 *Victorian Poetry* 79.

[77] J Rappoport, *Giving Women* (OUP, 2012) 101–05.

[78] A Harrison, 'Christina Rossetti: Illness and Ideology' (2007) 45 *Victorian Poetry* 415.

[79] D D'Amico, '"Equal before God": Christina Rossetti and the Fallen Women of Highgate Penitentiary' in A Harrison (ed), *Gender and Discourse in Victorian Literature and Art* (Northern Illinois University Press, 1992) 67. Marsh suggests that Rossetti's Highgate experience is still to come at the time *Goblin Market* is written and is perhaps instead a text in which Rossetti is reflecting on what she might encounter at Highgate: see J Marsh, 'Christina Rossetti's Vocation: The Importance of "Goblin Market"' (1994) 32 *Victorian Poetry* 233.

[80] L May, '"Eat Me, Drink Me, Love Me": Orality, Sexuality, and the Fruits of Sororal Desire in "Gob(b)lin(g) Market" and Beloved' in J Mink and J Ward (eds), *The Significance of Sibling Relationships in Literature* (Bowling Green State University Popular Press, 1993) 133. See M Carpenter, '"Eat Me, Drink Me, Love Me": The Consumable Female Body in Christina Rossetti's *Goblin Market*' (1991) 29 *Victorian Poetry* 415 for a comment on the possibilities of a homoerotic analysis of *Goblin Market*.

of different ways with the more simple and non-confrontational domestic life of the home. This group of accounts has been described as 'ones that put the *market* back in "Goblin Market"'.[81] The interplay between the poem as read out loud to an audience and the textually expressed oral cries of the Goblins embedded within the bustle of a market place is explained as a conversational interaction between Rossetti and the London streets that surrounded her home.[82] Stauffer builds on this to tie the Goblins' cries to particular contemporary songs and poems he terms the 'pedlar-cry microgenre' that might have been known to Rossetti.[83] For Tucker these cries are the embodiment of mid-nineteenth-century advertising. Their pitch focused on generating consumer desire; the Goblins' offer is one of a 'seductive merger of gustatory [pleasures] with verbal oralities'.[84] In Tucker's terms, Laura is an impulse buyer whilst Lizzie bests the Goblins by obtaining free fruit juice and fruit pulp to take home.[85]

The uncertain origins of the fruit the Goblins offer for sale ('[w]ho knows upon what soil they fed')[86] invites a detailed analysis of fruit-growing in mid-Victorian Britain. It appears that the winter of 1858 and the spring of 1859 were not conducive to fruit-growing, much of which would have been 'forced' under glass. Richard Menke suggests that the list of exotic fruit, which extends to some 19 lines of verse, is dreamlike, a fantasy of expectation for consumers.[87] He goes on to situate the fruit as a commodity in consumer capitalism which sets itself the task of reconstructing nature's cycles to fit the expanding market through the technology of new and improved transport and growing methods, say. The Goblin's market is contrasted with Laura and Lizzie's domestic life of cleaning, tending to farm animals and fetching water. Home is safety and the market is danger.[88] Home is the place where women in the Victorian economy, with its valourisation of production, are supposed to be; marginalised from capitalism. *Goblin Market* offers a counter-narrative to this by promoting a feminist economics centred on reproduction.[89] The home is also where autonomy might be found for Laura and

[81] H Tucker, 'Rossetti's Goblin Marketing: Sweet to Tongue and Sound to Eye' (2003) 82 *Representations* 117. The extent to which they do that is the subject of a rather stinging critique in V Coulson, 'Redemption and Representation in *Goblin Market*: Christina Rossetti and the Salvific Signifier' (2017) 55 *Victorian Poetry* 423.

[82] M Norcia, '"Come Buy, Come Buy": Christina Rossetti's "Goblin Market" and the Cries of London' (2012) 17 *Journal of Victorian Culture* 24. Norcia's account contains a very rich description of the sounds of the City and its inhabitants going about their daily business which would have assailed Rossetti from her house.

[83] A Stauffer, 'The Goblin Men and the Flower Girl: New Sources for "Goblin Market"' (2018) 56 *Victorian Poetry* 47.

[84] Tucker (n 81) 123.

[85] ibid 124 and 127.

[86] *GM* line 44.

[87] R Menke, 'The Political Economy of Fruit' in Arseneau et al (n 63) 105.

[88] ibid 118–19. See also T Holt, '"Men Sell not Such in any Town": Exchange in *Goblin Market*' (1990) 28 *Victorian Poetry* 51, 52.

[89] E Campbell, 'Of Mothers and Merchants: Female Economics in Christina Rossetti's "Goblin Market"' (1990) 33 *Victorian Studies* 393, 398.

Lizzie (and women in general). There they are engaged in active production of food (cream, butter, honey and cakes, for example) for themselves and others. Sowards sees this as Rossetti advocating for a 'stateless gift economy … [where] the means of production and the products themselves are held in common';[90] for him *Goblin Market* is not so much about the smallness and safety of the home versus the large and amorphous nature of the market but rather a contrast between a preferable intimacy and localism and the brutality and remoteness of capitalism.

Contracts within *Goblin Market*

Goblin Market is about systems of exchange from Laura and Lizzie's attempts to buy fruit through Rossetti's use of the language of economics[91] to, I will argue, the subtle overtones of prostitution and eventual marriage. Some of these exchanges are exchanges in the legal textbook tradition of contract, others of which are unenforceable contracts in that tradition but are nevertheless still creatures of the market as Laura and Lizzie move from using coins to their own bodies as consideration, from agency as subject to the object of exchange.[92] Macneil draws no distinction between contracts that possess the badge of legal enforceability and those, typically family and domestic arrangements, that do not.[93] The Goblins represent the potential brutality of the marketplace. The transactions that Laura and Lizzie undertake are not undertaken with Goblin 'men'[94] but with the abstract generality of the commercial system the Goblins represent, which Rossetti saw unfolding all around her. We know from her letters that Rossetti, despite being able to call upon her domestic staff, was fond of shopping in London and other locations she visited such as Frome, Bath and Torquay, although for household goods rather than food.[95] The women approach the marketplace as spinsters who are running their own home successfully not bound by social convention or law to anyone else's will. Perhaps the antagonism of the Goblins is explained by the fear of spinsters within Victorian society that Auchmuty identifies.[96]

[90] R Sowards, '*Goblin Market's* Localism' (2012) *Modern Philology* 114, 133. Sowards is reluctant to accept Menke's conclusions about the origin of the Goblin's fruit and his conclusions about the role of the fruit as 'pure commodity' (Menke (n 87) 126). However, their individual conclusions are closer than either might accept.

[91] Holt points to the use of words such as *inter alia* 'stock', 'money' and coin to conclude that the dominant motif of *GM* is economic, see Holt (n 88).

[92] See K Lysack, *Come Buy, Come Buy: Shopping and the Culture of Consumption in Victorian Women's Writing* (Ohio University Press, 2000) 1–14 and the literature contained therein.

[93] I Macneil, 'Exchange Revisited: Individual Utility and Social Solidarity' (1986) 96 *Ethics* 567, 585.

[94] Rossetti could not be clearer that the Goblins are not human: see line 375–76 'such fruits as these no man can carry' and lines 101 and 556 'men sell not such in any town'. She ascribes animalistic features to them, see lines 71–74 and 332–47.

[95] C Tarr, 'Covent Goblin Market' (2012) 50 *Victorian Poetry* 297.

[96] Auchmuty (n 39) 46.

For Macneil the philosophy of contract is one of relationships that are intertwined and evolve over time. Even what seems to be the barest of contexts is embedded in the social matrix of the parties' lives and the social and economic life of society.[97] Contract is social behaviour rooted in co-operation, the function of which is to plan exchange into the future. Within this notion of co-operation, the parties retain their separate goals; the significance of this is that Macneil believes that co-operation is key, not to the conclusion of the transaction, but to the attainment of these separate goals. By co-operation Macneil means not the sacrifice or subjugation of self-interest but rather a dynamic of self and shared interest between the parties that brings them together and keeps them together so that each can achieve their own aim.[98] Macneil places contracting behaviour in the third level of his three-tier structure.[99] The base level for any society is shared meanings around things like language. On those shared meaning are built the political and social structures of civic life such as laws against theft and guarantees that laws will uphold exchange behaviour, say. At the third level come Macneil's 10 external and internal norms (not rules) which he asserts will be present at different levels of intensity in every exchange and will change over time: role integrity, reciprocity, flexibility, consent, planning, contractual solidarity, power and the linking norms of reliance, expectation and restitution, propriety of means, and harmonisation of the social matrix.[100]

The first exchange scenario in *Goblin Market* is Laura's evening visit to the Goblins. Laura accepts the Goblins' terms for transacting – a lock of her hair as consideration for fruit that she then consumes immediately. She gives her hair, freely, in exchange for the fruit, maintaining her agency as a purchaser. In exchanging her hair for fruit,[101] is Laura signalling that she is offering herself in exchange for fruit? Is her contract one of prostitution?[102] Macneil's norm of consent is present, but whether his other norms such as power, contractual solidarity and genuine reciprocity are, or can ever be present, depends on how we construct the prostitution contract. If we take the view of radical feminists, prostitution represents the sale of women,[103] violence against women and the embodiment of male power over women. A liberal feminism sees prostitution as one of many forms of paid work for women,[104] and here we might situationally interrogate Macneil's

[97] I Macneil, 'Contract Adjustments of Long-Term Economic Relations under Classical, Neoclassical and Relational Contract Law' (1978) 72 *Northwestern University Law Review* 584.

[98] S Wheeler, 'Modelling the Contracts of the Future' (2017) 26 *Griffith Law Review* 593.

[99] I Macneil, 'Relational Contract Theory: Challenges and Queries' (2000) 94 *Northwestern University Law Review* 877.

[100] I Macneil, 'Values in Contract: Internal and External' (1983) 78 *Northwestern University Law Review* 340.

[101] For a discussion of the role of women's hair in Victorian literature, see E Gitter, 'The Power of Women's Hair in the Victorian Imagination' (1984) 99 *Publications of the Modern Language Association of America* 936.

[102] See Holt (n 88) 58.

[103] C Pateman, *The Sexual Contract* (Polity Press, 1988) 204–07.

[104] M Nussbaum, 'Whether from Reason or Prejudice: Taking Money for Bodily Services' (1998) 27 *Journal of Legal Studies* 693.

norms.[105] A critique grounded in postmodernism sits between these two positions centring on social, economic and cultural factors around money, migration and legal regulation.[106] For Helsinger, when Laura (and Lizzie, because Lizzie[107] does have a silver coin) leave the private space of their home and its domestic economy and move into the public economic space occupied by the market they cross a 'fictive' boundary that, within Victorian literature at least, only the prostitute can cross.[108] On this basis, despite her apparent agency as a purchaser, she also becomes, in Marxian terms,[109] the object of the exchange. The tear she 'dropp'd' simultaneously might be in recognition of the likely societal price (evidenced in *Goblin Market* by her physical decline)[110] that she would pay for this transaction;[111] this might have been the price that the shadowy figure of Jeanie paid. It seems clear that Laura was aware of the danger posed by contracting in public.[112] In that vein, rather than prostitution, what Laura's actions indicated was how disadvantaged women were in a market that did not value, in a monetary sense, any of the domestic activities around food production that she and her sister undertook in and around the home.

The final scene of *Goblin Market* describes Laura as the storyteller to an audience made up of her children and Lizzie's children. She tells them about the Goblins and their market, the fruit that they sold and the danger that came from this ('their fruits like honey to the throat [b]ut poison in the blood).[113] Solidarity was to be found in domestic relationships. Laura's contractual struggle with the Goblins in a setting where her means and systems of production are not acceptable to the masculine market can be set against Rossetti's own journey to commercially experienced author. We have already touched upon her position in relation to the status of women within the aesthetic market. In the early years of her literary career, six of her first eight published poems appeared in *The Germ*, the Pre-Raphaelite journal organised by her brothers, under a pseudonym, albeit a female one: Ellen

[105] See eg C Overall, 'What's Wrong with Prostitution?' (1992) 17 *Signs* 705, 715 for a discussion of reciprocity.

[106] J Scoular, 'The "Subject" of Prostitution: Interpreting the Discursive, Symbolic and Material Position of Sex/Work in Feminist Theory' (2004) 5 *Feminist Theory* 343, 348.

[107] A variety of different explanations have been offered for how Lizzie obtained the silver coin and what it means: see, for example, Menke (n 87) 127, and V Mendoza '"Come Buy": The Crossing of Sexual and Consumer Desire in Christina Rossetti's Goblin Market' (2006) 73 *Journal of English Literary History* 913, 929.

[108] E Helsinger, 'Consumer Power and the Utopia of Desire: Cristina Rossetti's "Goblin Market"' (1991) 58 *Journal of English Literary History* 903. Despite this comment Helsinger rejects the idea that Laura is a prostitute on the grounds that she is not excluded by Rossetti from polite society. What Helsinger seems rather to be suggesting is that Rossetti is constructing a female political economy in contrast to the mores and structures of the emerging retail economy.

[109] R Bowlby, *Just Looking* (CUP, 1985).

[110] *GM* lines 211, 264–68, 277–80 and 293–98.

[111] ibid 126 and 127.

[112] ibid 42, 43, 52 and 70.

[113] ibid 554–55.

Alleyn.[114] But from 1861 onwards Rossetti appears to be an experienced market actor conducting her own business affairs and determinedly keeping artistic control of her work, particularly around illustration.[115] She corresponds with Alexander Macmillan regarding cheques for publishing in *Macmillan's Magazine*, where poets were paid by the page and surrendered copyright.[116] In 1870 she breaks off negotiations with Macmillan over copyright retention in *Sing-Song* and then negotiates unsuccessfully with FS Ellis for its production.[117] She receives £35 from them for 'delay'.[118] *Sing-Song* is eventually published by Roberts Bros in Boston on copyright and royalty terms that Rossetti finds acceptable.[119] She places her next collection, *Speaking Likenesses*, with Macmillan in 1874,[120] and again she negotiates over copyright and the choice of illustrator.[121]

Many of Macneil's norms are present in Rossetti's contractual dealings, not least expectation, reliance and harmonisation of the social matrix. Alexander Macmillan typifies Macneil's explanation of co-operation[122] in contract in his construction of his long-term, interpersonal relationships with Rossetti and other authors.[123] This is not about a turn to altruism or to offering unconditional support of the arts on Macmillan's part but rather a recognition on his part that his self-interest is advanced by reaching sustainable arrangements on royalties and such like.[124] We might contrast this with Lizzie's experience. She is unable to agree the terms of her exchange with the Goblins. She wishes to purchase the fruit with her money and then remove herself and the fruit back to the home she shares with Laura – the fruit is for Laura after all. The Goblins want her to sit down and eat with them.[125] They want this so badly that they physically attack her.[126] Lizzie stood firm 'like a rock'[127] against this attack which we might see as an attempted rape,[128] or at least resistance by Lizzie to become the object of exchange.[129] The Goblins throw

[114] Harrison, *The Letters of Christina Rossetti* vol 1 (n 50) 30, letter 18.

[115] L Kooistra, *Christina Rossetti and Illustration: A Publishing History* (Ohio University Press, 2002) 93–101.

[116] Harrison (n 114) 143, 146, letters 131, 136.

[117] ibid letter 427 at p 355.

[118] L Kooistra, 'Copyright and Control: Christina Rossetti and her Publishers' in D Clifford and L Roussillon (eds), *Outsiders Looking In* (Anthem Press, 2004) 968.

[119] Harrison (n 114) 369, letter 446.

[120] This was offered first to Roberts but declined by them, see ibid 418, letter 509.

[121] A Harrison (ed), *The Letters of Christina Rossetti* vol 2 (University of Virginia Press, 1999) 6, 9, letters 543 and 548.

[122] I Macneil, 'A Primer of Contract Planning' (1975) 48 *Southern California Law Review* 627.

[123] M Joseph, *Victorian Literary Businesses* (Palgrave Macmillan/Springer Nature, 2019) 159ff.

[124] L Mulcahy, 'The Limitations of Love and Altruism – Feminist Perspectives on Contract Law' in Mulcahy and Wheeler (n 42) 1, 10–14, and I Macneil, 'Contracting Worlds and Essential Contract Theory' (2000) 9 *Social and Legal Studies* 431.

[125] *GM* line 380.

[126] ibid lines 424–30.

[127] ibid 410.

[128] D Mermin, 'Heroic Sisterhood in "Goblin Market"' (1983) 21 *Victorian Poetry* 107, 112.

[129] Helsinger (n 108) 923.

Lizzie's money back to her and squeeze fruit on her. This failed exchange takes place in Macneil's third layer of societal practices where his internal and external norms sit. It is hard to see how any of the ones we might expect to be present in a spot exchange designed like this – contractual solidarity, harmonisation of the social matrix, effectuation of consent, planning – are, in fact, present in Lizzie's interaction.

It becomes clear in this final scene that both Lizzie and Laura have married and have children post their encounters with the Goblins. Given Rossetti's own religious views and the position taken by 'polite' society in which she would have been immersed, it is unsurprising that redemption through marriage is Laura and Lizzie's fate. Exactly what they are being redeemed from – spinsterhood, prostitution, leaving their domestic idyll, exposure to danger – depends on one's interpretation of the poem. Rossetti saw marriage as a 'joy',[130] but not necessarily as the only route to happiness; Laura and Lizzie's life pre-marriage is referred to as 'those pleasant days long gone'.[131] The small number of Rossetti's contemporaries who railed against marriage saw it as a 'slave status'[132] or akin to prostitution because in both situations women are exchanging their bodies for subsistence.[133] Alongside her conception of marriage as a site of gendered power, Auchmuty describes it ironically as considered by the Victorians to be a woman's noblest vocation.[134]

In Macneil's terms, though, the marriage as an exchange relationship[135] rather than marriage as institution is seen as a positive illustration of the accuracy of his norms. For all the reasons that marriage can be described as a status relationship – the parties do not decide the terms, they cannot plan what breach of contract looks like or what the remedies for it will be, consent and also equality, until relatively recently, are problematic issues[136] – it is a contract that is embedded in a 'social matrix', one that exists against a backdrop of established social meanings and contains many non-promissory elements. Exchanges of terms either at the time of the marriage or before it could express the parties' emotional commitment and describe a standard of performance in ideological and general terms.[137] However, there is often no specificity or individualisation applied to marriage vows nor do the parties enter a pre-nuptial arrangement.[138] But whatever standard form promises are made, they remind the couple of the goal of maintaining a

[130] *GM* line 313.
[131] ibid line 550.
[132] JS Mill, *The Subjection of Women* (Longmans et al, 1870) 147.
[133] J Butler, 'Introduction' in J Butler (ed), *Women's Work and Women's Culture* (Macmillan, 1869) iv.
[134] Auchmuty (n 39) 41.
[135] I Macneil, in F Snyder (ed), 'Relational Contracting in a Digital Age' (2005) 11 *Texas Wesleyan Law Review* 675, 680ff.
[136] M Bergman, 'Status, Contract, and History: A Dialectical View' (1991) 13 *Cardozo Law Review* 171.
[137] E Scott and R Scott, 'Marriage as Relational Contract' (1998) 84 *Virginia Law Review* 1225.
[138] S Thompson, 'Feminist Relational Contract Theory: A New Model for Family Property Agreements' (2018) 45 *Journal of Law and Society* 617.

caring and co-operative relationship in which selfishness and commitment to the relationship will interchange.[139] As a putative long-term relationship, a marriage also requires flexibility and trust. Power is important in any context where social relations matter. It needs to be negotiated and sits alongside reciprocity as a key internal issue.

Endings

I hope that I have conveyed my admiration for Rosemary Auchmuty's scholarship. Her career stands testament to not only her engaging and rigorous work but also to her bringing to the foreground new areas of academic interest and methodologies within legal studies. In this contribution I have sought to return us to the world of Victoriana where Rosemary's work began and tie that to some of the observations she made some years later about the role of gender and power in contract law. Just as she brought together a discussion of how women's lives in the private sphere of the home were shaped by the very public social pressure of marrying, I have tried to explain the consequences in contract terms of the protagonists of *Goblin Market* leaving their domestic setting for more public market-based activity. Rosemary has reflected upon the potential negative consequences of heterosexual relationships where discussions between couples are 'mediated through social norms which limit the ability of the woman to negotiate'.[140] Macneil places all such interactions within his contract schema which offer us a variety of different norms for structuring individual negotiations. Above this *Goblin Market* models a particular sort of relationship; an interdependence. Laura and Lizzie enjoy an alliance where weakness and strength are constantly shifting between them, but each of them protects the other as this occurs. Theirs is a form of universal kinship but one which avoids the use of patriarchal language. It illustrates and underscores the importance of Macneil's enduring social relations.

[139] I Macneil, 'Political Exchange as Relational Contract' in J Martin (ed), *Generalised Political Exchange* (Westview Press, 1990) 151.

[140] R Auchmuty, 'The Rhetoric of Equality and the Problem of Heterosexuality' in Mulcahy and Wheeler (n 42) 51, 61.

8

The Heroines, the Underdogs, and Everything In-between: Injecting a Feminist Approach into Family Law History

SHARON THOMPSON

Introduction

To assume histories of family law have been hospitable spaces for feminist approaches is to misunderstand the history of family law. Though family law is inextricably *linked* with feminism – given the gendered power entrenched within legal questions about intimate relationships – it is perhaps more accurate to describe feminism and family law as having connected yet conflicting ideologies. Indeed, traditional descriptions of family law history tend to be based on the notion of family law as having evolved steadily, from being rooted in patriarchal structures towards a system which aims to protect the autonomy and equality of family members.[1] Such dominant accounts of legal developments are often blinkered, as those producing these accounts have focused mostly (or even solely) on the work of institutions: law reform bodies (most notably the Law Commission of England and Wales), the courtroom, and Parliament.[2] Understanding the processes of such institutions in reforming law has obvious importance. But in a world of law-making that has historically been led by men,[3] women – and the grass roots pressure groups led by women – have tended to be obliterated from histories of family law reform.

Rosemary Auchmuty has been at the forefront of challenging such historical accounts; rewriting stories of law by asking the 'woman' question, and thus

[1] As observed by M Minow, 'Forming underneath Everything that Grows: Toward a History of Family Law' (1985) 4 *Wisconsin Law Review* 819, 819.

[2] S Thompson, *Quiet Revolutionaries: The Married Women's Association and Family Law* (Hart, 2022) 14.

[3] S Fredman, *Women and the Law* (OUP, 1998) 2.

transforming understandings of the past. Yet while her work is valuable in encouraging us to locate women within legal scholarship in this first place, this chapter argues that her *critical* intervention has been exploring precisely what this entails, and how a feminist approach can be injected into legal histories, including family law. That is, there are numerous examples of feminist history in action, however, significantly less has been written about the discipline of feminist *legal* history and what this approach means.[4] Thus, Auchmuty's influence is perhaps best described as discipline-defining because she lifts the lid on feminist legal history and looks underneath its application to articulate both its importance and its strategies for the development of law.[5]

This chapter reflects upon how Auchmuty's work in this area has shaped my own perspective when writing family law history. It examines the influence of the Married Women's Association;[6] a feminist group that shaped married women's property rights in the twentieth century, yet whose work is not acknowledged in most family law accounts. Auchmuty and Rackley's guidelines for 'doing' feminist legal history help us understand why this is so. Part One explores Auchmuty and Rackley's assertions that 'heroine' narratives are to be avoided.[7] It argues that this not only has ramifications for our understanding of family law history. Rather, acknowledging this narrative tells us something about the feminists reforming family law too. In many cases, such reformists were themselves students of feminist history, inspired to campaign for women's emancipation by their feminist foremothers – and by heroine narratives. Then in Part Two, Auchmuty's approach to feminist history, and in particular her work on Olive Stone is considered in respect of the Married Women's Association's campaigns.[8] It shows how Stone worked closely with the Association on numerous unsuccessful Bills, suggesting that a feminist approach, which challenges orthodox views of 'failure' ultimately produces a more nuanced account of family law history. As this chapter concludes, such nuance is vital both when understanding the past, and also when navigating strategies for family law reform today.

Part One: The 'Heroines' and the 'Underdogs'

Ray Strachey was an important figure in the suffrage and post-suffrage movement, not just because of her activism, but because of her work as a feminist

[4] As Russell Sandberg has argued, there is also significantly more literature on the broader discipline of feminist legal studies than there is on feminist legal history: R Sandberg, *Subversive Legal History: A Manifesto for the Future of Legal Education* (Routledge, 2021).

[5] Minow (n 1) 819.

[6] Thompson (n 2).

[7] E Rackley and R Auchmuty, 'The Case for Feminist Legal History' (2020) 40 *Oxford Journal of Legal Studies* 878, 897.

[8] R Auchmuty and J Temkin, 'The Road to Olive Stone' in U Schultz, G Shaw, M Thornton and R Auchmuty (eds), *Gender and Careers in the Legal Academy*, Oñati International Series in Law and Society (Hart, 2021) 441.

historian. In *The Cause*,[9] Strachey charts the history of feminist campaigns from 1860 to 1920. The book has become a 'classic' of the nineteenth century women's movement.[10] It is a product of Strachey's insider status within the National Union of Women's Suffrage Societies (NUWSS) and as secretary to the NUWSS leader and prominent suffragette campaigner Millicent Fawcett. In it, Strachey tells of valiant individuals leading a series of successful campaigns to forge the path to women's suffrage and emancipation. The women in *The Cause* are united, and the story, as historian Rosalind Delmar has put it, 'is one of trials, vicissitudes, but eventual success'.[11] It highlights individual women as pioneers, and the heroic stories of their achievements.[12] Thus, while Strachey's book is still considered to be a major work of the women's movement, it arguably falls into the trap of the 'heroine narrative'.[13] And as Auchmuty and Rackley remind us, such 'pioneer narratives are not without pitfalls'.[14]

This section uses Auchmuty's work to explore the power of the heroine narrative and how it can limit the scope of what is included within histories of feminist activism. First, the heroine narrative is further explained, as are Auchmuty and Rackley's direct calls to identify and question it. Then, it is argued that Auchmuty's work challenges heroine narratives not only explicitly, but implicitly too, because she complicates our understandings of what makes women throughout history 'feminist'. Finally, this section concludes by considering how such narratives influenced the Married Women's Association, which the latter half of this chapter argues was an important organisation within family law history.

The Heroine Narrative

In questioning Strachey's *The Cause*, it is important not to undermine its significance as a text that is regarded as one of the best introductions to the history of feminism at the turn of the twentieth century. Thus, identifying the book's heroine narrative is certainly not grounds for its dismissal; it simply underlines the importance of critically evaluating its context, and of not treating any single source as definitive. But it *is* a trap of which one must be aware. And, as Barbara Caine has suggested, adopting an approach to the women's movement similar to Strachey's is 'no longer accepted as appropriate by historians of feminism'.[15]

Auchmuty and Rackley explain the 'heroine trap' as including 'inspirational women' who 'succeeded against all odds, and who negotiated – and defeated – patriarchal

[9] R Strachey, *The Cause: A Short History of the Women's Movement in Great Britain* (Virago, 1928).
[10] R Delmar, 'What is Feminism?' in J Mitchell and A Oakley (eds), *What is Feminism?* (Blackwell, 1986) 14.
[11] ibid 23.
[12] B Caine, 'Feminist Biography and Feminist History' (1994) 3 *Women's History Review* 247, 249.
[13] Rackley and Auchmuty (n 7) 897.
[14] ibid.
[15] Caine (n 12) 249.

hostility to make some important contribution to "mankind"'.[16] Furthermore, they explicitly identify the avoidance of heroine narratives as an important part of 'doing' feminist legal history. As they have put it: 'The danger is that if you set out with the intention of casting someone as a heroine or a role model, you are going to craft a life story to suit'[17] – a fiction that can obscure difficult personalities, fractious relationships and success tempered by setback. The attraction of such narratives is plain; the story is simple, accessible, encouraging, even soothing. But it is folklore. In the case of *The Cause*, the story is attractive in its portrayal of the women's movement as an undivided, consistent pursuit of women's suffrage; as Delmar suggests, 'it provides a certain reassurance in the example of women acting together in a united way'.[18] The 'climax', she notes, 'is the triumph of the vote'.[19] Underlying unity is assumed, and conflict is explained as resulting from diverging strategy and tactics rather than ideology.[20] Yet as we now know, the quest for suffrage was anything but linear, and was often fraught by dissention – Fawcett and Pankhurst did not speak with one voice[21] – and even within individual associations, there was frequent in-fighting.[22]

Strachey's focus on individuals as focal points within the women's movement is problematic too. Landmarks in feminist history cannot be explained by one heroine, or event, or idea. Just as progress tends to be neither steady nor united, feminist histories are inherently complicated, and are often fragmented by intellectual and cultural difference. However, it is understandable why Strachey presented the story of suffrage as she did. Her approach aligned with that of traditional biographies and legal histories, which have often been characterised as the 'study of great or exceptional people'.[23] Yet this is a mould which few women neatly fit into.[24] Focusing on the pioneers of the women's movement as Strachey has done skews the reality of collective activism. As Auchmuty and Rackley have put it:

> By ignoring feminists' situation within a wider movement, at best we risk (often following their lead) downplaying their significant achievements and sacrifices as (partly) consequences of being in the 'right place at the right time' (or some variant thereof). At worst, we ignore and silence the many, many women and supportive men whose names and stories we don't know.[25]

Challenging this model of pioneers presents a challenge to orthodox legal history. And this is one of the reasons Auchmuty's work is so significant. Instead of focusing

[16] Rackley and Auchmuty (n 7) 897.
[17] ibid 897–98.
[18] R Delmar (n 10) 23.
[19] ibid 21.
[20] ibid 17.
[21] See eg J Purvis (ed), *Women's History: Britain, 1850–1945: An Introduction* (Routledge, 2008); J Purvis, *Emmeline Pankhurst: A Biography* (Routledge, 2003).
[22] See eg Brian Harrison's work on Teresa Billington Greig: B Harrison, *Prudent Revolutionaries: Portraits of British Feminists between the Wars* (OUP, 1987) 45.
[23] Caine (n 12) 250.
[24] ibid.
[25] Rackley and Auchmuty (n 7) 899.

on public achievements, Auchmuty recovers the lives of figures such as Gwyneth Bebb and her role in women's admission to the legal profession.[26] Auchmuty's documentation of Bebb's experiences, while probing why she was previously ignored in historical records, is a direct challenge to traditional legal history.[27] It exemplifies how feminist legal history is distinctive from orthodox approaches. By seeking to understand the daily struggles of women[28] such as Bebb who are 'hidden from history',[29] Auchmuty's work looks in the opposite direction of those accounts that focus upon public achievements. Her work goes against the heroic model that Caine has suggested 'supplied the model for many studies of feminist activists'.[30] Furthermore, in delineating a method for feminist legal history which is conscious of avoiding stereotypes and superficial narratives, Auchmuty has played a vital role in elevating feminist legal history 'not simply as a niche or marginal sub-discipline, but an integral part of the story that must be told'.[31]

Avoiding the Trap

As well as warning us about the pitfalls of the heroine narrative, Auchmuty's work also uncovers the complexities of feminism, something that heroine narratives are at risk of riding roughshod over. By complicating our understandings of what 'feminist' means, Auchmuty is also implicitly challenging heroine narratives. This is because such narratives sometimes present a narrow and united view of feminism, and potentially exclude women who were not neatly siloed into 'the cause'. Returning to Strachey's work, for example, Delmar has argued that in failing to acknowledge the complexities of feminist ideology, *The Cause* unfairly omits prominent Victorian campaigner Caroline Norton, because of her apparent rejection of equality. Yet Norton played an important role in changes to the law on custody and divorce – significant landmarks in the history of women's emancipation.[32] However, her public views did not fit Strachey's united story. In her open letter to the Queen, Norton declared: 'The natural position of woman is inferiority to man … I never pretended to the wild and ridiculous doctrine of equality'.[33] Strachey accepts this as Norton's view, thus inferring Norton is not feminist because of her perception of women's emancipation. But Auchmuty's approach probes deeper.

[26] R Auchmuty, 'Whatever Happened to Miss Bebb? *Bebb v The Law Society* and Women's Legal History' (2011) 31 *Legal Studies* 199.
[27] R Auchmuty, 'Recovering Lost Lives: Researching Women in Legal History' (2015) 42 *Journal of Law and Society* 34.
[28] Caine (n 12) 250.
[29] S Rowbotham, *Hidden From History: 300 Years of Women's Oppression and the Fight* (Pluto Press, 1977).
[30] Caine (n 12) 250.
[31] Rackley and Auchmuty (n 7) 886.
[32] R Delmar (n 10) 23.
[33] C Norton, 'A Letter to the Queen on Lord Chancellor Cranworth's Marriage and Divorce Bill' (1855) in P Hollis (ed), *Women in Public: The Women's Movement 1850–1900* (George Allen & Unwin, 1979) 183.

The context of the Victorian women's movement is important, Auchmuty argues, for 'no one *seriously* argued that the sexes could be 'equal' in the modern sense; they 'were not fighting for "equality", but rather for justice'.[34] Auchmuty questions Norton's intentions instead of accepting them at face value, asking '*did she mean*' it when she said equality was 'wild and ridiculous', or was she being tactical?[35] After all, the context of these comments is important – Norton was appealing publicly for support from powerful, yet conservative individuals.

Thus, feminist legal history must acknowledge the complexity of feminist ideas, as Auchmuty does in her work. It is only by recognising the *fragmentation* of feminist ideas, that one can identify where feminist activism is actually happening. This is significant for family law history, as my work has shown.

Married Women's Association

Within family law history, an apposite example of a group fraught with infighting and constant setbacks was the Married Women's Association (MWA); a group formed in 1938 with the goal of equal partnership in marriage through law reform. They were active until the 1980s and demanded a 'new marriage law' – underscoring what Auchmuty has also sought to highlight in her own work – that is, the myth that marriage protects women economically during marriage.[36] The Married Women's Association wanted to provide spouses with rights in their partners' property during marriage – a proposal which was never implemented. But their ideology was interesting – it was politicising the family sphere and breaking down the barriers between public and private. By achieving legal and economic equality inside the home, so the argument went, married women of the 1940s, 1950s and 1960s would be better equipped to pursue equality also in the public sphere. And, by representing housewives in a legal setting, the Married Women's Association was mounting the first significant challenge against the legal status of married women since the Married Women's Property Act 1882. As MWA founder Juanita Frances put it: 'I'm not asking for protection [for married women], I'm asking for legal rights in hard cash'.[37] In the context of family law, this was radical and had huge significance. When the Association formed, married women had no rights over their husband's separate property, little opportunity to earn money outside the home, and depended on their spouse for housekeeping allowance. The Association's housewife-centred approach therefore made strategic sense

[34] Rackley and Auchmuty (n 7) 884 (emphasis added).

[35] R Auchmuty, 'The Married Women's Property Acts: Equality Was Not the Issue' in R Hunter (ed), *Rethinking Equality Projects in Law: Feminist Challenges* (Hart, 2008) 13, 26 (original emphasis).

[36] R Auchmuty, 'The Limits of Marriage Protection: In Defence of Property Law' (2016) 6 *Oñati Socio-Legal Series* 1196.

[37] From a leaflet by the Humanist lobby, as quoted in BH Lee, *Divorce Law Reform in England* (Peter Owen 1974) 201.

given the broader socio-political context, whereby the deeply entrenched roles of housewife and breadwinner represented the archetypal marriage of the 1940s and 1950s. By strengthening the domestic position of married women as different but of equal value to the breadwinning husband, the Married Women's Association could couch radical property reform in relatively conservative terms that did not threaten the conventional marriage contract of the day.

Recognising the importance of this group within family law history also exemplifies an approach that takes intellectual history seriously[38] because it forces us to assess conflicting ideologies about women's emancipation, as well as different beliefs about the meaning of equality within marriage. Even within the Association, there were intense disagreements over the best way to value women's work in the home. While some were in favour of husbands paying their wife a 'wage', others saw this as reinforcing unequal hierarchies within marriage and instead advocated the sharing of assets such as income and the home.

The work of the MWA is also connected to heroine narratives, as the members themselves exemplify how such narratives have impacted family law reformers. The members of the MWA were themselves feminist historians and were influenced by texts such as *The Cause*. MWA founder and Chair Juanita Frances credits *The Cause* for helping to educate her about the women's movement.[39] It was studying feminist history that made Frances political; after not knowing who to vote for in the 1935 general election, she joined the Fawcett library and read everything she could on the suffrage movement. Strachey's book, according to Frances, 'pointed the way'.[40] Frances' discovery of feminist politics in her thirties, thanks in part to *The Cause*, led her to meet former suffragette Dorothy Evans, who in turn recognised Frances' leadership potential and placed her in charge of the fledgling MWA. But while *The Cause* was, to Frances, a 'call to arms', there is also evidence to suggest it set her up for disappointment. Take, for example, her comment in the editorial of the MWA's publication *Wife and Citizen*: '[W]e of MWA are very chicken-hearted in our efforts compared with those of the very courageous pioneer suffragettes'.[41] Perhaps this rather disheartened remark is understandable. For the newsworthy, sometimes militant methods of those 'courageous pioneers' documented in *The Cause* did seem to contrast starkly with the behind-the-scenes efforts of the MWA to reform married women's property rights. As Barbara Caine suggests, the 'persistent yet always polite lobbying of MPs' helped make the work of the MWA and other similar groups "much less visible" than their predecessors.[42]

[38] See R Sandberg, and N Doe, 'Textual and Contextual Legal History' in N Doe and R Sandberg (eds), *Law and History, Vol 1: Critical Concepts in Law* (Routledge, 2016) 1; R Sandberg, 'The Time for Legal History: Some Reflections on Maitland and Milsom Fifty Years On' (2018) 180 *Law and Justice* 21.

[39] Brian Harrison interview with Juanita Frances, 14 November 1974, 8SUF/B/022, The Women's Library Archives, LSE, London.

[40] Michael Summerskill interview with Juanita Frances, SUMMERSKILL/1/46, The Women's Library Archives, LSE, London.

[41] *Wife and Citizen*, April 1951, 7TBG/1/32, The Women's Library Archives, LSE, London.

[42] B Caine, *English Feminism 1780–1980* (OUP, 1997) 174.

Militant methods had subsequently been abandoned because, once enfranchised, women felt they could not spurn parliamentary methods, and pursued a path of political pragmatism instead.[43] But did this make the MWA 'chicken-hearted', or worthy of exclusion from histories of family law? Clearly not. Indeed, Auchmuty's work sheds light on why heroine narratives can be harmful both to activism and histories of activism:

> There are many stereotypical narratives for pioneer women, each designed to inspire, but just as likely to produce the opposite effect. As well as the heroine and the role model, there is the straightforward narrative of success – she did this, and this, and this – with never a hint of disappointment or setback.[44]

This may help to explain why the MWA has been curiously ignored in histories of family law reform. Yet 'doing' feminist legal history as Auchmuty, Rackley, and others do[45] takes the emphasis away from greatness, removing 'the exceptional framework from the study of women's lives'.[46] In doing so, feminist legal history can redefine histories of family law. Omitted from institutional narratives of family law reform, the private experiences of women, and the lives of those in little-known Associations such as the MWA, cease to be viewed as historically irrelevant.[47]

While appearing to romanticise the work of the suffragettes in public, Juanita Frances appeared to be more realistic about the women's movement in private. When speaking to historian Brian Harrison towards the end of her life, she observed: '... any person or organisation are just cogs in a wheel. We do what we can but it doesn't rest on us if we go under and somebody else will come along'.[48] Such statements sit in direct contrast to the heroine narrative. It appears that the MWA did *not* expect to be recognised in legal histories as their foremothers were. But when studying their history, and their comparative lack of success, readers are not given an impression that with enough persistence reform will happen. Readers are not set up for failure. Rather, MWA stories of anti-climax and defeat rectify misleading, evolutionary narratives of progress.[49]

Part Two: The Importance of Studying 'Failure'

A corollary of the heroine narrative is that other stories are lost. Thus, a logical extension of debunking such stereotypical accounts is exploring feminist activism that has *not* necessarily resulted in success, yet has left some imprint on law.

[43] Harrison (n 22) 1.
[44] Rackley and Auchmuty (n 7) 898.
[45] F Batlan, 'Engendering Legal History' (2005) 30 *Law and Social Inquiry* 823.
[46] Caine (n 12) 252.
[47] Which Caine notes is a primary goal of women's history: ibid 250.
[48] Harrison interview with Juanita Frances (n 39).
[49] Delmar (n 10) 23.

Such instances may be regarded as 'failures' in an orthodox sense; the goal was not achieved, and the statute was not passed. But as Auchmuty has shown time and again, when viewed through a feminist lens, ostensible failures are in fact important interventions in legal history, unacknowledged in textbook accounts.[50] One example of this in Auchmuty's oeuvre is her biographical research on Olive Stone.[51] Olive Stone was an expert in family law, and supported reform of married women's property rights. She lectured in law at the London School of Economics (LSE) and bequeathed a proportion of her estate to the LSE for a scholarship for a female law student.[52] She challenged the Royal Commission on Marriage and Divorce in the 1950s for not doing enough to reform the law on maintenance, providing practical recommendations for reform that could benefit economically vulnerable married women.[53] And then in the 1960s and 1970s, she worked with feminist activists to push for reform of married women's property rights. Yet Olive Stone is not widely known. She was not the first female law lecturer (she was the third), nor did she ever become a professor. Her contribution to family law scholarship and reform has thus been overlooked until Auchmuty (with Jennifer Temkin) researched her life and career. This section reflects on the importance of this work for family law history, which is inextricably linked with my work on the MWA in obvious ways – Stone worked closely with the MWA – and in less obvious ways – both brought attention to the issue of married women's property rights at a time when the focus was reform of divorce.[54]

When writing about Olive Stone, Auchmuty does not identify Stone's successes and failures, but instead documents what Stone managed to achieve in spite of the obstacles she faced. Yet again, Auchmuty is challenging the heroine narrative by researching Olive Stone. Stone's work does not fit stereotypical accounts of pioneers and heroes; the legislation she helped draft did not make it onto the statute books, and the feminist groups she worked with did not have much success either when viewed in an orthodox way. But considering her participation behind the scenes of law reform processes is important and shows once again the significance of Auchmuty's contribution and perspective.

One example of Stone's participation within law making processes is her influence on family property law in the 1960s and 1970s. As Auchmuty documents in her work with Temkin, Stone played an integral role in discussions about reform to married women's property rights at this time,[55] and as my archival research has shown, she was an important contact for the MWA as they sought to promote legislation in this vein. She advised the Association on the law, drafted the

[50] Rackley and Auchmuty (n 7) 878.

[51] Auchmuty and Temkin (n 8) 441.

[52] Preferably women who were mature, single and childless: ibid, 441.

[53] OM Stone, 'The Royal Commission on Marriage and Divorce: Family Dependents and Their Maintenance' (1956) 19 *Modern Law Review* 601, 609.

[54] Auchmuty and Temkin (n 8) 441, Thompson (n 2); R Auchmuty, 'Feminism, Property and Divorce Law Reform in the 1960s' *Fifty Years of the Divorce Reform Act 1969* (Hart, 2022) 75.

[55] Auchmuty and Temkin (n 8) 449.

Association's bills and wrote letters on the group's behalf to the Law Commission and MPs. She operated as a valuable intermediary between the Association and policymakers because she provided guidance that highlighted the significance of the MWA's equal partnership proposals and translated legal documents into accessible language for MWA members with no legal training. She was also an important contact as she was influential in the world of law reform. For instance, she was consulted by the Law Commission and provided a report on legal rights of inheritance and general advice on the problems affecting family property law. Stephen Cretney has suggested that the 1970 seminar[56] at which she presented this report 'seems to have very much set the agenda for subsequent Law Commission work on the subject' of family property law reform.[57] Many of the conclusions reached at this seminar clearly fed into the Commission's *First Report on Family Property* in 1974.[58] Perhaps most importantly, Stone shared similar ambitions to the MWA for reform of property ownership during marriage.

One of these views was that reform of divorce should not overshadow the urgent need to reform married women's property rights. When the President of the Family Division Jocelyn Simon attacked the common law rules about matrimonial property as failing to value women's work in the home and leaving them economically vulnerable,[59] Stone stated that his views represented 'a long, cool look at the law of matrimonial property' and a 'witty attack' on the common law.[60] When the Divorce Reform Bill was before Parliament in the late 1960s, she agreed with the MWA – and their former President Edith Summerskill – that the reform should be delayed until matrimonial property reforms could be introduced. These views culminated in a significant, and now mostly forgotten Bill: the Matrimonial Property Bill 1969.

Matrimonial Property Reform

Stone and the MWA's powerful resistance to divorce reform morphed into a concrete obstacle: Edward Bishop's Matrimonial Property Bill in 1969. Before explaining this connection in more detail, however, it is important to understand the significance of the Bill itself. The Matrimonial Property Bill was a Private Member's Bill that held up the passage of the Divorce Reform Act 1969. It was an important bill because it was the closest England and Wales came to introducing

[56] For further details of this seminar, which took place in late September 1970 at Langdale Hall, University of Manchester, see Thompson (n 2) 205.

[57] S Cretney, *Family Law in the Twentieth Century* (OUP, 2005) 136.

[58] Law Commission, *First Report on Family Property: A New Approach* (Law Com No 52 HMSO 1974).

[59] J Simon, 'With all my Worldly Goods …', Presidential Address (Holdsworth Club, University of Birmingham, 1 January 1964).

[60] OM Stone, '"With all my Worldly Goods …"' (1965) 14 *International and Comparative Law Quarterly* 707, 707.

some form of community of property in marriage – in other words, automatic joint ownership of assets. Stephen Cretney argued that it was a 'significant historical landmark' as the last Bill on this issue 'ever to be fully debated in either House of Parliament'.[61] It is not typically seen as significant, however, because it never reached the statute books and was withdrawn. However, looking closer at the context of the Bill helps explain why it was so important. In return for the withdrawal of the Matrimonial Property Bill, the government agreed to support a Bill drafted by the Law Commission reforming the financial consequences of divorce, and by extension, married women's property rights. As a result, the Bishop Bill is an overlooked, yet significant part of family law history. It helped delay the Divorce Reform Act 1969 so that economic inequalities between husband and wife on relationship breakdown could be addressed. And it brought the debate about how to value women's work in the home to the House of Commons. This debate in the Commons appears to have been taken into account by the Law Commission when preparing what became the Matrimonial Proceedings and Property Act 1970.[62] This was a landmark reform that provided for property redistribution on divorce because it was able to account for the contributions made by spouses through looking after the home or caring for the family.[63] It gave women the right to share in the property earned directly by their husbands on divorce, in recognition of the unpaid work they had done throughout the relationship. And it continues to underpin the law of financial remedies in England and Wales today.[64]

The influence of the Bill is especially significant given that the Law Commission had originally planned to save its recommendations with respect to property division for a later report.[65] Documents in the National Archives indicate that while the Law Commission was interested in reforming the financial consequences of divorce, they did not plan to focus on this matter until after divorce reform was introduced.[66] The Matrimonial Property Bill and its widespread support amongst women's rights activists pressurised the Law Commission into acting sooner. This Bill brought married women's property rights to the top of the agenda, for the Law Commission and the Government feared that this Bill threatened to introduce community of property and to squash the passage of the Divorce Reform Act 1969, which in their view would be disastrous.[67]

[61] Cretney (n 57) 136.

[62] BC3/401, The National Archives; D Stetson, *A Woman's Issue: The Politics of Family Law Reform in England* (OUP, 1982) 202. Stetson also notes the influence of the concept of family assets developing in the courts in the late 1960s.

[63] Section 5(1)(f) Matrimonial Proceedings and Property Act 1970 and s 25(2)(f) of the consolidating Matrimonial Causes Act 1973.

[64] It was consolidated in the Matrimonial Causes Act 1973, which governs the financial consequences of divorce in England and Wales.

[65] Stetson (n 62) 202.

[66] Chairman of the Law Commission Leslie Scarman admitted in a letter to Leo Abse MP that he was 'certain' the reform culminating in the 1970 Act 'would not have been ready in time': Letter from Leslie Scarman to Leo Abse, 17 September 1969, BC3/410, The National Archives, London.

[67] Letter from Leslie Scarman to Gerald Gardiner, 20 December 1968, BC3/406, The National Archives, London.

A lesser-known aspect of the Matrimonial Property Bill 1969 is that although it is attributed to Edward Bishop (often known as the 'Bishop Bill'), it was originally the MWA's Bill (though its provisions differed).[68] And, when Edward Bishop agreed to take the MWA's Bill forward, it was none other than Olive Stone who agreed to draft it. It is possible, therefore, to draw a connection between the Married Women's Association, Olive Stone, the Bishop Bill and the radical reform of financial remedies in the 1970s.

This in turn also helped to ignite conversations about further reform during the 1970s and 1980s that went beyond the Matrimonial Proceedings and Property Act 1970. Both Stone and the MWA contributed to discussions matrimonial property reform that included automatic co-ownership of the matrimonial home and changes to inheritance. The MWA worked with Lord Simon and supported his 1980 Matrimonial Homes (Co-ownership) Bill, which was quashed in Parliament almost entirely by a lobby of MPs concerned about men's rights.[69] And, when this lobby of MPs helmed the Justice in Divorce Campaign in the 1980s seeking to abolish maintenance, Olive Stone and the MWA joined forces once again. In 1980, the Association included in its Bulletin a letter Olive Stone had sent to the *Times* on the Bill. In this letter, Stone asserted the Bill was important for two reasons:

1. Previous legislation has sought to regulate matrimonial property rights on relationship breakdown. This Bill is of 'far greater and more general significance' because it would grant equal rights and responsibilities by law to wives and husbands during the continuance of their marriage.
2. The law would make a decided shift from treating the married woman in the family home as her husband's dependant, to recognising her as his equal co-owner, 'with the status, responsibilities and rights that only ownership can bestow'.[70]

Stone's letter was never published in the *Times*. Stone and the MWA's calls for reform were ignored, married women's property rights were not extended, and their opponents within the Justice in Divorce Campaign had some success. By introducing 'clean break' orders, the Matrimonial and Family Proceedings Act 1984[71] greatly reduced the length of time for which husbands would be required to support financially their former wives after divorce. The consequences of the Act for women are perhaps summarised best by Smart, who argued it introduced: 'a firm principle into family law, namely that women must bear the full adverse consequences of their economic dependence on men – even though it is men who continue to accrue the benefits of that dependence'.[72] Indeed, at the time it was

[68] The MWA did not seek a community of property regime, and its Bill for equal partnership in marriage would instead have facilitated pooling of certain assets during marriage such as income.

[69] MWA Bulletin, April–May 1981, 5MWA/8/1, The Women's Library, London.

[70] MWA Bulletin, January–February 1980, 5MWA/8/1, The Women's Library, London.

[71] This Act inserted s 25A into the Matrimonial Causes Act 1973, imposing a duty upon the court to consider whether a clean break would be appropriate in the circumstances.

[72] C Smart, *The Ties That Bind* (Routledge, 1984) 242.

implemented a clean break was not a realistic option for spouses unable to become financially independent on divorce, and ever since the introduction of the clean break principle, research has consistently indicated that women take longer to recover financially from divorce than men do.[73] This is because, as Pamela Symes pointed out, a year after the Act's introduction, a coherent, clean break divorce would be unlikely unless the marital relationship had become 'a partnership of two economically independent individuals through the abolition of marital dependency and when the corresponding changes in the social infrastructure' were brought about.[74] And so, as the MWA had argued over the course of five decades, the goal of equal partnership in marriage needed to be attained if there was to be any hope of equality after divorce. In their view, the 1984 Act represented 'the first step to put back the clock on women's rights'.[75]

Rethinking Failure

This account of Stone's work with the MWA is typical of the indirect successes and myriad setbacks that define feminist legal history. As Auchmuty's work shows us, by focusing on individuals such as Stone, we can see how the history of feminist efforts to reform the law are characterised by disappointment, and at best, compromise.[76] It is also an example of how feminist legal history complicates understandings of failure. The work of Stone and the MWA are missing from family law textbooks, and their direct impact on successful legislation was limited. Though this may suggest 'failure', an approach influenced by Rackley and Auchmuty's guidebook to doing feminist legal history produces a wholly different view. Looking underneath law making processes uncovers how Stone and the MWA in fact played an integral role in building the foundations of our current law of financial remedies on divorce. As MWA Chair Dora Russell once argued:

> You can't just look at women's progress in terms of laws and Acts … you have to look at the area of relationships where women have been influential, and there you will see that there have been enormous changes.[77]

From *this* perspective, the word 'failure' is wholly inappropriate when applied to Stone's work with the MWA.

Despite this, Stone did appear to be frustrated and disappointed with the results of her efforts. In a letter to Helen Nutting – then Chair of the Council of Married Women – she expressed her disappointment that provisions for joint ownership in

[73] See eg H Fisher and H Low, 'Recovery from Divorce: Comparing High and Low Income Couples' (2016) 30 *International Journal of Law, Policy and the Family* 338.

[74] P Symes, 'Indissolubility and the Clean Break' (1985) 48 *Modern Law Review* 44, 60.

[75] MWA Bulletin, January–March 1983, 5MWA/8/1, The Women's Library, London.

[76] Rackley and Auchmuty (n 7).

[77] D Spender, *There's Always Been a Women's Movement This Century* (Harper Collins, 1983) 104.

the Bishop Bill (which she had helped draft) had not been incorporated into the 1970 reform:

> My own impression is that we shall delude ourselves if we think that the [Bishop] Bill had done its job. It has raised a real and substantial point and the judges have shown since that they largely agree with its aims. *But property is the holy of holies.* If women want it they will have to go in and get it. Nobody will offer it to them on a plate, but all sorts of smokescreens about bad drafting and the like will be raised to head them off. I hope they will keep on target.[78]

Stone therefore seemed well aware of the difficulties involved with pursuing reform of women's legal status, having experienced defeat in her own legislative efforts. And the MWA expressed very similar sentiments, stating that: 'Results have not been commensurate with effort and argument'.[79] Focusing on such ostensible failures produces nuanced and realistic accounts of feminist engagement with family law reform. This is important when understanding histories of feminist activism and is also vital when engaging with family law reform – both then, and now.

This shows the potential for rich histories to be uncovered when we heed Auchmuty's warning to avoid the trap of the heroine narrative. Stone's work with the MWA produces new accounts of family law history, and further debunks the notion that there was virtually no feminist activity between the first and second feminist 'waves', as Auchmuty has also noted.[80] While Stone and the MWA's work does not fit neatly within the Women's Liberation Movement – and is marginalised as a result – it nevertheless made a material difference to debates about the value of women's labour in the home.

Conclusion

Auchmuty's work demonstrates powerfully why it is important to inject a feminist approach into family law history. A feminist focus on family law reform provides important commentary *beyond* the family too, on how law is reformed more generally. Feminist analyses can usefully break down the boundaries between public and private, showing that far from being confined to the family unit, campaigns such as those instigated by the MWA could have broader policy implications for women's legal rights and responsibilities.

[78] Records of the Council of Married Women, 5CMW/B/22, The Women's Library, London (emphasis added), cited in D Stetson, *A Woman's Issue: The Politics of Family Law Reform in England* (OUP, 1982) 203.

[79] MWA Annual General Report, May 1963, 5MWA/3/1, The Women's Library, London.

[80] Auchmuty and Temkin (n 8) 441. See also C Beaumont, 'The Women's Movement, Politics and Citizenship 1918–1950s' in I Zweiniger-Bargielowska, *Women in Twentieth-Century Britain* (Routledge, 2001) 273.

But Auchmuty's work also goes further than the 'why' of feminist legal history. Rather, it is especially significant because it helps show feminist legal historians *how*. As well as Rackley and Auchmuty writing the 'guidebook', Auchmuty shows us how to do legal history through her biographical work uncovering the stories of women in law that have long been neglected. In doing so, she not only shows how the heroine narrative is an important trap to avoid, but also how it overshadows other important stories. In other words, Auchmuty presents a challenge to explore the opposite of heroine narratives, such as the Married Women's Association, whose work is absent from histories of family law because no direct legislative reform can be attributed to them. Yet exploring such work undoubtedly enriches our understanding of family law and its reform, for it highlights how indirect, behind-the-scenes work is often imperative for change to occur. Furthermore, a feminist approach if nuanced allows us to appreciate the messy, complex reality of reform and the context in which it operates. So, it reflects upon the nature of reform. And of law.

The MWA recognised this themselves, describing their work as being more notable for its 'ricochets' than its 'bulls'-eyes'.[81] The 'bulls'-eyes' are marked clearly by a new statute or precedent. The ricochets are the ostensible failures, that did in fact leave their mark. The MWA did not have many of the former to point to, noting instead: 'Experience has taught us not to expect the bulls'-eyes, but to view with satisfaction such ricochets as have furthered our cause'.[82] The MWA and Olive Stone's chronicle as family law reformers *is* perhaps best described in their own words as a series of 'ricochets', the impact of which can be seen by taking a feminist legal historical approach. Looking more closely at these ricochets and failed attempts at reform uncovers further evidence in support of the claims Auchmuty has long made in her work: that law is not a neutral arbiter, progress does not happen naturally, and institutions are not solely responsible for change.

This chapter has focused upon what Auchmuty's work teaches us about legal history. However, I want to conclude on a personal note, to acknowledge how the influence she has had through her published work is only part of the story. Just like the women she writes about, Rosemary Auchmuty has made a difference to the legal academy in innumerable, unrecorded ways, and for so many individuals, including me. When she examined my PhD, Auchmuty asked me what the role of feminist activism had been in the development of the law on prenuptial agreements. Though I had taken a feminist *theoretical* approach in my PhD, I had relied chiefly on legal, institutional sources when researching the *historical* context of these agreements. I had studied a history that was incomplete, because

[81] Quoting VS Pritchett, MWA Annual General Meeting, 11 May 1972, Secretary's Report for Year Ended 30 April 1972, 5MWA/3/1, The Women's Library, London: 'the long drawn out campaign for emancipation of women has been more noticeable for its ricochets than its bulls' eyes': MWA Annual General Meeting, 11 May 1972, Secretary's Report for year ended 30 April 1972, 5MWA/3/1, The Women's Library, London.

[82] ibid.

I had neglected the role of feminist activism. Discovering my omission changed the direction of my work. Auchmuty also influenced my work by inviting me to contribute a chapter on the Married Women's Property Act (MWPA) 1964 to *Women's Legal Landmarks*, a collection she co-edited with Erika Rackley.[83] In researching the history of the MWPA 1964 for this collection I discovered the members of the MWA – who had instigated this Act, and whom I'd never heard of previously, despite having studied family law for years. Thus, the scope of my own work has been transformed as a result of Rosemary Auchmuty. I am so grateful to her for opening my eyes to feminist legal history, and for encouraging me to investigate the history of family law through a different lens.

[83] E Rackley and R Auchmuty (eds), *Women's Legal Landmarks: Celebrating the History of Women and Law in the UK and Ireland* (Hart, 2019).

9

Change, Challenge and Resistance in Family Law

FELICITY KAGANAS AND ALISON DIDUCK

Introduction

In their introduction to *Women's Legal Landmarks*, Rosemary Auchmuty and Erika Rackley wrote: 'the process of law reform is presented as a tale in which enlightened institutions gradually reform themselves.'[1] Their feminist legal history challenges that view. They foreground women's role in effecting change and point to forces seeking to reverse it. So, while legal landmarks for women must be celebrated, whether they be policy achievements or court rulings, they are, as Auchmuty and Rackley remind us, 'almost always followed by a tightening of control by those whose power has been breached.'[2] In this chapter we will examine two 'landmarks' for women in family law. The first is the recognition within law and policy that domestic abuse is a serious social problem, that it goes beyond physical violence and that it includes coercive and controlling behaviour and so is best characterised as a pattern of behaviour rather than as individual incidents of violence. The second is law's promotion of non-discrimination and equality in the allocation of wealth on divorce and its acknowledgement of the value of homemaking and caregiving to the well-being of a family.

As important as these developments have been, Auchmuty and Rackley point out that 'the achievement of a landmark is rarely, if ever, the end of the story. Too often it signifies the start of another struggle; an even more bitter one since the impediments to justice and equality for women are no longer explicit but may be hidden, informal, and bolstered by practices not yet forbidden or even recognised'.[3] And they explain that feminist legal history sets out to challenge 'assumptions of

[1] E Rackley and R Auchmuty, 'Women's Legal Landmarks: An Introduction' in E Rackley and R Auchmuty (eds), *Women's Legal Landmarks* (Hart, 2019) 6.

[2] ibid 10.

[3] ibid 10–11.

unabated progress and liberal incrementalism by showing that legal reform is often messy, disjointed and episodic, that there is very often a backlash and regrouping by opponents, and that hard-won gains are easily lost …'[4] Nevertheless, they acknowledge that 'there have been and continue to be, important legal advances for women'.[5]

While each of the two landmarks we highlight is its own success story, we also highlight the 'impediments to justice and equality for women' as well as the backlash to these landmarks, now hidden within ideas of child welfare and women's autonomy and equality. Our aim is to adopt an approach consistent with Auchmuty and Rackley's feminist legal history which 'includes women's stories, experiences and voices' and focuses not only on law, but also on a 'nuanced view of how it operates'.[6]

Domestic Abuse

Evan Stark has observed that, 'the legal and policy responses to domestic violence are typically built on a violence model that equates partner abuse with discrete assaults or threats'.[7] He argues that this model fails to capture the entrapment of women in a pattern of abuse.[8] The seriousness of each incident is assessed separately and low level abuse is considered low risk.[9] He maintains that, '[d]espite the enormous accomplishments of the domestic violence revolution' it has not met its aim of improving women's prospects. This, he says:

> is largely the result of a paradigm that defines domestic violence as an incident-specific crime, equates abuse with physical and psychological assault, applies a 'calculus of harms' to assess severity (the more injury or trauma, the more serious the abuse), and rations intervention accordingly.[10]

Stark's criticism and his reframing of domestic abuse as a pattern of behaviour has, primarily as a result of feminist campaigning, led to the reform of both criminal and civil law. Yet in the long journey to reach this point, law reform has indeed been episodic and messy and its implementation continues to be grudging.

[4] ibid 5.
[5] ibid 1.
[6] ibid 5.
[7] E Stark, 'Re-Presenting Battered Women: Coercive Control and the Defense of Liberty', Prepared for Violence Against Women: Complex Realities and Violence in Changing World (Les Presses de l'Université du Québec, 2012) 1 www.stopvaw.org/uploads/evan_stark_article_final_100812.pdf.
[8] See also M Johnson, *A Typology of Domestic Violence: Intimate Terrorism, Violent Resistance and Situational Couple Violence* (University Press of New England, 2008).
[9] See C Wiener, 'Seeing What Is "Invisible in Plain sight": Policing Coercive Control' (2017) *The Howard Journal* 500, 504.
[10] E Stark, 'Rethinking Coercive Control' (2012) *Violence Against Women* 1509, 1510.

Criminal Law

Auchmuty has observed of the law in general that it has been implicated in the oppression of women and, in particular, '[l]aw's traditional reluctance to intervene in the private sphere allows some of the worst gendered oppression to go unchecked …'.[11]

Domestic violence is a paradigm example of law's reluctance to intervene in what was considered the private sphere.[12] Although there was a movement to improve the status and protection of wives in the 19th century,[13] it was only in the 1970s that there was a strong impetus for change and it came from feminist campaigners.[14] Feminist writers identified domestic violence as a serious social problem requiring action by public agencies. Feminist writers and campaigners also reframed domestic violence as being rooted in 'women's inferior status and dominant constructions of masculinity'.[15]

Yet, even so, the notion of family privacy persisted, particularly in relation to policing. The typical response was not to arrest but to treat domestic violence as a private family matter.[16] However after campaigners did succeed in making domestic violence a matter of public concern, police received instructions to adopt a more interventionist approach, including arresting perpetrators. New powers were conferred on the police too.[17] The terminology changed from that of violence to abuse. A new offence of Coercive or Controlling Behaviour in an Intimate or Family Relationship was enacted in 2015.[18] Most recently, the Domestic Abuse Act 2021 will broaden the language of statutory police powers from violence to abuse by means of Domestic Abuse Protection Notices and Orders.[19]

Yet despite this progress, several reports have been published over the years enumerating the shortcomings of the police and the CPS.[20] The same kinds of

[11] R Auchmuty, 'Introduction' in R Auchmuty (ed), *Great Debates in Gender and the Law* (Palgrave, 2018) xiv.

[12] A Diduck and F Kaganas, *Family Law, Gender and the State* (Hart, 2012) 552–54.

[13] ibid 554–56.

[14] ibid 556–58.

[15] ibid 559.

[16] RE Dobash and RP Dobash, *Violence Against Wives* (Free Press, 1979) 214. See generally Diduck and Kaganas (n 12) 464ff.

[17] Crime and Security Act 2010, ss 24–33. See below.

[18] Serious Crime Act 2015, s 76.

[19] See Domestic Abuse Act 2021, ss 22–49. See below. These provisions are not yet in force.

[20] See eg J Barron, *Not Worth the Paper … ? The Effectiveness of Legal Protection for Women and Children Experiencing Domestic Violence* (Women's Aid Federation of England, 1990); HM Crown Prosecution Inspectorate (HMCPSI) and HM Inspectorate of Constabulary (HMIC), *Violence at Home: A Joint Inspection of the Investigation and Prosecution of Cases Involving Domestic Violence* (Criminal Justice Joint Inspection, 2004); Home Department, *The Government Reply to the Sixth Report from the Home Affairs Committee Session 2007–8 HC263, Domestic Violence, Forced Marriage and "Honour"-Based Violence* (Cm 7450 2008); Association of Chief Police Officers and National Policing Improvement Agency, *Guidance on Investigating Domestic Abuse* (2008); HMIC, *Everyone's Business: Improving the Police Response to Domestic Abuse* (HMIC, 2014); HMIC, *Increasingly Everyone's*

problems have been repeatedly identified and it is by no means certain that the new Act will eliminate them. It was observed that the police were responding to women's accounts with disbelief, they were failing to arrest perpetrators, they were down-criming or no-criming, they were failing to use body-worn cameras and to build evidence-based cases, and they were failing to act on breaches of court orders. And while the most recent inspection report[21] noted improvements, still there were found to be 'unexplained variations' in the use of protective measures and some forces were 'not paying sufficient attention' to breaches of orders.[22] Police failure to pursue cases suggested that evidence-based cases were not being built[23] and the failure to pursue cases of coercive or controlling behaviour suggested that the police do not understand how to deal with these.[24] The report noted that 'the continued failure to identify patterns of behaviour, and the associated likely escalation of risk, is very worrying' and that the problems in the way breaches of orders were being dealt with could persist under the Domestic Abuse Act.[25] Another recent report[26] recorded that neither the police nor the CPS was identifying cases suitable for an evidence-led approach[27] and reasonable lines of enquiry were being missed.[28] Finally, it seems that sentencing has remained lenient[29] despite Sentencing Guidelines that were intended to ensure that courts treated offences more robustly.[30]

So, although the law has changed, its implementation has been patchy. Within the criminal justice system, understandings of domestic abuse and of how women and girls present as victims remain simplistic; assumptions about women's mendacity persist; and the trivialisation of abuse continues. These problems are manifested also in the implementation of the civil law.

Business: A Progress Report on the Police Response to Domestic Abuse (HMIC, 2015); Her Majesty's Inspectorate of Constabulary and Fire & Rescue Services (HMICFRS), *A Progress Report on the Police Response to Domestic Abuse* (HMICFRS, 2017); HMIC, *PEEL: Police Effectiveness 2016. A National Overview* (HMIC, 2017); HMICFRS, *The Police Response to Domestic Abuse; An Update Report* (HMICFRS, 2019); HMICFRS, *Police Response to Violence against Women and Girls. Final Inspection Report* (HMICFRS 2021). See, also, Solace Women's Aid and Justice Studio Ltd, *"When I Needed You to Protect Me, You Gave Him More Power Instead": Covid-10 Lockdown and Domestic Abuse* (2021) 23–24 www.solacewomensaid.org/sites/default/files/js_and_solace_when_i_needed_you_25.03.21_1_0.pdf. See, on the CPS, HMCPSI and HMICFRS, *Evidence Led Domestic Abuse Prosecutions* (2020).

[21] HMICFRS, *Final Inspection Report* (n 20).

[22] ibid 10, 12.

[23] ibid 12.

[24] ibid 39.

[25] ibid 70.

[26] HMCPSI and HMICFRS, *Evidence Led Domestic Abuse Prosecutions* (n 20).

[27] ibid para 1.2.

[28] ibid para 6.5.

[29] Women's Aid, *Transforming the Response to Domestic Abuse Consultation: Response from the Women's Aid Federation of England* (Women's Aid 2018) 57 www.womensaid.org.uk/wp-content/uploads/2018/05/Transforming-the-Response-to-Domestic-Abuse-Consultation-Response-from-Womens-Aid-31-May-2018.pdf; *R v Dalgarno* [2020] EWCA Crim 290.

[30] Sentencing Council, *Overarching Principles: Domestic Abuse* (2018) www.sentencingcouncil.org.uk/overarching-guides/crown-court/item/domestic-abuse/.

Civil Law

In 1975 a Select Committee was established to consider domestic violence and child abuse and to make recommendations.[31] McCabe records that these problems were brought to public attention by women's organisations[32] and that the Select Committee was set up in response to the new public awareness.

The Domestic Violence and Matrimonial Proceedings Act 1976 was passed as a result and introduced injunctions to prohibit molestation of victims and ouster orders by means of which the perpetrator could be excluded from the home. Further legislation followed[33] but still a number of problems were identified in relation to the scope and implementation of the law.[34]

Barron's research, published in 1990, showed that ouster orders were difficult to get and were referred to by judges as a last resort[35] since they interfered with the perpetrator's property rights.[36] The police and the courts did not respond appropriately to breaches of orders,[37] and courts were reluctant to send perpetrators to prison. In 1992 the Law Commission criticised the law too. It stated that the law was confusing and complex.[38] It did not address post-separation violence adequately and the criteria for ousters focused on the seriousness of the defendant's behaviour rather than its effect on the victim and children.[39]

The Family Law Act 1996 was intended to address some of these criticisms. It provided for non-molestation orders and occupation orders, which could be made to regulate occupation of the home. Unlike its predecessors, the statute covered a variety of relationships and extended to post-separation violence. Also, the degree of harm suffered by victims and children was included in the criteria for orders.

However, the reported cases suggest that courts continued to regard occupation orders as Draconian[40] and, it seems, until the decision in *Dolan v Corby*,[41] they were considered appropriate only in cases of serious[42] physical violence.[43] The police were still not using their powers of arrest; courts were not treating breaches

[31] S McCabe, 'Unfinished Business' (1977) *British Journal of Criminology* 280.

[32] E Pizzey, *Scream Quietly or the Neighbours Will Hear* (Penguin Books, 1974).

[33] Domestic Proceedings and Magistrates Court Act 1978, Matrimonial Homes Act 1967, Matrimonial Homes Act 1983. See also the Protection from Harassment Act 1997.

[34] See, generally, S Edwards, *Sex and Gender in the Legal Process* (Blackstone Press, 1996) 213ff.

[35] Barron (n 20) 50.

[36] Judges also called them draconian: Law Commission, *Family Law. Domestic Violence and Occupation of the Family* Home (Law Com No 207 HMSO 1992) para 2.26.

[37] Barron (n 20) 65 and 69.

[38] Law Commission (n 36) 1.2.

[39] ibid 2.26.

[40] *Chalmers v Johns* [1999] 1 FLR 392, 397.

[41] [2011] EWCA Civ 1664.

[42] *Chalmers v Johns* (n 40) 397.

[43] *G v G (Occupation Order: Conduct)* [2000] 2 FLR 36, 41. See M Burton, *Legal Responses to Domestic Violence* (Routledge-Cavendish, 2008) 39ff.

seriously; imprisonment was reserved for repeated breaches and sentences were short.[44] Humphreys and Thiara reported that lenient treatment emboldened abusers and made victims feel beyond protection.[45]

Yet further changes to the law were made[46] but again the law was declared confusing[47] and, as a result, the Domestic Abuse Act 2021 was passed.

On its face, this legislation might be called another women's legal landmark. It provides the first legal definition of domestic abuse,[48] building on the updated cross-government definition[49] and the offence of controlling or coercive behaviour. It adopts the terminology of abuse rather than violence[50] and the definition moves away from an incident focused approach. Instead, the definition centres on abusive behaviour which takes in a range of behaviours and can require an appraisal of the dynamics of the abusive relationship rather than limiting the court's deliberations to selected incidents.

In the light of all these changes, it can be said that the law now reflects a better understanding of the experiences of abused women and offers better protection. However, how the Domestic Abuse Act will be applied remains to be seen and there may well be regressive responses to it. The persistence of misogynistic tropes and stereotypical images of perpetrators and victims mean that this is almost certainly not the 'end of the story'.[51]

The reforms to the civil and criminal law have not always been understood or implemented as intended, and this seems to have been the result of entrenched attitudes, beliefs and myths about domestic abuse, about property and about false allegations. While this does not appear to have been the result of a 'backlash' or 'regrouping', there has been a severe backlash in another arena: the family courts dealing with disputes about children.

[44] Burton (n 43) 39ff.

[45] C Humphreys and R Thiara, *Routes to Safety* (Women's Aid Federation of England, 2002) 210.

[46] S10 Domestic Violence, Crime and Victims Act 2004.

[47] HM Government, *Transforming the Response to Domestic Abuse: Government Consultation* (HM Government, 2018) 34–35.

[48] The Act also replaces Domestic Violence Protection notices and orders with Domestic Abuse Protection notices and orders. However, when and if these provisions will come into force is not known. The Act also contains measures to make it easier for victims to go through the court processes. In addition, it extends the offence of controlling or coercive behaviour to cover post-separation abuse.

[49] See eg Home Office, *Information for Local Areas on the Change to the Definition of Domestic Violence and Abuse* (Home Office and AVA, 2013) assets.publishing.service.gov.uk/government/uploads/system/uploads/attachment_data/file/142701/guide-on-definition-of-dv.pdf.

[50] The heading of Part IV of the Family Law Act refers to domestic violence.

[51] The legislation while in Bill form was criticised: Women's Aid Federation England 2020, *Joint Recommendations Briefing for the Domestic Abuse Bill* (Women's Aid Federation England, 2020) 1 and 3. For the problems relating to the offence of coercive and controlling behaviour, see C Hanna, 'The Paradox of Progress: Translating Evan Stark's Coercive Control into Legal Doctrine for Abused Women' (2012) *Violence Against Women* 1459, 1465–67. See on evidential problems in the criminal law context, C Bishop and V Bettinson, 'Evidencing Domestic Violence including Behaviour that Falls under the new Offence Of "Controlling Or Coercive Behaviour"' (2018) *International Journal of Evidence and Proof* 3.

Contact/Child Arrangements Orders

For decades, the family courts have stressed the importance for children to have a relationship with both parents after divorce or separation. The courts have operated a de facto presumption in favour of contact with the non-resident (usually) father.[52] Hunt and Macleod, for example, observed that courts have been willing to 'bend over backwards' to establish or continue contact.[53]

The priority accorded to contact has been driven both by legal interpretations of 'psy' knowledge suggesting that a relationship with both parents is best for children[54] and by the intense lobbying of fathers' rights groups, arguing that the involvement of fathers should be given equal importance to that of mothers and that equal involvement is best for children.[55]

Carol Smart, writing in 1989, argued that prevailing constructions of welfare coupled with equality arguments from fathers' rights groups made fathers' claims almost unanswerable.[56] This has continued to be the case in spite of the fact that the evidence of the benefits of paternal involvement for children in general is far from unequivocal.[57]

It has been held that even domestic violence should not constitute a bar to contact,[58] although Practice Directions have been issued to promote safety. The most recent, Practice Direction 12J, 2010 Family Procedure Rules, requires the court to consider holding a fact finding hearing[59] and to ensure that any child arrangements order for contact does not expose the child or primary caretaking parent to a risk of harm.[60]

Barnett, reviewing the literature, reports that 'fact-finding hearings were usually restricted to allegations involving incidents of recent, very severe physical violence'.[61] Where there was no fact-finding, the judge would tend to ignore allegations of abuse.[62] And while post-2014 studies showed a better judicial and

[52] See eg *Re O (Contact: Imposition of Conditions)* [1995] 2 FLR 124, 128. See also eg *Re C (Direct Contact: Suspension)* [2011] EWCA Civ 521, para 47; *Re H (Minors) (Access)* [1992] 1 FLR 148, 152, See, for a discussion of the cases, Diduck and Kaganas (n 12) 446ff.

[53] J Hunt and A Macleod, *Outcomes of Applications to Court for Contact Orders After Separation or Divorce* (Ministry of Justice, 2008) 190; Diduck and Kaganas (n 12) 392ff.

[54] See Diduck and Kaganas (n 12) 391ff.

[55] ibid 391. See also *V v V (Contact: Implacable Hostility)* [2004] EWHC Fam 1215, para 4; *Re D (Intractable Contact Dispute: Publicity* [2004] EWHC Fam 727, para 4; *Re C (Residence Order)* [2007] EWCA Civ 866, para 24.

[56] C Smart, 'Power and the Politics of Child Custody' in C Smart and S Sevenhuijsen (eds), *Child Custody and the Politics of Gender* (Routledge, 1989) 9.

[57] See eg Diduck and Kaganas (n 12) 388–97.

[58] *Re L (Contact: Domestic Violence); Re V (Contact: Domestic Violence); Re M (Contact: Domestic Violence); Re H (Contact: Domestic Violence)* [2002] 2 [FLR] 334.

[59] PD 12J para 16.

[60] ibid para 5, 36.

[61] A Barnett, *Domestic Abuse and Private Law Children Cases, A Literature Review* (Ministry of Justice, 2020) 93.

[62] ibid.

professional 'theoretical' understanding of abuse as going beyond the physical, non-physical abuse is not necessarily taken seriously.[63]

The enactment of section 1(2A) of the Children Act 1989 has compounded the problems faced by mothers seeking to resist contact. This provision seems to have been, at least in part, a response to pressure from fathers' rights groups.[64] It has been seen as a bid to send a message[65] to those groups that their demands were being heard, and it is intended to impress on the public at large the importance of the involvement of both parents. The provision creates a presumption that the involvement of a parent seeking a section 8 child arrangements order under the Children Act is best for the child(ren) unless it can be shown that involvement will 'put the child at risk of suffering harm'.[66] And, importantly, it is also presumed that the involvement of the parent seeking an order will not cause such harm.[67]

The presumption has attracted criticism, notably in the Harm Report.[68] This report was commissioned by the Ministry of Justice to assess

> how effectively the family courts identify and respond to allegations of domestic abuse and other serious offences, in cases involving disputes between parents about the arrangements for their children.[69]

It reported that, in the family courts,

> abuse is systematically minimised, ranging from children's voices not being heard, allegations being ignored, dismissed or disbelieved, to inadequate assessment of risk, traumatic court processes, perceived unsafe child arrangements, and abusers exercising continued control through repeat litigation and the threat of repeat litigation.[70]

So, although it appears that the statutory presumption has had little effect on decision-making,[71] it has been suggested that it strengthens the pro-contact culture in the courts and should be reviewed.[72] And recently, in the courts themselves, there appears to be a nascent recognition of the dangers of abuse and the need to be alert to the presence of coercive control.[73]

[63] ibid 88–90.

[64] See eg F Kaganas, 'A Presumption that "Involvement" of Both Parents Is Best: Deciphering Law's Messages' (2013) *Child and Family Law Quarterly* 270.

[65] ibid.

[66] Section 1(6).

[67] Section 1(6).

[68] R Hunter, M Burton and L Trinder, *Assessing Risk of Harm to Children and Parents in Private Law Children Cases. Final Report* (Ministry of Justice, 2020).

[69] ibid, 'Executive Summary' para 2.

[70] ibid, 'Executive Summary' para 8.

[71] F Kaganas, 'Parental Involvement: A Discretionary Presumption' (2018) *Legal Studies* 549; J Harwood, 'Presuming the Status Quo? The Impact of the Statutory Presumption on Parental Involvement' (2021) *Journal of Social Welfare and Family Law* 119.

[72] Hunter et al (n 68) paras 7.3, 11.4; Ministry of Justice, *Assessing Risk of Harm to Children and Parents in Private Law Children Cases. Implementation Plan* (Ministry of Justice, 2020) 4; Harwood (n 71).

[73] *Re H-N and Others (children) (domestic abuse: finding of fact hearings)* [2021] EWCA Civ 448; *Re B-B (Domestic Abuse: Fact Finding)* [2022] EWHC 108 (Fam).

In *Re H-N*,[74] the Court of Appeal gave judgment in four appeals from decisions in fact finding hearings concerning allegations of domestic abuse made in the course of proceedings under the Children Act 1989. It provided guidance for family courts and considered, in particular, 'whether, where domestic abuse is alleged in proceedings affecting the welfare of children, the focus should in some cases be on a pattern of behaviour as opposed to specific incidents.'[75]

The court observed that the concept of domestic violence is outdated and that courts are recognising the need to focus on abusive patterns of behaviour;[76] coercive and/or controlling behaviour is central to current definitions of abuse.[77] The court also noted that children can be harmed by coercive control[78] and this suggests that, at least in some cases, contact with the non-resident parent may no longer be the overwhelming priority.

Another indication of progress is that a pilot is now in place to improve information sharing between agencies, including sharing of risk assessments to enable judges to gather information pre-trial 'so that more emphasis can be put into investigating and addressing allegations of domestic abuse'.[79] The Domestic Abuse Commissioner's monitoring and reporting mechanism is also being piloted to '[i]ncrease understanding' in and 'accountability' of family courts'.[80] In addition, a review of the presumption has begun.[81]

However, a recent report[82] notes that understandings of coercive control are still poor and that courts and professionals do not understand that fathers use child arrangements proceedings as a strategy of abuse. There is insufficient understanding of 'the impact of coercive control on survivors, and the ways perpetrators use it post-separation'.[83] Nor is the impact of domestic abuse on children understood. Courts did not seem cognisant with judgments such as *H-N* and, indeed, the report refers to the recent case of *K and K*[84] where abuse was minimised and the mother's allegations disbelieved. Although the court in that case did cite *H-N*, it focused on statements in the *H-N* judgment and in Courts and Tribunals Judiciary Guidance[85] that not all cases involving allegations of abuse require a fact-finding hearing. The authors of the report observe that:

[74] *Re H-N* (n 73).

[75] ibid para 1. See also *F v M* [2021] EWFC 4; *Re B-B* (n 73) paras 6(i), 94.

[76] *Re H-N* (n 73) paras 23–25, 52.

[77] ibid para 29.

[78] ibid paras 31, 52.

[79] Ministry of Justice, HM Courts and Tribunals Service, Lord Wolfson KC, 'Press Release: Pioneering Approach in Family Courts to Support Domestic Abuse Victims Better' (2022) www.gov.uk/government/news/pioneering-approach-in-family-courts-to-support-domestic-abuse-victims-better.

[80] Women's Aid, *Two Years, Too Long: Mapping Action on the Harm Panel's Findings* (Women's Aid, 2022) 21.

[81] ibid 24.

[82] ibid ch 3.

[83] ibid 26.

[84] [2022] EWCA Civ 468.

[85] Courts and Tribunals Judiciary, 'Fact-Finding Hearings and Domestic Abuse in Private Law Children Proceedings – Guidance for Judges and Magistrates' (5 May 2022) www.judiciary.uk/

> The guidance and judgment are examples demonstrating the argument that progress has stalled, and in some cases, gone backwards, since the publication of the Harm Report and the H-N judgment …. It appears that … a lack of both resources and understanding continues to operate as a barrier to the courts' effective consideration of domestic abuse allegations.[86]

In *K and K* the judge was of the view that despite serious allegations of abuse, the parents should have attended a MIAM (mediation information and assessment meeting). This emphasis on diversion from litigation is apparent also in the report of the Family Solutions Group[87] which has advocated change that contradicts the recommendations of the Harm Report. Instead of identifying the problem as a failure of the courts to protect women and children, it says the issue is that too many parents turn to the courts and that the solution is to divert them to mediation or counselling; the problem of domestic abuse is sidelined.[88]

K and K was also a case where the mother's allegations of rape and abuse were countered by the father's allegation of parental alienation, a strategy that has been increasingly used by abusers and that has been highlighted by Birchall and Choudhry.[89] It is a matter of concern that any reforms to ameliorate the problems facing mothers and children, particularly those subject to domestic abuse, stand to be undermined by the 'mainstreaming' of the notion of parental alienation.[90]

This concept has largely replaced 'implacable hostility', a label which was used to denote those mothers considered unreasonable and vengeful. Originally termed Parental Alienation Syndrome, it was described by Faller[91] as a 'circumstance in which a child demonstrates a strong affinity for one parent and alienation from the other'. Parental alienation has more recently been defined by Cafcass as 'an ongoing pattern of negative attitudes, beliefs and behaviours of one parent (or carer) that have the potential or expressed intent to undermine or obstruct the child's relationship with the other parent. It is one of a number of reasons why a child may

announcements/fact-finding-hearings-and-domestic-abuse-in-private-law-children-proceedings-guidance-for-judges-and-magistrates/.

[86] Women's Aid (n 80) 26.

[87] Sub-group of the Private Law Working Group.

[88] Women's Aid, *The Harm Report – One Year On* (The Transparency Project, 2021) www.transparencyproject.org.uk/the-harm-report-one-year-on/. See also Women's Aid (n 80) and Hunter et al (n 68). See Family Solutions Group, *'What About Me?' Reframing Support for Families Following Parental Separation* (Family Solutions Group, 2020) www.judiciary.uk/wp-content/uploads/2020/11/FamilySolutionsGroupReport_WhatAboutMe_12November2020-2.pdf-final-2.pdf.

[89] J Birchall and S Choudhry, *'What About My Right not to Be Abused?' Domestic Abuse, Human Rights and the Family Courts* (Women's Aid, 2018) 32–36.

[90] *Re S (A Child: Transfer of Residence)* [2011] 1 FLR 1787, para 46. See *RS v SS* [2013] EWHC B33 (Fam).

[91] K Faller, 'The Parental Alienation Syndrome: What Is It and What Data Support It?' (1998) *Child Maltreatment* 100. See also JR Johnston, 'Children of Divorce Who Reject a Parent and Refuse Visitation: Recent Research and Social Policy Implications for the Alienated Child' (2005) 38 *Family Law Quarterly* 757, 762.

reject or resist spending time with one parent post-separation'.[92] It applies only to false allegations of abuse; if the child's resistance is adjudged to be linked to child abuse or domestic abuse, it is not alienation.[93]

The term 'parental alienation syndrome' was coined by Richard Gardner, a psychiatrist, and the remedy, according to him, is to cut off contact with the alienating parent so that the child can be deprogrammed. Despite the fact that his work has largely been discredited and that the term 'syndrome' has been dropped,[94] parental alienation has been increasingly accepted by professionals and the courts as a valid 'diagnosis' or assessment. This has happened in spite of the fact that:

> There is no commonly accepted definition of parental alienation … as well as an absence of robust scientific and empirical studies on how it is or should be identified, understood, assessed and treated, the majority being US studies with methodological limitations.[95]

And while researchers espousing the concept of parental alienation concede that children's resistance to contact can be caused by multiple factors, including abuse, rather than simply the mother's hostility,[96] the theory is founded upon a belief that allegations of abuse are typically false and are 'merely evidence of an aligned parent's campaign of alienation'.[97] As long as an abuser can convince the court that the child has been alienated, the court is likely to transfer residence to the abuser; the protective parent (mother) is pathologised[98] and accused of emotional abuse.[99]

Birchall and Choudhry[100] report that participants in their study said that former partners or their legal representatives used allegations of alienation to 'rebut allegations of domestic or child abuse'.[101] Participants felt stereotyped as

[92] Cafcass, 'Alienating Behaviours' (Cafcass 2022) www.cafcass.gov.uk/grown-ups/parents-and-carers/divorce-and-separation/what-to-expect-from-cafcass/alienating-behaviours/.

[93] See Faller (n 91) 101. But see *F v M & Ors*: [2022] EWFC 89, paras 12, 14.

[94] Faller (n 91): J Meier, *Parental Alienation Syndrome and Parental Alienation: A Research Review* (National Resource Center on Domestic Violence, 2013); J Kelly and J Johnston, 'The Alienated Child: A Reformulation of Parental Alienation Syndrome' (2001) 39(3) *Family Court Review* 249; J Doughty, N Maxwell and T Slater, 'Professional Responses to "Parental Alienation": Research-Informed Practice' (2020) 42(1) *Journal of Social Welfare and Family Law* 68, 71–73.

[95] Barnett (n 61) 61 (references omitted).

[96] JR Johnston and JB Kelly, 'Commentary on Walker, Brantley, and Rigsbee's (2004) "A Critical Analysis of Parental Alienation Syndrome and Its Admissibility in the Family Court"' (2004) 1(4) *Journal of Child Custody* 77.

[97] Meier (n 94) 8.

[98] ibid 9–10.

[99] J Birchall and S Choudhry, '"I Was Punished for Telling the Truth": How Allegations of Parental Alienation are Used to Silence, Sideline and Disempower Survivors of Domestic Abuse in Family Law Proceedings' (2021) 6(1) *Journal of Gender-Based Violence* 1, 7; S Lapierre and I Cote, 'Abused Women and the Threat of Parental Alienation: Shelter Workers' Perspectives' (2016) *Children and Youth Services Review* 120, 125.

[100] Birchall and Choudhry (n 89) 8.

[101] See also A Barnett, 'A Genealogy of Hostility: Parental Alienation in England and Wales' (2020) 42(1) *Journal of Social Welfare and Family Law* 18.

vengeful or mentally unstable.[102] Children's wishes were discounted.[103] Measures to protect children such as withdrawing contact were construed as evidence of alienation:[104]

> participants' testimonies demonstrated the ways that mothers who are also survivors of domestic abuse can be positioned as overprotective, unable to put the past behind them, and blocking contact between child and parent for no good reason.[105]

Over one third of the mothers in the focus groups and interviews had children moved to live with the perpetrator as a result of allegations of alienation.[106] Other mothers were forced to send children for contact they considered unsafe for fear of losing their children.[107]

It is clear from Birchall and Choudhry's research that it is not only the notion of alienation that is problematic. It is also the stereotypes of mothers and uninformed perceptions of abuse that have been so prevalent in the courts. Allegations of abuse are met with disbelief[108] and mothers are frequently portrayed as obsessive[109] and overprotective as well as manipulative and vengeful liars.[110] These attitudes persist and may continue to do so, despite the sanguine view of the judge in *Re H-N* that judicial training and proper application of PD12J ensure that 'errors' are the exception.[111] As Burton and Bettinson remark, the submissions to the Harm Panel suggest that 'the idea that the cases where something goes wrong are isolated; a result of a few judges who do not understand the "modern approach", is not something which is entirely supported by the evidence'.[112] Mothers who are seen to be obstructing the father's relationship with his child are considered to pose a far greater danger to their children than abusive fathers, whose behaviour is played down. Damage to children is also brushed aside; they are moved despite the court's acknowledging, as in *Re H*,[113] that the move risks causing the child 'emotional harm and trauma'.

The backlash to changing perceptions of domestic abuse and the reform of the law to reflect them has come in the form of the concept of alienation which has been linked to the welfare principle and operationalised by abusive men.

[102] Birchall and Choudhry (n 89) 11–12.
[103] ibid 13.
[104] ibid 8.
[105] ibid 11.
[106] ibid 12.
[107] ibid 13–14.
[108] *Re H (Parental Alienation)* [2019] EWHC 2723 (Fam).
[109] *D (Children)* [2010] EWCA 496 Civ.
[110] In *RS v SS* (n 90) the court was critical of a mother who was found to be alienating. She was described as 'argumentative', 'wilful and angry' and as having a 'powerful personality'. She was not meeting the educational needs of the children and residence was transferred 70, 109, 104.
[111] *Re HN* (n 73) para 224.
[112] M Burton and V Bettinson, 'Domestic Abuse and Child Arrangement Proceedings: Identifying and Assessing the Risk of Harm, Including Coercive and Controlling Behaviour' (2022) *Child and Family Law Quarterly* 3, 10.
[113] *Re H (Parental Alienation)* [2019] EWHC 2723 (Fam), para 31.

And it is the support for the concept[114] and the attitudes in the courts and among professionals, rather than the letter of the law that leave mothers and children unprotected. As long as negative assumptions and stereotypes about mothers persist, and as long as children's views are discounted, 'errors' will occur.

Property and Finance on Divorce

Auchmuty's work as a feminist historian tells us much about law reform and its reverses and her analysis can be applied not only to the way law deals with domestic abuse, but also to the way in which law has addressed the financial consequences for women of marriage and divorce. She has offered us feminist histories of the Married Women's Property Acts[115] and the Divorce Reform Act.[116] She has also shed light upon how the law of property, rather than family law, may or may not help those in family relationships[117] including those in same sex relationships.[118] Her historical work focuses upon campaigns for legal change and the usually overlooked women who inspired and fought for those changes. Importantly, her work also tells us much about the tenacity of law's concern to protect its underlying principles of heteronormativity and male economic dominance in the family while at the same time it claims to protect and promote women's equality.

We have considered the way in which equality arguments together with particular constructions of welfare have been deployed to strengthen fathers' position in legal disputes over children. The aim of promoting equal parenting has taken priority and has eclipsed the issue of abuse. And this has been facilitated by entrenched myths about domestic abuse and women's mendacity. We saw, therefore, that the underlying norms of law, including formal equality, may do a disservice to women. Here we wish to consider the way equality claims play out in financial and property disputes after divorce. While the courts have made pronouncements about the equality of husbands and wives, perceptions of the value of parties' gendered contributions belie these pronouncements.

We wish, in particular, to consider the legal and social effects of one case, which most family law professionals consider to be a 'landmark' case.[119] With this case

[114] See the criticism of the judge below in *Re B (Children: Police Investigation)* [2022] EWCA Civ 982 54.

[115] R Auchmuty, 'The Married Women's Property Acts: Equality Was Not the Issue' in R Hunter (ed), *Rethinking Equality Projects in Law Feminist Challenges* (Hart, 2008).

[116] R Auchmuty, 'Feminism, Property and Divorce Reform Law in the 1960s' in J Miles, D Monk and R Probert (eds), *Fifty Years of the Divorce Reform Act 1969* (Hart, 2022) 75.

[117] R Auchmuty, 'The Limits of Marriage Protection: In Defence of Property Law' (2016) *Onati Socio-Legal Series* 1196.

[118] R Auchmuty, 'The Experience of Civil Partnership Dissolution: Not "Just Like Divorce"'(2016) *Journal of Social Welfare and Family Law* 152.

[119] J Herring, '*White v White* (2000)' in E Rackley and R Auchmuty (eds), *Women's Legal Landmarks* (Hart, 2019) and E Cooke, '*White v White* [2000] 1AC 596: A Late Instalment in a Long Story' in S Gilmore, J Herring and R Probert (eds), *Landmark Cases in Family Law* (Bloomsbury, 2011).

we see again the affirmation of the principle of equality and we see the assertion that this reflects 'changing times'. Yet the cases that followed show how women can be disadvantaged in the very name of their equality.

The case is *White v White*,[120] a decision of the House of Lords reported in 2000. In this case the House of Lords introduced a principle of fairness into the allocation of family assets on divorce. It observed that fairness is a subjective idea but said that there are 'generally accepted standards of fairness' which 'in a field such as this change and develop, sometimes quite radically, over comparatively short periods of time. … In the exercise of these discretions [in the MCA 1973] "the law is a living thing moving with the times and not a creature of dead or moribund ways of thought"'.[121]

The House of Lords went on to hold that fairness meant that the exercise of the statutory discretion in determining a financial award was to be measured by a yardstick of equality. And equality 'should only be departed from only if, and to the extent that, there are good reasons for doing so'.[122] In addition, fairness meant that there was to be no discrimination between the money earner and the home-maker. In Lord Nicholls' frequently quoted words:

> In seeking to achieve a fair outcome, there is no place for discrimination between husband and wife and their respective roles. … [W]hatever the division of labour chosen by the husband and wife, or forced upon them by circumstances, fairness requires that this should not prejudice or advantage either party … If, in their different spheres, each contributed equally to the family, then in principle it matters not which of them earned the money and built up the assets. There should be no bias in favour of the money-earner and against the home-maker and the child-carer.[123]

So, in addition to enumerating a principle of equality, this case is significant in the way it recognises and values care work in the home as equal to work done outside the home.

For these reasons, *White* is an important case for divorcing women. It values both equality and previously unseen and unvalued gendered work.

However we are sceptical of the view that this is an instance of the law simply 'moving with the times'. Indeed, Auchmuty cautions us away from this liberal view. She writes with Rackley that '[p]resenting hard-fought-for legal change, for example, as a simple response to shifts in "social attitudes", without saying who or what changed those attitudes is not merely inaccurate; it allows for the justification of inaction while waiting for the societal shift to happen.'[124]

Even by the 1950s, for example, women's domestic role was reconceived, 'by clever sleight of hand', as a 'symmetrical partnership with different, but essentially

[120] [2000] 1 AC 596.
[121] *White* (n 20) per Lord Nicholls (citing Sachs LJ in *Porter v Porter* [1969] 3 All ER 640, 644).
[122] ibid 605.
[123] ibid 605.
[124] E Rackley and R Auchmuty, 'The Case for Feminist Legal History' (2020) *Oxford Journal of Legal Studies* 878, 881–82.

equal roles',[125] but women were disappointed with the reality of that 'new' ideal and continued to campaign for change. Even though 'part of the explanation for the difficulty of voicing dissatisfaction [with women's homemaker role] was that it was so widely accepted that women had achieved full equality with men',[126] feminists throughout the 1960s campaigned strongly for a form of community property on divorce.[127] The Matrimonial Proceedings and Property Act 1970, which was the result of feminist lobbying,[128] fell short of this goal, but it did permit the courts for the first time to order capital transfers on divorce.

It is important, therefore, to acknowledge how and why attitudes changed, including acknowledging the setbacks, the discontinuities and the work of feminist campaigners. It is important also to acknowledge judicial statements about property and finance on divorce that came before *White* which challenged entrenched attitudes about family law's privacy and about gendered roles in marriage. Hale LJ, for example, noted in *SRJ v DWJ (Financial Provision)*:[129]

> [S]he gave up her place in the world of work to concentrate upon her husband, her home and her family. That must have been a mutual decision from which they both benefited. … It is not only in her interests but in the community's interests that parents, whether mothers or fathers, and spouses, whether wives or husbands, should have a real choice between concentrating on breadwinning and concentrating on home making and child rearing, and do not feel forced, for fear of what might happen should their marriage break down much later in life, to abandon looking after the home and the family to other people for the sake of maintaining a career.[130]

Yet even the 'welcome rhetoric'[131] of *White* which followed may be problematic. It values as equal the gendered contributions made to the well-being of the family, but still remains within law's labour desert frame when it speaks of homemaking contributions *deserving* recognition and only then creating entitlement. It does little to displace law's 'deeply patriarchal legal past'[132] 'in which property rights are justified only as a reward for the expenditure of one's labour'.[133] We see this rhetoric in play as the law and legal commentators struggle to value spouses' relative contributions to the family. Eekelaar, for example, suggests that on the basis of 'earned entitlement' the value of homemaking must be measured by its duration,

[125] Auchmuty (n 116) 82–83.
[126] ibid 83.
[127] ibid.
[128] ibid. See also S Thompson, 'Against Divorce? Revisiting the Charge of the Casanova's Charter' (2021) *Child and Family Law Quarterly* 193.
[129] [1999] 2 FLR 176.
[130] ibid para 82.
[131] Herring (n 119) 509.
[132] Rackley and Auchmuty, 'The Case for Feminist Legal History' (n 124) 885, quoting J Conaghan, *Law and Gender* (Clarendon, 2013).
[133] A Diduck, 'Family Law as Expression of Financial Relief in the English Courts' in E Aloni and R Tremblay (eds), *House Rules: Changing Families, Evolving Norms, and the Role of Law* (University of British Columbia Press, 2022) 87; A Diduck, 'Sharing Loss on Divorce – A Commentary' (2018) 32 *Australian Journal of Family Law* 132.

whereas the value of money-earning need not be.[134] And cases such as *Work v Gray*[135] have confirmed the 'special contribution' exception to treating as equal the spouses' contributions to the welfare of the family so as to justify departing from equality of division. While the court in *Work* also said that the concept is only relevant in a small number of cases, it is not surprising that it has been applied only to the money earner's contributions. Indeed, as the wife in *Work v Gray* argued, it is 'impossible' for a homemaker to evidence such a special contribution.[136]

Granted, *White* had come a long way from cases it implicitly overruled, such as *Page v Page*[137] and *Dart v Dart*.[138] In *Page* for example Ormrod LJ said:

> Forty years of marriage represents a large contribution by the wife, and the husband too, but this is not a case where the wife has been actively engaged in the husband's business either by working in it or by providing capital, though she must have helped him to save money to invest in his business activities. She has not, in that sense, 'earned' a share in the assets which in some cases gives the wife a considerable stake in them.[139]

And Dunn LJ said in the same case:

> Her contribution was over a forty-year marriage … looking after the husband and his home and bringing up the children. It is, of course, a substantial contribution but not one which entitled the wife *ipso facto* to a particular share in the family assets.[140]

In both *Dart v Dart*[141] and *Conran v Conran*,[142] the court agreed with the husband's submission that he was required only to meet his wife's 'reasonable requirements' from his considerable wealth. The cases immediately following *White* did not return to the blatant language of *Page* or the reasonable requirements ceiling of *Dart*, but they did challenge *White's* ideas of equality and non-discrimination. This litigation focused upon the question of when equality should be departed from. Courts found such departures justified when contributions to the family were not considered equal, such as the special contribution cases, or when the marriage was of short duration. When *Miller/McFarlane*[143] followed *White* in 2006, the judicially created means available for departing from equality only increased in number. *Miller/McFarlane* for example, introduced the concept of non-marital assets,[144] which are not available for equal sharing unless they are required to meet needs. Subsequent cases have identified the

[134] J Eekelaar, 'Asset Distribution on Divorce – Time and Property' (2003) *Family Law* 828.
[135] [2017] EWCA Civ 270.
[136] ibid para 51.
[137] (1981) 2 FLR 198.
[138] [1996] 2 FLR 286.
[139] *Page v Page* (n 137) 201.
[140] ibid 203.
[141] *Dart v Dart* (n 138).
[142] [1997] 2 FLR 615.
[143] [2006] UKHL 24.
[144] *Miller v Miller; McFarlane v McFarlane* ibid paras 21–29; 147–153; *Hart v Hart* [2017] EWCA Civ 1306.

category of unilateral property.[145] This is property acquired during the marriage by one spouse but kept separate from the family's joint use. This too is not considered shareable except to meet needs. In these ways, by creating exceptions to *White*'s equality principle, the law is said to have become more complex and confusing. As Herring notes, however, the complexity or confusing state of the current law has 'largely resulted from a reluctance to accept the principle of equality that was at the heart of … *White*. … [M]uch of the subsequent case law can be seen as an attempt to diminish the significance of that decision. … nearly always the post-*White* developments mean that the money earner gets to keep much more than half of the assets, to the disadvantage of the homemaker and child carer'.[146]

Interestingly, while courts were concerned to limit equality in these ways, public perception did not follow. London became known as the 'divorce capital of the world' for women motivated by the prospect of an equal share. In taking the unusual step of writing a postscript to his judgment in *Charman v Charman*,[147] Sir Mark Potter, then the President of the Family Division, commented upon the effect of the change to the law made by the *White* decision, saying that *White* was founded on 'profound social change, particularly in the recognition that marriage is a partnership of equals',[148] but that it 'has more than doubled the levels of award and it has been said by many that London has become the divorce capital of the world for aspiring wives'.[149] He lamented the loss of the certainty provided by the reasonable requirements principle and called for the Law Commission to review the law.[150] What he and other commentators failed to note, however, is that before *White*, London could conceivably have been called the divorce capital of the world for wealthy divorcing husbands, given the 'reasonable requirements' ceiling.

In cases where the concept of equality does survive, it has improved some women's position, but equality is a double-edged sword in the family court. If the spouses are equal, they must both be treated as free, rational and autonomous agents. In 2006, for example, the court refused to compensate a wife for the economic disparity between the spouses arising from their different roles: 'I am not persuaded at all that anything has been lost by the 7½ year gap in the applicant's employment, or as a result of the mutual agreement between the parties that she would not work …'.[151] And the assumption that spouses were 'similarly situated' and thus should accept the consequences of their family choices finally

[145] *Sharp v Sharp* [2017] EWCA Civ 408.
[146] J Herring, *Family Law* (Harlow Pearson, 2019) 296.
[147] [2007] EWCA Civ 503.
[148] ibid para 115.
[149] ibid para 116.
[150] ibid para 126.
[151] *S v S* [2006] EWHC 2793 (Fam) para 59.

received the imprimatur of the Supreme Court in 2010 in the context of upholding a prenuptial agreement:

> The Court should accord respect to the decision of a married couple as to the manner in which their financial affairs should be regulated. It would be paternalistic and patronising to override their agreement simply on the basis that the court knows best.[152]

There is a widely held assumption in the history of family law that we have moved with changing social times inexorably from coverture to equality and from status to contract.[153] But to see the 'achievement' of formal equality and 'autonomous rights-bearing individualism [within the family] as the destiny of progress'[154] is an over-simplification. Family law was and still is connected to the market, to productivity, to social security and to the gendered distribution of economic resources. Ascribing to the spouses an unnuanced autonomy, a 'freedom of contract' and formal equality ignores this connection and confines women's economic security within the private family.

The 'glosses' on *White* mean that despite its support for substantive equality principles in family law, without similar reformulations of other areas of law and policy, and challenges to law's underlying normative ideas of family privacy, formal equality and autonomy, women still lose out economically on divorce. Indeed, so long as these cases remain within the so-called 'private sphere,' they do little to encourage such policy change and may even deter it, as homemakers and child carers are seen to be 'looked after' by the family. In these 'big money' family finance cases from which come the principles to be applied to all cases, judges adopt an individualistic and private idea of equality between the spouses, and pray the principle of autonomy in support.

The result is that a 'consideration of the effect upon the public purse of divorce and the public revaluing of women's and men's labour inside and outside families have never been necessary,'[155] despite *White's* potential to encourage this revaluation. Instead, 'issues of family finances remain locked in the unsatisfactory "black box" of private family law and continue to appear to be unrelated to broader state policies concerned to sustain their privacy.'[156]

Yet, even while *White* has not led to social change, it can sometimes offer justice to individual women, many of whom are working 'double or triple shifts' combining employment, child care and care of dependent relatives.[157] Divorce exposes

[152] *Radmacher v Granatino* [2010] UKSC 42, para 78.

[153] HS Maine, *Ancient Law* (John Murray, 1861); M Minow, '"Forming Underneath Everything that Grows": Toward a History of Family Law' (1985) 4 *Wisconsin Law Review* 819; M Glendon, *The Transformation of Family Law* (University of Chicago Press, 1989); S Cretney, *Family Law in the Twentieth Century: A History* (OUP, 2005).

[154] Minow (n 153) 893.

[155] A Diduck, 'Fairness and Justice for All? The House of Lords in *White v White*' (2001) *Feminist Legal Studies* 173, 182.

[156] ibid.

[157] See Herring (n 146).

women's poverty or economic disadvantage and *White*, combined with the strands of needs and sharing referred to in *Miller/McFarlane*, could be invoked to at least partially compensate for this.

Conclusion

What we learn from Auchmuty's way of doing legal history is that reform is messy, and often a battleground. We learn the importance of recognising how women themselves always were and still are a part of those battles and, while some battles may appear to have been won, they are never over. Auchmuty's work alone and with Rackley allows us to develop a 'deeper understanding of the impact of law on the lived experience of women and the impact of women on law, to inform strategies adopted by those *currently* seeking social justice.'[158]

Our two examples of legal reform offer evidence that women themselves played a major part in effecting legal change and indeed, that that change can benefit them. But they also demonstrate that neither gendered cultural beliefs nor law's patriarchal ideological framework is so easily displaced. Even when the law looks to equality, it does so within these frameworks and this often means that it can become a tool for further and unanticipated difficulties, including backlash and turning gains into losses.

In the economic sphere, law's equality remains within the labour market desert frame, for example, and has difficulty assessing the value of gendered familial roles. It has also increasingly relied upon formal ideas of autonomy to suggest that the consequences of decisions made by women to leave work to care for children are theirs to bear alone, regardless of the social context of those decisions. In the case of domestic abuse, while law formally acknowledges that it is a matter of public concern and while there has been a shift from identifying incidents of violence to looking for patterns of abuse, the implementation of the law is fraught with misogynistic beliefs about women's propensity to make false allegations and to manipulate their children.[159] The result is that men's claims about equality of parenting together with the courts' interpretations of welfare end up harming women and children.

Rackley and Auchmuty remind us that both the law and the discipline of legal history are 'heavily invested in preserving the illusion of legal objectivity, neutrality and inevitability; in maintaining a narrative characterised by progress and liberal incrementalism.' And that the 'consequence of this pursuit of coherence is that the jumbled reality of law reform – the setbacks, compromises and failures – is lost'.[160]

[158] Rackley and Auchmuty, 'Women's Legal Landmarks' (n 1) 5.

[159] Neither has law escaped misogynist tropes about women in the economic sphere. See eg claims that women seek a 'meal ticket for life' from their ex-spouses.

[160] Rackley and Auchmuty (n 124) 882.

We hope that our two examples help to expose this incoherence and jumbled reality. We hope also however, that our examples demonstrate that while 'law is a blunt tool with which to try to secure, protect and enhance women's lives',[161] and that 'legal "reforms" rarely turn out to be what we want, as Rackley and Auchmuty ultimately conclude: 'in the hands of determined women law can prove a powerful mechanism for change.'[162]

[161] Rackley and Auchmuty, 'Women's Legal Landmarks' (n 1) 21.
[162] ibid.

10

Relationship Recognition: Feminism, Law, and Transformation

SUSAN BOYD AND CLAIRE YOUNG

Introduction

Rereading Rosemary's scholarly contributions, which reflect admirable clarity of argument and foresight, has been a pleasure. While our intention is to take some of the themes she has raised and expand upon them, the first thing that strikes us is how prescient she was. As we will show, her work raises many of the themes that have been central to debates about the role that marriage and cohabitation play in law and society. She highlighted the role of marriage (and marriage-like relationships) in state regulation, and the potential impact of that regulation for same-sex couples.[1] She also noted the increasing state abdication of public responsibility for the economic welfare of citizens and the consequent reinforcement of social and economic inequality by placing more of that responsibility on the private sector, especially the privatised family – and therefore on women.[2] In 2004 while discussing the proposals for a UK civil partnership registration scheme for same-sex couples and declaring herself as 'opposed to marriage', she noted nevertheless that 'I have come to the conclusion that same-sex marriage is inevitable'.[3] Although civil partnerships were being introduced by the government in an effort to avoid extending marriage to same-sex couples, she saw the writing on the wall.

Rosemary's lack of enthusiasm for marriage is one of the hallmarks of her work. Throughout she has insisted that feminists must tackle gendered inequalities rather than argue for legal remedies that purport to protect women through recognition of couple-based relationships. In order to tackle gendered inequalities in a transformative manner, women must be empowered, especially through financial independence. Instead of relying on remedies from intimate partners,

[1] See eg R Auchmuty, 'Same-Sex Marriage Revived: Feminist Critique and Legal Strategy' (2004) 14(1) *Feminism and Psychology* 101.

[2] See eg R Auchmuty, 'Feminist Responses to Same Sex Relationship Recognition' in C Ashford and A Maine (eds), *Research Handbook on Gender, Sexuality and the Law* (Edward Elgar, 2020) 164.

[3] Auchmuty (n 1) 103.

women must return to the earlier feminist demands of the *state*, including for pay equity, equal education and job opportunities, free contraception and abortion on demand, and universal, affordable childcare.[4] Despite their ongoing urgency, these demands remain largely unmet; in contrast, the move to legally recognise same sex relationships over the past two decades or so has been remarkably speedy.

We will first highlight two of Rosemary's contributions:

1. The importance of foregrounding lesbian lives and perspectives, and feminist analysis.
2. The history of marriage as a socio-legal institution that reinforces oppression.

We then elaborate upon the role of relationship recognition in the privatisation of social and economic responsibilities and the importance of looking at the intersections of class and gender. A discussion of strategising for the future follows, including the possibilities and pitfalls of abandoning the legal recognition of spousal status in socio-legal regulation and moving towards a more universal system of awarding benefits. Overall, we are less sanguine than Rosemary about modern marriage being a more benign and egalitarian institution than it once was or that it has moved to be a 'mere lifestyle choice'.[5] We are hesitant about any immediate proposal to diminish the protective role of law in redressing the impact of power imbalances that persist in many intimate relationships, in part due to the ongoing ideological power of marriage, and we offer ideas about avoiding an either/or approach.

Foregrounding Lesbian Lives and Perspectives and Feminist Analysis

A remarkable aspect of Rosemary's scholarship that sets it apart from much other feminist legal scholarship is her foregrounding of lesbian lives and perspectives. This focus informs her work on relationship recognition, as does her concern with single women, dating back to her doctoral work.[6] In 1992, her co-authored article on the rise of 'lesbian and gay studies' asked whether it was possible to offer such studies without rendering lesbian lives invisible or a pale reflection of the gay male experience.[7] In order to avoid those outcomes, she argued it was

[4] See R Auchmuty, 'Law and the Power of Feminism: How Marriage Lost its Power to Oppress Women' (2012) 20 *Feminist Legal Studies* 71, 81.

[5] ibid 72.

[6] R Auchmuty, *Victorian Spinsters*, PhD Thesis (Australian National University, 1975).

[7] R Auchmuty, S Jeffreys and E Miller, 'Lesbian History and Gay Studies: Keeping a Feminist Perspective' (1992) 1 *Women's History Review* 89. See also R Auchmuty, 'Feminist Approaches to Sexuality and Law Scholarship' (2015) 15 *Legal Information Management* 4.

crucial to study (hetero)patriarchy, which in turn requires a feminist analysis. Despite the common interest that lesbians and gay men share in developing a critical approach to heterosexist society and norms, gay men can demand equal rights with heterosexual men in ways that do not challenge or destabilise patriarchy, something that is key to women's liberation. She pointed out that gay men tend to be much more comfortable than lesbians in asserting that there is an essential lesbian/gay nature and that sexual preference is inborn.[8] In contrast, most feminist scholarship insists that sexuality is socially constructed, which is a key component of any argument for the possibility of social change. Arguing persuasively for the need for feminist analysis in considering lesbian studies, Rosemary and her co-authors noted that whether lesbians choose to make feminist struggle a priority in their own lives or not, all lesbians are affected by women's oppression.[9]

More recently, in her fascinating small interview study of (mostly female) 'pioneer' civil partners in the UK who had dissolved their partnerships,[10] Rosemary emphasises the importance of centring lesbian and gay experiences in research and not equating or comparing civil partnership (CP), which was then available only to same sex couples, with the heterosexual marriage model. She resists the tendency to adopt the 'sameness' model of equality, even in the research process, because this model prompts us to see only what is similar to the dominant group – which is itself part of the process of assimilation to dominant norms. Assuming an identity of interests between lesbians and gay men is also problematic. For example, older lesbian interviewees especially resisted the imposition of heterosexual family law norms upon their relationships. Many interviewees shared the misconception that marriage and CPs are generally protective of couples' rights, and were not infrequently alarmed at the time of dissolution to discover that one partner (usually the one with more wealth) had to share assets. Rosemary suggests that this assimilation to the marriage model via family law remedies detracts from innovative arrangements concerning finances that some same sex couples had made using contracts and wills, often before entering a CP, and sometimes not realising that a CP might void those documents. She concludes that the advent of same sex marriage and pressure to conform to marital norms means that there is less potential for lesbian and gay partners to provide models for autonomous, egalitarian relationships.

A review of Rosemary's longstanding critical research on marriage explicates why she reaches these conclusions.

[8] Auchmuty et al, 'Lesbian History' (n 7) 94.

[9] ibid 101.

[10] R Auchmuty, 'The Experience of Civil Partnership Dissolution: Not "Just Like Divorce"' (2016) 38 *Journal of Social Welfare and Family Law* 152–74; R Auchmuty, 'Dissolution or Disillusion? The Unravelling of Civil Partnerships' in N Barker and D Monk (eds), *From Civil Partnership to Same-Sex Marriage: Interdisciplinary Reflections* (Routledge, 2015) 199.

The History of Marriage as a Socio-Legal Institution that Reinforces Oppression

As a socio-legal institution that literally changes an individual's legal status as against all others (an *in rem* action), marriage is far more than a contract between two individuals. Marriage also plays numerous roles in society and the economic system and in the legal and regulatory systems. In many fields of law, including taxation, social assistance, and criminal law, one's marital (or spousal) status make a huge difference. As a powerful ideological influence in society, along with familial ideology, marriage also disciplines our choices and actions.

In a series of articles, Rosemary has traced the oppressive nature of marriage, greatly assisted by her legal history expertise. As she showed in 2016, the concept of marriage has shifted over time.[11] Throughout it has played a role in disciplining citizens, for example by offering tax incentives to marry and according elevated social status, while generating stigma against those who do not marry (especially women). Feminists have long criticised marriage for its subjection of women to the control and power of men, economically and otherwise. First wave feminists were, Rosemary argues, more radical in their critiques of marriage (for example, its contribution to domestic abuse) than we often think. Some such feminists referred to marriage as reducing women to a state of legal slavery due to how it affected their legal status, notably in relation to marital property and rape. Some resisted entering the marital institution themselves.

Early law reform initiatives (for example, those relating to marital property in the late nineteenth and early twentieth centuries, and to equal pay in the twentieth century) may not have fundamentally challenged the sexual division of labour or marriage *per se*, reflecting a middle class bias that there would be domestic help for wives.[12] But in the second wave of feminism, marriage did become the focus, as did the sexual division of labour and women's dependency within marriage (and common law relationships).[13] Much advocacy was for alternatives to marriage and for free public childcare. Some feminists, such as Carol Smart, argued for the abandonment of marriage and a new system of rights and duties not dependent on coupledom.[14] Rosemary has built consistently on this work. Interestingly, and possibly controversially, she has also argued that second wave feminist critiques of marriage became mainstream by the 2000s, contributing to the diminished appeal of marriage.[15] Indeed she has cast the 'widespread rejection of marriage' in favour of unmarried cohabitation and other modalities of living as playing a key role in challenging gender inequality and a '*wholesale social transformation*'.[16]

[11] R Auchmuty, 'Marriage and Civil Partnership: Law's Role, Feminism's Response' in VE Munro and M Davies (eds), *The Ashgate Research Companion to Feminist Legal Theory* (Routledge, 2016) 285.

[12] ibid 289.

[13] ibid 291.

[14] C Smart, *The Ties that Bind: Law, Marriage and the Reproduction of Patriarchal Relations* (Routledge & Kegan Paul, 1984) 146; quoted in Auchmuty (n 11) 293.

[15] R Auchmuty, 'What's So Special about Marriage? The Impact of Wilkinson v Kitzinger' (2008) 20 *Child and Family Quarterly* 475, 491.

[16] ibid; Auchmuty (n 4) 84.

Rosemary is particularly effective (and emphatic!) when she tackles the oft-made argument that marriage can be transformed by opening it to same sex partners. In 2004, in considering the proposal for civil partnerships she made the point, with some dismay, that the increasing irrelevance of marriage meant that same sex marriage was inevitable.[17] Rosemary insists that important alternative models of intimate living have been offered by same sex partnerships. She is equally insistent that marriage itself, as well as models such as civil partnerships, reinforce problematic gender roles and detract from such innovative models. In her review of different feminist approaches to same sex marriage, she notes how difficult it is to transform an institution that is so fundamentally embedded in state regulation.[18] Yet she argues that marriage is declining of its own accord, raising a potential contradiction.

Relationship Recognition, Privatisation, Class and Gender

In 2016 and 2020 Auchmuty refers to the privatising impact of the legal recognition of marriage and civil partnerships.[19] Privatisation is, *inter alia*, about placing responsibility on individuals to care for each other, thereby relieving the state of its own responsibility. Giving special state recognition to marriage (and, now, marriage-like relationships) literally saves the state money.[20] This outcome is not neutral. A key aspect to the ways in which marriage and the increasing legal recognition of marriage-like relationships have contributed to oppression in capitalist systems is how they are used to reinforce the privatisation of care and economic responsibilities within the family.[21] They encourage dependency within relationships, an often gender-based phenomenon. An individual's entitlement to social benefits can be lost because the state assumes (often falsely) that spouses will take financial responsibility for each other's economic well-being, both during and after a relationship. Indeed, in 1999 the Supreme Court of Canada acknowledged explicitly that a main purpose of spousal support law is to alleviate the burden on the public purse by shifting the obligations to provide support for needy persons to family members.[22] These assumptions are highly detrimental to those who have

[17] Auchmuty (n 1).
[18] Auchmuty (n 2) 169.
[19] Auchmuty (n 11) 294 and, especially, Auchmuty (n 2) 173–74.
[20] Smart (n 14) 21.
[21] SB Boyd and CFL Young, '"From Same-Sex to No Sex"? Trends Towards Recognition of (Same-Sex) Relationships in Canada' (2003) 1 *Seattle Journal for Social Justice* 757; C Young and S Boyd, 'Losing the Feminist Voice? Debates on the Legal Recognition of Same Sex Partnerships in Canada' (2006) 14 *Feminist Legal Studies* 213.
[22] *M v H* [1999] 2 SCR 3 at paras 4, 53, 106. See Young and Boyd (n 21) 220–21. For a discussion of the challenges for feminists of working on cases such as *M v H* that involve a privatising aspect, see

less income or wealth, with women especially suffering as social programmes are cut back based on the assumption of privatised remedies.

An example of the trend towards privatising economic responsibility in Canada is the spousal tax credit, which is available to a taxpayer who supports their spouse. Put simply, the taxpayer is entitled to a credit of almost $1,200 if their spouse has little or no income, with the credit being phased out as the spouse's income increases. As the Law Commission of Canada said, 'this credit appears to be designed to promote economic dependency in conjugal relationships'.[23] It clearly reinforces the private responsibility placed on the 'family' for its own economic welfare by affirming that economic dependency on one's spouse deserves tax relief. Many critiques could be made of this provision,[24] but in this context it should be noted that tax policy has responded to a spouse's lack of economic power (more often a woman's) by leaving it to the family (private sector) to assume responsibility for the lack of economic resources. Women's unpaid caregiving labour within the family is also an aspect of this privatised system.[25]

Rosemary's critical analysis of such couple-based privileges can be expanded by highlighting the intersections of class and gender.[26] We use as an example her 2009 case comment on *Burden v United Kingdom*.[27] In that case, two elderly sisters who lived in their family house argued they would be discriminated against when one of them died in comparison to married or civilly partnered couples because the surviving sister would not be eligible for the 'spousal exemption' from inheritance tax. Such a claim highlights the use of state subsidies to benefit those with wealth, in this case the family home, provided they are in a particular marriage or marriage-like relationship. Economic (inter)dependence in that relationship is rewarded, which in turn alleviates the state's potential future economic responsibility. The challenge by the Burden sisters was unsuccessful. Rosemary suggests that the case calls into question the legal and economic privileges enjoyed by legally-bound couples at the expense of everyone else. Yet not all couples benefit from such privileges.[28]

Looking at the impact of taking spousal relationships into account for tax purposes reveals that being treated as spouses for tax purposes does not always confer a benefit.[29] Indeed many couples pay more tax than they would if they were

SB Boyd. 'Family, Law and Sexuality: Feminist Engagements' (1999) 8(3) *Social and Legal Studies* 369–90, especially at 377–82 and 389–90.

[23] Law Commission of Canada, *Beyond Conjugality: Recognizing and Supporting Close Personal and Adult Relationships* (Law Commission of Canada, 2001) 74.

[24] See eg CFL Young, 'Taking Spousal Status into Account for Tax Purposes: The Pitfalls and Penalties' in A Bottomley and S Wong (eds), *Changing Contours of Domestic Life, Family and Law: Caring and Sharing* (Hart, 2009) 91, 100–02.

[25] Auchmuty (n 2) 173–74.

[26] Other social and economic inequalities such as race and disability also figure prominently, although we do not discuss them here.

[27] R Auchmuty, 'Beyond Couples: *Burden v United Kingdom*' (2009) 17 *Feminist Legal Studies* 205.

[28] Auchmuty (n 2) 173.

[29] See eg C Young, 'Beyond Conjugality: Time for the Tax System to Take That Concept Seriously' in K Brooks (ed), *The Quest for Tax Reform Continues: The Royal Commission on Taxation Fifty Years Later*

treated as individuals. The class implications are profound and given that women earn less than men and have less capital than men, they are particularly disadvantaged.[30] The general points relevant to Canadian tax law also apply in the UK and most other jurisdictions that take spousal status into account for tax purposes. While most jurisdictions, including Canada and the UK, do not tax spouses as one taxable unit, as we discuss below, they do take the spousal relationship into account for many tax purposes.[31] Generally speaking, a couple comprised of two low rate taxpayers will pay more tax when they are treated as a couple rather than as individuals. In contrast, couples in which there are two high-rate taxpayers and couples in which there is one high rate taxpayer and the other has little or no income both tend to benefit in terms of taxes saved when treated as a couple.

Why do low income couples pay more tax while the benefits of spousal status are accorded to those with high incomes? The *Burden* case illustrates one obvious example, which is the non-taxation on death of the appreciation in value of capital property owned by a taxpayer when that capital is passed on to their spouse. In Canada, even though there is no inheritance tax *per se*, numerous tax provisions allow capital to pass tax free from one spouse to another, a measure that mainly benefits higher income or property owning spouses and encourages dependency. The UK offers an exemption from inheritance tax for a taxpayer who leaves their capital property to their spouse. The gendered impact of these rules is clear. Men tend to have more wealth than women so it is mainly men who benefit directly from the exemptions. Certainly, to the extent that women in heterosexual relationships are the beneficiaries on death of capital property owned by their spouse, there may be a benefit to them as less tax is paid by the estate. But the assumption is that the tax savings will accrue to them, which is not always the case. The taxes saved go into the estate and whether a female spouse benefits from those funds depends on the terms of the will. Furthermore, in Canada where the rules allow the deceased to avoid capital gains that would accrue on death when property is left to a spouse, the spouse simply inherits the underlying tax liability and she is liable for the tax that would otherwise be payable when she disposes of the property.

As Rosemary notes, the Burden case is about 'spousal privilege', but it is also about class privilege. Tax policies that take spousal status into account are highly

(Carswell, 2013) 207; Young (n 24); and C Young, *What's Sex Got To Do With It? Tax and the Family in Canada* (Law Commission of Canada, 2000).

[30] While the gender pay gap has been narrowed over the years, it remains significant. In Canada, for example, in 2021 women in full-time work earned 11% less than men: Quality of Employment in Canada, 'Pay Gap 1998–2021' www150.statcan.gc.ca/n1/pub/14-28-0001/2020001/article/00003-eng.htm. Internationally, women earned 16.1% less than men in 2022, OECD iLibrary, 'Gender Wage Gap (Indicator)' (2022) doi:10.1787/7cee77aa-en. Lack of income contributes to women's lack of wealth. There are various estimates depending on how wealth is measured, with a recent estimate of women having less than 25% of the wealth owned by men: see, M Basi, *Measuring Wealth: A Key Step to Effectively Narrow The Gender Gap* (World Economic Forum, 13 June 2022) www.weforum.org/agenda/2022/07/women-wealth-equity-index-gender-gap/.

[31] For example, in the UK the marriage allowance permits an individual to transfer a portion of their personal allowance to their spouse, thereby reducing their overall tax bill.

implicated in that class privilege, with the benefits of the spousal exemptions from capital and inheritance tax benefitting only the very wealthy. For many couples, the only capital asset they own is their home and any disposition of that property is already exempt from tax, meaning that the spousal exemption on death is not required. The people who really benefit are high net worth individuals with significant other forms of capital, such as portfolios of stocks and shares, second homes, and other luxury items. Giving a spousal exemption from the very taxes that are intended to assist in the redistribution of income and wealth to those who are needy is, in our view, unconscionable.

A second important point to make about tax, class, gender and the legal recognition of spouses is that in Canada (and the same is probably true in the UK), when the definition of spouse in tax legislation was expanded to include same sex partners, the result was a revenue windfall for the government. The increased tax burden that resulted in that windfall was borne by taxpayers with low incomes, while as mentioned above, high income taxpayers benefitted. The reason for the increased tax burden for those with lower incomes is that some tax breaks have an income threshold level above which entitlement to the tax benefit is removed. In the case of spouses, incomes are aggregated for the purposes of that threshold. So, for example, the Child Tax Benefit in Canada is available to taxpayers with children, and is intended to help defray some of the cost of raising children. When lesbians were included as spouses for tax purposes many mothers lost that credit because when their income was aggregated with that of their spouse, the income threshold was exceeded. This sort of analysis confirms Rosemary's point that lesbians and gay men can have significantly different interests, based on their gender and their class.

Class and gender are thus inextricably entwined in the tax context (and elsewhere), in part because of women's lack of income and wealth. Teasing out the class implications strengthens Rosemary's call for the abolition of marriage (and the consequent legal recognition of spouses) as a legal concept. What would our tax systems look like if one took the negative impact on women and those with low incomes seriously? Can we still have a system that takes spousal status into account but that does not disadvantage these people? In the next section, we consider the possibilities of moving away from a system that makes spousal status central.

Strategising for the Future: Coupledom vs Universality vs Alternative Models

Rosemary has offered trenchant critiques of marriage as an historic embodiment of hetero-patriarchy, and made strong arguments for why allowing same sex partners to marry will not fundamentally challenge the role of marriage in capitalist patriarchy. We agree entirely with this assessment. Since the early 2000s, Rosemary has also suggested that marriage is increasingly irrelevant, as reflected in declining marriage rates in favour of unmarried cohabitation and living alone, and the declining stigma of raising children outside marriage (illegitimacy). In 2004, she argued that the increasing irrelevance of marriage meant that it was now just a personal choice, conferring few substantive legal or financial advantages.[32] We are unsure that marriage has lost that key role. In Canada, significant differences remain between the legal rights and responsibilities that attach to married versus unmarried cohabitants, especially economic remedies related to property.[33] We also think it important to consider the ongoing powerful ideology of marriage and its impact on the choices made by individuals and couples.

We now turn to some of the strategic challenges for the future that are raised by Rosemary's analysis of modern marriage and her argument that legal recognition of spousal relationships is unnecessary and, in some cases, damaging. Are there more transformational strategies that feminists should focus their energies on? Is it possible to see more than one strategy as a worthy terrain of struggle, especially during a period when it seems so hard to persuade governments that transformational strategies are needed and possible?

A consistent theme that crops up in Rosemary's work is the problematic privileging of couples in legal regulation (not that all benefit from that regulation; but, as we have shown, some do). As Carol Smart famously put it, as an ideological 'enclosure', marriage quintessentially prioritises coupledom and heterosexuality and makes them the norms against which all other relationships were measured. Marriage is thus 'as significant to the unmarried as to the married and to the homosexual as to the heterosexual'.[34] Marriage also becomes the privileged setting for the reproduction of children.[35] As we have discussed, Rosemary and other feminist legal scholars have further suggested that the trend to recognise 'marriage-like relationships' is almost as problematic as is marriage, especially in relation to the privatisation of social and economic responsibilities and the overlooking of the interests of those who live alone or otherwise fall outside of the marriage model. Rosemary goes back to second wave feminists such as Smart, who suggested alternatives to marriage and moving towards collectivism rather than individualism.[36] She suggests that realising this strategy would also diminish the privatisation of care work, still borne primarily by women. We share this vision but question how precisely to move towards it at this political juncture. In particular, should feminist strategies focus on the eradication of the legal privileging of

[32] Auchmuty (n 1) 121.

[33] Canadian family law is further complicated by the fact that it is regulated by both federal and provincial laws. Depending on where one lives, the definition of 'spouse' varies, and spousal rights and responsibilities can differ radically.

[34] Smart (n 14) 143.

[35] ibid 144.

[36] Auchmuty (n 11) 291–93. See also N Barker, *Not the Marrying Kind: A Feminist Critique of Same-Sex Marriage* (Palgrave Macmillan, 2012); MA Fineman, 'Cracking the Foundational Myths: Independence, Autonomy, and Self-Sufficiency' (2000) 8 *Journal of Gender, Social Policy and the Law* 13–30; SB Boyd, DE Chunn, F Kelly and W Wiegers, *Autonomous Motherhood: A Socio-Legal Study of Choice and Constraint* (University of Toronto Press, 2015) especially ch 7 at 212–35.

marriage and marriage-like relationships in favour of introducing universal benefits that would better benefit those who fall outside the bounds of coupledom, such as single people and the elderly? Or, as we discuss later, is there room for an alternative model?

The COVID-19 pandemic has provided us with an opportunity to rethink state regulation and benefits, and consider whether according rights and responsibilities on the basis of spousal status is a flawed state strategy. Apart from its huge impact on people's lives, the pandemic has prompted significant shifts in government fiscal policies. Certainly in its initial phase, many governments raced to provide some economic relief to individuals and businesses. In the Canadian context one example is the Canadian Emergency Response Benefit (CERB), a refundable tax credit of $500 a week to individuals who lost their job or who stopped working due to COVID-19.[37] CERB was available for just over six months in 2020 and during that time over $81B was spent, which made CERB the single largest tax expenditure in 2020.[38] Two key facts about CERB are that it was a refundable tax credit, and, significantly, it did not take spousal status into account. A refundable tax credit is available to *all* individuals, regardless of whether they pay tax or not. As with other tax benefits, it is of course contingent on filing a tax return. Governments are increasingly using the tax system to deliver money that otherwise might have been a grant programme because of the efficiencies involved. Rather than requiring a complicated application process, much of the data respecting the applicant is already in the tax system and the funds can be deposited in bank accounts as soon as a short application online is made. In this case, payments were made within two weeks of initial applications being made.

Other examples of refundable tax credits are the Canada Child Tax Benefit and the GST tax credit, which is intended to help defray the cost of the GST (VAT) for low-income individuals. In contrast to CERB, both those credits take spousal status into account, which means that the income of spouses is aggregated, resulting in a decline in the amount of the payment or elimination of the tax break when the income threshold is reached. Income aggregation for the purpose of entitlement to a refundable tax credit is, to a certain extent, based on the theory of economies of scale. That is, two people living together incur fewer expenses than two individuals who live alone.

The fact that CERB did *not* take spousal status into account is key to our discussion. Could one say that the government realised the flaws in tax provisions that take spousal status into account? In terms of theories of economies of scale, one could easily argue that many others enjoy economies of scale, including anyone who shares accommodation with a family member or a roommate. Using spousal status as the marker does not take these relationships and associated economies of

[37] Canada Emergency Response Benefit Act, SC 2020, c 5.

[38] Government of Canada, *Report on Federal Tax Expenditures: Concepts, Estimates and Evaluation* (Department of Finance, Canada 2021) www.canada.ca/en/department-finance/services/publications/federal-tax-expenditures/2021.html.

scale into account. Policy makers probably did not intend CERB to be a change of policy, but it sets a potentially important precedent for a different approach. CERB was introduced in a moment of extreme pressure on governments and given the speed with which it was introduced, it is unlikely that it was subject to the usual review of tax measures. Rather it was a measure intended to provide an immediate response to the loss of income incurred by many Canadians due to the impact of COVID-19.

The next question is can we see the pandemic and measures such as CERB as a moment to move forward with respect to rethinking how we deliver benefits, including those delivered through the tax system? Can we make them more universal and at the same time move away from taking spousal status into account in their delivery? In the early days of the pandemic, various socially progressive organisations resurrected proposals for a Guaranteed Basic Income. These proposals differed in their details, but the general proposal was that in order to reduce poverty in Canada, some form of basic annual income should be provided to Canadians. Instead of using measures such as social assistance or tax expenditures to assist those living in poverty, the concept is, as one organisation put it, is to provide 'an unconditional cash grant to enable everyone to meet their basic needs, participate in society and live with dignity, regardless of work status'.[39]

A guaranteed basic income has periodically been discussed and researched over the years, but during the early days of the pandemic the concept seemed to gain traction.[40] Precisely how to deliver such as programme has been the subject of much debate. How should it be delivered? Should it be a direct payment or a negative income tax? What should the amount be? Importantly, should it take family and/or spousal income into account? How universal should it be? How should it be funded? Embedded in these questions is one broader theme that resonates with the question of moving away from taking spousal status into account and using the individual as the marker for benefits. That is the interrelationship of the various measures. A Guaranteed Basic Income programme will not operate in a vacuum, and neither does the current tax system. So, for example, if one were to argue that the tax system should treat taxpayers as individuals for all purposes, how does that interact with other provisions that make spousal status relevant? What about family law, immigration law, or pension law, or any other rules that take spousal status into account? All these measures are inextricably linked, and cannot be

[39] C Pasma and S Regehr, *Basic Income: Some Policy Options for Canada* (report prepared for the Basic Income Canada Network, 2019) 2: https://basicincomecanada.org/policy_options/; Basic Income Network, *Signposts to Success: Report of the BICN Survey of Ontario Basic Income Recipients* (Basic Income Network, 2019) basicincome.org/news/2019/06/canada-report-signposts-to-success-shows-how-beneficial-the-cancelled-ontario-basic-income-experiment-was-being/.

[40] K Pate, *Why a Guaranteed Livable Income?* (Office of Kim Pate, Independent Senator, 10 May 2020) sencanada.ca/media/366776/senpate_glibi-perspective-document_10-05-2020_e.pdf; and S Kimpson, 'Basic Income, Gender and Disability' (Women's Legal Education and Action Fund (LEAF), 2022) www.leaf.ca/publication/basic-income-gender-and-disability/.

addressed as discrete questions, which returns us to the question of whether we should advocate for abolition of the legal regulation of marriage and marriage-like relationships in the course of advocating for a guaranteed basic income.

Abolishing Marriage and Family Law

We have suggested that marriage has not become quite as irrelevant or more egalitarian and benign as Rosemary may think,[41] nor has it become simply one amongst several personal lifestyles from which to choose. It remains a very powerful ideology, infecting unmarried relationships as well. In Canada, even if statistics indicate that unmarried couples are on the rise and marriage rates are somewhat diminished, marriage remains the predominant type of union. In 2021, 77 per cent of couples were married, with the remaining 23 per cent living common law. Although Canada has the highest share of couples living common law among G7 countries (23 per cent), this number mainly reflects the popularity of unmarried unions in the province of Quebec, which is home to 43 per cent of Canada's common-law couples.[42] Excluding Quebec, the share of common-law couples in Canada would have been 17 per cent. Moreover, the prevalence of living common law drops sharply after young adulthood in most provinces and territories, suggesting that living common law tends to be a 'prelude' to marriage. (To a lesser extent, living common law is gaining popularity at older ages as well.) This trend also suggests that unmarried couples may marry when they have children (except in Quebec), meaning that illegitimacy – or having children outside wedlock – remains a stigma to some extent and that marriage remains the privileged form of relationship.[43] The choice to live together unmarried is no guarantee that spouses will adopt more egalitarian patterns within their relationships, for example in relation to who assumes more responsibility for childcare.

Even in Quebec, which has the highest rate of living unmarried, yet offers the least protection for unmarried couples of all Canadian provinces, research suggests that 45 per cent of Quebec *de facto* spouses believe that they have the same legal status as married people.[44] Forty-nine per cent believe that their assets would be shared equally in the event of a breakup and 39 per cent believe that

[41] Rosemary has acknowledged that the institution of marriage is not entirely free of oppressive features: Auchmuty (n 2) 169.

[42] From 1981 to 2021, the number of common-law couples increased by 447%, whereas married couples increased by only 26%. Statistics Canada, 'State of the Union: Canada Leads the G7 with Nearly One-Quarter of Couples Living Common Law, Driven by Quebec' *The Daily* (13 July 2022) www150.statcan.gc.ca/n1/daily-quotidien/220713/dq220713b-eng.htm.

[43] Living common law drops rapidly from ages 25 to 34, then declines more slowly to reach its lowest levels in the oldest age group: ibid.

[44] H Belleau, 'One Myth Leads to Another: From Ignorance of the Laws to the Presumption of Informed Choice among de Facto Spouses' in E Aloni and R Tremblay (eds), *House Rules: Changing Families, Evolving Norms, and the Role of Law* (University of British Columbia Press, 2022) 213, 220, citing H Belleau, C Lavallée and A Seery, *Unions et désunions conjugales au Québec: rapport de recherche.*

the financially weaker spouse would be entitled to spousal support upon breakup. Given that some degree of inequality will almost inevitably exist at the time of many relationship breakdowns, especially in opposite sex relationships where the gender-based income gap and the motherhood penalty are pertinent,[45] it appears that a significant number of unmarried partners will be left economically vulnerable should a breakup occur, not to mention disappointed.

More couples still fall into patterns of economic dependency than we would like to think in these modern times, including lesbian and gay couples. Rosemary notes the possibility of unequal same sex relationships, observing that the gay men she interviewed in particular seemed to ignore the repercussions of power dynamics.[46] Younger civil partners too seemed less concerned by feminist concerns about resisting gender roles and dependency, with many embracing terms such as 'wife', 'husband', and 'marriage'. Surely remedies are still needed for individuals who adopt a role that contributes to them suffering negative economic repercussions if the relationship ends. Gendered patterns have shifted somewhat over recent decades, but women carry a greater load of childcare and household labour, as well as mental and emotional labour and the pandemic has exacerbated these patterns.[47] Considerable gendered behaviour thus persists in this third decade of the twenty-first century, which leads to socio-economic inequalities both within society and within relationships, including, it seems, same sex relationships.

Rosemary has consistently advocated for better conveyancing practices and more use of and better public legal education about the use of contracts, joint ownership, and wills to govern relationships, rather than family law remedies. We wonder, however, whether most individuals entering intimate partnerships will be sufficiently informed and rational to utilise these remedies effectively. Will persisting power relations between intimate partners allow for reasonably equal negotiations for contracts that will govern their relationship? Will relationships not change over time in ways that exacerbate inter-personal inequalities and depart from the assumptions that might have underpinned negotiation of a contract? Rosemary acknowledges this problem to some extent when discussing marriage.[48]

In relation to private remedies such as contract and wills, the more economically powerful person tends to protect their own interests. As Rosemary notes, the reaction of the lesbian with the greater assets is similar to that of a wealthy husband finding out that his carefully negotiated marriage contract might be varied in a

Première partie: le couple, l'argent et le droit (INRS Centre Urbanisation Culture Société, 2017) espace.inrs.ca/5763/1/belleau-2017-unionsA.pdf.

[45] See discussion of gender wage and wealth gaps above (n 30). A Crittenden, *The Price of Motherhood* (Metropolitan Books, 2001).

[46] Auchmuty, 'Dissolution or disillusion?' (n 10). See also Barker (n 36) 200, suggesting that we refer to the impact of the 'marriage model' rather than marriage itself as we consider the consequences of expanding relationship recognition.

[47] R Pettigrew, 'An Untenable Workload: COVID-19 and the Disproportionate Impact on Women's Work–Family Demands' (2021) 113 *Journal of Family and Consumer Sciences* 8.

[48] Auchmuty (n 2) 169.

divorce order.[49] Yet she argues that the ideal of individual autonomy characterising (some) non-heterosexual relationships is worthy of attention. Can public legal education and knowledge of law proceed to the point that individuals with less economic or psychic power can use private remedies to protect themselves? Younger heterosexual women may 'choose' to have separate bank accounts from their spouses in a spirit of independence and autonomy, but they still tend to earn less while sometimes contributing the same amounts to the household in the name of 'equality'. This form of equality is, we suggest, not meaningful or substantive. Yet courts sometimes affirm unequal economic consequences at the end of a relationship as acceptable on the grounds that they reflect the (earlier) 'choice' of an (unequal) arrangement or dynamic in the relationship.[50] This argument is based on the much criticised concepts of liberal individualism and choice that constrain decisions at various points in negotiating an intimate relationship. Even assuming that a strong degree of legal literacy is possible in the general cohabiting public, an 'optimism bias' among other factors may deter individuals from negotiating an arrangement that will adequately protect their interests.[51]

As a result of these problems, we are reluctant to suggest that family law remedies resting on spousal status (eg matrimonial property, spousal support) can be abandoned (yet) in favour of more universal remedies. Even Carol Smart in her response to Rosemary's reflections on Smart's *Law and the Power of Feminism* suggested that there is ongoing need for feminist interventions in family law, notably in relation to children and post separation care and support.[52] We too remain reluctant to abandon this terrain of discursive struggle. At the same time, we appreciate that family law financial remedies assist only a subset of those with spousal status who suffer economic inequality, mainly those who have been in a relationship with a reasonably well off person and who are able to negotiate or litigate a good remedy. Universal remedies are ultimately far more effective and desirable and arguably more likely to tackle material inequalities. Can we strive on both fronts to redress inequalities? Should family law be conceptualised as one part only of a larger system of public law – a sort of social insurance scheme – that allocates the risk of life events including poverty, disability, mental illness as well as family breakup?[53]

We agree with Rosemary that it is necessary to work more forcefully towards transformation of unequal social and economic relations. Capitalism still relies

[49] Auchmuty, 'The Experience of Civil Partnership Dissolution' (n 10) 168–69.

[50] See A Diduck, 'Family Law as Expression: Financial Relief in the English Courts' in Aloni and Tremblay (n 44) 91.

[51] See Belleau (n 44) 223–26.

[52] C Smart, 'Reflection' (2012) 20 *Feminist Legal Studies* 161–65, at 162–63.

[53] A Alstott, 'Private Tragedies? Family Law as Social Insurance' (2010) 4(1) *Harvard Law and Policy Review* 3; see also J Halley and K Rittich, 'Critical Directions in Comparative Family Law: Genealogies and Contemporary Studies of Family Law Exceptionalism' (2010) 58(4) *American Journal of Comparative Law* 753. Building on this sort of work, Brenda Cossman attempts a thought experiment that would move family law away from the current private civil law system towards a more public form of social law and simplified dispute resolution: 'Abolishing Family Law (as We Know It)' in Aloni and Tremblay (n 44) 303.

on the privatisation of responsibility for care and dependency within the family, perhaps increasingly so, and opening marriage to same sex partners clearly has not transformed that deeply material problem. Indeed the same sex marriage campaigns arguably distracted from these more important issues.[54] But until we address those large issues of capitalist patriarchy, can we abandon family law remedies and the struggle to improve them? Do we therefore need to continue to legally recognise certain types of intimate relationships, at least for certain purposes? Is there a way to accomplish both strategies without losing sight of an overall transformational goal? Can we avoid an 'either/or' approach in this context?[55]

Alternative Models of Relationship Regulation?

In relation to pursuing multiple strategies, we ask whether there is any form of recognition and regulation of relationships, at least for certain purposes, that allows us to redress many of the inequities we have discussed?

Numerous feminist legal scholars have proposed innovative models for recognising relationships beyond the marriage model. They have often done so in the course of critically analysing the marriage model and its relationship to the lack of universal remedies for economic equality, and lack of access to health care in the American context. For example, as Rosemary discusses, Martha Fineman has famously argued that instead of couples, the primary relationship that should be legally protected is the mother/child bond, with the idea being to confer legal protection, and therefore resources, to care relationships.[56] Fineman's rationale is that the inevitable dependency of young children generates a derivative (economic and structural) dependency in their caregivers, who are usually women. The state should accordingly recognise this structural dependency and organise social and economic support around it. Other benefits such as health care could be extended on an individual basis. Building on this work, Nancy Polikoff has argued that instead of prioritising marriage relationships, law should recognise households that are raising children and also allow registration of 'designated family relationships'.[57] These could be partners or spouses, but equally they might be committed friends, thus expanding the range of legally recognised relationships beyond traditional markers of biology and marriage. Along these lines, Régine Tremblay proposes that the test for legal recognition of relationships should be functional rather than conjugality or formal criteria, notably emotional and economic interdependency, with various tests being available to rebut any

[54] Auchmuty (n 2) 174–75.

[55] See Boyd and Young (n 21) 778–85.

[56] Auchmuty (n 11) 295. MA Fineman, *The Neutered Mother, The Sexual Family and Other Twentieth Century Tragedies* (Routledge, 1995). See also Barker (n 36).

[57] N Polikoff, *Beyond (Straight and Gay) Marriage: Valuing All Families under the* Law (Beacon Press, 2008).

presumption of interdependency.[58] It is worth pointing out that many models of ascription of relationship status already allow for some degree of contracting out, thus allowing some flexibility to craft innovative relationships that depart from norms, while protecting against certain vulnerabilities.[59]

In relation to the significance of friendship relationships, Rosemary notes that 'families we choose'[60] often arose when families of gay men and lesbians rejected or abandoned them, providing alternative models for support that depart from nuclear family and biological networks. Families we choose mostly fall outside the couple model, as do friendship support networks or sibling supports, such as the Burden sisters. Rosemary points out that with the rise of same sex marriage, these alternative models have been marginalised once again. Will moving towards legal recognition of these models promote equality and more transformative remedies, or is this strategy risky given the privatising impetus of most states in the current era?

Proposed alternatives for relationship recognition have appeal, but we return to the question of how such legal regulation would work and whether once again, in a capitalist system, law and policy might reinforce the privatisation of care relationships.[61] Will the neo-liberal state inevitably be tempted to use recognition of an expanded range of relationships in order to further privatise economic responsibilities? While from the point of view of simplicity and improving legal literacy it may be desirable to strive for consistency in definitions of legal relationships across various areas of law,[62] the repercussions of standardising relationship recognition in various realms can be radically different, and not always positive (for example when spousal status is used to claw back benefits for single mothers).

Rosemary also raises concerns about legal regulation of alternative models.[63] To follow her logic, we worry that to recognise and regulate such models would endanger more innovative relationships with assimilation into a 'familial' model, just as same sex couples have been assimilated into a nuclear model that tends towards traditionalism, and that state interests in privatisation of financial responsibility may colonise them. As well, will advocates for universal remedies be distracted or thwarted by such initiatives to recognise alternative models of living? These, we think, are some key questions for future researchers to explore, based on Rosemary's work and that of other feminist legal scholars who point to the dangers of limiting our legal imaginations about transformative strategies. Thinking beyond disciplinary boundaries to consider strategies and their potentially varying implications across fields such as tax, family law, immigration, and poverty law will be crucial, as well as looking beyond the limits of law.

[58] R Tremblay, 'Recoding Family Law: Towards a Theory of Relationships of Economic and Emotional Interdependency in the Civil Code of Québec' (forthcoming) 68 *McGill Law Journal*. See also Law Commission of Canada (n 23).

[59] See eg British Columbia's Family Law Act, SBC 2011, c 25, s 6(5).

[60] K Weston, *Families We Choose: Lesbians, Gays, Kinship* (Columbia University Press, 1991).

[61] Barker (n 36) 202–03.

[62] Belleau (n 44) 225–26.

[63] Auchmuty (n 11) 297, 298.

11

Until Marriage Do Us Part: Women Teachers and the Marriage Bar in the 1920s

HARRIET SAMUELS

Introduction

During the 1920s many local authorities in England and Wales adopted a policy of dismissing married women teachers in their employment. The marriage bar, as it was known, was contested in the courts and the litigation provides an early twentieth century example of a series of test cases that attempted to overturn a discriminatory policy. The legal claims failed, and the courts rejected the argument that local authorities had acted beyond their statutory powers. In *Price v Rhondda Urban District Council*, the court held that the marriage bar was not inconsistent with the Sex Disqualification (Removal) Act 1919 or in restraint of marriage.[1] The Court of Appeal subsequently upheld the marriage bar in *Short v Poole Corporation*,[2] and this case was followed in *Fennell v East Ham Corporation*, ending the attempt in the courts to halt the dismissal of married women teachers.[3] When the litigation failed, the campaign to abolish the marriage bar continued through political lobbying, achieving limited success, with the bar being lifted in some local authorities.[4] The marriage bar for teachers was finally abolished in England and Wales by the Education Act 1944.[5]

The nature of the losses in the courts and the precedent set by the Court of Appeal in *Short v Poole Corporation* would appear to caution against the use of law to advance feminist aims. One view is that such cases reveal the impervious nature of legal reasoning to women's demand for equality and the limitations of law as a

[1] *Price v Rhondda Urban District Council* [1923] 2 CH 372 (hereafter *Price v Rhondda UDC*).
[2] *Short v Poole Corporation* [1926] Ch 66.
[3] *Fennell v East Ham Corporation* [1926] Ch 641.
[4] A Oram, *Women Teachers and Feminist Politics 1900–39* (Manchester University Press, 1996) 26.
[5] See further H Samuels, 'Education Act 1944' in E Rackley and R Auchmuty (eds), *Women's Legal Landmarks: Celebrating the History of Women and the Law in the UK and Ireland* (Hart, 2018).

progressive force.[6] The result of the cases could serve as warning against litigation on the grounds that court-based challenges are expensive, can deplete activists' energy and may set unfortunate legal precedents.[7]

This chapter shifts the focus away from the outcome of the cases to concentrate on the tenacity and collective endeavour of the women who challenged the marriage bar. Whilst there are excellent historical accounts of the resistance to the bar, the discussion of the litigation is scattered throughout much of the historical literature, and there is no standalone analysis of the litigation's place within feminist legal history.[8] Compared with other legal challenges such as the suffrage and person cases it has received little attention.[9] The intention here is to fill this gap by exploring why the women were so determined to challenge the marriage bar in court, and despite their failure why it should be considered an important act of resistance. Adopting this perspective is consistent with the goals of feminist legal history as it identifies women as agents of change and explores how they tried to effect improvements and overcome the legal and political obstacles in their way.[10] To fully understand the context of the cases on the marriage bar, the chapter gives a detailed examination of the judgments, but also looks beyond the law reports to the reporting of the cases in the popular press and the newsletters or gazettes of the relevant trade unions and campaigning organisations. It uses feminist legal method to 'ask the woman question' to illuminate the gendered nature of the decision making.[11] Feminist legal method enables a deeper understanding of the loss that the married women teachers suffered and the impact the marriage bar had on their everyday life. Throughout the chapter there is a deliberate use of the women's full names and an identification of the schools they worked at. Their personal circumstances and the impact of the marriage bar on their lives is made plain as part of the feminist method of writing women's lived experience back into law. It is also a reminder that there are real people before the court who deserve to be addressed, and for whose treatment the court should be accountable.

The struggle against the marriage bar lasted decades, and there were many twists and turns before it was finally overturned. It was fought in the courts, in Parliament, in government, in local councils and within trade unions. Writing

[6] MJ Mossman, 'Feminism and Legal Method: The Difference It Makes' (1987) 3 *Wisconsin Women's Law Journal* 147.

[7] For the history of public interest litigation in the UK, see C Harlow and R Rawlings, *Pressure through Law* (Routledge, 1992) and J Cooper and R Dhavan, *Public Interest Law* (Basil Blackwell, 1987).

[8] See eg Oram (n 4).

[9] See A Sachs and J Hoff Wilson, *Sexism and the Law: A Study of Male Beliefs and Judicial Bias* (Martin Robertson, 1978).

[10] E Rackley and R Auchmuty, 'The Case for Feminist Legal History' (2020) 4 *Oxford Journal of Legal Studies* 878, 879.

[11] See KT Bartlett, 'Feminist Legal Method' (1990) 4 *Harvard Law Review* 829. See also R Hunter, 'An Account of Feminist Judging' in R Hunter, C McGlynn and E Rackley (eds), *Feminist Judgments: From Theory to Practice* (Hart, 2010) 30.

about the failure of the claim in the case of *Price v Rhondda UDC*, the editors of *The Common Cause* write:

> We condole with them; but we congratulate them warmly on their courage since by their action they have undoubtedly defended the 'common cause'.[12]

For legal feminists there is a need to reflect on the place of law within a long and difficult campaign. What does the episode tell us about the use of litigation as part of a campaign and does it reflect a naivety about the law? Even if this is so, it is still appropriate to acknowledge the courage and spirit of ordinary women in standing up for their rights before the law and to recognise the collective effort that was necessary to shape society and to attempt to imbue equality norms throughout law, policy and politics.[13]

The Background to the Marriage Bar in the Teaching Profession

The vigorous implementation of the marriage bar in teaching in the 1920s needs to be seen in the context of the political, social and economic policies of the time. After the First World War there had been some limited political gains for women subsequent to the long campaign of the suffrage movement. Women over 30 had obtained the right to vote in the Representation of the People Act 1918, and women were able to stand for Parliament.[14] Parliament had also passed the Sex Disqualification (Removal) Act 1919 removing barriers preventing women from entering various professions such as the law.

During the war, women, as a reserve labour force, were used to carry out many jobs that were previously only open to men, and they were widely praised for their contribution and competence. Yet once the war ended women were pressured to give up their jobs and return to the home. One example of this was the enactment of the Pre-War Trade Practices Act 1919 which restored trade practices to their pre-1914 position. It was intended to ensure that soldiers could come back to their pre-war jobs in industry on similar terms and conditions. This wiped out many of the gains women had made: for instance, it made it illegal for women to be employed in engineering processes whether skilled or unskilled. It meant that women's skill and knowledge gained in industry during the war were disregarded, as well as denying women continued employment opportunities.[15]

[12] 'Editorial: The Right to Marry' *The Common Cause* (London, 11 May 1923). *The Common Cause* was the weekly journal of the National Union of Women's Suffrage Societies.

[13] For an example of this approach, see R Auchmuty, 'Whatever Happened to Miss Bebb? *Bebb v The Law Society* and Women's Legal History' (2011) 31 *Legal Studies* 199.

[14] Parliament (Qualification) Act 2019.

[15] S Law, *Suffrage and Power: The Women's Movement 1918–1928* (IB Taurus, 1997) 75.

The reasons why there was hostility to women remaining in the workforce and hindrance of further progress towards equality after the First World War were complex. They were partly economic as there was a financial slump, after a brief economic boom, in the early 1920s. The rate of unemployment increased, compounded by demobilisation and the Government not being prepared for peace.[16] In these circumstances married women wanting to work were seen as greedy because it was assumed their husbands would provide for them. They were also perceived as selfish in preventing single women from being employed and depriving men, especially former soldiers, of a job. Having been praised during the war for undertaking work which contributed to the war effort, they were then vilified for wanting to continue in employment after the war.[17]

This more reactionary era was fuelled by concerns about population decline and alarm by some at the fraying of classical gender roles.[18] The response was to push women out of the workforce and require them to return to the family, where their primary role was in the domestic sphere raising children and where men earned a wage that supported the family. Kingsley Kent explains there was a backlash against feminism that extended beyond employment and a 'kinder, kuche, kirche ideology stressing traditional femininity and motherhood permeated British culture'.[19] She suggests that, after the turmoil and anxiety of the war, the traditional family was seen as an antidote to the confusion and unfamiliarity of that period and a prerequisite for social peace.[20] The marriage bar, which had always been applied in some local areas, was now being promoted and applied more vigorously as it fitted with the move to domesticate married women and confine them to the private sphere. The reasons given by local authorities for the reintroduction of the marriage bar varied, but they were a combination of economic necessity and a desire to give jobs to men and single women who had recently trained as teachers but could not find work. Yet this reasoning was usually reinforced by tropes about the lack of efficiency of married women who, it was said, took too much time off work and whose central preoccupation was or should be attending to the needs of their husbands and children.

The realisation that the enthusiastic reintroduction of the marriage bar spoke to a politics that went beyond the economic was obvious to many feminist activists.[21] For example, at the National Union of Women Teachers (hereafter

[16] S Rowbotham, *A Century of Women: The History of Women in Britain and the United States* (Viking, 1997) 89 and Law (n 15) 63.

[17] S Kingsley Kent, 'The Politics of Sexual Difference: World War 1 and the Demise of British Feminism' (1988) 27 *Journal of British Studies* 232.

[18] HL Smith, 'British Feminism in the 1920's' in HL Smith (ed), *British Feminism in the Twentieth Century* (Edward Elgar, 1990) 47–65.

[19] Kingsley Kent (n 17) 239. *Kinder, kuche and kirche* means children, kitchen and church. It is a German phrase indicating that women's responsibilities should be restricted to looking after their children and household, cooking and fulfilling their religious obligations.

[20] S Kingsley Kent, 'Gender Reconstruction after the First World War' in Smith (n 18) 66–80, 71.

[21] Law (n 15) 67.

NUWT) conference in Cardiff in 1923 a London representative, Mrs Tidswall, is reported as saying: 'the reactionaries wanted to stab women in the back. If the movement for the dismissal of married women succeeded women would be driven back to the position of marrying to be kept. I hoped we had advanced beyond that stage.'[22]

Unfortunately, this was not the situation and to retain some of the economic power and status that women had earned during the war required a determined political and legal struggle.

Challenging the Marriage Bar Through the Courts

The three documented legal challenges to the marriage bar occurred in the areas of Rhondda in Wales, East Ham in London, and Poole in Dorset. They were very widely reported in the national press and in the local press throughout England and Wales. This may have been because similar disputes on the marriage bar were taking place at the local level across the country, the results of the cases were relevant as each local area had to decide whether the bar should be imposed on schools in its jurisdiction. So regional newspapers reported the proceedings in some depth, and this fed into the heated debates about the marriage bar.

In each reported case there was a lead plaintiff who gave evidence and was cross-examined, but it was understood that these were test cases, and the courts refer to them accordingly. The litigation in *Short v Poole Corporation* was funded by the National Union of Teachers (hereafter NUT) whilst the women in *Fennell v East Ham Corporation* received financial backing from the NUWT.[23] The earliest case, *Price v Rhondda UDC*, was funded by the plaintiffs themselves as the NUT had refused to provide funding, claiming that it had received legal advice that the case was unwinnable.[24] This was resented by its married women members, and the NUT was seen as not fighting hard enough to protect their interests.

The arguments made in the three cases varied slightly, but they mainly focused on the exercise of statutory power by the local authorities, although in *Price v Rhondda* there was an important attempt to rely on the Sex Disqualification (Removal Act) 2019.

Price v Rhondda Urban District Council

The dispute in this case arose because in December 1919 Rhondda Urban District Council resolved to reinstate a marriage bar that had been suspended during the war.

[22] 'The Married Woman's Right to Work: Teachers Claim Equality' *Manchester Guardian* (Manchester, 6 January 1923).
[23] Oram (n 4) 167–68.
[24] ibid.

The council gave notice that the dismissal of married women would take effect on 31 July 1920, but that those women who needed to complete minimum qualifying periods to receive their pension would be allowed to continue working until they qualified. However, in July 1922 the council went back on this promise and decided that all married women should be dismissed even if they had not worked long enough to safeguard their pension. The reasons given were that there were many single women who had graduated from college as certified teachers but who were unable to find work. In addition, it was said that the married women teachers were undesirable employees as they had to take periodical absences, presumably for pregnancy and childbirth, that were inconvenient for the school as substitute teachers had to be found. There were exemptions to the bar for married women whose husbands were infirm and unable to support them, although any exceptions were strictly interpreted and applied.[25]

The married women in Rhondda, as the case report shows, were treated particularly shabbily by the local authority.[26] They lost their jobs, their income, and their career prospects. Some were also deprived of their pensions after the council reneged on its promise. To compound matters they were told that any time off to have a child would not count towards their pension qualifying period. It is therefore unsurprising that the married women teachers were eager to challenge the decision by any means possible, and this included through the courts.

The lead plaintiff was Elizabeth Price, an assistant teacher at Cwm Clydach, Ystradyfodwg in Glamorgan, who sued on behalf of 57 other teachers including some headteachers. The argument based on contract, specific to the situation in the Rhondda, that related to the promise to allow the teachers to remain until they had qualified for their pension was rejected. Then, in common with the other two marriage bar cases, it was argued that the dismissals of married women took the council outside of its statutory powers. Section 35 of the Elementary Education Act 1870 required the local authority to act for the statutory purpose of maintaining the efficiency of the school (educational efficiency).[27] It was argued that the married women teachers were not dismissed for the statutory purpose of educational efficiency, but for the economic reason of reducing unemployment amongst newly certified single teachers. Eve J rejects this argument, holding that the authority acted for an educational purpose. He holds that the council honestly believed that in the long-term harm would be done to the education of the children in the area if so many newly qualified women teachers were unemployed. The council could therefore justify the married women teachers' dismissal in order to find jobs for new teachers.[28]

[25] ibid 62.
[26] *Price v Rhondda Urban District Council* (n 1) 373–80.
[27] Subsequently Education Act 1921, s 17.
[28] *Price v Rhondda Urban District Council* (n 1) 390.

The plaintiffs also argued that the local authority's policy was in restraint of marriage and public policy. Knowing they would be dismissed might cause women teachers to reject marriage. The judge did not accept this stating that:

> it would, in my opinion be pressing public policy to intolerable lengths to hold that it was outraged by this Authority expressing a preference for unmarried over married women as teachers, [since] the services of the latter are frequently not continuous but are liable to be interrupted by absences extending over several months.[29]

So, in other words, it is not in restraint of marriage and contrary to public policy to prefer to employ unmarried women as teachers as they do not get pregnant and take time off work to give birth and expect to come back to a job.

One of the most important arguments made centred on the Sex Disqualification (Removal) Act 1919. This legislation was the consequence of a long campaign to remove disqualifications that prevented women from entering the professions. It had been introduced by the Government to kill off a more radical bill that had been proposed to Parliament by the Labour Party and that had the support of most feminists.[30] The Sex Disqualification (Removal) Act 1919 did not explicitly outlaw the marriage bar. Nevertheless, many feminists still hoped that the legislation was wide enough to prohibit marriage bars being implemented, and that it would be interpreted by the courts to forbid discrimination on the grounds of marriage. Section 1 of the Sex Disqualification (Removal) Act 1919 states that:

> A person shall not be disqualified by sex or marriage from the exercise of any public function, or from being appointed to or holding any civil or judicial office or post, or from entering or assuming or carrying on any civil profession or vocation, or for admission to any incorporated society.

It was argued that the local authority's marriage bar infringed the letter and the spirit of the legislation. Disappointing the plaintiffs and their supporters, the judge dismisses the argument in a few lines, not even calling on counsel for Rhondda to respond to the plaintiffs' argument, stating that:

> I cannot accept that view. The Act, as appears from its title, is an act to remove certain disqualifications arising from sex, and I am not prepared to hold that an authority commits a breach of that Act if in some of its appointments it indicates that applications from one sex only can be received. Consider the absurdity to which such a conclusion might lead.[31]

Having rejected the plaintiffs' arguments, showing himself to be completely closed-minded, adopting a rather mocking tone, and dismissing the action with costs, he

[29] ibid 391.

[30] See M Takayanagi, 'Sacred Year or Broken Reed? The Sex Disqualification (Removal) Act 1919' (2020) 29 *Women's History Review* 563.

[31] *Price v Rhondda UDC* (n 1) 391.

goes on to say that he feels sympathy towards the married women, especially those near the pensionable qualifying period, and he hopes the council will take this into account. He continues:

> It only remains for me to say that no one can feel anything but very genuine sympathy for these ladies, and I earnestly hope that the Authority will take into consideration the question whether it is not possible to alleviate the hardship which results from its action, at any rate, in those cases where the teacher has had a comparatively short period to serve before becoming entitled to the superannuation benefit.[32]

Reading the summary of the proceedings and the discussions that took place in court in non-legal sources Eve J's sympathy appears rather hollow. Referring to the fact that pregnant women teachers took time off to give birth he jokes that: 'I suppose when we have women judges the court will be closed in similar circumstances for twelve months.'[33] The report notes that this comment was followed by laughter. Eve J also banters about the position of unemployed single women teachers. He quips that '[t]hey can make cooks of them which would be more useful!' to which counsel for the local authority replies '[b]ut according to the other side you would not be able to discharge the cook when she married'. Eve J responds '[t]he trouble is to get one first'.[34] Humour may sometimes relieve tension in a difficult situation such as a courtroom, but when reading these accounts of the hearing there is a sense of the male judge and lawyers finding the idea of the married women protesting their treatment as mildly amusing, and that the idea of equality is something to make light of and not to be taken entirely seriously.

The imposition of the marriage bar locally rather than nationally meant that it was not long before a second case came before the courts a few years later. This time the NUT did agree to support the married women and fund the litigation as a test case.

Short v Poole Corporation

This case was heard at first instance by Romer J in July 1925. The plaintiff, Mrs Ethel Florence Short was successful at first instance, but the decision was reversed in the Court of Appeal. There were at least 16 other married women teachers who worked in elementary schools in Poole in a similar position to Ethel Short. There was some uncertainty as to the exact reason for the council's decision to dismiss married women teachers. However, the judge accepted, based on a letter written by the town clerk to some of the schools where the women worked, that the reasons were the belief that married women could not effectively attend

[32] ibid 392.
[33] (1923) *Times Educational Supplement.*
[34] 'Ought Wives to be Teachers: Judge Suggests Making Our Girls Cooks' *The Daily Herald* (London, 18 April 1923).

to their work and domestic duties. Also, that it was unfair for married women, whose husbands could keep them, to occupy jobs when there were many unmarried teachers without teaching positions.[35]

Ethel Short had been employed by the council since 1905 as a certificated assistant teacher at the girl's department of the Branksome Heath Council Elementary School. In 1914 she took up a position as an assistant mistress at Heatherlands Council School, Parkstone, Dorset, a public elementary school. In August 1921 she married Mr Short, and she carried on teaching until July 1924 when she received a notice informing her of the council's decision to cease to employ married women whose husbands 'were living and capable of supporting them'.[36] Along with the other married teachers, she was invited to write to the council to persuade them that she should continue to be engaged as a teacher. This was intended to allow for the retention of a married woman teacher on compassionate grounds if, for example, her husband could not keep her due to illness or infirmity. Ethel Short replied informing the council that she had no domestic ties to hinder her 'in the smallest sense', that her husband earned 4/ (shillings) a week and that she hired help in the home.[37] Her mother who lived with her supervised in her absence, and therefore she could give her duties as a teacher her 'whole and undivided attention'.[38] From the newspaper accounts it is also reported that Ethel Short earned more money than her husband who was the chief librarian in Poole and on a much smaller salary than her own, therefore the loss of income would be significant.[39] So Ethel Short does not fit the stereotype of a married woman occupied by domesticity, and her desire to pursue a career as a teacher and to be the main breadwinner for her family is alien to the ideology being imposed through the marriage bar.

In *Short v Poole Corporation*, the argument was focused almost exclusively on whether the reasons for the dismissal were consistent with the statutory purpose of educational efficiency. It was argued that terminating the married women teachers' employment to provide jobs for unmarried and newly qualified women teachers was not a policy adopted to further educational objectives. In addition, counsel for Ethel Short made the case forcefully that the authority had adopted this policy because its members believed that married women should not work. It was therefore acting for 'alien and irrelevant purposes' as opposed to the statutory purpose of educational efficiency.[40] By inquiring into the financial circumstances of the married women teachers and their husbands, the authority was trying to 'regulate the domestic and sociological conditions of the district'.[41] This was not an educational purpose as required by the statute.

[35] *Short v Poole Corporation* (n 2) 77.
[36] ibid 73.
[37] ibid 76.
[38] ibid 76.
[39] 'Married Teacher Wins her Case' *Yorkshire Evening Post* (York, 31 July 1925).
[40] *Short v Poole Corporation* (n 2) 68.
[41] ibid 68.

The judge, Mr Justice Romer, agrees with the plaintiff noting that Ethel Sharp is, 'exceptionally free from ties that might interfere with the discharge of her duties as a teacher'.[42] He holds that the authority had not acted on educational grounds but because it wanted to 'remove … any inducement to married women teachers to neglect their domestic concerns'.[43] In other words, he agrees that the council was imposing its view of the division of labour between husband and wife by introducing the marriage bar. The judge also finds that the council believed that the primary duty of married women was their domestic obligations and that unmarried women teachers were in greater need of work. He holds that these were irrelevant and alien reasons and inconsistent with the council's statutory powers which required it to act for the purpose of educational efficiency.

He also points out the inconsistency of the council's reasoning that married women were less efficient than single women. The judge states that:

> I cannot understand what the Education Committee or the Council had to do with the financial position of the teachers and their husbands. If … the Council were really of the opinion that the best interest of education in their district demanded that married women teachers should no longer be employed, the amount of the husband's salary or the teacher's income from outside sources was surely an irrelevant consideration …[44]

The judge maintains that if the council genuinely believed that married women were poor teachers due to distractions in their home life then their financial situation was irrelevant. The judge also highlights the indignity and intrusion of privacy that the married women and their families underwent. Many of the newspaper and journal reports pick up on this salient point and quote this part of the judgment verbatim. This is because Romer J strongly indicates that he suspects the council's policy is more about imposing traditional familial values than about educating the young.

Unfortunately, the Court of Appeal in *Short v Poole Corporation* reversed the decision and upheld the marriage bar. It found that the judge at first instance had adopted a very narrow view of what was an educational purpose. It held that the local authority was entitled to consider educational policy more generally that went beyond a decision about a particular school and or teacher. The court was mindful of the broad statutory discretion given to the council and emphasised judicial restraint in not interfering with the decision of an elected body. It held that the court could only interfere with the decision of an authority if it was made in bad faith or for corrupt, alien or irrelevant motives.[45] Warrington LJ notes that:

> a determination to employ as far as possible women who are devoting their lives and energies entirely to the business of teaching without assuming the privilege and the

[42] ibid 74.
[43] ibid 78.
[44] ibid 77.
[45] ibid 91.

> burden of domestic ties, cannot in my judgment be irrelevant to the maintenance of the efficiency of the schools or the course of education …[46]

He finds that a decision made in good faith would only be irrelevant if it was frivolous or foolish, for example a teacher being dismissed because she had red hair.[47] He goes on to explain that a desire to make sure that single women teachers are able to obtain employment and that parents continue to invest in their daughters' careers as teachers was relevant to the broader cause of education and was therefore a lawful factor.

So, Warrington LJ is quite sure that it was rational for the council to assume that single women were more reliable teachers than married women as they were not preoccupied by their domestic life. He appears to be equally of the view that the married women teachers should give up their careers to make way for the single women who have just qualified even though the logic of this proposition is highly questionable as discussed below.

Many of the same arguments are raised again in the third case in the trilogy.[48] This case had already been heard, but the judgment had not been given when the decision of the Court of Appeal in *Short v Poole Corporation* was handed down.

Fennell v East Ham Corporation

This case, backed by the NUWT, was brought by Katherine Ellen Fennell, Eleanor Mary Harbott and Edith Sarah Hern-Ebdon, who were employed as assistant mistresses at elementary schools in East Ham. They were all certified teachers and were married when they were appointed, with Mrs Fennell having worked as a teacher at the Shaftsbury Road Infant School since April 1910 and the other two women being appointed at the Brompton Road Girls' School in April 1919. The women are described in the judgment as 'efficient teachers', and there is no suggestion that there was any complaint about their work or how they discharged their duties. On 1 November 1924, they were given notices of dismissal because East Ham Council had adopted a policy of no longer employing married teachers. The council reached this decision after a series of heated meetings in the Education Committee and in the full council meeting, including one meeting of the Education Committee where the women had led a deputation and made representations to the council to no avail.[49]

The court following *Short v Poole Corporation* rejected the argument that the council had acted *ultra vires*. Lawrence J found that dismissing the married

[46] ibid 92.
[47] ibid 89.
[48] On the NUWT see generally, E Phipps, *History of the National Union of Women Teachers* (NUWT, 1928) 44.
[49] 'Dismissal of Married Women Teachers: Women Fight Against Dismissal', *Echo, Mail and Chronicle* (London, Friday 6 November 1925).

women to secure positions for newly qualified single teachers was for reasons of educational efficiency. He explains that there were different views on the desirability of employing married women and whether it was wrong for two salaries to go into the same home, but, in his view, the council was entitled to draw its own conclusion without the interference of the court.[50]

The law report in *Fennell v East Ham* draws attention to an additional external pressure on the council to dismiss the married women teachers. It is argued unsuccessfully by the plaintiffs that in adopting its policy on married women it had been acting under the domination of the Ratepayer's Association, a body preoccupied with financial prudence. This is contrary to the legal principle that a council must exercise its own discretionary powers independently as required by statute.[51] Evidence is given by one councillor, Mr Pope, that the reason why the married women were dismissed to make way for the single women teachers was at the instigation of the Ratepayer's Association which had demanded information about the number of married women teachers at the schools in the area and had pressed for their dismissal.[52] Even though the judge holds that the Ratepayers Association's action was the direct cause of the council pursuing the matter of the married women teachers, he finds that the council took the final decision and had exercised its discretion independently as required by law.[53]

The visceral nature of the debate over the marriage bar comes across very strongly in this judgment and in the newspaper reports. This is evident from the lobbying against the married women by the Ratepayer's Association in East Ham, the long, drawn-out meetings reported in depth in the local papers and the personal motives ascribed to the councillors. One councillor is accused of siding with the married women because his wife is a teacher and he in turn accuses a member of the Ratepayer's Association of acting out of political spite.[54] Another councillor claims the Ratepayer's Association is motivated by the fact that several members have daughters who are unmarried teachers looking for work. This reflects that what is at stake is not just a matter of economic expediency but deep-seated questions as to social values and personal convictions about social and domestic life.

The Marriage Bar Cases and Feminist Legal Method

The marriage bar cases appear to demonstrate the intransigence of legal method to feminist ideas. Mossman explains that legal method defines its own boundaries, and it is the court that decides what is a matter of law, politics and morals.[55]

[50] *Fennell v East Ham Corporation* (n 3) 655.
[51] ibid 653.
[52] ibid.
[53] ibid.
[54] ibid 644.
[55] Mossman (n 6) 164.

This enables the court to appear neutral and facilitates its assertion that it is the law and not the judges that are responsible for the result. Legal method also allows considerable choice in deciding the selection of precedent to be followed, the interpretation of statutes and whether ideas of the mainstream or margins are preferred.[56] Mossman concludes that legal method appears resistant to the changes that feminists want to see and '[t]hat legal method is structured in such a way that it is impervious to a feminist perspective'.[57] She insists that feminists must take seriously the capacity of law to reinforce and legitimate patriarchal norms and to resist the possibility of feminist transformation.

The marriage bar litigation provides good examples of the courts' use of legal method to reject credible legal arguments and to uphold the status quo. At every opportunity, with the exception of the first instance decision in *Short v Poole Corporation*, the judges choose to adopt interpretations of the facts, evidence, policy and precedent that rejected more favourable outcomes for the married women. This is despite equally credible and more progressive conclusions being possible in law.

Feminist activists at the time, commenting on the cases, see the outcomes as evidence of judicial partiality and hostility to married women who want to work. Crystal Eastman, a feminist activist and lawyer during the 1920s, highlights that in other situations the courts have been prepared to prevent the dismissal of teachers when councils have gone beyond their statutory powers.[58] She cites the case of *Sadler v Sheffield Corporation*.[59] Here the decision of a local authority to dismiss half of its teachers over 60 and to appoint younger teachers was held to be unlawful. The decision was found to have been taken for financial reasons and not the educational reasons required by the Education Act 1921. The court further held that, even if the reasons for the dismissal could be said to be partly educational, the decision could not stand as mixed grounds for the decision could not be said to be educational. Illustrating Mossman's point about the courts' discretion to choose which precedents to follow, the court in *Fennell v East Ham Corporation* declined to follow *Sadler v Sheffield Corporation* holding unconvincingly that this was a different situation.

In essence, the court shuts down the fraught debate on the marriage bar by categorising the decision to dismiss married women, to provide jobs for the newly qualified teachers, as being for reasons of educational efficiency rather than for financial prudence or prejudice against married women. It held further discussion would be to consider the merits of the policy and therefore outside the court's proper jurisdiction.

Resultantly, the counter-arguments to the marriage bar are not examined by the court. These are that public funds have been used to train both married and

[56] ibid 164.

[57] ibid 165.

[58] C Eastman, 'London Letter – The Married Teacher', *Equal Rights* (1926) in BW Cook (ed), *Crystal Eastman: On Women and Revolution* (OUP, 1978) 172–76.

[59] [1924] 1 Ch 483.

unmarried women teachers, the unfairness of the two-income household is only a 'problem' for married women and not for other two-income households. Besides, the newly trained women teachers are incapable of replacing many of the married women who hold more senior posts. One headteacher, Dr Isabel Turnadge, writing in *Time and Tide*, writes indignantly that:

> [t]he kind of post which has to be filled must be considered. In my own case it has been urged in the press that I should not be allowed to retain the post of the headmistress of Twickenham County School while numbers of young women from the elementary training colleges of the country are unable to find work. Does the general public believe that these young people could do the work I do, or even that an older woman with their qualifications would be chosen for the post that is now vacant?[60]

The fact that the newly qualified teachers will be unable to take over the work of more senior teachers is not contemplated by the courts nor is the loss of the married women teachers' life experience in enriching the children's education.

There is also no proper scrutiny of the financial arguments. In the case of East Ham, the council has provided bursaries and given money to local colleges to support the training of newly qualified teachers, and it is argued this money will be wasted if they cannot find jobs.[61] By the same token the married women's teacher training has also been supported by public money that would be 'wasted' if they are dismissed. The claim that young women, and their parents may not want to go to the expense of training as teachers if they cannot find work immediately is not adequately evidenced. Moreover, the argument that young women may not want to enter the teaching profession, at all, if their careers terminate on marriage is ignored.

By allowing the council to juxtapose the single and married women, men and other types of households can be ignored completely. For instance, households where a single teacher lived with a mother, father or brother who were in employment also enjoyed two incomes or more. The NUWT notes that:

> As to two incomes going into one home, this is just as applicable to two incomes from any source whatever and not merely from marriage. If a man marries a wife who has say 200 a year of her own, on this view he should be dismissed. If a man acquires an income by the operation of a will, equally he should be dismissed, if this theory is sound. Why limit it only to the income brought by the wife and obtained through teaching only.[62]

Once it has been decided by the court that favouring single over married women is for the reason of 'educational efficiency', the arguments as to whether there are alternative methods to achieve the councils' supposed aim, of finding jobs for single women teachers, become a policy matter not to be reviewed by the

[60] I Turnadge, 'The Merits of the Case' *Time and Tide* (London, 3 December 1926).
[61] Above n 3 at 643.
[62] 'Dismissal of Married Women Teachers' *The Woman Teacher* (London, 18 December 1925).

courts. The court can therefore ignore the argument that the underlying motive for targeting the married women for dismissal, as opposed to the male teachers, was based on a belief that required women to be mothers and homemakers kept by their husbands.

There is a wealth of evidence that illustrates that the reasons for the dismissals were the councillors' views about married women's rightful place. Despite this, the courts exclude or minimise the weight of such evidence. In *Fennell v East Ham Corporation*, the judge rejects the attempt to introduce evidence of the councillors' speeches supporting the marriage bar, this is on the grounds that they believed married women should remain at home and be supported by their spouse. Lawrence J holds that the newspaper accounts are 'fair enough as far as they went' but were not complete reports and were likely to be sensationalised.[63] Whilst the judge's concerns about reliability are not completely unfounded, the same attitude of giving little weight to alternative accounts to that of the councils is also seen in *Short v Poole Corporation*. Here, as mentioned above, one key piece of evidence put forward to show that the council is acting for ulterior motives is found in a letter written by the town clerk to the managers of some of the schools in the area. In the letter he summarises the reason for the policy to dismiss the married teachers as, first, that it is the primary duty of married women to attend to domestic concerns, and secondly the unfairness to unmarried teachers seeking work to have their positions 'occupied by married women who presumably had husbands capable of maintaining them'.[64] In the first instance judgment, in favour of the married women teachers, the judge accepted this as evidence that 'strongly suggested' the council and committee acted for ulterior motives.[65] Whereas in the Court of Appeal it was not given much weight, with it being said that it should be read 'without sinister bias', and that the council was just trying to balance the interests of married and unmarried women for educational reasons.[66]

In addition, the judges appear anxious to defend the local authorities, and to make their actions appear as reasonable as possible by presenting them in the best possible light. In the three cases, the judges seize on the fact that the councils try to take some steps to alleviate the harshness of the policy on married women whose husbands cannot support them. So, for example in *Fennell v East Ham Corporation*, Lawrence J states that what the Council eventually decided on 'was not a policy of ruthlessly terminating the engagements of all married women teachers, but was the more considerate and humane policy of reducing the number of married teachers'.[67] It involved looking at 'the domestic circumstances of the teachers and the means and earning capacity of their husbands'.[68] This framing of

[63] *Fennell v East Ham Corporation* (n 3) 656.
[64] *Short v Poole Corporation* (n 2) 78.
[65] ibid 78.
[66] ibid 86.
[67] *Fennell v East Ham Corporation* (n 3) 656.
[68] ibid 656.

the issues allowed the council and the court to appear reasonable and sympathetic whilst the intrusiveness and ruthlessness of the policy is disguised.[69] It is only in the first instance decision in *Short v Poole Corporation* that Romer J highlights the inconsistency in the reasoning, and is willing to hold the that the council's action was unlawful and an intrusion on the married women's personal life.

Overall, the courts' reasoning distracts from the sexist policy and enables the married women to be portrayed as self-centred and uncaring. This can be seen in the questions put to the women when they were cross-examined. For example, Mrs Price is asked if she has considered the impact of there being so many unemployed young teachers. She is reported as saying that it has nothing to do with her but that she 'had sympathy with everyone out of employment'.[70] The women are also accused of undermining the sanctity of marriage and not knowing their rightful place. In the case law, this is a theme that emerges from the evidence of the heated council meetings and the reasons given by the councillors for the dismissal of the married women teachers. The married women's insistence that their teaching jobs should not be sacrificed to save the jobs of a generation of young teachers is seen as self-indulgent and mercenary generating considerable hostility towards them as demonstrated by many of the newspaper headlines and the angry exchanges in the letter pages of the local and national press.[71]

In sum, the judges in the marriage bar cases proclaim their intention not to take sides on the rights and wrongs of the married women teachers' dismissals. Despite these judicial protestations, their use of legal method, treatment of the evidence and their language reveal that their decision making is far from impartial.

Evaluating the Challenges to the Marriage Bar

Whilst bringing the legal challenges did involve financial loss, and the result was ultimately disappointing, there were sound reasons for taking the risk of pursuing the litigation. These included the need to test the legislation in the courts, to expose the injustice on a personal level, challenge the stereotypes of women, circulate feminist knowledge and, if the case was lost, to energise the political campaign.

There had been a considerable investment by feminist activists in campaigning for the Sex Disqualification (Removal) Act 1919, and though the legislation did not go as far as feminists wanted it was still hoped that it might be broad enough to overturn the marriage bar. Feminists were invested in its success and wanted to

[69] 'Dismissal of Teachers, Action by Three Women Fails, Judge on Council's Humane Policy' *The Daily News* (London, 11 December 1925).

[70] 'Ought Wives to Be Teachers: Judge Suggests Making Our Girls Cooks' *The Daily Herald*, (London, 18 April 1923).

[71] A Oram, 'Serving Two Masters? The Introduction of a Marriage Bar in Teaching in the 1920s' in The London Feminist History Group (ed), *The Sexual Dynamics of History: Men's Power, Women's Resistance* (Pluto Press, 1983) 134–48.

take the opportunity to enforce it. There were some early signs that the legislation might disappoint. When the House of Lords had refused to allow Lady Rhondda to inherit her father's peerage, and to take his seat in the House of Lords, this was held to be lawful and not contrary to the 1919 Act.[72] There had also been negative legal advice received by the NUT that led it to refuse to fund the married teachers in the Rhondda in Wales.[73] However, there was still a degree of legal uncertainty about the more general arguments on statutory purpose and educational efficiency: for example, the councillors on the Education Committee in East Ham were unclear about the legal position and the advice they had received.[74] The solicitors' firm advising the NUWT thought the case was winnable. So, there was quite a lot of support in favour of testing the marriage bar. The NUWT was also keen to show that it was supporting its members, and it received many letters from married women teachers describing their financial difficulties after dismissal.[75]

The concern, which often arises when bringing a test case, that it might set an unhelpful precedent if the case is unsuccessful was used by the NUT to avoid funding the litigation in *Price v Rhondda*.[76] Ultimately, this did not prevent the litigation from going ahead as the women in *Price v Rhondda* were desperate to try to remedy the injustice being perpetrated against them. The NUT subsequently supported the legal action in Poole, and the NUWT did not want to back down in the East Ham case. It may be that so many local authorities were in the process of dismissing married teachers, despite the opaque legal position, that there was little to lose in trying to overturn the ban. At least if the limit of the legislation was understood feminists might begin to lobby politically for its amendment or replacement. So, when it became obvious that the Sex Disqualification (Removal) Act 1919 did not prevent the implementation of the marriage bar, feminist organisations turned their attention to political activism. This change of strategic direction is urged by the editors of *The Common Cause*. In a note added to a detailed summary of the negative appellate court's decision in *Short v Poole Corporation*, written by Mrs Maud Croft, a solicitor, the editors state that:

> The moral to be drawn from this able report of the case is surely that it is imperative that new legislation should be passed to safeguard the interests of married women public employees. The Sex Disqualification (Removal) Act has been shown to be a hollow sham in this respect.[77]

The feminist campaigners were aware of the possibility that their claims might be rebuffed and understood the courts might be resistant. Writing in 1922 the

[72] *Viscountess Rhondda's Claim* [1922] 2 AC 339.

[73] See Oram (n 4) 167.

[74] 'Married Women Teachers in East Ham Schools, Arrangements for Terminating their Engagement, Another Lively Committee Debate' *Chronicle* (London, 6 June 1924).

[75] Archives of the NUWT UWT/D/11/10-Married Women Teachers-East Ham case, Institute of Education, London.

[76] Oram (n 4) 183.

[77] 'Editors' Note', *The Common Cause* (London, 18 May 1923).

former president of the NUWT, AS Byett, stresses the need for a legal challenge. She admits that, 'legal processes are costly, and the law courts in this country are dominated by men and men's ideas'. She asserts that it is necessary to test the legality of the marriage bar and, if the court finds such bars are lawful, the union's membership should be instructed to refuse to sign unsatisfactory contracts and the union should shame the offending local authorities. She argues that women have been trained for generations in 'submission and subservience' and need to understand their own value.[78]

This illustrates that the NUWT saw the court action as part of a process of protest and resistance. It hoped that the considerable publicity generated by the cases would spark debates in the national and local press and would supply a platform to make the feminist arguments against the bar and provide the impetus to mount a strong political campaign. Indeed, this is what happened, and after the litigation there were two unsuccessful attempts to introduce a Private Members' bill.[79] After these bills failed the campaigners then shifted their attention from national institutions to working at the local level where they pressured local authorities, and sometimes stood for election as councillors, so they could remove the marriage bar. There were notable successes in various areas including London and Manchester.[80] However, it took further intense campaigning before the eventual repeal of the marriage bar in the Education Act 1944 after the Second World War.

Conclusion

Social change often happens very slowly, and in hindsight it may seem inevitable in a way that was not so at the time. As Rosemary Auchmuty reminds us, there is a tendency to ascribe women's legal advances to changes in social attitudes without asking why they occurred.[81] She identifies that law is presented as a series of 'top-down reforms', and the 'long arduous battle' fought by women to achieve change is often forgotten.[82]

Applying feminist legal methods to the analysis of the marriage bar cases reveals not only the gendered nature of the decision-making by the judges, but how much the married women personally had to lose. In addition to the economic suffering, there was also the emotional pain for some women of losing their career. This is expressed poignantly by Freda Corbet, who later went on to become a lawyer and a Labour Member of Parliament:

[78] AS Byett, 'Married Women' *The Woman Teacher* (NUWT, 1922).

[79] See the Married Women (Employment) Bill 1927 and Married Women Teachers (Employment).

[80] See Oram (n 4) 171.

[81] R Auchmuty, 'Recovering Lost Lives: Researching Women in Legal History (2015) 42 *Journal of Law and Society* 34, 51.

[82] ibid 51.

> I threw my career to the winds in 1925 and got married. It was a very incautious thing to do; it was a very rash thing and perhaps a very unwise thing. For ten years I have eaten my heart out because I have not been able to do the thing I liked and loved.[83]

Bringing the legal claims involved personal courage. The married women had to give evidence in court, were subject to cross-examination and had to disclose personal information about their domestic arrangements. Much of the detail was published in the national and local press, including photos of both Ethel Short and Elizabeth Price. This was in an atmosphere of backlash when patriarchal ideals were being re-asserted. They were accused of being self-centred, ungrateful and neglecting their husbands and families. Nevertheless, with their jobs and pensions on the line, they thought it was vital to take their cases to court, to tell their stories, expose the injustice of the marriage bar and to obtain redress. They were agents of change whose actions were part of the uneven journey that eventually led to the change in the law. The women teachers and the feminist activists who supported them rejected the regressive attempt to limit the horizons of married women to the home and to deprive them of their economic and personal independence. They were determined to articulate, in both legal and political institutions, a feminist vision of the domestic and working life that they believed all women were entitled to pursue.

[83] *The School Master*, 23 July 1935 as cited in G Partington, *Women Teachers in the 20th Century in England and Wales* (NFER Publishing Company, 1976) 33.

12

Women and Publishing in Family and Property Law Journals

VICTORIA BARNES AND NORA HONKALA*

Introduction

It is difficult to articulate exactly how one person matters to you and has contributed to your development in a way that is both clear and succinct. It is common in British middle-class culture (within which the academic world is embedded) to stay muted in the belief that there is some general dignity in silence. Indeed, this route would be far easier. But this is not what is demanded here on this occasion. This a *festschrift*. The tradition here is by contrast rather different and as such, it differs from any ordinary edited collection.[1] The tradition is to begin by commenting briefly on the author's relationship to the honouree and to summarise their life with overt flattery. We propose to offer some expression on our relationships with Rosemary Auchmuty,[2] but to dispense with the abject hyperbole and disingenuous laudation. We instead display what is a modicum of heart-felt and rather honest admiration. This perhaps reflects our cultural interpretation (or adaptation) of what *festschrift* ought to look like.

Such a task of balancing laudation with honesty is an act that is fraught with complexity generally speaking, but, even more so in this chapter. This is because it is far more challenging to write about your relationship with a person, when the

* We would like to thank, in particular, Sally Wheeler, Rosemary Hunter and all other contributors to the workshop on this *Festschrift* where we presented our ideas. We are also grateful for those who participated in the Brunel Law School Staff Seminar and especially to Adrienne Barnett and Felicity Kaganas, who commented on this text. We also owe Carl Stychin our thanks for his thoughts on and support of this project. All errors and omissions remain our own.

[1] Michael Taggart, 'Gardens or Graveyards of Scholarship? Festschriften in the Literature of the Common Law' (2002) 22 *Oxford Journal of Legal Studies* 227.

[2] We propose here to use Rosemary's full name throughout, as odd as it sounds. This navigates the thorny issue of referring to her by her first name, as is common in informal circles (and we do normally), or her last name, as is more common in scholarship and the normal attribution of scholar. The full name fits both of those positions.

authors are, in fact, two people. This is, after all is said and done, a joint paper. This chapter is a shared one and it is collectively written – and deliberately so. To put it simply, the authors are two different people with a separate rather than a joint set of relationships. People thus mean different things to one another. Individuals quite frequently and quite understandably have different relationships. No two (or three!) relationships are the exact same. The paragraphs that follow will nevertheless try to achieve our aim of writing about our relationships with Rosemary Auchmuty without the gratuitous detail, fictionalised accounts and the hagiographic bent. We will briefly summarise our connection to Rosemary Auchmuty and relationships with her, before moving onto the substantive aspects of the chapter and the details about its core claims in relation to scholarship.

Throughout her career, Rosemary Auchmuty has contributed to the lives of a wide range of scholars, not only in law and not only to our lives, but also in other ways. She has mentored both of the authors of this chapter. Nora Honkala has known Rosemary Auchmuty for 15 years (to date) during which Rosemary Auchmuty supervised Nora's Masters dissertation, as well as her PhD on gender and refugees in international law. Both the LLM and the PhD were undertaken at the University of Reading. Nora also had the pleasure of contributing to two projects of Rosemary Auchmuty's; the *Women's Legal Landmarks Project*, which Rosemary Auchmuty led and edited with Erika Rackley, and the *Great Debates in Gender and Law*. Both of these were valuable opportunities to work with groups of feminist scholars, and they showed how feminist projects could be different to other collective academic projects. They also provided a learning opportunity to reflect on the importance of mentoring in academia in general.

Victoria Barnes's connection to Rosemary Auchmuty is equally longstanding, but perhaps not as intense. Rosemary Auchmuty was not Victoria's PhD supervisor. She was, in Reading's lexicon of the time, her monitor.[3] In essence, each year, Rosemary Auchmuty would verify that Victoria's PhD was on track and, if we use the lexicon of today, check on her wellbeing. In other words, Rosemary Auchmuty would verify that the relationship between Victoria and her supervisors was satisfactory. Victoria gave her first paper to the Society of Legal Scholars in the Legal History section, which Rosemary Auchmuty then led. Although it is impossible to prove a counterfactual point, Victoria probably would not have presented in this section and certainly not without Rosemary Auchmuty's encouragement. This point is perhaps easy to overlook or forget many years on, where a conference presentation matters little. Small gestures do matter, though. To a PhD student with very little experience, that gesture mattered even more. It is demonstrative of the kindness and support that Rosemary Auchmuty offered, for example, by contributing to the special issue of the *Journal of Legal History* organised by Victoria (and Catharine MacMillan and Stefan Vogenauer). There Rosemary Auchmuty

[3] In other institutions, this is the Research Development Officer.

represented an important and understated viewpoint by defending the importance of a socio-legal approach to legal history, fairly unabashedly.[4]

Aside from shaping our research and beliefs about the direction of scholarship, Rosemary Auchmuty has also played a tremendous role in our academic lives and their pathways. For most of our careers, Rosemary Auchmuty was not associated with what are now her obvious research strengths. Indeed, this realisation has come for some other people, only rather recently.[5] It may be difficult to believe now that her academic leadership was for the most part concentrated around teaching rather than research. These routes have been for too long bifurcated with one being seen, by some, as lesser than the other. Contempt is often plain to see.[6]

Having been the Director of Teaching and Learning at Reading for many years, Rosemary Auchmuty was always involved closely in the discussion of legal education. Then research was (and is) more prestigious. At that time, she was, without a doubt, the leading voice on these matters and in supporting those on the teaching side.[7] It was there, in that position, that Rosemary Auchmuty encouraged greater dialogue about teaching and more reflection, but, essentially, she pushed for change in culture.[8] In the beginning of both Nora and Victoria's academic careers, Rosemary Auchmuty was instrumental in the development of our teaching in law schools. Given her prominent position in the Law School at Reading, she was influential in our first academic appointments there as teaching fellows. This was an important first stepping-stone for both of us. Rosemary Auchmuty's role here demonstrated a point that should be plain for all to see. Namely, this was an admission that teaching and mentoring others, whether formally or informally, was an academic's first priority.

In sum, we owe a debt to Rosemary Auchmuty that can never quite be repaid. Our labour in the writing of this chapter and the organisation and the editing of this *festschrift* is but a small gesture in the grand scheme of things. It is a token of our gratitude and a celebration of someone with an academic career marked by an unusual commitment to both teaching and research. Her commitment was genuine and, even after her research successes, unwavering. In this sense, Rosemary Auchmuty's scholarly ethos is unique, remarkable and, above all, exceptional.

[4] R Auchmuty and E Rackley, 'Feminist Legal Biography: A Model for *All* Legal Life Stories' (2020) 41 *Journal of Legal History* 186.

[5] For the under-recognition of women's research as measured through citations, see CA Cotropia and L Petherbridge, 'Gender Disparity in Law Review Citation Rates' (2017) 59 *William and Mary Law Review* 771.

[6] For a wider discussion, see AC McGinley, 'Reproducing Gender on Law School Faculties' (2009) 2009 *Brigham Young University Law Review* 99 and, in relation to those in adjacent academic support roles, SP Liemer and HS Temple, 'Did Your Legal Writing Professor Go to Harvard? The Credentials of Legal Writing Faculty at Hiring Time' (2007) 46 *University of Louisville Law Review* 383.

[7] For a discussion of why this matters and is important, see KM Stanchi, 'Who Next, the Janitors – A Socio-Feminist Critique of the Status Hierarchy of Law Professors' (2004) 73 *University of Missouri–Kansas City Law Review* 467.

[8] R Auchmuty, 'Using Feminist Judgments in the Property Law Classroom' (2012) 46 *The Law Teacher* 227.

Over the course of those years, we have spent many hours over coffees talking about gender and women and the law, feminism(s), issues of discrimination, equality and equity. These conversations have enriched our research careers. Many a time we have agreed, although not always. Those conversations have always been productive, with Rosemary Auchmuty taking perhaps what might be best described as unusually clear and less than opaque positions. There was always room to toy with ideas, debate and even disagree, sometimes vehemently so, on scholarly issues. Just as two persons do not share the same relationship with the third, three people do not always share the exact same world view, although, as you can see, there are enough similarities in our various positions, aims and drives.

Rosemary Auchmuty's scholarship and interests span the three broad specialist fields of law examined here; namely property, trusts and family law.[9] In many respects, Rosemary Auchmuty is a first mover. She was a pioneering feminist within an academy mostly dominated by male legal scholars and scholarship, having started her career in law in 1989, when she took up a lectureship at Westminster. But to what extent has this situation changed? This was our inspiration and motivation for this chapter. Our aim is to try to document what the gender balance and situation for women is like now? One of the ways to measure and understand the research landscape in the areas of law that we have chosen is to look at the gender of the authors of the literature in these fields.

This chapter examines the key journals, several of which Rosemary Auchmuty has contributed to,[10] and the participation of women in these publications. It considers the authors in five leading law journals in property, trusts and family law. For its data points, it takes each author of an article in the *Child and Family Law Quarterly*, the *Journal of Social Welfare and Family Law*, *Conveyancer and Property Lawyer*, *Trusts and Trustees* and the *International Journal of Law, Policy,*

[9] A selection of Rosemary Auchmuty's recent scholarship in these fields includes: R Auchmuty, 'What's so Special about Marriage? The Impact of Wilkinson v Kitzinger' (2008) 20(4) *Child and Family Law Quarterly* 479; R Auchmuty, 'The Married Women's Property Acts: Equality Was Not the Issue' in R Hunter (ed), *Rethinking Equality Projects in Law: Feminist Challenges* (Hart, 2008); R Auchmuty, 'Land Law and Equity and Trust' in C Hunter (ed), *Integrating Socio-Legal Studies into the Law Curriculum* (Palgrave Macmillan, 2012); R Auchmuty, 'Law and the Power of Feminism: How Marriage Lost Its Power to Oppress Women' (2012) 20 *Feminist Legal Studies* 71; R Auchmuty, 'Marriage and Civil Partnership: Law's Role, Feminism's Response' in M Davies and V Munro (eds), *The Ashgate Research Companion to Feminist Legal Theory* (Ashgate, 2013); R Auchmuty, 'Dissolution or Disillusion: The Unravelling of Civil Partnerships' in N Barker and D Monk (eds), *From Civil Partnership to Same-Sex Marriage: Interdisciplinary Reflections* (Routledge, 2015); R Auchmuty, 'The Experience of Civil Partnership Dissolution: Not "Just like Divorce"' (2016) 38 *Journal of Social Welfare and Family Law* 152; R Auchmuty, 'The Limits of Marriage Protection: In Defence of Property Law' (2016) 6(6) *Oñati Socio-Legal Series* 1196; R Auchmuty, 'The Limits of Marriage Protection in Property Allocation When a Relationship Ends' (2016) 28 *Child and Family Law Quarterly* 303; R Auchmuty, 'Feminist Responses to Same Sex Relationship Recognition' in C Ashford and A Maine (eds), *Research Handbook on Gender, Sexuality and the Law* (Routledge, 2020).

[10] She has published in the *Conveyancer*, *Child and Family Law Quarterly* and the *Journal of Social Welfare and Family Law*. See Rosemary Auchmuty, 'Not Just a Good Children's Story: A tribute to adverse possession' (2004) 63 *Conveyancer* 293; Auchmuty, 'What's so Special about Marriage?' (n 9); Auchmuty, 'The Limits of Marriage Protection' (n 9); Auchmuty, 'The Experience of Civil Partnership Dissolution' (n 9).

and the Family. Our dataset runs from 2016 to 2020 and considers the gender of authors of articles in these five journals. Altogether, there are around 1,500 authors in this dataset.

The analysis of these results reveals that although there has been some change, wide discrepancies still exist between men and women in legal publishing. This suggests that factors such as networking as well as an absence of openness act as barriers for women. The exclusion and underrepresentation of women in the scholarly literature not only has an impact on individual careers, but also on the shape and scope of the legal field as a whole. Our aim here is to shed light, identifying issues of representation in the publishing field. We view this as essential. Such an empirical approach allows for a systematic exploration of what is often chalked up to be – and otherwise, dismissed and, in short, rubbished – an individual experience. The results here show that this is not the case. With greater understanding of general trends and a clear statement that these experiences are not anecdotal, solutions can be found. It is to this pragmatic goal that our work in this chapter speaks the most.

Theories about Women Publishing

To date, there have been various studies, in fields other than law, exploring men's and women's publication rates in academic journals. Some large studies have been undertaken – especially in science, technology, engineering and mathematics (STEM) subjects – looking into this issue. For example, a study of 15 different journals which published the work of researchers from the American Society for Microbiology found that senior women were underrepresented as authors, when compared to global and the society's estimates of microbiology researchers.[11] Furthermore, they found that manuscripts submitted by corresponding authors that were women received more negative outcomes than those submitted by men.[12] Other studies have also demonstrated a lower percentage of women-authored publications compared to their share in the professional fields, such as a 20-year study of five high impact journals in gastroenterology by Long

[11] AK Hagan et al, 'Women Are Underrepresented and Receive Differential Outcomes at ASM Journals: A Six-Year Retrospective Analysis' (2020) 11 mBio e01680, 1.

[12] ibid. A corresponding author is the person among the team who is tasked with correspondence about a paper. It is sometimes a pride of place and given to the lead or head author. For others, it is just about the division of labour and who submits the paper. Frequently, readers misunderstand this and ignore this label; they contact, whomever they like out of the author team and generally without explanation. For some, these positions are vital to them because they are an archaic feature that gives rise to status. It makes dominance visible and it is a sign that egos have no bounds. Others operate in a non-hierarchical setting and like to not subordinate each other. They share things equally and try to operate democratically. The world of principal investigators and co-investigators sits quite unhappily with them. The latter world view is, of course, allied to, but not quite the same as, subverting the hierarchy.

et al,[13] as well as a 15-year study of 10 high profile political science journals by Teele and Thelen.[14] Teele and Thelen also observed that women had not benefited equally from co-authorship and that the methodological leanings of top journals were more likely to reflect the type of work men disproportionately engaged with.[15] Prothero and McDonagh's study of marketing journals noted a lack of women on editorial and advisory boards, as well as a lack of women among recipients of awards given and works celebrated.[16]

In addition, there has also been engagement with gender representation of authorship in individual journals, such as *The Lancet*,[17] as well as smaller reviews undertaken by editors or editorial boards, such as the *Journal of Mental Health*,[18] the *Journal of Roman Studies*[19] and the *American Journal of Political Science*[20] to name a few. Some of the STEM subject-specific studies have additionally focused on analysis of last-named and corresponding authors,[21] as different fields have different conventions as to authorships.[22] For example, some conventions include analysis of last authors as they could be serving as a proxy for seniority, or to represent a project lead, whereas corresponding authors are often considered to have contributed the most to a publication. Some STEM fields also have a convention of including supervisors, listed as authors in students' publications, a tradition that does not exist in legal publishing.

Currently, on average, women represent 49 per cent of academic staff and 66 per cent of part-time staff in United Kingdom (UK) Higher Education institutions.[23] The proportion of women professors overall is merely 28 per cent.[24]

[13] MT Long et al, 'Female Authorship in Major Academic Gastroenterology Journals: A Look over 20 Years' (2015) 81 *Gastrointestinal Endoscopy* 1440.

[14] D Langan Teele and K Thelen, 'Gender in the Journals: Publication Patterns in Political Science' (2017) 50 *PS: Political Science and Politics* 433.

[15] ibid 434.

[16] A Prothero and P McDonagh, '"It's Hard to Be What You Can't See" – Gender Representation in Marketing's Academic Journals' (2021) 37 *Journal of Marketing Management* 28.

[17] J González-Alvarez, 'Author Gender in The Lancet Journals' (2018) 391 *The Lancet* 2601; J Clark and R Horton, 'What Is The Lancet Doing about Gender and Diversity?' (2019) 393 *The Lancet* 508; R Morgan et al, 'Gendered Geography: An Analysis of Authors in The Lancet Global Health' (2019) 7 *The Lancet Global Health* e1619.

[18] T Wykes and J Evans, 'Gender Diversity in the Journal of Mental Health – How Are We Doing and What Do We Need to Do?' (2020) 29 *Journal of Mental Health* 493.

[19] C Kelly et al, 'Gender Bias and the Journal of Roman Studies' (2019) 109 *Journal of Roman Studies* 441.

[20] K Dolan and JL Lawless, 'It Takes a Submission: Gendered Patterns in the Pages of AJPS' (*American Journal of Political Science*, 20 April 2020) ajps.org/2020/04/20/it-takes-a-submission-gendered-patterns-in-the-pages-of-ajps/.

[21] See eg J Overbaugh, 'Defining the Barriers to Women Publishing in High-Impact Journals' (2018) 92 *Journal of Virology* e02127, 1–4.

[22] For an explanation of what a corresponding author is in different circles, please see n 11 above. Last-named and first-named authors are similar positions to that of corresponding authors in that these positions, correctly or incorrectly, imply seniority and status. It says little of the division of labour or who did what.

[23] Higher Education Statistics Authority Bulletin 2020–2021 www.hesa.ac.uk/news/01-02-2022/sb261-higher-education-staff-statistics.

[24] ibid.

Law, however, is rather different and has more women professors than many other fields.[25] Nevertheless, the percentage is still markedly lower for women than men, currently at 37 per cent.[26] The proportion of women decreases as seniority increases, and women are also overrepresented in the ranks of part-time workers.[27] Furthermore, academia, just as most other sectors of employment, suffers from a persistent gender pay gap. Currently, the professorial gender pay gap in the UK is at 6.2 per cent, well above the 5 per cent which the Equality and Human Rights Commission defines as a significant gender pay gap.[28] If we were to make a general hypothesis, based on the representation of women in academic institutions, a corresponding level of representation in legal publishing would constitute a reasonable expectation.

That said, these figures do not only document the trends in legal academia. The practices and habits that lead to these figures perpetuate them. Where you publish matters. It matters to individual careers, and to the collective. If hiring committees and promotion committees use journal names as a proxy or shorthand for research excellence – such practice seems logical given that we cannot all be specialists in everything – and if the 'top' journal does not publish pieces written by women at the same rate as men, then it will be harder for women to occupy middling or senior positions – or, at the very least, to be seen as solid researchers.

Many journals are prestigious because they are exclusive and difficult to get into. But perhaps they are merely exclusionary. In the British academic world, scholarship and editorial decisions are couched in terms of 'quality', 'originality' and 'rigour', but that is not necessarily the case in reality. It cannot be true that only men write research that is of a sufficiently high quality, originality and rigour. Arguably, we need a better way of assessing, monitoring and, ultimately, changing what journal editors do because their decisions have such a tremendous impact on individual careers. It is hoped that the data in this chapter will help to begin conversations around this. This is a worthwhile aim because questions about gendered inequalities matter.

[25] The first woman, Claire Palley, was appointed to chair in 1970. F Cownie, 'The United Kingdom's First Woman Law Professor: An Archerian Analysis' (2015) 42 *Journal of Law and Society* 127. For more on the legal academy, see C McGlynn, 'Women, Representation and the Legal Academy' (1999) 19 *Legal Studies* 68; C Wells, 'Working out Women in Law Schools' (2001) 21 *Legal Studies* 116; L Duff and L Webley, 'Gender and the Legal Academy in the UK: A Product of Proxies and Hiring and Promotion Practices' in U Schultz, G Shaw, M Thornton and R Auchmuty (eds), *Gender and Careers in the Legal Academy*, Oñati International Series in Law and Society (Hart, 2021). There are a number of studies outside of the UK, see R West, 'Women in the Legal Academy: A Brief History of Feminist Legal Theory' (2018) 87 *Fordham Law Review* 977; U Schultz, 'Gender in Socio-Legal Teaching and Research in Germany' (2020) 21 *German Law Journal* 1345; A Melville and A Barrow, 'Persistence Despite Change: The Academic Gender Gap in Australian Law Schools' (2022) 47 *Law and Social Inquiry* 607.

[26] Higher Education Statistics Authority Dataset for 2021.

[27] Higher Education Statistics Authority Bulletin 2020–2021 (n 23).

[28] Universities and Colleges Association for Employers, 'Examining the Gender Pay Gap in Higher Education' (June 2022) www.ucea.ac.uk/library/infographics/gender-pay/.

Submission rates have recently been under much scrutiny in the general academic field.[29] This is because the impact of the COVID-19 pandemic has exacerbated age-old gendered inequities in the academic and non-academic world and so brought increased attention to academic publishing. It has been shown, for example, that women have been disproportionately affected by the pandemic.[30] Once again we see, especially in STEM-subject fields, academic figures addressing, or at least making visible, the disproportionate effect the pandemic has had on women's research productivity.[31] King and Frederikson have, for instance, found that, across STEM disciplines, women's publishing rate has fallen relative to men's amid the pandemic. Here, they note that the 'publish or perish' culture of academia alongside the pandemic could be setting back hard-won progress of women in STEM.[32]

There are of course limitations to viewing a significantly large and varied sector as a whole, including using aggregate results as we often do here. Looking at results from a bird's eye view reveals very little of the best and worst performers. It gives individuals a cloak and enables them to remain hidden and obscured by the average. Uncovering the gaps – working out which journals publish the work of most women and the fewest women – is what this chapter aims to achieve.

Method

For the purposes of our analysis here we have taken every published journal article in the five leading property, equity and family law journals: namely, *Child and Family Law Quarterly*, the *Journal of Social Welfare and Family Law*, *Conveyancer and Property Lawyer*, *Trusts and Trustees* and the *International Journal of Law, Policy, and the Family* over five years from 2016 to 2020. The reason these journals that have been chosen for this chapter are due to them representing the broad specialist fields that Rosemary Auchmuty's work has engaged with. The data has then been broken down further to examine all of the authors on co-authored journal articles and each of those authors – whether single or co-author – have been weighted equally. This chapter only focuses on journal articles, rather than all types of publications, including, for example, case commentaries and book reviews. This

[29] MM King and ME Frederickson, 'The Pandemic Penalty: The Gendered Effects of COVID-19 on Scientific Productivity' (2021) 7 *Socius* 23780231211006976; R Cui, H Ding and F Zhu, 'Gender Inequality in Research Productivity during the COVID-19 Pandemic' (2022) 24 *Manufacturing and Service Operations Management* 707.

[30] Indeed, this has a wider impact on the shape of the system, see M Oleschuk, 'Gender Equity Considerations for Tenure and Promotion during COVID-19' (2020) 57 *Canadian Review of Sociology* 502.

[31] See eg G Viglione, 'Are Women Publishing Less during the Pandemic? Here's What the Data Say' (2020) 581 *Nature* 365.

[32] King and Frederickson (n 29) 1, 14.

is primarily for the reason that journal articles in the main go through similar processes of review, which is, in short, an editor-screening followed by peer review.[33]

The articles were then gender coded by a combination of first-name coding and, if needed, a follow up internet search conducted to assign authors to men and women categories. This is a common method in the literature concerning gender statistics in publishing.[34] Authors were coded by men's first names to 'M', women's names to 'F' and others to 'O'. For any first name that was not obvious – for example Alex could be Alexander or Alexandra, as with Nic and so on – a manual check on the person's website was performed where the gender was either evident from the photograph or the biography. The category 'O' is intended for others, including corporations and those who use the pronoun 'they'. There are, of course, some limitations to this way of coding. It is possible that there remains some misgendering in the dataset. For example, if the author is trans and has a gender-ambiguous name, but does not use 'they' as a pronoun on their webpage, they may be categorised based on the gender implied conventionally and traditionally by the appearance in their photograph. Indeed, it is commonplace to simply use a first name in a biography and so trans authors could use a first name alone and this would otherwise obscure their gender. Another example would be if an author had published an article under a man's name in 2016 and subsequently changed their gender, now identifying as a woman: this would not be reflected in the dataset. *Modern Law Review* is one of the few journals that has a policy where authors who at a later stage change their name after publication can retrospectively update the name listed as the author of the article.[35] The remaining journals do not have such a policy (at the time of writing) or, at least, if they do, it is not publicly shared information. In other words, each name in the dataset appears as it is written on the journal article at the time of publication. And this also means that if one author publishes in each of the five journals reviewed, their name appears five times in the dataset.

There are several different stages at which gender equality in terms of representation could be evaluated, for example at submission stage, in editorial decisions, or in the review processes. The data for this present study does not include submission numbers. These are held by individual journals and publishers and, as such, are not currently accessible to the public. The decrease in the rate of publication for women is consistent with women performing disproportionately more of the care work at home (and in the workplace). Evidence from scientific fields also shows that women academics are more likely to have a partner who is also an academic, and therefore less likely to have full-time support at home, whereas men, who are scientists, are more likely to have partners who are not working for pay outside the

[33] It is worthwhile to note that there are some journals which have their own process of peer review, for example by the whole editorial board reviewing each piece that is published in the journal. An example of this is the journal *Feminist Legal Studies*.

[34] See eg D Card et al, 'Are Referees and Editors in Economics Gender Neutral?' (2020) 135 *Quarterly Journal of Economics* 269.

[35] This has traditionally been an issue for women, who change their names upon marriage.

home.[36] Undoubtedly, further studies comparing submission and publication rates would be required to further understand this field. Even though our current data also does not tell us specifically about women's lived experiences of publishing or of the distribution of labour in the home, there is much to be gained by counting women, and men, in this way. Let us consider how persistent inequalities are in the academy and the aims and objectives of law in creating just and fair results. It is somehow paradoxical how little engagement there has been in systematically analysing representation of men and women in legal publishing.

This study conducts the first stage in a process of understanding the system of academic publishing in law journals. This is, first, to merely know the numbers of women publishing, when and where, which is in and of itself important. It makes visible a matter that has hitherto been invisible. It allows the public to see the publication rates of women authors in journals. These raw numbers have previously only been visible to editors and publishers. Individual journals will be collecting this type of data, and clearly conversations happen internally. It is also clear that these conversations even mean that action is taken by some editorial boards to address these issues. For example, the *Modern Law Review* offered a public seminar to encourage further submissions from women in particular, while women on the journal's editorial board noted that although the journal does indeed receive fewer submissions from women, it has a higher rate of acceptance of women-authored publications.[37] Given, however, the various studies in other fields and the considerably higher visibility of engaging with questions of gendered research productivity or editorial practices in other subject areas, legal studies lag significantly behind on these questions. We now turn to discuss the journals that are relevant to the research of Rosemary Auchmuty and the extent to which women publish in them.

Results

The overall numbers across the five journals are represented in Figure 1, with about 58 per cent of the publications having been authored by men, represented by the pillar on the left, and about 42 per cent women, represented by the pillar on the right. However, this pattern is not universal across the journals examined. As Figure 2 shows, there is a wide discrepancy across these five journals. They each have markedly different gender profiles, with none of them representing this average. Furthermore, the peaks and troughs among the journals are extreme. The journal with the highest number of women authors, at 87 per cent in 2019, is *Child and Family Law Quarterly*. By a marked contrast in 2019, only 6 per cent of authors in *Conveyancer and Property Lawyer* were women. The gap between these two journals is marked and, in percentile, this is a difference of 81 per cent.

[36] King and Frederickson (n 29) 4.

[37] V Mantalou, V Munro, J Braithwaite, K Greasley, O Lynskey and C Gearty, 'Modern Law Information Session for Female Academics' (10 June 2020) onlinelibrary.wiley.com/page/journal/14682230/homepage/zoom_info_session.

Figure 1 Numbers of men and women authors

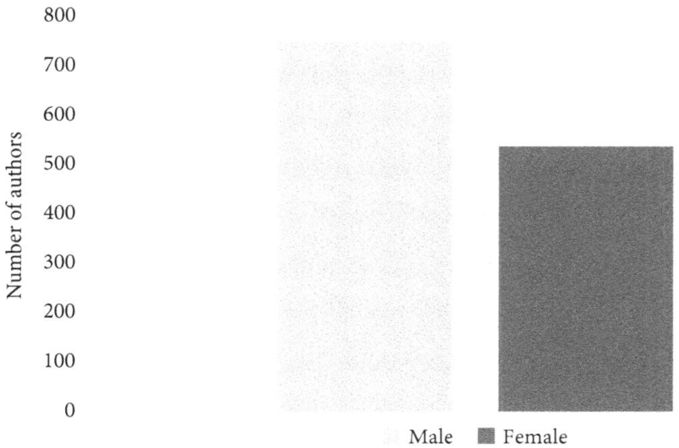

Source: Dataset.

Figure 2 Percentage of women authors by journal, by year

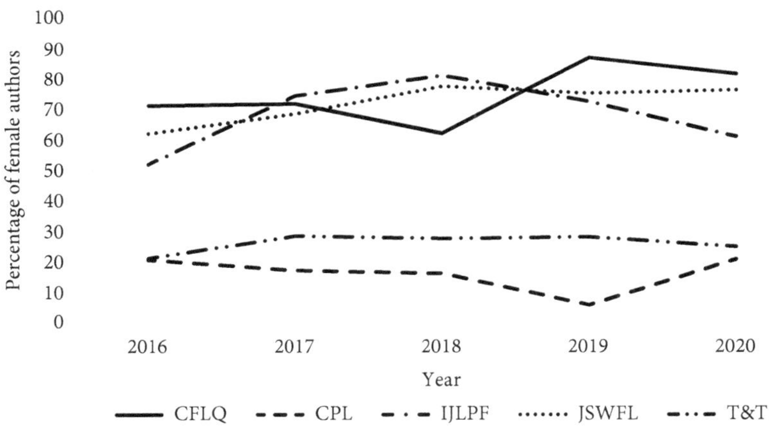

Source: Dataset.

More generally, there is a notable bifurcation in these journals. In more detail, we see the percentages of women authors in *Child and Family Law Quarterly* varying between around 60 and 90 per cent, the *International Journal of Law, Policy, and the Family* varying between just above 50 to 80 per cent, and the *Journal of Social Welfare and Family Law* between just above 60 and almost 80 per cent. On the other hand, for *Trusts and Trustees*, the percentage of women authors over the five-year period varies from only just above 10 per cent to a high of less than 30 per cent. Lastly, in *Conveyancer and Property Law*, the percentage of women authors varies from the lowest in the dataset of 6 per cent to a high of around 20 per cent. To put it crudely, it is evident that *Child and Family Law Quarterly*, the *Journal of Social Welfare and Family Law*, and the *International Journal of Law, Policy, and the Family* are 'women's journals'. They publish – predominantly – the work of women. *Conveyancer and Property Lawyer* and *Trust and Trustees* are 'men's journals'. They publish – predominantly – the work of men. This leaves a segregation where women are in one place but not in another. Much of the work in family and property law focuses on the family home, as has much of Rosemary Auchmuty's work.[38] If we think of these journals like Georgian and Victorian homes, there is a drawing room (that is for women) and a dining room (this is for men).

If we return here to the question of the pandemic and the potential that the disparity could be in part explained by a decrease in the ability of women to participate in publishing, there are three journals that are noteworthy in the dataset. The onset of the pandemic was in 2019 and by March 2020, it was in full swing. We see that the *International Journal of Law, Policy and the Family* sees a dip in the percentage of women authors in 2020, although this decrease is a continuation from the previous year. The journal *Trust and Trustees* sees a dip from a relatively low percentage of women authors to even lower in 2020. *Child and Family Law Quarterly* also sees a drop in the number of women authors from 2019 to 2020, although this is only by a few percentage points. It is possible that some of these decreases could be explained by a drop off in women's submissions due to the effects of the pandemic or that they were unable to complete revisions at an ordinary pace. With the data that we have, we cannot conclude this definitely. Our data shows trends that require explanation. The data does not itself explain them. Nevertheless, it ought to be noted that it seems unlikely that the disparities in the publications overall could be explained merely by the number of submissions. The discrepancies between the rates in the journals remain quite significant. This is an issue that we return to for further consideration in the 'Discussion' section below.

Figure 3 Gender balance in authors by journal

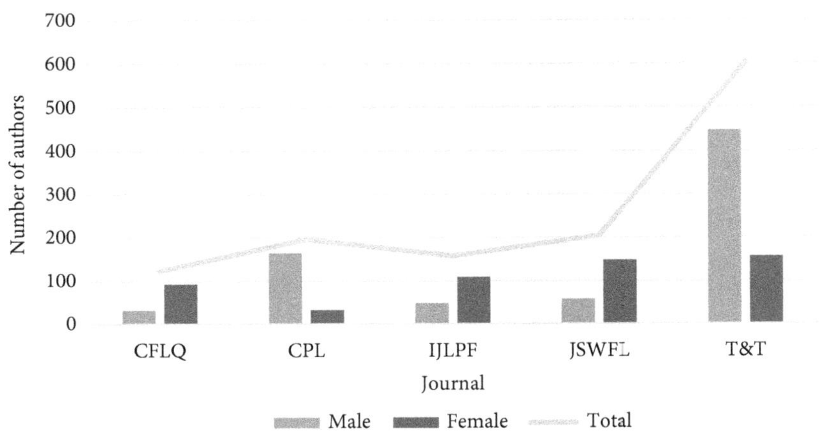

Source: Dataset.

[38] See, for instance, the forthcoming monograph: R Auchmuty, *Women and the Family Home: Legal and Social Change in Post-War England*.

Figure 4 Gender balance of single and multi-authored manuscripts

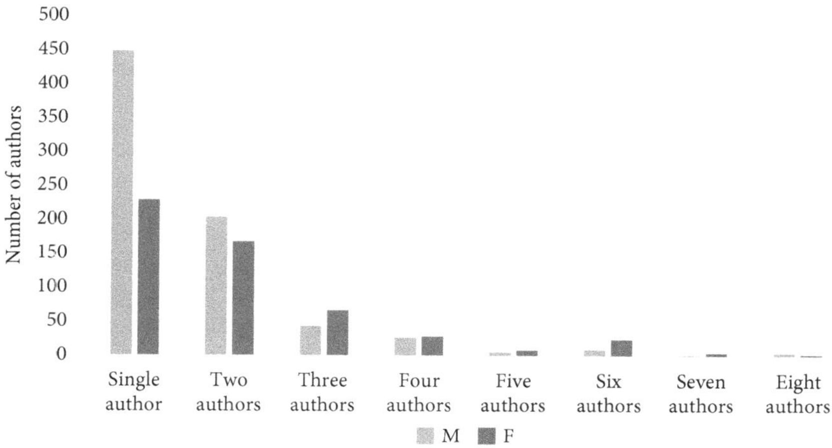

Source: Dataset.

Figure 3 represents the numbers of authors rather than percentages. It allows for a more nuanced view, which shows the scale and size of these journals more prominently. Scale and size are particularly important, and we discuss this in detail in the analysis in the following section. There is also another factor to consider, which is the gender balance of single- and multi-authored manuscripts.

What is clearly evident from Figure 4 is that men are significantly more likely to write single-authored pieces, and women are more likely to collaborate. In fact, men are almost twice as likely than women overall to publish single-authored pieces. The cross-over between more men or more women seems to happen at the three-author stage. There are, of course, multiple possible explanations for this. For example, some may view women as more collaborative than competitive in their outlook, considering them as being socialised to be more relational than men.[39] Others may prefer a more structural explanation derived from feminist critiques of gendered labour practices in the workplace and at home. These might explain why women as a group, as compared to men, lack time to do research, as they perform disproportionately more of the care and administrative tasks at work, as well as more unpaid labour in the home, in the form of housework, and care work, whether childcare/elderly care or care of the disabled.[40] Furthermore, in academia, women are also disproportionately represented as part-time workers, as noted above, as well as working on teaching-intensive contracts as opposed to teaching and research contracts. This may have an effect on women's choices to undertake collaborative work. Collaborative projects alleviate pressure but are

[39] See eg C Gilligan, *In a Different Voice: Psychological Theory and Women's Development*, reprint edn (Harvard University Press, 2016).

[40] C Westoby et al, 'What Are the Barriers and Facilitators to Success for Female Academics in UK HEIs? A Narrative Review' (2021) 33 *Gender and Education* 1033.

not necessarily efficient nor a way of producing more research, more quickly. The nature of collaboration (in an ideal world) entails far greater levels of communication because all parties involved in authoring should participate and agree on the direction of the research.

Discussion

The most notable finding from our dataset is the clear bifurcation between 'men's journals' (*Conveyancer and Property Lawyer* and *Trust and Trustees*) and 'women's journals' (*Child and Family Law Quarterly*, the *International Journal of Law, Policy and the Family* and the *Journal of Social Welfare and Family Law*). When we examine the patterns further, the following observations can be made. Our data says little of the wider fields and gender.

Patterns in 'Women's Journals'

Comparing the journals, we can find that the high numbers of women authors for *Child and Family Law Quarterly*, for example, can partly be explained by their higher numbers of co-authored manuscripts. Whether or not this co-operation would be explained through women being more collaborative than men or gendered labour practices, we suggest that this trend is not something editors need necessarily be concerned about. Or, in other words, it is not suggestive of bias on their part. It is also notable that these journals encourage socio-legal research in their mission statements. *Child and Family Law Quarterly*, for example, notes that the journal 'embraces a wide variety of approaches to child and family law: empirical, doctrinal, historical, socio-legal, and comparative'.[41] The *International Journal of Law, Policy and the Family* notes that it includes theoretical analysis of law, sociological literature concerning the family, which is of special interest to law and legal policy, and social policy literature of special interest to law and the family, as well as literature in related fields.[42] The *Journal of Social Welfare and Family Law* publishes 'interdisciplinary research and analysis of social welfare, family law and policy issues from a UK and international perspective'.[43] By contrast, the mission statements of *Trusts and Trustees* and *Conveyancer and Property Lawyer* describe themselves as 'the leading', and 'most authoritative' journals in their fields respectively. They also demonstrate that as journals they are more practice-oriented and make no mention of socio-legal approaches.

[41] About *Child and Family Law Quarterly* www.familylaw.co.uk/child-and-family-law-quarterly.
[42] About *Journal of Law, Policy and the Family* academic.oup.com/lawfam/pages/About.
[43] Overview of *Journal of Social Welfare and Family Law* www.tandfonline.com/journals/rjsf20.

It may be the case that the scientific data-driven analyses often published in *Child and Family Law Quarterly*, the *International Journal of Law, Policy and the Family* and the *Journal of Social Welfare and Family Law* may lend themselves to co-authorship, while writing narratives, interpretations or critiques potentially lends itself more easily to working independently at a desk without a team. To write a narrative – to research and carry out those tasks together with someone else – would require finding someone who agrees with your world view to an astonishingly high degree, which is not impossible, but can be difficult. It is, therefore, possible that the high numbers of women's publications in these journals reflect the higher proportion of women in the legal field engaging in socio-legal work. It is also possible that the data reflects the higher representation of women in the sub-field of family law. To be clear, it may be that the broader and persistent gender stereotypes, gender biases and gender segregation in the academic system and questions of different socialisation of men and women explain the gender-segregation in certain legal fields, such as a high proportion of women in family law. Previous studies have shown, for instance, how legal academia privileges courses such as constitutional law, which as a field remains dominated by men, while viewing women-dominated 'softer' subjects, such as family law or gender and law, as less prestigious.[44] In this literature, skills-based courses, such as Legal Method, Legal Practice, Advocacy and Lawyering Skills are known as 'the pink ghetto'.[45]

Patterns in 'Men's Journals'

Our data shows here that, where the journal is smaller in size (as measured by the number of authors), fewer women are publishing original articles in it. Where the journal is larger in size (as measured by the number of authors), there are more women. This is shown by the line of best fit on Figure 5 with brings together each of the journals here as a reference point. The relationship between the number of authors and women is disproportionate. Bear in mind that the scale on Figure 5 is not the same on the y and x axis. This suggests that the part of the issue here is in the openness or closedness of the network. In other words, if the network of authors in a given area is small, there are likely to be fewer 'outsiders' and more 'insiders'. There are fewer women because they are outsiders in a profession that has historically been dominated by men.

If we apply this logic and bear the theory in the paragraph above in mind, *Conveyancer and Property Lawyer* is arguably less of a concern. Why? This is

[44] ME Kornhauser, 'Rooms of their Own: An Empirical Study of Occupational Segregation by Gender among Law Professors' (2004) 73 *University of Missouri–Kansas City* 293.

[45] ibid and see eg C Haight Farley, 'Confronting Expectations: Women in the Legal Academy' (1996) 8 *Yale Journal of Law and Feminism* 333, 352–53.

because *Conveyancer and Property Lawyer* is the first point from the left in Figure 5. It is a small journal and it behaves in a way that is typical of the smaller journals. It is a closed network made up of 'insiders' and with few women. If it were to expand and become a bigger journal and follow the pattern set out by Figure 5, then more 'outsiders' and more women would publish in it. Where the journal is larger in size and publishes more articles, it is generally open, and there are disproportionately more women. Yet, this is not what appears with *Trust and Trustees*. The pattern here cannot be explained with a small insider or male-dominated network. In around five years, the journal published the work of around 650 authors, only a quarter of whom were women. Something else, then is at play.

Figure 5 Journal length and women authors for family, property and trust law journals

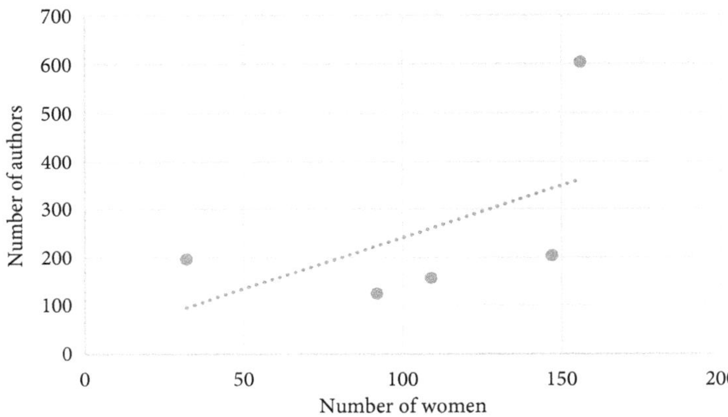

Source: Dataset.

Journal editors badge their decisions around 'quality', 'originality' and 'rigour', but Figure 5 suggests it is a difficult position to hold when faced with these details. It is not tenable to argue that in one year, a journal only accepted the work of a handful of women because all of the other women submitted manuscripts that were unoriginal and lacking in quality and/or rigour. It could, of course, be argued that women do not submit enough to a particular journal. However, one of the tasks of an editor is to go out there and talk to interesting people, doing what is perceived to potentially be good quality written work, and encourage them to submit. One possibility is that some editorial teams are not doing this enough or that they may be having conversations which are restricted to a small network. Indeed, these patterns suggest an exclusiveness, as if editors are either not soliciting articles openly or only talking to one gender. This of course, ties into a wider conversation about the composition of editorial teams and the necessity of widening participation on editorial boards, keeping in mind representation as to sex, ethnicity, seniority and class.

Conclusion

The academic world has, no doubt, changed in several different ways since Rosemary Auchmuty began her career. How much have the journals which have been allied to her work changed? Family law, unlike some other fields of legal inquiry, has always been a place for women scholars. Andrew Bainham, Stephen Cretney and Stephen Parker were important male figures, but there were also female figures, such as Ruth Deech, Christina Lyon, Judith Masson and Joanna Miles. Has there been a proliferation of women since then? Are they publishing now? If so, where? Our answer to this question is not built upon stories of individual women or men as is the traditional method in Rosemary Auchmuty's research. This is the method in legal biography to which she has contributed significantly.[46] Instead, here we have taken an approach that aims to be more systematic. It is an approach that deliberately speaks of unnamed individuals in order to document and then improve the participation of a collective. This aim is, of course, one that Rosemary Auchmuty has equally promoted, most notably for us in her leadership and teaching.[47] This study is a quantitative and empirically driven view of the authors in leading journals in family and property law.

Here, we have not only documented the extent to which women are part of the scholarship but have also suggested ways to increase this rate of participation. In doing so, the findings are not merely descriptive, but also push for change. Our data shows that family law is a field of scholarship that is dominated by women writing. But this is not necessarily a worry for the editors of these journals. The data shows that in the journals studied here women collaborate more often and so publish as teams, thus we hear more voices and those voices happen to be women's. This can only be a positive for editors, who are not in control of how their authors write. It may well be that women collaborate because socio-legal work is often about data and, as such, it is far more divisible than traditional black letter legal research which is desk-based and often revolves around perceptions of a claim to superior interpretation.

These points about methodological divisions and the fact that socio-legal journals have more women authors aside, there are some key takeaways for editors. Editors do, of course, have control of what they publish. Journals that do not have a socio-legal emphasis have relatively few women authors. Why is it that women do not publish single-authored manuscripts and engage in black letter desk-based research at the same rate as men? Possible explanations are that women are socialised to help and collaborate, so they do. Another is simply that they collaborate in order to do research in a busy world with competing demands for time. Both are equally possible. Collaborative projects are not necessarily quicker, as the nature of collaboration demands both greater levels of communication and consent. As

[46] See the chapters by Bourne, Derry and Cownie in this volume.
[47] See the chapter by Hunter in this volume.

such, they can in themselves be slow. This means in an academic setting, where efficiency and results are prioritised, that those writing with a feminist ethos can be at a disadvantage. The same applies to those in leadership positions.[48] While journal editors are not in control of how their authors write nor of the academic system in which they inhabit, they are able to influence a journal's profile and the manuscripts that they accept. This gives much pause for thought.

Finally, this study hopefully also offers some thought to those in the wider academic system. Publications remain at the heart of opportunities for promotion in the academy. Failures to address systematic differences in men and women's publication rates directly contributes to the persistent inequalities in the academy. Though the data presented here offers merely a snapshot of publications in the legal field, it ought to make us pause as we go ahead. Any assumptions that the academy is a place where women now enjoy equality in research cannot be sustained. Journals which exclude women by accident or by design should not be considered to be solid places for legal research. The findings here ought to be a concern for doctrinal law journals. Equality is more than an aim and a goal that is aspirational.[49] It is evident that these journals lack the equality and diversity in authors which is now needed to be perceived as a suitable outlet of important research. We suggest this ought to be considered by hiring managers, promotion committees or authors, who seek for greater equality and opportunity for all.

[48] ibid.

[49] L Carasik, 'Renaissance or Retrenchment: Legal Education at a Crossroads' (2010) 44 *Indiana Law Review* 735.

13

Locating Feminist Scholars and Scholarship in the Legal Academy

ROSEMARY HUNTER

Introduction

In this chapter I engage with Rosemary Auchmuty's argument that feminist legal scholars have come to play a valuable – and indeed central – role in the legal academy, as teachers, researchers and managers. This argument can be found in particular in three of Rosemary's publications: 'Feminists as Stakeholders in the Law School',[1] 'Using Feminist Judgments in the Property Law Classroom',[2] and 'The Road to Olive Stone'.[3] All three appeared in edited collections (the Feminist Judgments article was part of a special issue of the *Law Teacher*, edited by myself and Helen Carr, reflecting on the uses of the Feminist Judgments Project in teaching).[4] This in itself provides an indication of the collaborative and interlocutory nature of Rosemary's scholarship. She was constantly in dialogue with other scholars, both feminist and non-feminist, contributing her own distinct perspective to doctrinal, theoretical and policy debates. These dialogues occurred both in print and in person. The chapter also draws upon many informal conversations with Rosemary over the years, at conferences and workshops, on trains and buses and over coffee and online, as well as two formal conversations in the course of writing the chapter, the first at the workshop held in July 2022 at which first drafts of essays for this collection were shared with other contributors and with Rosemary,[5] and the second a follow-up discussion with Rosemary in October

[1] R Auchmuty, 'Feminists as Stakeholders in the Law School' in F Cownie (ed), *Stakeholders in the Law School* (Hart, 2010) 35.

[2] R Auchmuty, 'Using Feminist Judgments in the Property Law Classroom' (2012) 46 *The Law Teacher* 227.

[3] R Auchmuty and J Temkin, 'The Road to Olive Stone' in U Schultz, G Shaw, M Thornton and R Auchmuty (eds), *Gender and Careers in the Legal Academy* (Hart, 2021) 441.

[4] H Carr and R Hunter (2012) 46 *The Law Teacher* Special Issue on the Feminist Judgments Project 214.

[5] 'Women, their Lives and the Law' Workshop Discussion, Scarman Conference Centre, University of Warwick, 19 July 2022.

2022.[6] The chapter first sets out Rosemary's view on the value of feminist scholars to the legal academy and then engages with her argument in light of the literature on feminism in the neoliberal university.

Feminist Teachers

Rosemary's argument about the value of feminist law teachers was multi-faceted. First, she contended that feminist law teachers provide a corrective to the exclusion of feminist agency from mainstream – malestream – legal education. She consistently noted that textbooks invariably explain progressive law reforms for women in terms of an inevitable response to social change, and/or as the work of benevolent male legislators.[7] They fail to refer to the feminist activism lying behind many of the reforms, or the fact that feminists conceptualised, demanded and struggled for them. This was, of course, part of the impetus behind her edited collection with Erika Rackley, *Women's Legal Landmarks*.[8] Here, they aimed to remedy the omissions of the textbooks, to provide the real back story to many reforms of significance for women and to ensure that feminist struggles were acknowledged and given their due.

Secondly, Rosemary argued that feminist law teachers play an important role in teaching students to question the status quo and the gendered operations of law.[9] Her own aim as a feminist educator was to enable students to acquire sufficient insight to recognise law's role in creating and accommodating harmful and discriminatory practices against women, while professing to treat women equally.[10] This critical project was aimed at legal formalism and the myth of legal neutrality and objectivity. Feminist law teachers crucially expose the notion of legal objectivity as a myth and enable students to understand how it can function to obscure the reality of inequality and to insulate such inequality from questioning.

Thirdly, and conversely, Rosemary argued that feminist law teaching can also galvanise reform ideas and activism by suggesting alternatives and empowering students to work for change.[11] In her view, as well as enabling insight and critique, one of the goals of legal education is to empower students by equipping them with the knowledge and skills to take greater control of their lives.[12] Thus, for example, in the process of countering dominant narratives which erase feminist activism

[6] Rosemary Auchmuty, discussion with the author, 10 October 2022.

[7] For a counterpoint, see Bourne, ch 1, this volume.

[8] E Rackley and R Auchmuty (eds), *Women's Legal Landmarks: Celebrating the History of Women and Law in the UK and Ireland* (Hart, 2018).

[9] Auchmuty (n 1) 35.

[10] Auchmuty (n 2) 227.

[11] Auchmuty (n 1) 35–36.

[12] Auchmuty (n 2) 227.

from the history of law reforms, *Women's Legal Landmarks* ensured that feminist achievements were celebrated and could inspire further activism.

These arguments chime with the observations of Heijstraa and Pétursdóttir, who conducted interviews with a number of senior academic feminists in Iceland. Their interviewees similarly described introducing feminist perspectives in their teaching 'in the hope of creating awareness of the topic and effecting change',[13] and giving students 'wings to enact change'.[14] They comment that:

> Our participants' activism is thus not least through relational work of educating and empowering others who then go on to have an impact on society through their different professions and work. We call this the ripple effect, which they see as their greatest reward and accomplishment and a strategy to effect change within academia and society.[15]

Heijstraa and Pétursdóttir note, however, that such activism only goes so far when only a limited number of students enrol on 'gender' courses and feminist academics find themselves mainly preaching to the choir.[16] Rosemary acknowledged that the feminist message is not always easy to transmit in a context in which students (as well as many teaching colleagues) tend to be at best indifferent or, at worst, resistant to feminist content.[17] In the 'Feminist Judgments' article she presented a strategy for overcoming such obstacles and exposing all students to feminist ideas, not only those choosing to take an optional gender and law module. She described her integration of feminist perspectives into a core module – Property Law – via a core legal method – reading and analysing cases. Given that textbooks present cases in digested versions stripped of context or critique,[18] and in particular eschew feminist legal scholarship,[19] the module required students to read cases in full and presented them in their historical and social context.[20] The cases chosen involved facts that lent themselves to a feminist analysis. Thus, while developing students' legal skills, they could also be convinced of the relevance of gender by seeing it for themselves. Rosemary dubbed this 'feminist legal education by stealth'.[21] This was cemented by the assessment for the module, which included writing an alternative judgment in a property law case. While the case again raised gender issues, there was no requirement that the alternative judgment students produced should be a feminist judgment. However, the book *Feminist Judgments:*

[13] TM Heijstraa and GM Pétursdóttir, 'Feminist Academics Strategically Playing Offense/Defense in Pursuit of Academic and Societal Change' (2022) *Nora: Nordic Journal of Feminist and Gender Research* 6, online May 2022 doi.org/10.1080/08038740.2022.2080255.
[14] ibid.
[15] ibid, references omitted.
[16] ibid 7.
[17] Auchmuty (n 2) 228.
[18] ibid 230–32.
[19] ibid 229.
[20] ibid 230.
[21] ibid 238.

From Theory to Practice[22] provided an obvious source of models for alternative judgments and by referring students to the book, further 'feminist legal education by stealth' could occur. By incorporating feminist perspectives into mainstream teaching, Rosemary hoped to educate future generations of lawyers, judges and policy makers to be alert to gendered disadvantage and the need to address it, and thereby to make a difference in the world.[23]

As well as raising the question of where feminist content can be included in the curriculum (in compulsory or optional modules), Heijstraa and Pétursdóttir comment on the apparently limited temporality of feminist approaches to teaching, and 'the need for constant repetition of the feminist agenda for it not to slide into the background and eventually get lost'.[24] Two of their interviewees identify this point in particular:

> Marta describes how a feminist course she has taught for decades will presumably be cancelled when she retires. Mjöll is very aware that when she goes on sabbatical, there will be no one to step in, which means that a whole class will miss her feminist course.[25]

This prompted me to ask Rosemary what had happened to the module that she wrote about in 2012. Was it still being taught in the same way in 2022? Her response was that the module had run for a number of years, and while students initially found it difficult, they came to like it and it received very good evaluations. In particular, students were able to achieve good marks by getting the law right and being able to emulate the style of a judgment. However, the module had not survived the last redesign of the LLB in response to the introduction of the Solicitors Qualifying Examination (SQE).[26] This may say something about the anti-intellectual nature of the SQE, or about the willingness of law schools to revise their curricula to reflect its narrower focus. In either case, the effect was to exclude a feminist perspective (and presumably other critical perspectives) once again. Subsequently, Rosemary told me that she had been inspired by our discussion to reintroduce lectures and coursework assessment on alternative (feminist) judgments into the Land Law module she was now convening.

But even if the introduction of feminist perspectives in legal education has remained a matter for individual feminist scholars rather than becoming mainstreamed, and hence has been contingent and time-limited, Rosemary was clear that feminist legal pedagogy is better legal pedagogy.[27] The Property Law module

[22] R Hunter, C McGlynn and E Rackley (eds), *Feminist Judgments: From Theory to Practice* (Hart, 2010).

[23] Auchmuty (n 1) 61.

[24] Heijstraa and Pétursdóttir (n 13) 8.

[25] ibid.

[26] The SQE replaced the requirement for a Qualifying Law Degree and a vocational training course in order to qualify as a solicitor with the simple requirement to pass the qualifying exam, with legal knowledge tested in stage 1 exclusively by means of multiple-choice questions.

[27] For a similar point in relation to the writing of feminist judgments, see eg R Hunter, 'More Than Just a Different Face? Judicial Diversity and Decision-Making' (2015) 68 *Current Legal Problems* 119; R Hunter, 'Feminist Judgments in the "Real World"' (2018) 8(9) *Oñati Socio-Legal Series* 1275; R Hunter

discussed in 'Feminist Judgments', for example, got all students to read cases, used case law as a vehicle for learning legal rules and problem-solving techniques, fostered students' critical skills, exposed them to socio-legal context in a way that was central rather than peripheral to their learning, introduced an innovative form of assessment (moving away from reliance on exams),[28] and facilitated student attainment. All of these attributes are lauded in contemporary (legal) educational literature and practice. In Rosemary's argument, feminist legal scholars design and teach innovative courses and teach traditional courses in innovative ways, both of which have proved popular with an increasingly female and diverse student body.[29] In the contemporary higher education environment, popularity with students translates into success on various educational performance indicators, including the Teaching Excellence Framework (TEF), the National Student Survey (NSS) and law school league tables.

The final element of Rosemary's argument in relation to teaching was that feminist legal scholars play an important role as mentors and role models for students.[30] This is illustrated in the chapter on Olive Stone, which highlights Stone's mentoring of women students.[31] Taking this role even further, Stone left most of her estate to the LSE for the benefit of law students, especially those with life experiences similar to her own, ie women students who were childless, unmarried or fatherless, and older students.[32] By this means, Stone could be seen as an early proponent of the widening participation agenda.

Feminist Researchers

In addition to good teaching, Rosemary maintained that law schools have become reliant on feminist scholars for excellent research performance. In 'Stakeholders', she wrote about the transformation brought about by the UK Research Assessment Exercise (RAE), which meant that research could no longer be regarded as an occasional or optional activity. Suddenly law schools needed active researchers, and feminist legal scholars fitted the bill. Indeed, she argued that the RAE legitimised feminist legal research,[33] which went from being regarded as marginal and lacking in intellectual credibility to being considered a valid and respectable form of legal scholarship, albeit one that continued to

and E Rackley, 'Feminist Judgments on the UK Supreme Court' (2020) 32 *Canadian Journal of Women and the Law* 85; R Hunter, K Mack and S Roach Anleu, 'Feminist Judgments in Lower Courts' (2021) 48 *Journal of Law and Society* 595.

[28] Auchmuty (n 2) 237.

[29] Auchmuty (n 1) 61.

[30] ibid.

[31] Auchmuty and Temkin (n 3) 450.

[32] ibid 452–53.

[33] Auchmuty (n 1) 57.

be treated as a niche area of specialisation with which non-feminist legal scholars felt no imperative to engage. In other words, while the content of feminist work might still be ignored, its institutional usefulness was accepted.[34] Feminist scholars produced outputs and those outputs were capable of a high degree of originality, significance and rigour, and hence were good value in RAE (and now Research Excellence Framework (REF)) terms.

Rosemary also noted that when external research funding became a desirable commodity, feminists showed they were capable of attracting large amounts of funding, with the leading example being the then Arts and Humanities Research Board (AHRB)-funded Centre for Law, Gender and Sexuality.[35] The Centre LGS was a collaboration between the Universities of Kent, Keele and Westminster, with Rosemary being the Westminster lead before her move to Reading in 2007. Arguably, feminist traditions and experience of collaborative working equipped them well to mobilise often cross-institutional research teams capable of securing substantial grant funding.

Since 'Stakeholders' was published in 2010, feminist legal scholars have only strengthened their institutional value as researchers. When 'impact' (some kind of change or effect in the outside world produced by academic research) was included in the 2014 REF, the long-standing concern of feminist legal scholars to influence the law-making process through their scholarship and policy writing[36] made them very adept at responding to the impact agenda. In the 2021 REF, quite a number of impact case studies were submitted by feminist legal scholars and/or were based on feminist work across a range of areas of law.[37]

The centrality of policy-relevant research to feminist legal scholarship can also be seen in Rosemary's chapter on Olive Stone. Stone was an outspoken proponent of women's rights to matrimonial property, and of fairness to wives on divorce when their contribution to the marriage had consisted of unpaid labour in the home.[38] This academic advocacy was translated into policy influence through Stone's role as legal adviser to the National Council of Women.[39] In contemporary terms, Stone was developing pathways to impact and having an impact beyond academia in ways that would now be regarded as exemplary. The freedom provided by academia for feminist legal scholars to incorporate their politics into their work, as Rosemary identified,[40] has been turned to advantage, with that politically-motivated activity now also serving strategic institutional goals.

[34] ibid 60.
[35] ibid.
[36] ibid 61.
[37] On a rough count by the author, around 10% of impact cases studies included feminist authors or content. See Impact case study database, REF 2021. results2021.ref.ac.uk/impact.
[38] Auchmuty and Temkin (n 3) 449–50.
[39] ibid 450.
[40] Auchmuty (n 1) 61.

Feminist Managers

Rosemary also observed in 'Stakeholders' how feminists had moved into senior positions in the academy, including on the RAE, in learned societies, as Heads of School, and in other management roles,[41] such that law schools had also come to rely on feminists for their management skills. Again, this trend has only intensified in the years since 'Stakeholders' was written. The editors of and contributors to this collection of essays include several former and current Chairs of learned societies, Deputy Vice Chancellors, Pro-Vice Chancellors, REF panellists, grant panellists, Heads of School, and School and Faculty Directors of Research, Directors of Research Centres, REF Directors and Directors of Learning and Teaching. Some, including Rosemary herself, have held several of these roles. Feminist legal scholars have proved themselves to be effective, highly competent and efficient academic managers, and have brought a different (and again, arguably better) leadership style, that is less hierarchical, less patriarchal, and more inclusive, supportive and nurturing than the traditional masculine style of academic authority. Implicitly, in Rosemary's work, this is all cause for celebration.

However the notion that feminists are thriving as institutional and disciplinary managers must give some pause for thought. In the first place, Rosemary's account of feminist success in the legal academy, while finding some support in the legal education literature,[42] is notably at odds with that of many other commentators who argue that feminist scholars and other critical voices are marginalised in the neoliberal university because they do not offer instrumental knowledge,[43] their pedagogical approaches are antithetical to neoliberal institutional structures,[44] and their knowledge and political commitments are incompatible with neoliberalism's competitive individualism.[45] As suggested above, feminist knowledge may

[41] ibid 59–60.

[42] See eg A Bradney, *Conversations, Choices and Chances: The Liberal Law School in the Twenty-First Century* (Hart, 2003); F Cownie, *Legal Academics: Culture and Identities* (Hart, 2004); A Bradney and F Cownie, 'Gothic Horror? A Response to Margaret Thornton' (2005) 14 *Social and Legal Studies* 277. Bradney and Cownie both point to the flourishing of socio-legal scholarship in recent decades in the UK, including work on gender, as also noted by R Collier, '"Love Law, Love Life": Neoliberalism, Wellbeing and Gender in the Legal Profession – The Case of Law School' (2014) 17 *Legal Ethics* 202, 217.

[43] See eg M Thornton, *Privatising the Public University: The Case of Law* (Routledge, 2012) 77–78, 157; F Jenkins, 'Gendered Hierarchies of Knowledge and the Prestige Factor: How Philosophy Survives Market Rationality' in M Thornton (ed), *Through a Glass Darkly: The Social Sciences Look at the Neoliberal University* (Australian National University Press, 2015) 49; J Blackmore, 'Disciplining Academic Women: Gender Restructuring and the Labour of Research in Entrepreneurial Universities' in ibid 179.

[44] E Bussea, M Krauschb and W Liao, 'How the "Neutral" University Makes Critical Feminist Pedagogy Impossible: Intersectional Analysis from Marginalized Faculty on Three Campuses' (2021) 41 *Sociological Spectrum* 29.

[45] L Girerd and V Bonnot, 'Neoliberalism: An Ideological Barrier to Feminist Identification and Collective Action' (2020) 33 *Social Justice Research* 81; CA Taylor, 'Slow Singularities for Collective Mattering: New Material Feminist Praxis in the Accelerated Academy' (2020) 39 *Irish Educational Studies* 255, 257.

have become instrumental with its ability to score highly on measures of student satisfaction and research quality, and to attract grant funding and create impact, although as Heijstraa and Pétursdóttir observe, the marginalisation of feminism within higher education:

> manifests itself as a push and pull; either feminism is pushed back or pulled in, whichever suits the days' criteria and institutional and political climate. Feminism is pulled in if feminist programmes become revenue building in the neoliberal academy, even though feminism's epistemic grounds are always suspect and under scrutiny.[46]

More generally it appears that competing accounts of feminist inclusion vs marginalisation in the neoliberal academy can be reconciled by distinguishing between feminist scholars and their scholarship. Margaret Thornton's observation that law schools tolerate feminist content in courses offered by feminists but there is no feeling that anyone else should include it in their courses,[47] chimes precisely with Rosemary's concerns about the ghettoisation of feminist knowledge and her efforts to counteract this by including feminist content in a core module. Rosemary would probably also agree with Thornton's point that students have become resistant to any courses with 'feminist' in the title because they are worried about how this will look on their CV and impact on their employability[48] – hence the need for 'feminist legal education by stealth'. The key to the divergent analyses lies in something that Rosemary presents as a conundrum: 'the entrenched marginalisation of feminist scholarship in the academy … sits so oddly alongside the increasing institutional importance of feminists themselves'.[49] If this separation turns out to be not a conundrum but the condition under which feminist scholars have been 'let in' to the neoliberal academy, then the position becomes clearer, if also somewhat darker.

The second pause therefore, is to reflect on the implications if Rosemary is right – that feminist legal scholars have found a home, flourished in and are now often involved in running, neoliberal law schools, while their actual scholarship remains peripheral. Have feminist legal scholars proved themselves to be the perfect neoliberal institutional fodder, all process and no substance? Have they been instrumentalised or co-opted by neoliberal institutional agendas or, worse, have they become active proponents of them? It is clearly observable that feminist legal scholars are delivering on the full range of audited performance measures: research excellence, teaching excellence, knowledge exchange, EDI credentialling (particularly Athena SWAN), widening participation, student wellbeing, success, attainment and employability. In the words of Heijstraa and Pétursdóttir:

[46] TM Heijstraa and GM Pétursdóttir, 'Sisterly Advice for Feminists in Academia when Playing the Game and Working the Cracks' (2022) 34 *Gender and Education* 247, 249.

[47] Thornton, *Privatising* (n 43) 77–78. See also Heijstraa and Pétursdóttir (n 13) 6: feminist 'actions in the ivory basement (Eveline, 2004) go largely unnoticed as their colleagues find it unworthy of attention'.

[48] Thornton, *Privatising* (n 43) 78.

[49] Auchmuty (n 1) 61.

> Our participants, many of whom were hired in the pre-neoliberal era, are in many ways poster children of the neoliberal system, bearing strong resemblances to workaholics; successful in obtaining funding and popular among students, which is what the neoliberal academic system thrives on.[50]

But have feminists been so focused on becoming compliant and responsible neoliberal institutional subjects that they've been willing to accept the side-lining of their scholarship? As Fiona Mackay reflects:

> I have sometimes wondered whether it is a particularly tempting form of neoliberal 'seduction'... for academic feminists to be offered positions of institutional power in the neoliberal academy. Such positions bring apparent prestige and power – tantalising opportunities to gain capital in the 'prestige economy' of HE and in marked contrast to the marginal position of academic feminists and the precarious status of their scholarship.[51]

Similarly, Heijstraa and Pétursdóttir refer to the 'elastic self' that senior feminists have cultivated in response to institutional demands, but note that the 'wiggle room' obtained by excelling at the academic game comes at the potential cost of becoming 'unrecognisable to ourselves'. They caution that, 'In our interpretation, and in line with Pereira's (2017) conclusion warning feminists in academia against losing sight of their initial goal of changing society, this might mean that, to fit into the academy, we become the misfits in our movements, and vice versa.'[52]

Feminist Neoliberals?

As a significant body of feminist academic literature attests, when women began to enter the academy in greater numbers in the 1970s–80s, the climate that greeted them was distinctly chilly.[53] Rosemary has noted the earlier struggles of women academics to survive and gain a foothold in the face of misogyny, homophobia, sexual harassment, family unfriendliness,[54] and processes of homosocial reproduction – the appointment and promotion of bright young chaps with potential, while women had to prove they were twice as good to receive the same recognition and rewards. Likewise, both Celia Wells and Richard Collier have remarked on the formerly dominant culture of heteronormative and homosocial male collegiality, a

[50] Heijstraa and Petursdottir (n 46) 251 (references omitted).

[51] F Mackay, 'Dilemmas of an Academic Feminist as Manager in the Neoliberal Academy: Negotiating Institutional Authority, Oppositional Knowledge and Change' (2021) 19 *Political Studies Review* 75, 85 (references omitted).

[52] Heijstraa and Petursdottir (n 46) 249–50, citing Maria do Mar Pereira, *Power, Knowledge and Feminist Scholarship: An Ethnography of Academia* (Routledge, 2017).

[53] See eg The Chilly Collective (eds), *Breaking Anonymity: The Chilly Climate for Women Faculty* (Wilfrid Laurier University Press, 1995).

[54] Workshop Discussion (n 5).

culture marked by patronage, male privilege, clear-cut gender divisions[55] and, one might add, sexual predation by male lecturers on female students.

By contrast, the structures of the neoliberal university – students as consumers, research assessment and top-down management – have proved more welcoming for women. As Fiona Mackay notes:

> not all trends associated with neoliberalism and managerialism need be inherently unprogressive (including professionalisation, accreditation, accountability and quality assurance). Many of these trends – particularly those that have increased transparency – have been helpful in easing the entry of marginalised groups and knowledges into the academy.[56]

And Richard Collier similarly observes that:

> Interlinking economically rational gender-neutral imperatives associated with neoliberalism … the changes that have taken place can be read as – far from entrenching gender divisions – having 'opened out' a university system (and with it, their law schools) hitherto based on patronage, elitism and unaccountability to what are, for all their limitations, more egalitarian processes and cultures in relation to areas such as recruitment and promotion.[57]

When Thornton refers to the appointment of Deans and Heads of School by management rather than being elected by their peers, and line managers being accountable to senior management rather than to their colleagues, as representing a weakening of democratic norms and collegial bonds,[58] this may also be seen as a weakening of traditional academic hierarchies, values and practices which operated to exclude women. And when Thornton associates top-down managerialism with masculinity and collegiality, connectedness and community with the feminine, in line with Gilligan's 'different voice' thesis,[59] the reality (as in other areas where feminine 'difference' has been argued) may in fact be more complex. As feminist scholars and critics of Gilligan have pointed out, communitarianism is not necessarily feminine, let alone feminist.[60] It depends on whose norms are enshrined in cultural traditions and whose voices are the loudest, and these rarely operate to the benefit of women.

Feminist legal scholars have participated in women's greater success in the neoliberal university and, as Rosemary argued, have also brought distinct additional institutional skills and competencies by virtue of their feminist political commitments. Thus, feminists may have become key players in academic

[55] C Wells, 'Working Out Women in Law Schools' (2001) 21 *Legal Studies* 116; Collier (n 42) 216. See also the British campus novels of eg David Lodge.

[56] Mackay (n 51) 83.

[57] Collier (n 42) 217.

[58] Thornton, *Privatising* (n 43) 16.

[59] ibid 133.

[60] See eg E Frazer and N Lacey, *The Politics of Community: A Feminist Critique of the Liberal–Communitarian Debate* (Harvester Press, 1993); E Feder Kittay, 'A Feminist Public Ethic of Care Meets the New Communitarian Family Policy' (2001) 111 *Ethics* 523.

managerialism because they are at least equally, and possibly more, capable of playing the management game, and of turning that game, at least to some extent, to their own ends. Rather than a simple picture of co-optation, there does appear to have been an element of reverse co-optation or at least mutual benefit between feminist scholars and the neoliberal university. The more welcoming climate for women has included space for feminist legal scholars to be valued and rewarded for pursuing their political commitments outside academia. This pursuit is no longer something they are expected to do in their own time as an entirely separate activity, which might be at the expense of research, but can be understood *as* research, dissemination, knowledge transfer and/or public engagement, that is, as legitimate and strategically important academic activity.

Likewise, there is (some) space to pursue feminist political commitments inside the academy, through the production of high-quality outputs (open to any theoretical content), obtaining research grants for feminist projects, and the recognition and valuing of more 'caring', creative and egalitarian educational practices. For example, while Thornton decries 'the shift away from radical critique and the social in favour of the technical and the applied' when it comes to teaching in the neoliberal law school,[61] the feminist judgment projects show how 'the technical and the applied' can also be feminist and, as Rosemary's article demonstrated, can be used as a vehicle for the social and for the critique of law in teaching. For such reasons, at least in British academia, it does not appear to be the case, as Thornton claimed, that women engaged in feminist scholarship find it difficult to get promoted.[62]

While there might be a variety of ways in which feminist and neoliberal institutional agendas coincide and become mutually reinforcing, however, this does not fundamentally challenge the latter. The relative 'success' of feminist scholars and managers in the neoliberal university has been accompanied by strengthened authoritarianism, greater enslavement to market and regulatory demands, increased workloads and stress, and correspondingly shrinking opportunities for reflection and critique. Furthermore, not all feminists have benefited, with empowerment linked to intersections of gender with race, class and sexuality.[63] Collier argues that 'Changes associated with the neoliberal corporatisation of universities may … be serving not so much to *diminish* the significance of gender … rather, alongside the embedding of formal equality … they are *re-gendering* universities in some problematic and often contradictory ways.'[64] These include the emergence of a form of business-entrepreneurial masculinity (rational, disembodied, instrumental, fratriarchal) in place of older style paternalistic masculinity.[65] They may also include a new form of feminism – or what some have contended is post-feminism, 'in

[61] Thornton, *Privatising* (n 43) 80.
[62] ibid 140.
[63] Heijstraa and Petursdottir (n 46) 248.
[64] Collier (n 42) 218 (emphasis in original).
[65] ibid 223, 228.

which what matters … is performative achievement through individual striving, and feminine identity as constructed through ambition, confidence, hard work and success'.[66] In this environment, feminism is regarded as 'an already "achieved project" whose collective feminist politics we can dispense with'.[67]

Feminist Resistance?

Both Auchmuty and Thornton observe that academics have generally offered little resistance to the new managerialism in universities.[68] They have for the most part been compliant, accepted the managerial turn, adapted to it, and got on with their careers as best they could. Feminist scholars have not been different from their non-feminist colleagues in this respect. Heath and Burdon identify a number of possible explanations for academics' lack of resistance to neoliberal reforms. One is:

> the hostile, precarious and overloaded nature of academic work which has resulted from changes to governance including performance management, quality assurance processes, restructuring and budgetary devolution … Academics are simply too overworked, exhausted and overwhelmed to resist even when they do not live in fear of losing their jobs or failing to get another contract or casual position.[69]

A second argument is that neoliberal reforms have actively disabled resistance in order to achieve the desired efficiencies:

> Parker and Jary, for example, explain diminished academic autonomy and reductions in democratic and collegial decision making in universities as prerequisites for the intensification of academic labour. They argue that the degree of intensification of academic work which has occurred would not have been possible without significantly decreasing the role and power of academics in decision making as well as restricting the democratic nature of decision making. They also suggest that the public pillorying of the university as a 'bastion of parochialism rather than the cutting edge of the intellect' has limited academic preparedness to counter neoliberal changes, which are often articulated as being essential to ensure efficiency, productivity and market capacity.[70]

Thirdly, it has been argued that '"neoliberal governance has imposed panoptic surveillance regimes" on academics: regimes of oversight, accountability and audit which ensure every academic knows that s/he is constantly being watched and judged'.[71] This sense of constant surveillance 'produces academics who exercise

[66] Taylor (n 45) 259.
[67] ibid.
[68] Workshop Discussion (n 5); Thornton, *Privatising* (n 43) 114.
[69] M Heath and PD Burdon, 'Academic Resistance to the Neoliberal University' (2013) 23 *Legal Education Review* 379, 383 (footnotes omitted).
[70] ibid 384, citing M Parker and D Jary, 'The McUniversity: Organization, Management and Academic Subjectivity' (1995) 2 *Organization* 319 (footnotes omitted).
[71] ibid 385.

self-surveillance and self-monitoring rather than requiring the imposition of external forms of coercion'.[72] In this account, resistance is stifled by self-restraint without any need for institutional intervention.

Nevertheless, like any other system of power, neoliberalism must be understood as hegemonic rather than totalising. As Collier points out, the reconfiguration of universities and reconstitution of academic subjectivities does not mean that those processes are fixed or final or that resistance is impossible.[73] Similarly, Heath and Burdon argue that 'Formations of power are in a constant process of being undermined and re-formed by the resistance of active agents. There is always something that "escapes them"'.[74] Thus, while their review found little evidence of organised or collective resistance to neoliberal university reforms, it did discover 'visible and hidden acts of individual resistance that are both creative and effective'.[75] This suggests that feminist scholars and managers do have (some) scope not just for contributing impressively to neoliberal metrics but for political agency against the process of academic commodification.

Rosemary has suggested that while feminists in the law school may occupy positions of power, they are not rulers, and their continued occupation of these roles is conditional on good behaviour. Thus, feminist managers have not been authorised or felt able to use their positions of power to try to transform the academy.[76] But this is both too much of a disclaimer – feminists cannot avoid accountability for how they exercise power – and perhaps also concedes too much. One form of resistance demonstrated by feminist managers has been in relation to leadership styles, and the capacity – or deliberate strategy – of feminists, as mentioned above, to subvert the managerial paradigm by adopting more collaborative, relational, democratic and nurturing practices of leadership.[77]

Thornton argues that feminist academics in managerial roles in the corporatised university are in a difficult position, damned if they do and damned if they don't. Since management, in her account, is inherently masculine, if feminist managers adopt a different style they are perceived as ineffectual and weak, or if they adopt the standard masculine style they are unable to perform it as convincingly as a man and so are not valued in the same way as men.[78] She concludes, 'It would seem that there is no acceptable subject position for women in authority within the corporatised academy.'[79]

Yet Thornton also concedes that, 'The personal managerial style of the vice-chancellor and line managers determines whether collegial practices, such as regular meeting and consultation, are retained or not.'[80] This suggests that there

[72] ibid.
[73] Collier (n 42) 219.
[74] Heath and Burden (n 69) 390.
[75] ibid 381.
[76] Discussion with the author (n 6).
[77] See eg N Loveless and C Smith, 'Attunement in the Cracks: Feminist Collaboration and the University as Broken Machine' (2022) 34(1) *Feminist Formations* 272.
[78] Thornton, *Privatising* (n 43) 156–57.
[79] ibid 157.
[80] ibid 114.

is scope at least for personal difference in management (as in teaching) practices. And if a manager's personal commitments are feminist (or otherwise critical or democratic), then it is possible within their field of managerial responsibility to maintain cultures and practices of collegiality, transparency, consultation and collaboration that buck the trend of top-down command. Likewise, line managers can treat their colleagues not simply as units of performance for the school and the university but as individuals with their own lives, commitments and aspirations to be nurtured and facilitated.

The literature identifies a variety of feminist managerial strategies of resistance, including collaborative leadership;[81] everyday practices of care and relationality;[82] capacity-building[83] and community-building,[84] supporting slow scholarship;[85] and sharing knowledge and giving advice.[86] Rosemary notes that as mentors, feminists have been good at advising junior colleagues on 'how to play the game',[87] but more than that, feminist managers can maintain a critical stance towards 'the game' and communicate that to colleagues as well. Sotiropoulou and Cranston in fact distinguish between mentoring and what they term 'critical academic friendship'. As a counter to the individualist structures of neoliberal academia, friendship implies partnership, a mutually supportive relationship between equals, as opposed to the hierarchical instrumentalism of mentoring. The focus of friendship is on the process of engagement and support rather than on working towards a particular career goal.[88]

More generally, Fiona Mackay distinguishes between (feminist) management, which is hierarchical and instrumental, focused on getting things done, and (feminist) leadership, which is a relation of influence involving motivating, understanding and inspiring others, and possibly also striving for organisational transformation.[89] While the two may overlap, they are not coterminous. Management may or may not require leadership, while leadership may be exercised outside formal managerial roles.[90] In her view:

> While I am sceptical there is a distinct set of rules comprising a 'feminist' style of management, feminist academic practice consists of a 'disposition'... including attentiveness to unequal power relations and social justice, to relationships, to boundaries

[81] Loveless and Smith (n 77) 274.
[82] ibid 283; L Morley and RWB Lund, 'The Affective Economy of Feminist Leadership in Finnish Universities: Class-Based Knowledge for Navigating Neoliberalism and Neuroliberalism' (2021) 42 *Discourse: Studies in the Cultural Politics of Education* 114, 122; P Sotiropoulou and S Cranston, 'Critical Friendship: An Alternative, "Care-full" Way to Play the Academic Game' (2022) *Gender, Place and Culture* 5, online 3 May 2022: DOI: 10.1080/0966369X.2022.20696845; Taylor (n 45) 260.
[83] Taylor (n 45) 260.
[84] Morley and Lund (n 82) 122.
[85] Sotiropoulou and Cranston (n 82) 6.
[86] Heijstraa and Petursdottir (n 46) 249, 255.
[87] Workshop Discussion (n 5).
[88] Sotiropoulou and Cranston (n 82) 6–8.
[89] Mackay (n 51) 79.
[90] ibid.

> of inclusion and exclusions and forms of marginalisation, and to self-reflection. At a minimum then, a feminist style of management would attempt to steer clear of control, domination and competitiveness. It would be open to one's own vulnerabilities and limitations, would seek to use positional power to open up opportunities for other people, and endeavour to build shared capacity. It is apparent that there is considerable overlap between feminist management and the markers of feminist leadership … in seeking to hold and exercise power 'helpfully'.[91]

Mackay acknowledges the caution that 'the belief that academic feminists can lead differently in the contemporary managerialised global academy can be a form of "cruel optimism"'.[92] However she sees feminist academic leaders – like civil service 'femocrats' before them[93] – as 'tempered radicals', outsider insiders who can and do make use of their particular positionality to achieve small but significant changes:

> Tempered radicals, according to Meyerson and Scully (1995), are individuals who are committed both to their organisations and to a cause, identity or ideology that is at odds with the dominant institutional culture. Their radicalism drives them to challenge the status quo (as does their very presence as individuals who do not 'fit'). Their temperedness reflects the way they have been toughened by their sense of struggle and ambivalence, and angered by the 'incongruities between their own values and beliefs about social justice and the values and beliefs they see enacted in their organizations' (Meyerson and Scully, 1995: 587). Importantly, they are tempered in their inclination to practice moderation in their interactions with power-holders, and in their efforts to effect change: 'In this sense, tempered radicals must be simultaneously hot- and cool-headed. The heat fuels action and change; the coolness shapes the action and change into legitimate and viable forms' (Meyerson and Scully, 1995: 587). The emphasis is on insider strategies of seeking incremental change through 'small wins'.[94]

Mackay's account offers a convincing analysis of how feminist managers engage in acts of resistance through feminist leadership in the neoliberal university. Indeed, her account arguably provides a compelling description of Rosemary's own practice as a feminist leader. It is usefully supplemented, however, by Morley and Lund's critical observation that descriptions of feminist leadership often focus exclusively on affective labour – the work of 'mediating and applying understandings of power relations and systems to soothe, comfort, and reassure colleagues',[95] of 'creating a sustainable work environment in which people can actually work,

[91] ibid 79 (references omitted).

[92] ibid 78. The reference is to L Berlant, *Cruel Optimism* (Duke University Press, 2011).

[93] ibid 80; see also eg H Eisenstein, *Inside Agitators: Australian Femocrats and the State* (Temple University Press, 1996); M Sawer, *Sisters in Suits: Women and Public Policy in Australia* (Allen & Unwin, 1991); M Thomson, 'Femocrats and Babes: Women and Power' (2001) 16(35) *Australian Feminist Studies* 193; A Yeatman, *Bureaucrats, Technocrats, Femocrats: Essays on the Contemporary Australian State* (Allen & Unwin, 1990).

[94] Mackay (n 51) 76, quoting DE Myerson and MA Scully, 'Tempered Radicalism and the Politics of Ambivalence and Change' (1995) 6 *Organization Science* 585.

[95] Morley and Lund (n 82) 125.

rather than a negative atmosphere',[96] and of making 'affective interventions to counter the corrosive effects of the neoliberal … academy'.[97] While this kind of 'soft managerialism', making neoliberal institutions more livable, is important, it should not represent the limits of feminist leadership practice or potentiality. As Morley and Lund argue:

> feminist knowledge should not be reduced solely to [the] … affective labour of soothing, comforting, and reassuring anxious colleagues struggling to survive in the neoliberal university, but should also be used effectively to rethink, together with those colleagues, what the good academic organisation and working life could be instead … A key question is how feminist leadership knowledge can be used for imagination and actualisation, rather than mitigation.[98]

Ultimately, though, I think Rosemary would agree with Fiona Mackay's conclusion:

> Should feminists aspire to take on positions of authority with top-down power dynamics and the perils of complicity in the neoliberal academy? I think the question is an important one, and the potential pitfalls serious, but it needs to be considered along with its corollary: is it better then to leave it to non-feminists to steer, shape and exert power in the academy?[99]

Conclusion

Rosemary was acutely aware of and troubled by the fact that for all that feminist legal scholars have become indispensable to the effective operation of contemporary law schools (for better or for worse), the marginalisation of feminist legal scholarship remains entrenched. Substantive feminist critiques of the gendered nature of law, its complicity in perpetuating the oppression of women in society, and feminist arguments for change have not become part of mainstream law teaching, textbooks, or legal scholarship. On the contrary, other forms of oppression are seen as more morally compelling (ignoring their intersectionality with gender) and critiques of feminism tend to get plenty of air time.[100] Are feminists presiding over institutions engaged in undermining their own project? Or has the feminist project in law instead expanded – or shifted – to embrace the quiet mitigation or stealthy subversion of neoliberal governance in law schools?

These questions are, of course, not susceptible to simple answers. But they are important questions for feminist legal scholars to stop and ponder. To the extent that Rosemary's work has directed attention to the role of feminist scholars and

[96] ibid 122.
[97] ibid 126.
[98] ibid 126.
[99] Mackay (n 51) 90.
[100] Discussion with the author (n 6). Critiques of feminism have come from a variety of different sources over time. See eg whatever is most salient at the time you are reading this.

scholarship in the contemporary legal academy it has usefully prompted these reflections. But Rosemary was also not one to spend too long pondering. She was a pragmatic woman of action, and her response was very often to get on and do it – to redesign a core module and its assessment, to write a textbook, to champion feminist activism, to take on leadership roles, and to support and mentor junior colleagues. Her unwavering goal was to fight women's oppression wherever she found it, and to encourage and inspire students and colleagues to do the same. We are indebted to both her thoughts and her practical example.

14

Auchmuty, Legal Education and Equality

LISA WEBLEY

Introduction

In this chapter I hope to connect the three elements of the title: legal education, equality and Rosemary Auchmuty's contribution to them both within the framework of Women, Their Lives and the Law. I have been fortunate to work with Rosemary since the turn of the millennium, to learn from her and to have her as a friend. We have spent many hours talking about the purpose of legal education, how it has changed over time and how it has become more apparently equal as student and academic demographics have shifted while structural inequality, or as Rosemary would say injustice, persists just below the surface. Auchmuty's contribution both to gender and law discourse and feminist activism, as well as her ongoing commitment to legal education, are woven into the warp and weft of countless law schools in which she has worked, along with many others besides. The invitation to contribute to this collection has provided an opportunity for me to reflect on her approach to education and to scholarship during a time of intense change in university law schools in England and Wales.

This chapter begins with a thumbnail biography of Auchmuty's contribution to education, to legal education and to scholarship from Australia to the UK. It draws upon her approach to biographies as access points to consider the lived experience of women, including as a means to examine context and structural inequality, injustice, the silences, barriers and supports that pervade study and careers. Alongside this I super-impose the trajectory of continuity and change in (largely English) legal education during the period covered by Auchmuty's time within it. I locate her contribution to gender in teaching, leadership and scholarship within that. Thirdly I touch upon gender equality in the academy, which Auchmuty has championed socially, politically and professionally. In concluding I hope to draw out a few of the issues that Auchmuty and other feminists continue to grapple with in their experience of legal education practice and scholarship.

Auchmuty

Auchmuty read for her undergraduate degree in history at the Australian National University from 1967–71. Following successful completion, she went on to undertake a PhD in history between 1972–75, which included time in London, something she thoroughly enjoyed. Thereafter she spent three years at Wollongong Institute of Education, now the University of Wollongong, where she taught history and social science and during which she studied for a primary teaching diploma in education and undertook teaching in schools. She experimented with experiential learning, keeping a diary during this time entitled 'Half a Teacher'. The diary has yet to be serialised but may prove both enlightening as a window into the life of one woman at a time of great change and, knowing Rosemary, also an entertaining read. It was a turbulent time for her which foreshadowed her later interest in law and legal fairness alongside harnessing her feminist activism. In 1978 she lost her job, took her employer to court and won her claim for unfair dismissal. Themes of precarity, resistance and the ricochets evident in women's lives pervade this collection. Auchmuty's early career is an exemplar of these things.

Auchmuty moved to London in 1978 with the firm intention of making it her home, which it became. During a period that Auchmuty describes as 'a sojourn in the hospitality industry', waitressing and undertaking bar work, she was invited to speak to a local group of the National Housewives Register[1] by a former housemate from her student days in London. Following the event and on the train home she was talking to another speaker, who was an organiser for the London University Extra-Mural Department (EMD) and she offered Auchmuty part-time work for the EMD, where Auchmuty first taught social history classes and later women's studies classes for many years. Additionally, she taught for the Workers Education Association (WEA) and for local Adult Education Institutes. Later she was employed as a local tutor on the Arts Foundation courses and subsequently also on the Women's Studies courses of the Open University, which were year-long contracts of part-time work. She also taught on both their summer schools for years. In time she taught on the Postgraduate Diploma in Women's Studies at the Polytechnic of Central London (PCL), which was the first postgraduate Women's Studies course in the UK.

She was called to take part in jury service and this ignited her interest in law for the first time; prior to that she had been interested in law only as it affected women. At this stage, the substance of the law, its constituent parts, the nature of the rules became intriguing. It brought together her overlapping commitments to justice, fairness, women's empowerment and workers' rights. She successfully applied to be part of the first intake of part-time day LLB (Hons) students at PCL, the forerunner institution of her later employer the University of Westminster, reading for

[1] Data from 1970–80 from the National Housewives Register is archived in the Women's Library held at the London School of Economics.

the LLB between 1985–89. On graduating, she applied for and accepted a full-time lectureship at PCL, and within a few years was promoted to Senior Lecturer. This was her first experience of permanent employment, some 10 years after she had first begun to teach. She could finally put down firm roots. At the time she was the only person in the Law School who held a PhD qualification. She remained at PCL/ Westminster for 18 years in total during which time she was funded by Westminster to read for the University of London LLM (at UCL), and she studied Spanish and French through the University of Westminster Polylang language programme. She was promoted to Principal Lecturer, Head of Department and Reader and subsequently left in 2007 to take up a Chair at the University of Reading. There she remains having been both the Director of Learning and Teaching for Law and also having been a full member of the Law REF2014 sub-panel. Law became her adopted primary discipline, yet in many ways for an extended period early in her career she had stood in a liminal space, spanning disciplines and traditions. She was and is an inter-disciplinary scholar and educator.

In my telling of the account I have emphasised the precarity of those part-time teaching years, but to Auchmuty it did not feel like that and she notes how much the world has changed. Then it was possible to live quite comfortably without full-time work and it was, in her experience, normal within her social circle. She lived in a council flat, available because of its position in a high rise building which had made it hard for the council to rent out. It meant her housing situation was secure and the rent was modest. She had the time to be heavily involved in the women's movement in which she was very active politically and socially. She co-founded the Lesbian History Group in 1988. Subsequently she was able to buy a flat when she secured her lectureship at PCL although she had to make something of a leap of faith to do this given her financial circumstances at the time. For those of you who are devoted contract law scholars, it may be amusing to know that Auchmuty's flat was in High Trees House.[2]

Auchmuty's scholarship has been as similarly diverse as her teaching career, taking in girl's school stories,[3] the position of housewives in society,[4] gender in land law and equity and trusts,[5] sexuality and marriage,[6] the biographies of women

[2] *Central London Property Trust Ltd v High Trees House Ltd* [1947] KB 130, an important High Court case in which the then Mr Justice Denning reaffirmed and extended the doctrine of promissory estoppel.

[3] R Auchmuty, *A World of Girls* (The Women's Press, 1992); R Auchmuty, *A World of Women: Growing up in the girl's school story* (The Women's Press, 2008).

[4] R Auchmuty, 'The Married Women's Property Acts: Equality was not the issue' in R Hunter (ed), *Rethinking Equality Projects in Law: Feminist Challenges* (Hart, 2008).

[5] See eg R Auchmuty, 'Men Behaving Badly: an analysis of English undue influence cases' (2002) 11 *Social and Legal Studies* 257.

[6] See eg R Auchmuty, 'Same-sex Marriage Revived: Feminist critique and legal strategy' (2004) 14 *Feminism and Psychology* 101; R Auchmuty, 'Law and the Power of Feminism: How marriage lost its power to oppress women' (2012) 20 *Feminist Legal Studies* 71; R Auchmuty, 'The experience of civil partnership dissolution: not "just like divorce"' (2016) 38 *Journal of Social Welfare and Family Law* 152. Rosemary was a member of the Advisory Board of the AHRC Research Centre for Law, Gender and

in law[7] and much more. She has been one of the foundational scholars in the Feminist Judgments projects, bringing together historical understandings, with doctrinal and feminist scholarship, activism and critique.[8] She has highlighted the importance of positionality and how rich, nuanced, detailed understandings of biographies of women uncover structural inequality and injustice in the public sphere and experiences of denial, sacrifice and sometimes of fulfilment and liberation in the private sphere.

Auchmuty has been keen to stress that many of her projects (teaching and writing) have been team efforts, bringing together junior and established scholars. She champions early career and senior faculty alike, through support, guidance, mentoring and, on occasion, advocacy. She has been willing to make herself unpopular to those in positions of power by challenging notions of 'excellence' whether in terms of the value placed on different forms of scholarship, on different types of role, on the differing weights placed on education, research and leadership, on how confirmation bias privileges those already imbued with additional power, and on publicity campaigns by a book publisher that she and others considered sexist and wrong. Her contribution has been emblematic of much of the work that has needed to be done to make the legal academy a fairer place to work and to study and she has been one of the leaders of this work. Yet she has been less inclined to make much of her contribution, instead choosing to push others forward and to shine a light on their contributions. It has been a career that demonstrates differing fortunes at distinct times, depending on the extent to which one's work (teaching, scholarship, approach to leadership) is viewed, of outsider/insider status, the role of women mentoring women, the drive to make criteria for advancement transparent. Her multi-disciplinary education and research profile has been lauded as a strength by some and been entirely discounted by others who have wished to assess her contributions through a purely legal academic lens. Promotion to Chair came later than for some given this, and yet the assessment of worth can change quite quickly when the proxies for excellence pivot to meet new higher education metrics and policy objectives. This has been the story of many women, particularly lesbian law academics, who having been identified as outsiders at one point in their career subsequently found that their scholarship

Sexuality between the Universities of Keele, Kent and Westminster 2004–2009, having been involved in Centre events while at Westminster.

[7] See eg R Auchmuty, 'Early Women Law Students at Cambridge and Oxford' (2008) 29 *The Journal of Legal History* 63; R Auchmuty, 'Whatever Happened to Miss Bebb? Bebb v The Law Society and women's legal history' (2011) 31 *Legal Studies* 199; R Auchmuty, 'Recovering Lost Lives: researching women in legal history' (2015) 42 *Journal of Law and Society* 34; R Auchmuty and E Rackley, 'Feminist Legal Biography: A Model for All Legal Life Stories' (2020) 41(2) *The Journal of Legal History* 186; E Rackley and R Auchmuty, 'The Case for Feminist Legal History' (2020) 40 *Oxford Journal of Legal Studies* 878.

[8] See eg R Auchmuty, 'Out of the shadows: Feminist silence and liberal law 1' in V Munro and C Stychin (eds), *Sexuality and the Law: Feminist Engagements* (Routledge-Cavendish, 2007) 91; R Auchmuty, S Jeffreys and E Miller, 'Lesbian history and gay studies: keeping a feminist perspective' (1992) 1 *Women's History Review* 89.

and teaching interests have been reimagined by the academy to be considered closer to the 'mainstream' over time.

Rosemary is likely one of a very small number of law academics in Australia and the UK, who has taught at primary and secondary education level, further education for adult learners, undergraduate, postgraduate taught and supervised postgraduate research students. Her teaching practice has spanned differing pedagogic traditions, social science, humanities, the arts and law, across two different hemispheres, in institutions with differing pedagogic/andragogic traditions, student populations and foci. Throughout her teaching has encompassed the teaching of gender and sexuality, of equality whether through history, women's studies or law. Her law teaching has focused on the importance she places on knowledge of case law and statute, both to identify sites of oppression and the tools for emancipation, as well as socio-legal engagement including the role of retelling the stories of women's lives as a means to engage in searching critical reflection about the differing fates of men and women, those of different classes, identities and backgrounds. She has managed to do this not only in niche elective subjects taken by students who identify with feminism and justice. She has integrated these concepts into the teaching of two core, and therefore compulsory, undergraduate subjects: land law and equity and trusts. Other trail-blazers have done similarly, such as Mulcahy and Wheeler in contract law.[9] By taking this approach, feminist critiques are experienced by all students of undergraduate law degrees, rather than those who actively select engagement opportunities. I argue that this is a relatively unusual level of disruption to the traditional approach to core substantive modules in law schools, as indicated in the next section in which I focus on some of the changes to the status quo in legal education during Auchmuty's time in academia noting that she has been present during many, has contributed to some and pushed hard at the forefront of others.

Legal Education

In this section I chart the nature of undergraduate legal education in England and Wales during the time covered by Rosemary's university career. The treatment is necessarily brief; I aim to show the constancy of the undergraduate core curriculum alongside real changes in focus in scholarship which may be juxtaposed against the incredible change in the make-up of the student and staff populations as set out in the subsequent section on (gender) equality. The undergraduate curriculum, the bread and butter of English law schools, has yet to be profoundly reshaped across the sector, and instead has been punctuated by sporadic disruption, whether, for example, through individual modules on women or gender and the law, recent

[9] See L Mulcahy and S Wheeler, *Feminist Perspectives on Contract Law*, (Routledge- Cavendish, 2005).

developments to decolonise the curriculum[10] and earlier attempts to 'feminise' and further diversify reading lists. Individuals and small groups working together have effected some change, which has sometimes been unwound once those colleagues are no longer available to teach those modules. There is, though, a real sense of constancy in the undergraduate legal cannon.

Law as a discipline has a long tradition of awkwardness within the academy, with its roots spread deep into the legal profession, the humanities, the arts and the social sciences. Auchmuty has been ideally placed to sit within this discomfort given her education and teaching experiences prior to coming to law. Some in the academy have reduced the identity of law schools to vocational or trade schools, designed to deliver technical legal instruction for legal professional life, focussing on the principles of law with an overlay of the formal theory or theories of jurisprudence to give an air of respectability associated with practice that is informed by theory. Others have sought to inject real theoretical critique within the study of law.[11] There have been ebbs and flows in the identity politics of law, as legal professional regulators have asserted more and then increasingly less control over the undergraduate legal curriculum. There have been shifts in the proportion of law academics who considers themselves as legal practitioners who teach law compared with those who identify as legal academics who research and undertake research led teaching, moving the preponderance from legal practitioner dominance to relative numeric equality between the two groups.[12] The identity of law, law schools and law academics seems to be in a constant state of flux.

Academic legal research has also changed markedly, as the Research Assessment Exercise (1986, 1989, 1992, 1996, 2001 and 2008) and then Research Excellence Framework (2014, 2021) has shaped the research agenda within law schools as in other disciplines in universities in the UK.[13] Where once there was a concentration on domestic and doctrinal investigations more akin to legal advocacy undertaken by senior barristers (what the legal rules are in England and Wales, how they apply and what they should be) research projects have diversified to include far more work on international doctrinal law (human rights and international law),

[10] For details see *Towards Anti-racist Legal Pedagogy: A Resource* A Social and Legal Studies Association (SLSA) funded research project led by Dr S Jivraj, University of Kent research.kent.ac.uk/decolonising-law-schools/.

[11] W Twining, *Blackstone's Tower: The English Law School* (Sweet and Maxwell, 1994); R Pring, *Closing the Gap: Liberal Education and Vocational Preparation* (Hodder and Staughton, 1995); F Cownie (ed), *The Law School-Global Issues, Local Questions* (Routledge Revivals, 2020 original publication 1999); F Cownie, 'The Importance of Theory in Law Teaching' (2000) 7 *International Journal of the Legal Profession* 225.

[12] F Cownie, 'Women Legal Academics – a new research agenda?' (1998) 25 (1) *Journal of Law and Society* 102; F Cownie, *Legal Academics: Culture and Identities* (Hart, 2004); A Sherr, R Moorhead and H Sommerlad (eds), *Legal Education at the Crossroads: Education and the Legal Profession* (Routledge, 2018).

[13] To compare how the legal research terrain and its emphasis has changed see: H Genn, S Wheeler and M Partington, *Law in the Real World: Improving Our Understanding of How Law Works: Final Report and Recommendations* (The Nuffield Foundation, 2006); F Cownie and A Bradney, 'Socio-legal Studies: a challenge to the doctrinal approach' in *Research Methods in Law* (Routledge, 2013) 42.

socio-legal, empirical, policy based, and theoretical, philosophical and critical enquiries.[14] This may be attributable, in part, to greater academic staff mobility between jurisdictions, a lessening of the influence of professional practice as the training ground for legal educators as the importance of holding a doctorate has replaced this, as well as the influence of the REF which ascribes greater value to new knowledge creation over application of existing knowledge to new contexts, running counter to traditional legal scholarship.

Such tensions, transitions and change would suggest a melting pot of ideas and creativity that should shape the curriculum decisively.[15] Undergraduate programmes are a major site of struggle for a shared understanding of the purpose of university legal education, and the curriculum and law teacher practice reflects this. Strong-willed core module leaders have been able to introduce context into the core curriculum, to require students to critique the substance of the rules rather than simply learning what they are and how to apply them. Yet that approach has rarely solidified within core modules and once that pioneer module leader has stepped away from leadership there is a regular reversal back to tradition. Real embedded change has been difficult to discern other than in pockets of innovation associated with electives and topics on gender, equality, decolonisation, inter-sexuality, context and technology located often, if not always, as an adjunct to a module.[16] Why might that be?

The pull of the statutory legal professional regulators has, until relatively recently, had more than a subtle impact on the undergraduate curriculum. This has been supplemented by the influence of any number of stakeholders who have been invited or who have chosen to insert themselves into debates about the purpose of an undergraduate legal education and the nature of the curriculum and assessment in ways that disciplines not directly connected with a profession are rarely subjected to.[17] There have been many reviews of legal education in the past 30 years.[18] Most recently, in 2011 the three main legal professional regulators

[14] See the REF2014 (2015) Overview Report by Main Panel C, 2015: 70–75, REF2021 (2022) Overview Report by Main Panel C of Sub-groups 13–23, sub-panel 18: 104–115.

[15] A Sherr, 'Legal Education, Legal Competence and Little Bo Peep' (1998) 32 *The Law Teacher* 37; A Sherr and D Sugarman, 'Theory in legal education' (2000) 7(3) *International Journal of the Legal Profession* 165; A Boon, J Flood and J Webb, 'Postmodern Professions? The Fragmentation of Legal Education and the Legal Profession' (2005) 32 *Journal of Law and Society* 473; A Boon and J Webb, 'Legal Education and Training in England and Wales: Back to the future' (2008) *Journal of Legal Education* 58; P Baron and L Corbin, 'Thinking Like A Lawyer/Acting Like a Professional: communities of practice as a means of challenging orthodox legal education' (2012) 46 *The Law Teacher* 100.

[16] See K Galloway, J Webb, F Bartlett, J Flood and L Webley, 'The Legal Academy's Engagements with Lawtech: Technology Narratives and Archetypes as Drivers of Change' (2019) *Law, Technology and Humans* lthj.qut.edu.au/article/view/1337.

[17] The UK Centre for Legal Education (UKCLE) Research Consortium, led by Julian Webb with Jane Ching, Paul Maharg and Avrom Sherr was appointed to conduct the research stage of the Review in May 2011. See *Setting Standards The Future Of Legal Services Education And Training Regulation In England And Wales: the Final report of the Legal Education Training Review in England and Wales Independent Research Team* (2013).

[18] See eg Lord Chancellor's Advisory Committee on Legal Education and Conduct, *First Report on Legal Education and Training* (ACLEC, 1996); K Economides (ed), *Ethical Challenges to Legal Education*

in England and Wales examined the life-cycle of education from undergraduate to post-qualification continuing professional development. The review followed three stages. The first was a national empirical academic research project, involving legal academics, legal professionals and other stakeholders. Stage two was a consultation on proposed reforms, and stage three was to effect regulatory change viz legal professional qualification pathways, admission and continuing professional development. The review findings have not put an end to the soul-searching about how we should address the differing conceptions of the undergraduate degree's primary purpose.[19] The liberal legal education[20] vs vocational technical education fault line persists although it has been addressed in some law schools which have pivoted towards vocationalism (mostly the post-92 sector) in order to be part of what may be an important solicitor qualifying market for students by embedding the Solicitor Qualifying Exam 1 content into not just 'the core' but also the optional or elective undergraduate curriculum. The pre-92 sector has so far tended to span the academic vocational divide and kept the curriculum relatively unchanged to date, while overseas regulators whose recognitions attract large numbers of overseas students and so whose influence is growing for some Russell Group institutions in particular, consider how best to respond to the apparent abolition of the concept of a Qualifying Law Degree (QLD) that is professionally overseen (even if it has not been meaningfully regulated by the professions for decades).

Discussions within law schools, across law schools, within the academy and with legitimate stakeholders about purpose,[21] curriculum design and ways to respond to the future legal services market, if at all, were already emotive and at times polarised in the light of reforms to the legal profession/legal services market that flowed from understandings about the Legal Services Act 2007.[22] The reforms had greater psychological impact than they did palpable change. Few things were made permissible that had historically been impermissible but for changes to law

and Conduct (Hart, 1998); N Duncan, 'The Skill of Learning: Implications of the ACLEC First Report for Teaching Skills on Undergraduate Law Course' (1997) 5 *Web Journal of Current Legal Information.*

[19] See eg W Twining, 'LETR: the role of academics in legal education and training: 10 theses' (2014) 48 *The Law Teacher* 94; J Guth and C Ashford, 'The Legal Education and Training Review: regulating socio-legal and liberal legal education?'(2014) 48 *The Law Teacher* 5–19; R Abel, '"You never want a serious crisis to go to waste." Reflections on the reform of legal education in the US, UK and Australia' (2015) 22 *International Journal of the Legal Profession* 3; J Ching, P Maharg, A Sherr and J Webb, 'An overture for well-tempered regulators: four variations on a LETR theme' (2015) 49 *The Law Teacher* 143; J Ching, P Maharg, A Sherr and J Webb, 'Legal Education and Training Review: a five-year retro/prospective' (2018) 52 *The Law Teacher* 384.

[20] See A Bradney and F Cownie (eds), *Transformative Visions of Legal Education* (Wiley-Blackwell, 1999).

[21] See F Cownie (ed), *Stakeholders in the Law School* (Hart, 2010).

[22] See P Maharg, *Transforming Legal Education: Learning and Teaching the Law and the Early 21st Century* (Ashgate, 2007); D Edmonds, 'Training the Lawyers of the Future – A regulator's view' (2011) 45 *The Law Teacher* 4; R Huxley-Binns, 'Tripping over thresholds: a reflection on legal andragogy' (2016) 50 *The Law Teacher* 1.

firm business ownership rules.[23] Yet, for a brief period, the attention the reforms attracted appeared to upend some of the traditional thinking about law and legal education. There appeared to be a moment when many law school leaders considered whether the profession was dying, whether its apparent grip was lessening, whether outsiders would take over the reins of law firm business ownership and reshape practice. Other key factors in shaping curriculum discussions include the influence of the parents of law students who increasingly attend law school open days along with their children, and whose questions often focus on post qualification employability and a curriculum fit for life as a practising lawyer. Law student career aspirations, legal employer preferences and the changing career patterns of lawyers in the newly de(re)regulated legal services market have all had an influence on the way in which some in law schools have viewed appropriate construction and assessment of the undergraduate curriculum. The influence of the Office for Students as the higher education regulator, government rhetoric, coupled with student learning preferences and their reasons for choosing law over other subjects has instantiated a conservatism within the undergraduate curriculum with an ongoing eye on professional qualification than would have seemed unlikely given the way in which the legal professional regulators have stepped away from being prescriptive. Some law schools have fought hard to retain the link with the profession and were concerned that the introduction of the Solicitors Qualifying Examinations would sever the connection. For others, the link has always been tenuous and although observed by many as part of the marketing copy to attract students to study law, has never had the same icy grip on the content of their classes that others have felt necessary or desirable.

Competition for undergraduate law students from higher education providers, if not in the higher ranked institutions that remain extremely over-subscribed, has led to an avowedly market led approach in some parts of the sector. Students' choice of undergraduate law is overwhelmingly motivated by their desire to become a solicitor or barrister,[24] which stands in sharp relief to their likelihood of securing a traditional legal professional career.[25] Eighteen thousand students graduate with an undergraduate law degree each year,[26] far more than the legal professions can or at least have been willing to absorb through formal training and admission routes. The indefatigable influence of 'The Joint Statement' setting out what an

[23] L Webley, 'Legal Professional De(Re)Regulation, Equality, And Inclusion, And The Contested Space Of Professionalism Within The Legal Market In England And Wales' (2015) 83 *Fordham Law Review* 2349.

[24] A range of surveys over the years have suggested that as many as 9 in 10 first year law students have this aspiration: P Childs, N Frith and H de Rijke, 'The gap between law student career aspirations and employment opportunities' (2014) 48 *The Law Teacher* 51 at 55.

[25] A fairly static figure of c.35% enter the two main legal professions: L Webley, J Tomlinson, H Sommerlad, D Muzio and L Duff, 'Access to a Career in the Legal Profession in England and Wales: Race, Class and the Role of Educational Background' in R Nelson, S Headworth, R Dinovitzer and D Wilkins (eds), *Diversity in Practice* (CUP, 2016).

[26] *Trends in the Solicitors' Profession Annual Statistics Report 2021* (London, the Law Society of England and Wales, 2022) 41.

LLB must include, agreed between the solicitor and barrister professions and the academic community, or the often erroneous perceptions about the contents of 'The Joint Statement', pervades the undergraduate law degree, even though it was only ever one step on the way to some branches of the legal profession, and is not and never has been a fully exempting qualification.[27] The continued dominance of the conservatively drawn, domestically bounded compulsory English and Welsh law modules that make up the majority of credits studied during undergraduate legal education, is perhaps therefore unsurprising, with the optional modules providing space for research led teaching in the sense of teaching that aligns with academics research interests, ideologies and stances.[28] The core is often taught by larger teams of colleagues collaborating on content, and it takes a persuasive module leader to take a whole team in the direction of a feminist approach to land law or equity and trusts, such as Auchmuty. The options provide more space for idiosyncratic approaches, lenses and content and the pairing of like-minded teachers coming together out of choice to teach an elective together. Innovation has often come about as a result of these collaborations as feminist academics have moved through institutions and paired up with others to create time-limited but excellent, challenging options that have waned when they have moved on. Such has been Auchmuty's contribution to legal education, as an innovator in optional modules and as a disrupter of the core albeit in a way that made it difficult to challenge as for her the rules and the cases are key to understanding how law shapes society, women's lives and their futures. On the teaching of the rules she and traditional doctrinal scholars agree.

(Gender) Equality

Law schools have been subject to marked demographic change since the 1980s when Auchmuty joined her first one as a mature undergraduate. In the late 1980s in England and Wales the law graduate cohort has transformed to being c. 50 per cent female on entry. Now 69 per cent of entrants to undergraduate law degrees are female.[29] Total populations of law graduates have increased substantially too, now

[27] The General Council of the Bar and Law Society of England and Wales, in force from 2002, still relevant for qualification through the Bar route in most instances and also still of relevance for qualification as a solicitor if making use of the transition arrangements while the Legal Practice Course remains open to some current students reading for a Qualifying Law Degree during the phasing in of the Solicitors Qualifying Exam and Qualifying Work Experience pathway. It is noteworthy that the QAA Law Benchmarks are only as prescriptive as are the QAA Benchmarks for other disciplines, see *Subject Benchmark Statement Law March 2023* 5ed (Gloucester: Quality Assurance Agency, 2023) www.qaa.ac.uk/the-quality-code/subject-benchmark-statements/subject-benchmark-statement-law.

[28] LETR (n17) and K Clegg, *Playing Safe: Learning and Teaching in Undergraduate Law* (UKCLE, 2004).

[29] *Trends in the Solicitors' Profession Annual Statistics Report 2021* (London, the Law Society of England and Wales, 2022) at 39, 41: 26,290 law students accepted places onto a first degree in law of

at c. 18,000 per year with more year on year.[30] As graduating lawyers move into legal practice we have seen substantial change in the practising population, albeit at a slower speed particularly in the more senior echelons which remain stubbornly male, white and drawn from higher socio-economic groups in-keeping with the previous dominance of these groups in an old profession. This homogeneity is being gradually eroded but at glacial pace compared to the rate of downstream change, something that critics of trickle-up theory have persistently noted.[31] Even the business case for diversity, a beloved rallying cry in the profession aimed at harnessing the power of the market to effect change, has not produced the results expected at senior levels.[32] This may speak to the foundations of the business case, which is underpinned by the focus on the profitability that a diverse workforce may produce, rather than a focus on unpicking the power structures that act as a means to push some up and hold others down. Either the structures do not promote advancement on equal merit grounds, or there are unequal levels of ambitions between lawyers from different backgrounds (which is not borne out by the research evidence). As I have said elsewhere: 'concerns about social reproduction and the ongoing power of dominant groups are not unique to the legal profession, of course, but they are pronounced, persistent and antithetical to a profession that is the guardian of the rule of law and a champion in the fight against discrimination'.[33] That has been a primary concern for Auchmuty, both as regards how the profession views the value of women and is willing to engage with the biases inherent in old, and not so old, legislation and case law and how it reflects on its own role in promoting the status quo at the expense of women and minority groups. Education is often suggested as the key to changing this.

What of the legal academy, then? Is the academy mirroring the diversity of the law student population or is it prey to similar blockers experienced by women within the practising legal profession? Far less research has been undertaken on gender in the legal academy although there have been a number of important studies including those by Collier, Cownie, McGlynn, Thornton (Australia), Vaughan

which 69% were female. In 2011 there were 14,859 law graduates (63% female), in 2016 this was 15,950 law graduates (64% female) in 2021 it was 18,927 in total (66% female).

[30] ibid.

[31] On trickle up theory and related see: C McGlynn, 'The Business of Equality in the Solicitors' Profession' (2000) 63 *Modern Law Review* 42; C McGlynn, 'Strategies for Reforming the English Solicitors' Profession: An Analysis of the Business Case for Sex Equality' in U Schultz and G Shaw (eds), *Women in the World's Legal Professions* (Hart, 2003) 159; M Thornton, *Dissonance and Distrust: women in the legal profession* (OUP, 1996); L Webley and L Duff, 'Women Solicitors as a Barometer for Problems Within the Legal Profession – Time to Put Values before Profits?' (2007) 34 *Journal of Law and Society* 374; H Sommerlad, L Webley, D Muzio, J Tomlinson and L Duff, *Diversity in the Legal Profession in England and Wales: A Qualitative Study of Barriers and Individual Choices* (University of Westminster Press and the Legal Services Board, 2013).

[32] L Webley, 'Great Debates in Gender and the Legal Profession' in R Auchmuty (ed), *Great Debates in Gender and Law* (Palgrave MacMillan, 2017).

[33] L. Webley, 'Sociology of the Legal Professions' in J Přibán (ed), *Research Handbook on the Sociology of Law* (Edward Elgar, 2020) 215. This sets out in detail the underlying evidence base for the claims made in this section of the chapter.

and Wells which we can draw upon as well as research undertaken more recently by me and Duff.[34] McGlynn's early study, in 1998, considered not only female representation in the academy and legal practice but also courses that included feminist legal studies. At that time she noted that only 4 per cent of law professors were women, compared to 9 per cent across all disciplines, but that women academics were increasing and made up over a third of law academics.[35] Once again, trickle-up theory would suggest that women would rise to the top in greater numbers over time, although Collier in his work noted that there was a formal and substantive equality gap in UK law schools that may act as a brake on this, including the masculine culture of law schools which dissociated women from conceptions of authority and held on to a narrow normative ideal of a successful law academic.[36] Cownie's study determined that even in the early 2000s there was still a lack of awareness about gender inequality, making it difficult to embed a critique of gender dynamics within either the curriculum or teaching practice.[37] At a similar time in Australia, Thornton's studies identified a very male dominated senior management culture in universities more generally, with a lack of acknowledgement of patterned inequality as between male and female academics.[38] Some feminist law academics were looking into the academy as well as examining sites beyond it, with others bringing the importance of the historical perspective of women as legal practitioners and law academics into full consciousness.[39]

Duff and I examined the differential numbers of men and women in each of the seniority levels in the legal academy through analysis of the UK Higher Education Statistical Agency's systematically collected data of the population of 5,335 full and part-time legal academics derived from all higher education institutions in the

[34] See R Collier, '"Nutty Professors", "Men in Suits" and "New Entrepreneurs": Corporeality, Subjectivity and Change in the Law School and Legal Practice' (1998) 7 *Social and Legal Studies* 27; R Collier, 'The Changing University and the (Legal) Academic Career – Rethinking the Relationship between Women, Men and the "Private Life" of the Law School' (2002) 22 *Legal Studies* 1; Cownie, 'Women Legal Academics' (n 12); Cownie, *Legal Academics* (n 12); C McGlynn, 'Women, Representation and the Legal Academy' (1999) 19 *Legal Studies* 68; C McGlynn, 'The Status of Women Lawyers in the United Kingdom' and 'Strategies for Reforming the English Solicitors' Profession: An Analysis of the Business Case for Sex Equality' in U Schultz and G Shaw (eds), *Women in the World's Legal Professions* (Hart, 2003) 139 and 159; S Vaughan, 'The State of the Nation: Diversity and the British Legal Academy' (2016) 50 *The Law Teacher* 255; C Wells, 'Ladies in Waiting: The Women Law Professors' Story' (2001) 23 *Sydney Law Review* 167; C Wells, 'The Remains of the Day: The Women Law Professors Project' in U Schultz and G Shaw (eds), *Women in the World's Legal Professions* (Hart, 2003) 225; and L Duff and L Webley, 'Gender and the Legal Academy in the UK: a Product of Proxies and Hiring and Promotion Practices' in U Schultz, G Shaw, R Auchmuty and M Thornton (eds), *Gender and Careers in the Legal Academy* (Hart, 2021).

[35] C McGlynn, *The Woman Lawyer* (Butterworths, 1998) 41.

[36] Collier, 'The Changing University' (n 34) 8–9, 28.

[37] Cownie, *Legal Academics* (n 12).

[38] M Thornton, 'Neo-liberal Melancholia: The Case of Feminist Legal Scholarship' (2004) 20 *Australian Feminist Law Journal* 77; M Thornton, 'Corrosive Leadership (or Bullying by Another Name): A Corollary of the Corporatised Academy' (2004) 17 *Australian Journal of Labour Law* 161.

[39] See eg E Rackley and R Auchmuty, 'Introduction' in E Rackley and R Auchmuty (eds), *Women's Legal Landmarks: Celebrating the History of Women and Law in the UK and Ireland* (Hart, 2019) 7–11.

United Kingdom.[40] The data is now a little out of date (2015–16 data made available in 2017). Having said that, I would suggest that the fundamental landscape has not altered that dramatically, and the conclusions we came to are likely to still have currency. The female to male ratio had increased from a third being female at McGlynn's census point in the late 1990s to 50 per cent female in 2015–16. Women were slightly over-represented in the more junior levels of legal academy and under-represented in the higher levels (Professors: 31 per cent female: 69 per cent male; Law School Heads: 38 per cent female: 62 per cent male). We concluded that the ongoing differentials between female and male promotion trajectories are at least partly associated with the way in which we in the academy assess and value excellence, merit, and contribution. While new research outputs and grants, 'new business' in the terminology of the legal profession, are prized more greatly than the maintenance of relationships, the development of colleagues, the management of workloads, service to the institution and others, in some sectors undergraduate teaching, then these disparities will persist. Collier's previous studies had identified the importance of being perceived to be excellent and productive in research in order to secure advancement within the legal academy.[41] Cownie's informants valued intellectual curiosity and communication skills,[42] with those in 'old' universities also adding strong organisational skills and persistence (often in research). And yet when it came to discussions about the reasons for promotion to Chair they noted that research was the key factor whereas good citizenship was neither necessary nor seemingly valued.[43] In short, some tasks were to be avoided if one was ambitious for promotion, and an individual focus on building an individual internationally recognised research profile was crucial.

Many academics would recognise the depictions from those earlier studies even now, some 20 years on, and even given that there have been a number of significant changes in higher education since they were undertaken. These include the introduction of undergraduate student fees, the National Student Survey and related surveys, the introduction of the Office for Students, the increasing grip of new public management and the breakdown of collegiate self-governance or benign neglect[44] and the development of a culture of competition between academics in pursuit of prestige which as Collier notes as gendered impacts.[45] We still place a good deal of weight on identifying and hiring the 'exceptional' candidate, someone who comes with scholarships, awards, high status publications and earlier than expected research grants or a greater than average research grant profile and research impact for someone at their stage. Few of us hire with

[40] Duff and Webley (n 34).
[41] Collier, 'The Changing University' (n 34).
[42] Cownie, *Legal Academics* (n 12) 81.
[43] Cownie, *Legal Academics* (n 12) 87–88.
[44] On top-down management and the breakdown of collegiate governance see M Thornton, *Privatising the Public University: The Case of Law* (Routledge, 2012).
[45] On the gendered impacts of competition within academic life see Collier 'The Changing University' (n 34).

education and leadership in mind, and, when we do, it is a function of necessity rather than status, power, excitement about working with a colleague who has that kind of track record. We have largely bought in to the ideology of gifted and talented rather than of excellence as a product of development, collegial nurturing and hard work and dedication.[46] Institutionally colleagues are expected to self-propel through their careers, with junior colleagues encouraged to seek out mentors who may be guides and facilitate opportunities for research collaborations, rather than teaching opportunities, so as to build their profiles.[47] This is in real contrast to the way in which we treat those same colleagues at an earlier stage of their relationships with us, as students.

There is nothing showy about service, the term that tends to be used in many institutions in place of 'leadership' which has self-sacrificial rather than more authoritative overtones. Without strong, effective academics willing to undertake service the whole edifice of an organisation, whether a school or a department soon crumbles. We have seen it in many law schools when new leadership or an absence of leadership whether in education, research, staff development or the School as a whole fails to live up to what is needed to create community, drive positive change and to allow the academics and the students to thrive. Much of our educational endeavour is also a form of service to the next generation of lawyers and law academics, to our students. Much of the work of educators is hidden even if it can be self-fulfilling, supportive of colleagues as well as students, developmental, and crucial to the academy. Service involves giving others time, advocating for and in some instances seeking to repel change and bureaucracy, unwarranted measurement and much more. It is about doing what one can to enable others to thrive, whether colleagues or students. The time spent on these forms of important work cannot be spent on other things such as research outputs, research grant applications, building research impact, winning awards. Without a rebalancing of the notion of talent from exceptionality in individual endeavour to striving as part of a team, we are unlikely to redress many of the imbalances in promotion rates even when we assess achievement in relation to opportunities or recognise that higher education metrics and league tables can have pernicious and perverse impacts. This is a conversation to be had well beyond the legal academy but an essential one to have. It is one that Auchmuty has had in all the law schools in which she has worked both substantively in the context of women's lives and the law but also in the context of those who do the hidden work in law schools not just

[46] For details of good practice see T Mottershead (ed), *The Art and Science of Strategic Talent Management in Law Firms* (Thomson Reuters, 2010); and further on the misrecognition of 'talent' see C Tansley, 'What do we mean by the term "talent" in talent management?' (2011) 43 *Industrial and Commercial Training* 266 and on distinctions between western and eastern conceptions of talent see F Gagné, 'Understanding the Complex Choreography of Talent Development through DMGT-based analysis"' in K Heller, F Mönks, R Sternberg and R Subotnik (eds), *International Handbook of Giftedness and Talent*, 2nd edn (Elsevier Science, 2001) 67.

[47] See D Collings and K Mellahi, 'Strategic Talent Management: A review and research agenda' (2009) 19 *Human Resource Management Review* 304.

in broader society. Many other feminist scholars have had similar conversations. They are conversations we must continue to have.

Conclusions

A number of threads have run throughout this chapter, the contribution that Auchmuty has made to introducing gender and power dynamics into the study of law by an increasingly diverse student population, her influence on feminist scholarship including doctrinal and socio-legal research and her challenge of the proxies that pervade our everyday assessments of the value we place on roles, tasks and performance in academic life. Her career has developed alongside great change in the academy, in the profession, in society. We have experienced progress, retrenchment, the opening up of debate at the same time as we have seen it shut down. She, along with other feminist legal academics, have played their part in bringing an activist lens to leadership in research and teaching, using their outsider status to support other outsiders while harnessing the power available to them when called to leadership to challenge dominant understandings. Leadership in positions of power, in law schools as in other areas of management, requires compromise in a way that opposition from the side lines does not. As we see greater numbers of women in the more senior levels of the legal academy, will we see them taking on positions of authority in formal leadership that enable them to effect change from within, or will those increasingly managerial roles position them as responsible, accountable and yet of lower status because their service takes them away from research that is valued more highly within the academy? Time will tell whether the market overtakes the ability for leaders in law to bring about meaningful change in any way other than through research with impact.

ROSEMARY AUCHMUTY PUBLICATIONS

Authored Books

(1978) *Australia's Daughters* (Methuen)
(1983) (with Ken Methold) *Ancient History* (Longman)
(1992) *A World of Girls: The Appeal of the Girls' School Story* (The Women's Press)
(2nd edn Bettany Press 2004)
(1999) *A World of Women: Growing up in the Girls' School Story* (The Women's Press)
(2nd edn Bettany Press 2008)

Edited Books

(1989) (with Sheila Jeffreys as Lesbian History Group) (ed) *Not a Passing Phase: Reclaiming Lesbians in History 1840–1985* (The Women's Press)
(2nd edn The Women's Press 1993)
(German ed) *Und Sie lieben sich doch! Lesbische Frauen in der Geschichte 1840–1985* (Daphne 1991)
(1994) (with Juliet Gosling) *The Chalet School Revisited* (Bettany Press)
(2000) (with Joy Wotton) *The Encyclopaedia of Boys' School Stories* (Ashgate)
(2000) (with Joy Wotton) *The Encyclopaedia of Girls' School Stories* (Ashgate)
(2018) *Great Debates in Gender and Law* (Palgrave Macmillan)
(2019) (with Erika Rackley) *Women's Legal Landmarks: Celebrating the History of Women and Law in the UK and Ireland* (Hart)
(2021) (with Ulrike Schultz, Gisela Shaw and Margaret Thornton) *Gender and Careers in the Legal Academy* (Hart)

Chapters in Books

(1975) 'Spinsters and Trade Unions in Victorian Britain' in Ann Curthoys, Susan Eade and Peter Spearritt (eds), *Women at Work* (Australian Society for the Study of Labour History) 109–122
(1979) 'The Truth about Sex' in Peter Spearritt and David Walker (eds), *Australian Popular Culture* (George Allen & Unwin) 169–89

(1989) 'By Their Friends We Shall Know Them: the Lives and Networks of Some Women in North Lambeth, 1880–1940' in Lesbian History Group ed. *Not a Passing Phase: Reclaiming lesbians in history 1840-1985* (The Women's Press) 77–98
(1989) 'You're a Dyke, Angela! Elsie Oxenham and the Rise and Fall of the Schoolgirl Story' in Lesbian History Group (ed), *Not a Passing Phase: Reclaiming Lesbians in History 1840–1985* (The Women's Press) 119–40
(1994) 'The Chalet School Guides: Girls' Organisations in Girls' School Stories' in Rosemary Auchmuty and Juliet Gosling (eds), *The Chalet School Revisited* (Bettany Press) 173–12
(1995) (with Alex Warwick) 'Women's Studies as Feminist Activism' in Gabriele Griffin (ed), *Feminist Activism in the 1990s* (Taylor & Francis) 182–91
(1996) 'Lesbian Studies: Politics or Lifestyle?' in Lynne Harne and Elaine Miller (eds), *All the Rage: Reasserting Radical Lesbian Feminism* (The Women's Press) 200–14
(1997) 'Enid Blyton and the School Story' in Nicholas Tucker and Kimberley Reynolds (eds), *Enid Blyton: A Celebration and Reappraisal* (National Centre for Research in Children's Literature) NCRCL Papers 2, 79–95
(1997) 'Lesbian Law, Lesbian Legal Theory' in Gabriele Griffin and Sonya Andermahr (eds), *Straight Studies Modified: Lesbian Interventions in the Academy* (Cassell) 39–56
(1999) 'The School Story: from Brazil to Bunty' in Nicholas Tucker (ed), *School Stories from Bunter to Buckeridge* (National Centre for Research in Children's Literature) NCRCL Papers 4, 52–62
(2001) 'The Fiction of Equity' in Susan Scott-Hunt and Hilary Lim (eds), *Feminist Perspectives on Equity and Trusts* (Cavendish) 1–25
(2005) 'The Rhetoric of Equality and the Problem of Heterosexuality' in Linda Mulcahy and Sally Wheeler (eds), *Feminist Perspectives on Contract* (Glass House Press) 51–74
(2007) 'Out of the Shadows: Feminist Silence and Liberal Law' in Carl Stychin and Vanessa Munro (eds), *Sexuality and the Law: Feminist Engagements* (Routledge)
(2007) 'Unfair Shares for Women: The Rhetoric of Equality and the Reality of Inequality' in Anne Bottomley and Hilary Lim (eds), *Feminist Perspectives on Land Law* (Glass House Press)
(2008) 'The Married Women's Property Acts: Equality was not the Issue' in Rosemary Hunter (ed), *Rethinking Equality Projects in Law: Feminist Challenges* (Hart)
(2010) 'Feminists as Stakeholders in the Law School' in Fiona Cownie (ed), *Stakeholders in the Law School* (Hart) 35–64
(2010) 'Judgment: *Royal Bank of Scotland v Etridge (No 2)*' in Rosemary Hunter, Clare McGlynn and Erika Rackley (eds), *Feminist Judgments: From Theory to Practice* (Hart) 155–69
(2012) 'Land Law and Equity and Trusts' in Caroline Hunter (ed), *Integrating Socio-Legal Studies into the Law Curriculum* (Palgrave Macmillan) 69–103
(2013) 'Marriage and Civil Partnership: Law's Role, Feminism's Response' in Margaret Davies and Vanessa Munro (eds), *The Ashgate Research Companion to Feminist Legal Theory* (Ashgate) 285–302
(2015) 'Dissolution or Disillusion: The Unravelling of Civil Partnerships' in Nicola Barker and Daniel Monk (eds), *From Civil Partnership to Same-Sex Marriage: Interdisciplinary Reflections* (Routledge) 199–219
(2015) 'Why Study Law? The English Experience' in Kishor Vaidya (ed), *Law for the Curious: Why Study Law?* Online Book

(2016) 'Gender Issues in HE Management' in Chris Ashford and Jess Guth (eds), *The Legal Academic's Handbook* (Palgrave Macmillan)
(2018) 'Introduction', 'Legal History' and 'Sexuality' in Rosemary Auchmuty (ed), *Great Debates in Gender and Law* (Palgrave Macmillan) xi–xv, 173–83, 199–210
(2019) 'Feminist Responses to Relationship Recognition' in Chris Ashford (ed), *Research Handbook on Gender, Sexuality and Law* (Edward Elgar)
(2019) (with Erika Rackley) 'Introduction' in Erika Rackley and Rosemary Auchmuty (eds), *Women's Legal Landmarks: Celebrating the History of Women and Law in the UK and Ireland* (Hart) 1–21
(2019) '*The Slave Grace* (1827)', 'Married Women (Restraint Upon Anticipation) Act 1949' and '*Williams & Glyn's Bank v Boland* (1980)' in Erika Rackley and Rosemary Auchmuty (eds), *Women's Legal Landmarks: Celebrating the History of Women and Law in the UK and Ireland* (Hart) 47–53, 241–47, 357–62
(2020) 'Uses and Abuses of Heroines' in Elizabeth Conaghan (ed), *Celebrating 100 Years of Women's Voices* (University of Reading)
(2021) 'The Road to Olive Stone' in Ulrike Schultz, Gisela Shaw, Margaret Thornton and Rosemary Auchmuty (eds), *Gender and Careers in the Legal Academy* (Hart) 441–55
(2022) 'Feminism, Property, and Divorce Law Reform in the 1960s' in Jo Miles, Daniel Monk and Rebecca Probert (eds), *Fifty Years of the Divorce Reform Act* (Hart) 71–92

Special Issue of Journal

(2012) (with Karen van Marle) 'Carol Smart's Feminism and the Power of Law' 20(2 August) *Feminist Legal Studies*

Articles

(1976) 'History without Women' 11 *Refractory Girl* 10–17
(1976) 'The Victorian Theory of Spinsterhood' 2 *University of Wollongong Historical Journal* 38–73
(1977) 'Out of the Gutter and into the Classroom: The Debate over Sex Education in Schools' 15 *Refractory Girl* 19–23
(1977) 'The Schoolgirl Formula' *Meanjin* 391–99
(1980) 'City Building in Newcastle in the Interwar Years' *Australia 1938 Bulletin* 1
(1982) 'Women's Forgotten Friendships' 10 *Revolutionary and Radical Feminist Newsletter* 23–30
(1983) (with Peter Spearritt) 'Building: Interwar Sydney' *Australia 1938 Bulletin*
(1983) (with Peter Spearritt) 'Surf and Steel: Wollongong and Port Kembla in the Interwar Years' (Winter) *Heritage Australia* 16–21; reprinted in Australian Council of National Trusts, *Australia in Trust: A Selection of the Best Writings from 'Heritage Australia'* (Collins 1986) 120–29
(1983) (with Frances Borzello and Cheri Davis Langdell) 'The Image of Women's Studies' 6 *Women's Studies International Forum* 291–98

(1987) (with Jane Allen, Siriol Davies and Jackie Scutt) 'Lesbian Input, Women's Studies and Education' 10/11 *GEN* 26–28

(1987) 'You're a Dyke, Angela! The Rise and Fall of the Schoolgirl Story' 10 *Trouble and Strife* 23–30; reprinted in Deborah Cameron and Joan Scanlon (eds), *The Trouble and Strife Reader* (Bloomsbury 2010) 169–177

(1991) 'Hannah Barlow' (Lambeth Libraries broadsheet in series on Lambeth women)

(1991) 'Community Projects and Students' *New Law Journal* 16 November, 1561

(1992) (with Sheila Jeffreys and Elaine Miller) 'Lesbian History and Gay Studies: Keeping the Feminist Perspective' 1 *Women's History Review* 89–108

(1994) 'InVersions: A Tribute to the Late All-Women Publishing House, Open Letters' 3 *Women's History Review* 439–43

(1994) Student-Centred Assessment' *Reflections* 1 (University of Westminster)

(1997) 'Last In, First Out: Lesbian and Gay Legal Studies' 5 *Feminist Legal Studies* 235–53

(2000) '*The Encyclopaedia [of School Stories]*: Origins and Organisation' 31 *Children's Literature in Education* 145–58

(2002) 'Men Behaving Badly: An Analysis of Undue Influence Cases' 11 *Social and Legal Studies* 257–82

(2003) 'Agenda for a Feminist Legal Curriculum' 23 *Legal Studies* 377–401

(2003) 'When Equality is Not Equity: Homosexual Inclusion in Undue Influence Law' 11 *Feminist Legal Studies* 163–90

(2004) 'Not Just a Good Children's Story: A Tribute to Adverse Possession' 63 *Conveyancer* 293–307

(2004) 'Same-Sex Marriage Revived: Feminist Critique and Legal Strategy' 14 *Feminism and Psychology* 101–26; reprinted in Leslie J Moran (ed), *Sexuality and Identity* (Ashgate 2006)

(2007) 'Girls' School Stories: The Critical Response' 128 *Children's Literature Review*

(2007) 'The Woman Law Student and the Girls' College Novel' 19 *Canadian Journal of Women and the Law* 37–72

(2008) 'What's So Special about Marriage? The impact of *Wilkinson v Kitzinger*' 20 *Child and Family Law Quarterly* 479–98

(2008) 'Early Women Law Students at Cambridge and Oxford' 29 *Journal of Legal History* 63–97

(2009) 'Beyond Couples? *Burden v the United Kingdom* (2008)' 17 *Feminist Legal Studies* 205–218

(2011) 'Whatever Happened to Miss Bebb? *Bebb v The Law Society* and Women's History' 31 *Legal Studies* 71–87

(2012) 'Law and the Power of Feminism: How Marriage Lost its Power to Oppress Women' 20 *Feminist Legal Studies* 71–87

(2012) 'Using Feminist Judgments in the Property Law Classroom' 46 *The Law Teacher* 227–38

(2015) 'Feminist Approaches to Sexuality and Law Scholarship' 15 *Legal Information Management* 4–7

(2015) 'Recovering Lost Lives: Researching Women in Legal History' 42 *Journal of Law and Society* 34–52; also published in Linda Mulcahy and David Sugarman (eds), *Legal Life Writing: Marginalized Subjects and Sources* (Wiley Blackwell) 34–52

(2016) (with Erika Rackley) 'The Women's Legal Landmarks Project: Celebrating 100 Years of Women in the Law in the UK and Ireland' 16 *Legal Information Management* 30–34

(2016) 'The Experience of Civil Partnership Dissolution: *Not* "Just Like Divorce"' 38 *Journal of Social Welfare and Family Law* 152–74
(2016) 'The Limits of Marriage Protection: In Defence of Property Law' 6 *Oñati Socio-Legal Series* 1196–224
(2016) 'The Limits of Marriage Protection in Property Allocation when a Relationship Ends' 28 *Child and Family Law Quarterly* 303–24; in Spanish (2018) 'La experiencia de la disolución civil: no es exactamente "lo mismo que un divorcio"' special issue 'Genero y derecho' 43 *Revista Jurídica de Buenos Aires* 99–132
(2019) 'The Past Is Another Truth' 1 *ANU Historical Journal II* 35–38
(2020) (with Erika Rackley) 'Feminist Legal Biography: A Model for *All* Legal Life Stories' 41 *Journal of Legal History* 186–211
(2020) (with Erika Rackley) 'The Case for Feminist Legal History' 40 *Oxford Journal of Legal Studies* 878–904

Entries in Reference Books

(2000) Four entries ('Child Custody', 'Children's Books and Stories', 'Feminism' and 'UK Law') in Timothy F Murphy (ed), *Reader's Guide to Lesbian and Gay Studies* (Fitzroy Dearborn Publishers) 127–28, 129–30, 216–17 and 600–02
(2000) 'The Critical Response' in Rosemary Auchmuty and Joy Wotton (ed), *The Encyclopaedia of Girls' School Stories* (Ashgate)
(2000) 'United Kingdom' in Bonnie Zimmerman (ed), *Lesbian Histories and Cultures: An Encyclopedia* (Garland Publishing) 781–85
(2004) 'Cicely Hale' and 'Henrietta Mueller' in HCG Matthew and Brian Harrison (eds), *Oxford Dictionary of National Biography* (Oxford University Press)
(2006) nine entries, including the long entry (3,600 words) on 'School Stories' in Jack Zipes (ed), *Oxford Encyclopedia of Children's Literature* (4 vols, Oxford University Press and online)
(2008) two entries ('Lesbian' and 'Women Lawyers, Distinguished') in Peter Cane and Joanne Conaghan (eds), *The New Oxford Companion to Law* (Oxford University Press) 728, 1256–57.
(2011) 'Bebb, Gwyneth Marjory' *Oxford Dictionary of National Biography* (Oxford University Press) www.oxforddnb.com

Essays

(2010) Preface to the Greyladies edition of Gladys Mitchell, *Convent on Styx*
(2012) Preface to the Greyladies edition of Josephine Elder, *The Mystery of the Purple Bentley*
(2015) 'Crush and the Girls' School Story', programme note for the musical 'Crush'
Regular contributions to the *Abbey Chronicle, New Chalet Club Journal, Scribbler etc*

BIBLIOGRAPHY

Abel, R, '"You never want a serious crisis to go to waste." Reflections on the reform of legal education in the US, UK and Australia' (2015) 22 *International Journal of the Legal Profession* 3

Adams, JA, 'Clive Schmitthoff (1903–1990)' in J Beatson and R Zimmermann (eds), *Jurists Uprooted. German-speaking Émigré Lawyers in Twentieth-century Britain* (OUP, 2004) 367–80

Aiston, SJ and Fo, C, 'The Silence/ing of Academic Women' (2021) 33 *Gender and Education* 138

Alden Franz, N, *English Women Enter the Professions* (Cincinnati, Ohio, privately published 1965)

Aronson, J, 'When I use a word ... Festschrift' (The BMJ Opinion, 31 May 2019)

Arseneau, M, 'Incarnation and Interpretation: Christina Rossetti, the Oxford Movement, and Goblin Market' (1993) 31 *Victorian Poetry* 79

Association of Chief Police Officers and National Policing Improvement Agency, *Guidance on Investigating Domestic Abuse* (2008)

Auchmuty, R, 'The Past is Another Truth' (2019) II(1) *ANU Historical Journal* 35

Auchmuty, R and Rackley, E, 'Feminist Legal Biography: A Model for *All* Legal Life Stories' (2020) 41 *Journal of Legal History* 186

Auchmuty, R and Rackley, E, 'Feminist Legal Biography: A Model for All Legal Life Stories' (2020) 41 *Journal of Legal History* 186

Auchmuty, R, 'Agenda for a Feminist Legal Curriculum' (2003) 23(3) *Legal Studies* 377

Auchmuty, R, 'Beyond Couples: *Burden v United Kingdom*' (2009) 17 *Feminist Legal Studies* 205

Auchmuty, R, 'By their Friends We Shall Know Them: The Lives and Networks of Some Women in North Lambeth, 1880–1940' in Lesbian History Group (ed), *Not a Passing Phase: Reclaiming Lesbians in History 1840–1985* (The Women's Press, 1989)

Auchmuty, R, 'Dissolution or Disillusion? The Unravelling of Civil Partnerships' in N Barker and D Monk (eds), *From Civil Partnership to Same-Sex Marriage: Interdisciplinary Reflections* (Routledge, 2015)

Auchmuty, R, 'Early Women Law Students at Cambridge and Oxford' (2008) 29 *Journal of Legal History* 63

Auchmuty, R, 'Feminism, Property and Divorce Reform Law in the 1960s' in J Miles, D Monk and R Probert (eds), *Fifty Years of the Divorce Reform Act 1969* (Hart, 2022)

Auchmuty, R, 'Feminist Approaches to Sexuality and Law Scholarship' (2015) 15 *Legal Information Management* 4

Auchmuty, R, 'Feminist Responses to Same Sex Relationship Recognition' in C Ashford, and A Maine, (eds), *Research Handbook on Gender, Sexuality and the Law* (Edward Elgar, 2020)

Auchmuty, R, 'Feminists as Stakeholders in the Law School' in F Cownie (ed), *Stakeholders in the Law School* (Hart, 2010)

Auchmuty, R, 'Introduction' in R Auchmuty, (ed), *Great Debates in Gender and the Law* (Palgrave, 2018)

Auchmuty, R, 'Law and the Power of Feminism: How Marriage Lost its Power to Oppress Women' (2012) 20 *Feminist Legal Studies* 71

Auchmuty, R, 'Legal History' in R Auchmuty (ed), *Great Debates in Gender and Law* (Red Globe Press, 2018)

Auchmuty, R, 'Marriage and Civil Partnership: Law's Role, Feminism's Response' in VE Munro and M Davies (eds), *The Ashgate Research Companion to Feminist Legal Theory* (Routledge, 2016)

Auchmuty, R, 'Marriage and Civil Partnership: Law's Role, Feminism's Response' in M Davies and V Munro (eds), *The Ashgate Research Companion to Feminist Legal Theory* (Ashgate, 2013)

Auchmuty, R, 'Men Behaving Badly: An Analysis of English Undue Influence Cases' (2002) 11 *Social and Legal Studies* 257

Auchmuty, R, 'Out of the Shadows: Feminist Silence and Liberal Law' in C Stychin and V Munro (eds), *Sexuality and the Law: Feminist Engagements* (Routledge, 2007)

Auchmuty, R, 'Recovering Lost Lives: Researching Women in Legal History' (2015) 42 *Journal of Law and Society* 34

Auchmuty, R, 'Researching Women in Legal History: The Case of Miss Bebb' (2014) 14 *Legal Information Management* 19

Auchmuty, R, 'Same-Sex Marriage Revived: Feminist Critique and Legal Strategy' (2004) 14(1) *Feminism and Psychology* 101

Auchmuty, R, 'Spinsters and Trade Unions in Victorian Britain' (1975) *Labour History* 109

Auchmuty, R, 'The Experience of Civil Partnership Dissolution: Not "Just Like Divorce"' (2016) 38 *Journal of Social Welfare and Family Law* 152

Auchmuty, R, 'The Limits of Marriage Protection in Property Allocation When a Relationship Ends' (2016) 28 *Child and Family Law Quarterly* 303

Auchmuty, R, 'The Limits of Marriage Protection: In Defence of Property Law' (2016) 6 *Oñati Socio-Legal Series* 1196

Auchmuty, R, 'The Married Women's Property Acts: Equality Was Not the Issue' in R Hunter (ed), *Rethinking Equality Projects in Law: Feminist Challenges* (Hart, 2008)

Auchmuty, R, 'The Rhetoric of Equality and the Problem of Heterosexuality' in L Mulcahy and S Wheeler (eds), *Feminist Perspectives on Contract Law* (Routledge-Cavendish, 2005)

Auchmuty, R, 'The Victorian Theory of Spinsterhood' (1976) 2 *University of Wollongong Historical Journal* 38

Auchmuty, R, 'Using Feminist Judgments in the Property Law Classroom' (2012) 46 *The Law Teacher* 227

Auchmuty, R, 'What's So Special about Marriage? The Impact of Wilkinson v Kitzinger' (2008) 20(4) *Child and Family Quarterly* 475

Auchmuty, R, 'Whatever Happened to Miss Bebb? *Bebb v The Law Society* and Women's Legal History' (2011) 31 *Legal Studies* 199

Auchmuty, R, *A World of Girls* (The Women's Press, 1992)

Auchmuty, R, *A World of Women: Growing up in the Girls' School Story* (The Women's Press, 1999)

Auchmuty, R, *Victorian Spinsters* PhD Thesis (Australian National University, 1975)

Auchmuty, R, *Women and the Family Home: Legal and Social Change in Post-War England* (forthcoming)

Auchmuty, R, Jeffreys, S and Miller, E, 'Lesbian History and Gay Studies: Keeping a Feminist Perspective' (1992) 1(1) *Women's History Review* 89

Auchmuty, R and Temkin, J, 'The Road to Olive Stone' in U Schultz, G Shaw, M Thornton and R Auchmuty (eds), *Gender and Careers in the Legal Academy*, Onati International Series in Law and Society (Hart, 2021)

Bajohr, S and Rödiger-Bajohr, K, 'Die Diskriminierung der Juristin in Deutschland Bis 1945' (1980) 13(1) *Kritische Justiz* 39–50

Baker, V, 'Women in Higher Education: Re-Imagining Leadership in the Academy in Times of Crisis' (2021) 35 *Journal of Faculty Development* 57

Balham Neighbourhood Law Centre, 'A Case for Change: Annual Report, 1975–76' (Balham Neighbourhood Law Centre, 1976)

Balham Neighbourhood Law Centre, 'Inside Story: Annual Report, 1974–75' (Balham Neighbourhood Law Centre, 1975)

Banks, S and Carpenter, M, 'Researching the Local Politics and Practices of Radical Community Development Projects in 1970s Britain' (2017) 52(2) *Community Development Journal* 226–46

Barker, N, *Not the Marrying Kind: A Feminist Critique of Same-Sex Marriage* (Palgrave Macmillan, 2012)

Barnes, V, 'Interrogating the Self-Told Narrative: Lord Lindley's Autobiography, His Life and His Legal Biography' (2020) 41 *Journal of Legal History* 143

Barnes, V, MacMillan, C and Vogenauer, S, 'On Legal Biography' (2020) 41 *The Journal of Legal History* 115

Barnes, V and Newton, L, 'Visualizing Organizational Identity: The History of a Capitalist Enterprise' (2018) 13 *Management and Organizational History* 24

Barnett, A, 'A Genealogy of Hostility: Parental Alienation in England and Wales' (2020) 42 *Journal of Social Welfare and Family Law* 18

Barnett, A, *Domestic Abuse and Private Law Children Cases, A Literature Review* (Ministry of Justice 2020)

Baron, P and Corbin, L, 'Thinking Like A Lawyer/Acting Like a Professional: communities of practice as a means of challenging orthodox legal education' (2012) 46 *The Law Teacher* 100.

Barron, J, *Not Worth the Paper ...? The Effectiveness of Legal Protection for Women and Children Experiencing Domestic Violence* (Women's Aid Federation of England, 1990)

Bartlett, KT, 'Feminist Legal Method' (1990) 4 *Harvard Law Review* 829

Bartley, P, *Women's Activism in Twentieth Century Britain: Making a Difference across the Political Spectrum* (Palgrave, 2022)

Basi, M, *Measuring Wealth: A Key Step to Effectively Narrow The Gender Gap* (World Economic Forum, 13 June 2022)

Batlan, F, 'Engendering Legal History' (2005) 30 *Law and Social Inquiry* 823

Batlan, F, 'The Birth of Legal Aid: Gender Ideologies, Women, and the Bar in New York City, 1863–1910' (2010) 28(4) *Law and History Review* 931

Batlan, F, *Women and Justice for the Poor: A History of Legal Aid 1863–1945* (CUP, 2015)

Beatson, J, 'Aliens, Enemy Aliens, and Friendly Enemy Aliens. Britain as a Home for Emigré and Refugee Lawyers' in J Beatson and R Zimmermann (eds), *Jurists Uprooted. German-speaking Émigré Lawyers in Twentieth-century Britain* (OUP, 2004) 73–104

Beatson, J and Zimmermann, R (eds), *Jurists Uprooted. German-speaking Émigré Lawyers in Twentieth-century Britain* (OUP, 2004)

Beaumont, C, 'The Women's Movement, Politics and Citizenship 1918–1950s' in I Zweiniger-Bargielowska, *Women in Twentieth-Century Britain* (Routledge, 2001)

Bell, M, *Christina Rossetti: A Biographical and Critical Study* (Roberts Brothers, 1898)

Belleau, H, 'One Myth Leads to Another: From Ignorance of the Laws to the Presumption of Informed Choice among de Facto Spouses' in E Aloni and R Tremblay (eds), *House Rules: Changing Families, Evolving Norms, and the Role of Law* (University of British Columbia Press, 2022)

Belleau, H, Lavallée, C and Seery, A, *Unions et désunions conjugales au Québec: rapport de recherche. Première partie: le couple, l'argent et le droit* (INRS Centre Urbanisation Culture Société, 2017)

Benöhr, H-P, 'Review of Jurists uprooted. German-speaking émigré lawyers in twentieth-century Britain ed. by Jack Beatson and Reinhard Zimmermann 2004' (2007) *Zeitschrift der Savigny-Stiftung für Rechtsgeschichte. Germanistische Abteilung* 124

Benwell Community Law Project, 'Annual Report, 1975' (Benwell Community Law Project, 1975)

Bergman, M, 'Status, Contract, and History: A Dialectical View' (1991) 13 *Cardozo Law Review* 171

Berlant, L, *Cruel Optimism* (Duke University Press, 2011)

Birchall, J and Choudhry, S, '"I Was Punished for Telling the Truth": How Allegations of Parental Alienation are Used to Silence, Sideline and Disempower Survivors of Domestic Abuse in Family Law Proceedings' (2021) 6(1) *Journal of Gender-Based Violence* 1

Birchall, J and Choudhry, S, '*"What About My Right not to Be Abused?" Domestic Abuse, Human Rights and the Family Courts*' (Women's Aid, 2018)

Bishop, C and Bettinson, V, 'Evidencing Domestic Violence including Behaviour that Falls under the new Offence Of "Controlling Or Coercive Behaviour"' (2018) *International Journal of Evidence and Proof* 3

Blackmore, J, 'Disciplining Academic Women: Gender Restructuring and the Labour of Research in Entrepreneurial Universities' in M Thornton (ed), *Through a Glass Darkly: The Social Sciences Look at the Neoliberal University* (Australian National University Press, 2015)

Blackstone, W, *The Commentaries of the Law of England* 4 vols, WR Prest, DSS Lemmings, TP Gallanis and R Paley (eds), (OUP, 2016) vol 1
Boedeker, E and Meyer-Plath, M, *50 Jahre Habilitation in Deutschland* (Otto Schwartz, 1974)
Boon, A, Flood, J and Webb, J 'Postmodern Professions? The Fragmentation of Legal Education and the Legal Profession' (2005) 32 *Journal of Law and Society* 473
Boon, A and Webb, J 'Legal Education and Training in England and Wales: Back to the future' (2008) *Journal of Legal Education* 58
Borkowski, JA and Thomas, HG, *The Bristol Law Faculty – The First Fifty Years* (University of Bristol, 1984)
Böttger, B, *Das Recht auf Gleichheit und Differenz* (Westfälisches Dampfboot, 1990)
Bourne, J, 'Gwyneth Bebb: The Past Explaining the Present' *Law Society Gazette* 29 April 2019
Bourne, J, *Helena Normanton and the Opening of the Bar to Women* (Hook Waterside Press, 2016)
Bourne, J, 'First Woman to Be Admitted to an Inn of Court, Helena Normanton, 1919' in E Rackley and R Auchmuty (eds), *Women's Legal Landmarks: Celebrating the History of Women and Law in the UK and Ireland* (Hart, 2018)
Bourne, J, *Helena Normanton and the Opening of the Bar to Women* (Waterside Press, 2016)
Boyce, D, 'Palmer, William Waldegrave, Second Earl of Selborne (1859–1942), Politician' *Oxford Dictionary of National Biography* (DNB, 2004)
Boycott, O, '"We are the A&E of Law": The First UK Law Centre for Poor People Turns 50' *The Guardian* (London, 28 July 2020)
Boyd, SB and Young, CFL, '"From Same-Sex to No Sex"? Trends Towards Recognition of (Same-Sex) Relationships in Canada' (2003) 1 *Seattle Journal for Social Justice* 757
Boyd, SB, Chunn, DE, Kelly, F and Wiegers, W, *Autonomous Motherhood: A Socio-Legal Study of Choice and Constraint* (University of Toronto Press, 2015)
Boyd. B, 'Family, Law and Sexuality: Feminist Engagements' (1999) 8 *Social and Legal Studies* 369
Bradney, A, *Conversations, Choices and Chances: The Liberal Law School in the Twenty-First Century* (Hart, 2003)
Bradney, A and Cownie, F, 'Gothic Horror? A Response to Margaret Thornton' (2005) 14 *Social and Legal Studies* 277
Bradney, A and Cownie, F, (eds), *Transformative Visions of Legal Education* (Wiley-Blackwell, 1999)
Brandt, K, *Christina Rossetti's 'Goblin Market'* (Åbo Akademi University Press, 2006)
Brent Community Law Centre, 'Annual Report, 1976' (Brent Community Law Centre, 1976)
Brent Community Law Centre, 'Annual Report, 1978' (Brent Community Law Centre, 1978)
Brent Community Law Centre, 'Annual Report, 1979' (Brent Community Law Centre, 1979)
Breunung, L and Walther, M, *Die Emigration deutscher Rechtswissenschaftler ab 1933 / Westeuropäische Staaten, Türkei, Palästina/Israel, lateinamerikanische Staaten, Südafrikanische Union* (De Gruyter Saur, 2012)
Broomfield, K, 'Enid Rosser Locket' (Celebrating the Centenary of Women Lawyers, 2017)
Buchdahl, Gerd, 'Nagel's Message' (1971) 231 *Nature* 399
Budde, G-F, *Frauen der Intelligenz. Akademikerinnen in der DDR. 1945 bis 1975* (Vandenhoeck und Rupprecht, 2003)
Burdett, J, 'Professional Accountability and Community Control in Legal Services Provision: A Study of Community Law Centres in England' (PhD thesis, London School of Economics, 2004)
Burton, M, *Legal Responses to Domestic Violence* (Routledge-Cavendish, 2008)
Bussea, E, Krauschb, M and Liao, W, 'How the "Neutral" University Makes Critical Feminist Pedagogy Impossible: Intersectional Analysis from Marginalized Faculty on Three Campuses' (2021) 41 *Sociological Spectrum* 29
Butler, J, 'Introduction' in J Butler (ed), *Women's Work and Women's Culture* (Macmillan, 1869)
Byles, A and Morris, P, *Unmet Need: The Case of the Neighbourhood Law Centre* (Routledge, 1977)
Cafcass, 'Alienating Behaviours' (Cafcass, 2022)
Caine, B, 'Feminist Biography and Feminist History' (1994) 3 *Women's History Review* 247
Caine, B, *English Feminism 1780–1980* (OUP, 1997)

Camden Community Law Centre, 'Annual Report and Five Year Review, 1977–78' (Camden Community Law Centre, 1978)
Camden Community Law Centre, 'Half-Yearly Report, 1973' (Camden Community Law Centre, 1973)
Campbell, E, 'Of Mothers and Merchants: Female Economics in Christina Rossetti's "Goblin Market"' (1990) 33 *Victorian Studies* 393
Campbell, J, 'Smith, Frederick Edwin, First Earl of Birkenhead (1872–1930), Lawyer and Politician' *Oxford Dictionary of National Biography* (DNB, online edn)
Carasik, L, 'Renaissance or Retrenchment: Legal Education at a Crossroads' (2010) 44 *Indiana Law Review* 735
Card, D et al, 'Are Referees and Editors in Economics Gender Neutral?' (2020) 135 *Quarterly Journal of Economics* 269
Carpenter, M, '"Eat Me, Drink Me, Love Me": The Consumable Female Body in Christina Rossetti's *Goblin Market*' (1991) 29 *Victorian Poetry* 415
Carpenter, M and Kyneswood, B, 'From Self-Help to Class Struggle: Revisiting Coventry Community Development Project's 1970s Journey of Discovery' (2017) 52 *Community Development Journal* 247
Carr, EH, *What Is History?* (Penguin, 1961)
Carr, H and Hunter, R (2012) 46 *The Law Teacher* Special Issue on the Feminist Judgments Project 214
Ceadel, M, 'Cecil, (Edgar Algernon) Robert Gascoyne- [known as Lord Robert Cecil], Viscount Cecil of Chelwood (1864–1958), Politician and Peace Campaigner' *Oxford Dictionary of National Biography* (DNB, 2004)
Cevasco, G, 'Douglas, Lord Alfred Bruce (1870–1945), Poet and Biographer' *Oxford Dictionary of National Biography* (DNB, 2004)
Chapman, C, *The Poor Man's Court of Justice: Twenty-Five Years as a Metropolitan Magistrate* (Hodder & Stoughton, 1925)
Clegg, K, *Playing Safe: Learning and Teaching in Undergraduate Law* (UKCLE, 2004).
Clemens, W, 'Die ersten Rechtsanwältinnen in München' in Münchener Anwaltverein (ed), *12 Jahrzehnte Münchener Anwaltverein. Festschrift* (Deutscher Anwaltverlag, 2000) 19–25
Childs, P, Frith, N and de Rijke, H, 'The gap between law student career aspirations and employment opportunities' (2014) 48 *The Law Teacher* 51
Chilly Collective, The (eds), *Breaking Anonymity: The Chilly Climate for Women Faculty* (Wilfrid Laurier University Press, 1995)
Ching, J, Maharg, P, Sherr, A and Webb, J, 'An overture for well-tempered regulators: four variations on a LETR theme' (2015) 49 *The Law Teacher* 143
Ching, J, Maharg, P, Sherr, A and Webb, J, 'Legal Education and Training Review: a five-year retro/prospective' (2018) 52 *The Law Teacher* 384
Clark, J and Horton, R, 'What Is The Lancet Doing about Gender and Diversity?' (2019) 393 *The Lancet* 508
Clarkson, P and Presmeg, N, *Critical Issues in Mathematics Education: Major Contributions of Alan Bishop* (Springer, 2008)
Collier, R, '"Love Law, Love Life": Neoliberalism, Wellbeing and Gender in the Legal Profession – The Case of Law School' (2014) 17 *Legal Ethics* 202
Collier, R, '"Nutty Professors", "Men in Suits" and "New Entrepreneurs": Corporeality, Subjectivity and Change in the Law School and Legal Practice' (1998) 7 *Social and Legal Studies* 27
Collier, R, 'The Changing University and the (Legal) Academic Career – Rethinking the Relationship between Women, Men and the "Private Life" of the Law School' (2002) 22 *Legal Studies* 1
Collings, D and Mellahi, D, 'Strategic Talent Management: A Review and Research Agenda' (2009) 19 *Human Resource Management Review* 304
Common Cause, The, 'Editorial: The Right to Marry' (London, 11 May 1923)
Conaghan, J, *Law and Gender* (Clarendon, 2013)
Cooke, E, '*White v White* [2000] 1AC 596: A Late Instalment in a Long Story' in S Gilmore, J Herring and R Probert (eds), *Landmark Cases in Family Law* (Bloomsbury, 2011)
Cooper, J and Dhavan, R, *Public Interest Law* (Basil Blackwell, 1987)

Cordes, O, *Frauen als Wegbereiter des Rechts: Die ersten deutschen Juristinnen und ihre Reformforderungen in der Weimarer Republik* (Diplomica, 2012)
Oda Cordes, *Marie Munk (1885–1978) Leben und Werk* (Böhlau, 2015)
Cosgrove, R, 'Pollock, Sir Frederick, Third Baronet (1845–1937), Jurist' *Oxford Dictionary of National Biography* (DNB, 2004)
Cossman, B, 'Abolishing Family Law (as We Know It)' in E Aloni and R Tremblay (eds), *House Rules: Changing Families, Evolving Norms, and the Role of Law* (University of British Columbia Press, 2022)
Cotropia, CA and Petherbridge, L, 'Gender Disparity in Law Review Citation Rates' (2017) 59 *William and Mary Law Review* 771
Coulson, V, 'Redemption and Representation in *Goblin Market*: Christina Rossetti and the Salvific Signifier' (2017) 55 *Victorian Poetry* 423
Courts and Tribunals Judiciary, 'Fact-Finding Hearings and Domestic Abuse in Private Law Children Proceedings – Guidance for Judges and Magistrates' (5 May 2022)
Covert, J, 'Creighton [née von Glehn], Louise Hume (1850–1936), Social Activist and Writer of Popular History and Biography' *Oxford Dictionary of National Biography* (DNB, 2004)
Cowan, D, *Housing Law and Policy* (CUP, 2011)
Cownie, F, *Legal Academics: Culture and Identities* (Hart, 2004)
Cownie, F, (ed) *Stakeholders in the Law School* (Hart, 2010)
Cownie, F, (ed) *The Law School-Global Issues, Local Questions* (Routledge Revivals, 2020 original publication 1999)
Cownie F, 'The Importance of Theory in Law Teaching' (2000) 7 *International Journal of the Legal Profession* 225
Cownie, F, 'The United Kingdom's First Woman Law Professor: An Archerian Analysis' (2015) 42 *Journal of Law and Society* 127
Cownie, F 'Women Legal Academics–a new research agenda?' (1998) 25(1) *Journal of Law and Society* 102
Cownie, F and Bradney, A 'Socio-legal Studies: a challenge to the doctrinal approach' in *Research Methods in Law* (Routledge, 2013) 42
Crawford, E, *The Women's Suffrage Movement in Britain and Ireland: A Regional Survey* (Routledge, 2006) 125
Cretney, S, *Family Law in the Twentieth Century* (OUP, 2005)
Crittenden, A, *The Price of Motherhood* (Metropolitan Books, 2001)
Crossland, R, 'Indo-European Origins: The Linguistic Evidence' (1957) 12 *Past and Present* 16
Cui, R, Ding, H and Zhu, F, 'Gender Inequality in Research Productivity during the COVID-19 Pandemic' (2022) 24 *Manufacturing and Service Operations Management* 707
D'Amico, D, '"Equal before God": Christina Rossetti and the Fallen Women of Highgate Penitentiary' in A Harrison (ed), *Gender and Discourse in Victorian Literature and Art* (Northern Illinois University Press, 1992)
D'Amico, D and Kent, D, 'Rossetti and the Tractarians' (2006) 44 *Victorian Poetry* 93
Delmar, R, 'What is Feminism?' in J Mitchell and A Oakley (eds), *What is Feminism?* (Blackwell, 1986)
Derry, C, 'Clapham, Olive Catherine [Married Name Miles] (1898–1973)' *Oxford Dictionary of National Biography* (DNB, 2018)
Derry, C, 'Cobb, Monica Mary Geikie (1891–1946)' *Oxford Dictionary of National Biography* (DNB, 2018)
Derry, C, 'Ethel Bright Ashford: More or Less than a Role Model' (2000) 129 *Women's History Review* 615
Derry, C, 'Ethel Bright Ashford: More and Less than a Role Model' (2020) 29 *Women's History Review* 615 *English Women Enter the Professions* (Cincinnati, Ohio, privately published, 1965)
Derry, C, *Legal Temporalities of Sexual Consent* (Edinburgh University Press, 2024 forthcoming)
Deutscher Juristinnenbund (ed), *Juristinnen in Deutschland. Eine Dokumentation* (1900–84) (Nomos, 1984)
Deutscher Juristinnenbund (ed), *Juristinnen in Deutschland. Die Zeit von 1900 bis 1998* (Nomos, 1998)

Deutscher Juristinnenbund (ed), *Juristinnen in Deutschland. Die Zeit von 1900 bis 2003*, 4th edn (Nomos, 2003)

Deutscher Juristinnenbund (ed), *Jüdische Juristinnen* (Beck, 2019)

Diduck, A, 'Fairness and Justice for All? The House of Lords in *White v White*' (2001) *Feminist Legal Studies* 173

Diduck, A, 'Family Law as Expression: Financial Relief in the English Courts' in E Aloni and R Tremblay (eds), *House Rules: Changing Families, Evolving Norms, and the Role of Law* (University of British Columbia Press, 2022)

Diduck, A, 'First Rape Crisis Centre 1976' in E Rackley and R Auchmuty (ed), *Women's Legal Landmarks: Celebrating Feminist Legal History* (Hart, 2018)

Diduck, A, 'Sharing Loss on Divorce – A Commentary' (2018) 32 *Australian Journal of Family Law* 132

Diduck, A and Kaganas, F, *Family Law, Gender and the State* (Hart, 2012)

do Mar Pereira, Maria, *Power, Knowledge and Feminist Scholarship: An Ethnography of Academia* (Routledge, 2017)

Dobash, RE and Dobash, RP, *Violence Against Wives* (Free Press, 1979)

Doughty, J, Maxwell, N and Slater, T, 'Professional Responses to "Parental Alienation": Research-Informed Practice' (2020) 42 *Journal of Social Welfare and Family Law* 68

Drachman, VG, *Sisters in Law: Women Lawyers in Modern American History* (Harvard University Press, 1998) 123–26

Duff, L and Webley, L, 'Gender and the Legal Academy in the UK: A Product of Proxies and Hiring and Promotion Practices' in U Schultz, G Shaw, M Thornton, and R Auchmuty (eds), *Gender and Careers in the Legal Academy* (Hart, 2021)

Duncan, N, 'The Skill of Learning: Implications of the ACLEC First Report for Teaching Skills on Undergraduate Law Course' (1997) 5 *Web Journal of Current Legal Information.*

Dutton, K, 'Auchmuty, James Johnston (1909–1981)' (2007) 17 *Australian Dictionary of Biography*

Dutton, K, *Auchmuty* (Boombana, 2000)

Eastman, C, 'London Letter – The Married Teacher', *Equal Rights* (1926) in BW Cook (ed), *Crystal Eastman: On Women and Revolution* (OUP, 1978)

Economides, K, (ed), *Ethical Challenges to Legal Education and Conduct* (Hart, 1998)

Edel, Leon, 'Biography: A Manifesto' (1978) 1 *Biography* 1

Edmonds, D, 'Training the Lawyers of the Future – A regulator's view' (2011) 45 *The Law Teacher* 4

Edwards, S, *Sex and Gender in the Legal Process* (Blackstone Press, 1996)

Eekelaar, J, 'Asset Distribution on Divorce – Time and Property' (2003) *Family Law* 828

Eisenstein, H, *Inside Agitators: Australian Femocrats and the State* (Temple University Press, 1996)

Ender, A and Wälchli, B, 'The Making of a Festschrift, Is It a Ritual?' in A Ender, A Leemann and B Wälchli (eds), *Methods in Contemporary Linguistics* (De Gruyter Mouton, 2012) 143

Enright, M, 'Contract Law' in R Auchmuty (ed), *Great Debates in Gender and the Law* (Red Globe Press, 2018)

von Erffa, M and Richarz-Simons, I, 'Der weibliche Rechtsanwalt' in J Magnus (ed), *Die Rechtsanwaltschaft* (W Moeser, 1929) 471–85

Faine, J, *Lawyers in the Alice: Aboriginals and Whitefellas' Law* (Federation Press, 1993)

Faller, K, 'The Parental Alienation Syndrome: What Is It and What Data Support It?' (1998) *Child Maltreatment* 100

Family Solutions Group, *'What About Me?' Reframing Support for Families Following Parental Separation*' (Family Solutions Group, 2020)

Feder Kittay, E, 'A Feminist Public Ethic of Care Meets the New Communitarian Family Policy' (2001) 111 *Ethics* 523

Felz, S, 'Das Judentum in der Rechtswissenschaft. Die deutsche Rechtswissenschaft im Kampf gegen den jüdischen Geist Eine "Wissenschaftliche Tagung" im Oktober 1936 in Berlin' in *ZNR* 2017, 87–99

Fernald, A, *The Oxford Handbook of Virginia Woolf* (OUP, 2021)

Ferris, S, Parr, N, Markey, R and Kyng, T, 'Long Service Leave: Past, Present and Future' (2015) 3 *Australian Journal of Actuarial Practice* 5

Fieberg, G, *Catalogue for the exhibition of the German Ministry of Justice 'Im Namen des Deutschen Volkes. Justiz und Nationalsozialismus'* (Verl. Wiss. u. Politik, 1989)

Fikentscher, R, *Liebe Arbeit Einsamkeit. Wilhelm Schubart, Papyrologe. Gertrud Schubart-Fikentscher, Rechtshistorikerin. Ein Gelehrtenpaar in zwei Diktaturen* (Mitteldeutscher Verlag, 2014)

Fineman, MA, *The Neutered Mother, The Sexual Family and Other Twentieth Century Tragedies* (Routledge, 1995)

Fineman, MA, 'Cracking the Foundational Myths: Independence, Autonomy, and Self-Sufficiency' (2000) 8(1) *Journal of Gender, Social Policy and the Law* 13

Fisher, H and Low, H, 'Recovery from Divorce: Comparing High and Low Income Couples' (2016) 30 *International Journal of Law, Policy and the Family* 338

Fitzgerald, LF, 'Still the Last Great Open Secret: Sexual Harassment as Systemic Trauma' (2017) 18 *Journal of Trauma and Dissociation* 483

Fobear, K, 'Do You Understand? Unsettling Interpretative Authority in Feminist Oral History' (2016) 10 *Journal of Feminist Scholarship* 61

Foot, M, 'Palmer, Roundell Cecil, Third Earl of Selborne (1887–1971), Politician' *Oxford Dictionary of National Biography* (DNB, 2004)

Forster, S and Varghese, M, *The Making of the Australian National University* (ANU Press, 2009)

Foucault, M, *The History of Sexuality*, vol 1 (Vintage Books, 1980)

Fox, H, 'Williams, Ivy (1877–1966)' in *Oxford Dictionary of National Biography*, D Cannadine (ed) (DNB, 2020)

Fraser, R, 'Beginnings – Some Reflections on the ANU Historical Journal 1964–70' (2019) II *ANU Historical Journal* 3

Frazer, E and Lacey, N, *The Politics of Community: A Feminist Critique of the Liberal–Communitarian Debate* (Harvester Press, 1993)

Fredman, S, *Women and the Law* (OUP, 1998)

Freeman, R and Maybin, L, 'Documents, Practices and Policy' (2011) 7 *Evidence and Policy* 158

Freeman, R, 'Learning by Meeting' (2008) 2 *Critical Policy Analysis* 1

Gagné, F, 'Understanding the Complex Choreography of Talent Development through DMGT-based analysis' in K Heller, F Mönks, R Sternberg and R Subotnik (eds), *International Handbook of Giftedness and Talent*, 2nd edn (Elsevier Science, 2001)

Galloway, K, Webb, J, Bartlett, F, Flood, J and Webley, L 'The Legal Academy's Engagements with Lawtech: Technology Narratives and Archetypes as Drivers of Change' (2019) *Law, Technology and Humans* (open access)

Gates, GE (ed), *The Woman's Year Book 1923–1924* (NUSEC, 1924) 42

Gee, D, 'Guest Editorial: Legal Biography' (2014) 14 *Legal Information Management* 15

Genn, H, Wheeler, S and Partington, M *Law in the Real World: Improving Our Understanding of How Law Works: Final Report and Recommendations* (The Nuffield Foundation, 2006)

Gibson, M, 'Tchk, tchk, tchk: *Skippy the Bush Kangaroo* and the Question of Australian Seriousness' (2014) 28 *Continuum* 574

Gidart, K, Howell, D and Kirk, N, *Dictionary of Labour Biography*, vol 11 (Palgrave MacMillan, 2016)

Gilbert, S and Gubar, S, *The Madwoman in the Attic: The Woman Writer and the Nineteenth-Century Literary Imagination* (Yale University Press, 1997)

Gilligan, C, *In a Different Voice: Psychological Theory and Women's Development*, reprint edn (Harvard University Press, 2016)

Girerd, L and Bonnot, V, 'Neoliberalism: An Ideological Barrier to Feminist Identification and Collective Action' (2020) 33 *Social Justice Research* 81

Gitter, E, 'The Power of Women's Hair in the Victorian Imagination' (1984) 99 *Publications of the Modern Language Association of America* 936

Glendenning, V, *Leonard Woolf: A Biography* (New York Free Press, 2006)

Glendon, M, *The Transformation of Family Law* (University of Chicago Press, 1989)

Gluck, S, 'Has Feminist Oral History Lost its Radical/Subversive Edge?' (2011) 39 *Oral History* 63
Goldthorpe, L, 'First Woman to Practise as a Barrister in Ireland and the (Then) United Kingdom, Averil Deverell, 1921' in E Rackley and R Auchmuty (eds), *Women's Legal Landmarks: Celebrating the History of Women and Law in the UK and Ireland* (Hart, 2018)
Golub, E, 'Untying Goblin Apron Strings: A Psychoanalytic Reading of "Goblin Market"' (1975) 25 *Literature and Psychology* 158
González-Alvarez, J, 'Author Gender in The Lancet Journals' (2018) 391 *The Lancet* 2601
Goodhart, W, 'Buckmaster, Stanley Owen, First Viscount Buckmaster (1861–1934) Lord Chancellor' *Oxford Dictionary of National Biography* (DNB, 2004)
Goodman, J, 'Afterword: Histories of Women's Higher Education, Time, and Temporalities' (2020) 56 *Paedagogica Historica* 6
Göppinger, H, *Juristen jüdischer Abstammung im 'Dritten Reich'*, 2nd edn (Beck, 1990) (1st edn *'Die Verfolgung der Juristen jüdischer Abstammung durch den Nationalsozialismus'* 1963)
Government of Canada, *Report on Federal Tax Expenditures: Concepts, Estimates and Evaluation* (Department of Finance, Canada, 2021)
Grabham, E, *Brewing Legal Times: Things, Forms and the Enactment of Law* (University of Toronto Press, 2016)
Grace, C and Lefevre, P, 'Draining the Swamp' (1985) 7 *Law and Policy* 97
Green, E, 'Hills, John Waller (1867–1938), Politician and Angler' *Oxford Dictionary of National Biography* (DNB, 2004)
Green, J and Chapman, A, 'The British Community Development Project: Lessons for Today' (1992) 27 *Community Development Journal* 242
Green, J, 'Action-Research in Context: Revisiting the 1970s Benwell Community Development Project' (2017) 52 *Community Development Journal* 269
Grosz, E, 'Histories of a Feminist Future' (2000) 25 *Signs* 1017
Grosz, E, 'Thinking the New: of Futures Yet Unthought,' (1998) 6 *Symploke* 38
Guth, J and Ashford, C, 'The Legal Education and Training Review: regulating socio-legal and liberal legal education?'(2014) 48 *The Law Teacher* 5–19
Hackney Advice Bureau and Law Centre, 'Annual Report, 1976–1977' (Hackney Advice Bureau and Law Centre, 1977)
Hagan, AK et al, 'Women Are Underrepresented and Receive Differential Outcomes at ASM Journals: A Six-Year Retrospective Analysis' (2020) 11 mBio e01680
Haight Farley, C, 'Confronting Expectations: Women in the Legal Academy' (1996) 8 *Yale Journal of Law and Feminism* 333
Hanbury, H and Mooney, H, 'Joyce, Sir Matthew Ingle (1839–1930)' *Oxford Dictionary of National Biography* (DNB, 2004)
Hanna, C, 'The Paradox of Progress: Translating Evan Stark's Coercive Control into Legal Doctrine for Abused Women' (2012) *Violence Against Women* 1459
Häntzschel, H and Bußmann, H, *Bedrohlich, Gescheit – Ein Jahrhundert Frauen und Wissenschaft in Bayern* (Beck, 1997)
Hansen, M, *Erna Scheffler (1893–1983). Erste Richterin am Bundesverfassungsgericht und Wegbereiterin einer geschlechtergerechten Gesellschaft* (Mohr Siebeck, 2019)
Harford, J, 'The Perspectives of Women Professors on the Professoriate: A Missing Piece in the Narrative on Gender Equality in the University' (2018) 8 *Education Science* 50
Harlow, C and Rawlings, R, *Pressure through Law* (Routledge, 1992)
Harrison, A (ed), *The Letters of Christina Rossetti Vol 1* (University of Virginia Press, 1997)
Harrison, A, 'Christina Rossetti: Illness and Ideology' (2007) 45 *Victorian Poetry* 415
Harrison, B, *Prudent Revolutionaries: Portraits of British Feminists between the Wars* (OUP, 1987)
Harwood, J, 'Presuming the Status Quo? The Impact of the Statutory Presumption on Parental Involvement' (2021) *Journal of Social Welfare and Family Law* 119
Hasler, Eveline, *Die Wachsflügelfrau*, 13th edn (Nagel & Kimche, 1991)
Hassett, C, *Christina Rossetti* (University of Virginia Press, 2005)

Heath, M and Burdon, PD, 'Academic Resistance to the Neoliberal University' (2013) 23 *Legal Education Review* 379
Heijstraa, TM and Pétursdóttir, GM, 'Feminist Academics Strategically Playing Offense/Defense in Pursuit of Academic and Societal Change' (2022) *Nora: Nordic Journal of Feminist and Gender Research* 6
Heijstraa, TM and Pétursdóttir, GM, 'Sisterly Advice for Feminists in Academia when Playing the Game and Working the Cracks' (2022) 34 *Gender and Education* 247
Heilbron, H, *Rose QC – The Remarkable Story of Rose Heilbron: Trailblazer and Legal Icon* (Hart, 2019)
Heilbron, H, 'Women at the Bar: A Historical Perspective' (31 May 2013) *Counsel*
Heim, S (ed) *Die Verfolgung und Ermordung der europäischen Juden durch das nationalsozialistische Deutschland 1933–1945 (Quellensammlung) vol 2: Deutsches Reich 1938–August 1939* (R. Oldenbourg, 2009)
Helsinger, E, 'Consumer Power and the Utopia of Desire: Cristina Rossetti's "Goblin Market"' (1991) 58 *Journal of English Literary History* 903
Her Majesty's Inspectorate of Constabulary and Fire & Rescue Services (HMICFRS), *A Progress Report on the Police Response to Domestic Abuse* (HMICFRS, 2017)
Her Majesty's Inspectorate of Constabulary and Fire & Rescue Services (HMICFRS), *The Police Response to Domestic Abuse; An Update Report* (HMICFRS, 2019)
Her Majesty's Inspectorate of Constabulary and Fire & Rescue Services (HMICFRS), *Police Response to Violence against Women and Girls. Final Inspection Report* (HMICFRS, 2021)
Herman, D, *An Unfortunate Coincidence: Jews, Jewishness, and English Law* (OUP, 2011)
Herring, J, '*White v White* (2000)' in E Rackley and R Auchmuty (eds), *Women's Legal Landmarks* (Hart, 2019)
Herring, J, *Family Law* (Harlow Pearson, 2019)
HM Crown Prosecution Inspectorate (HMCPSI) and Her Majesty's Inspectorate of Constabulary and Fire & Rescue Services (HMICFRS), *Evidence Led Domestic Abuse Prosecutions* (2020)
HM Crown Prosecution Inspectorate (HMCPSI) and HM Inspectorate of Constabulary (HMIC), *Violence at Home: A Joint Inspection of the Investigation and Prosecution of Cases Involving Domestic Violence* (Criminal Justice Joint Inspection, 2004)
HM Government, *Transforming the Response to Domestic Abuse: Government Consultation* (HM Government, 2018)
HM Inspectorate of Constabulary (HMIC), *Everyone's Business: Improving the Police Response to Domestic Abuse* (HMIC, 2014)
HM Inspectorate of Constabulary (HMIC), *Increasingly Everyone's Business: A Progress Report on the Police Response to Domestic Abuse* (HMIC, 2015)
HM Inspectorate of Constabulary (HMIC), *PEEL: Police Effectiveness 2016. A National Overview* (HMIC, 2017)
Höpel, S, 'Die Säuberung der deutschen Rechtswissenschaft – Ausmaß und Dimensionen der Vertreibung nach 1933' (1993) 26(4) *Kritische Justiz* 438–60
Holt, T, '"Men Sell Not Such in Any Town": Exchange in *Goblin Market*' (1990) 28 *Victorian Poetry* 51
Home Department, *The Government Reply to the Sixth Report from the Home Affairs Committee Session 2007-8 HC263, Domestic Violence, Forced Marriage and 'Honour'-Based Violence* (Cm 7450 2008)
Home Office, *Information for Local Areas on the Change to the Definition of Domestic Violence and Abuse* (Home Office and AVA, 2013)
Houston, H, *The Real Horatio Bottomley* (Hurst & Blackett, 1923)
Howarth, J, 'Fawcett, Dame Millicent Garrett [née Millicent Garrett] (1847–1929), Leader of the Constitutional Women's Suffrage Movement and Author' *Oxford Dictionary of National Biography* (DNB, 2004)
Howe-Walsh, L and Turnbull, S, 'Barriers to Women Leaders in Academia: Tales from Academia and Technology' (2016) 41 *Studies in Higher Education* 415
Huxley-Binns, R, 'Tripping over thresholds: a reflection on legal andragogy' (2016) 50 *The Law Teacher* 1
Humphreys, C, and Thiara, R, *Routes to Safety* (Women's Aid Federation of England, 2002)

Hunt, J and Macleod, A, *Outcomes of Applications to Court for Contact Orders After Separation or Divorce* (Ministry of Justice, 2008)
Huerkamp, C, *Bildungsbürgerinnen. Frauen im Studium und in akademischen Berufen 1900–1945* (Vandenhoek und Ruprecht, 1996)
Huerkamp, C, 'Jüdische Akademikerinnen in Deutschland 1900-1938' (1993) 19(3) *Geschichte und Gesellschaft* 311–31
Hunter, R and Rackley, E, 'Feminist Judgments on the UK Supreme Court' (2020) 32 *Canadian Journal of Women and the Law* 85
Hunter, R, 'An Account of Feminist Judging' in R Hunter, C McGlynn and E Rackley (eds), *Feminist Judgments: From Theory to Practice* (Hart, 2010)
Hunter, R, 'Feminist Judgments in the "Real World"' (2018) 8(9) *Oñati Socio-Legal Series* 1275
Hunter, R, 'More Than Just a Different Face? Judicial Diversity and Decision-Making' (2015) 68 *Current Legal Problems* 119
Hunter, R, Burton, M and Trinder, L, *Assessing Risk of Harm to Children and Parents in Private Law Children Cases. Final Report* (Ministry of Justice, 2020)
Hunter, R, Mack, K and Roach Anleu, S, 'Feminist Judgments in Lower Courts' (2021) 48 *Journal of Law and Society* 595
Hunter, R, McGlynn, C and Rackley, E (eds), *Feminist Judgments: From Theory to Practice* (Hart, 2010)
Hurdley, R, 'Dismantling Mantelpieces: Narrating Identities and Materializing Culture in the Home' (2006) 40(4) *Sociology* 717
Hyman, A, *The Rise and Fall of Horatio Bottomley, The Biography of a Swindler* (Cassell, 1972)
Jane, EA, 'Systemic Misogyny Exposed: Translating Rapeglish from the Manosphere with a Random Rape Threat Generator' (2018) 21 *International Journal of Cultural Studies* 661
Jenkins, F, 'Gendered Hierarchies of Knowledge and the Prestige Factor: How Philosophy Survives Market Rationality' in M Thornton (ed), *Through a Glass Darkly: The Social Sciences Look at the Neoliberal University* (ANU Press, 2015)
John, A, 'Between Cause and the Courts: The Curious Case of Cecil Chapman' in C Eustance, J Ryan and L Ugolini (eds), *Suffrage Reader, Charting Directions in British Suffrage History* (Bloomsbury, 2000)
Johnson, M, 'Spoor, Benjamin Charles [Ben] (1878–1928), Politician' *Oxford Dictionary of National Biography* (DNB, 2004)
Johnson, M, *A Typology of Domestic Violence: Intimate Terrorism, Violent Resistance and Situational Couple Violence* (University Press of New England, 2008)
Johnston, JR, 'Children of Divorce Who Reject a Parent and Refuse Visitation: Recent Research and Social Policy Implications for the Alienated Child' (2005) 38 *Family Law Quarterly* 757
Johnston, JR and Kelly, JB, 'Commentary on Walker, Brantley, and Rigsbee's (2004) "A Critical Analysis of Parental Alienation Syndrome and Its Admissibility in the Family Court"' (2004) 1(4) *Journal of Child Custody* 77
Jolly, M and Huibo, L, 'Hearing Her: Comparing Feminist Oral History in the UK and China' (2019) 45 *The Oral History Review* 48
Jolly, M, Russell, P and Cohen, R, 'Sisterhood and After: Individualism, Ethics and an Oral History of the Women's Liberation Movement' (2012) 11 *Social Movement Studies* 211
Jolly, M, *Sisterhood and After: An Oral History of the UK Women's Liberation Movement, 1968–Present* (OUP, 2019)
Jörn-Schellenberg, S, 'Die erste Anwältin: Maria Ottos Weg in die Anwaltschaft' (Anwaltsblatt online, 24 May 2022) anwaltsblatt.anwaltverein.de/de/anwaeltinnen-anwaelte/anwaltspraxis/maria-ottos-weg-in-die-anwaltschaft
Joseph, M, *Victorian Literary Businesses* (Palgrave Macmillan/Springer Nature, 2019)
Kaganas, F, 'A Presumption that "Involvement" of Both Parents Is Best: Deciphering Law's Messages' (2013) *Child and Family Law Quarterly* 270
Kaganas, F, 'First Women's Refuge 1971' in E Rackley and R Auchmuty (ed), *Women's Legal Landmarks: Celebrating Feminist Legal History* (Hart, 2018)

Kaganas, F, 'Parental Involvement: A Discretionary Presumption' (2018) *Legal Studies* 549
Kandler, P, 'North Kensington Law Centre: Reflections 40 Years On' (2010) *Socialist Lawyer* 29
Kelliher, D, 'Striking Solidarity: Friendship and the 1984–5 Miners' Strike' (History Workshop, 17 June 2020)
Kelly, C et al, 'Gender Bias and the Journal of Roman Studies' (2019) 109 *Journal of Roman Studies* 441
Kelly, J and Johnston, J, 'The Alienated Child: A Reformulation of Parental Alienation Syndrome' (2001) 39 *Family Court Review* 249
Kelly, S 'Garrett, Agnes (1845–1935), Interior Designer and Suffragist' *Oxford Dictionary of National Biography* (DNB, 2004)
Kelly, S, 'Janes, Emily (1846–1928), Women's Welfare Activist' *Oxford Dictionary of National Biography* (DNB, 2004)
Kelly, S, 'Ridding [née Palmer], Lady Laura Elizabeth (1849–1939), Suffragist and Philanthropist' *Oxford Dictionary of National Biography* (DNB, 2004)
Kilian, M, and Schultz, U, 'Germany. Resistance and Reactions to Demands of Modernisation' in R Abel, H Sommerlad, O Hammerslev and U Schultz (eds), *Lawyers in 21st Century Societies*, vol 1 (Hart, 2020) 209–33
King, MM and Frederickson, ME, 'The Pandemic Penalty: The Gendered Effects of COVID-19 on Scientific Productivity' (2021) 7 *Socius* 23780231211006976
Kingsley Kent, S 'Gender Reconstruction after the First World War' in HL Smith (ed), *British Feminism in the Twentieth Century* (Edward Elgar, 1990)
Kingsley Kent, S, 'The Politics of Sexual Difference: World War 1 and the Demise of British Feminism' (1988) 27 *Journal of British Studies* 232
Kingsley, T, 'Meet the "Rock n Roll" Lawyers of Kensington who Started in an Old Butcher's Shop' *West London News* (London, 11 June 2020)
Kling, G, 'Die rechtliche Konstruktion des "weiblichen Beamten". Frauen im öffentlichen Dienst des Großherzogtums Baden im 19. und frühen 20. Jahrhundert' in U Gerhard (ed), *Frauen in der Geschichte des Rechts* (Beck, 1999) 600–16
Kooistra, L, 'Copyright and Control: Christina Rossetti and her Publishers' in D Clifford and L Roussillon (eds), *Outsiders Looking In* (Anthem Press, 2004)
Kooistra, L, 'Modern Markets for "Goblin Market"' (1994) 32 *Victorian Poetry* 249
Kooistra, L, 'Visualizing the Fantastic Subject' in M Arseneau, A Harrison and L Kooistra (eds), *The Culture of Christina Rossetti* (Ohio University Press, 1999)
Kooistra, L, *Christina Rossetti and Illustration: A Publishing History* (Ohio University Press, 2002)
Kornhauser, ME, 'Rooms of Their Own: An Empirical Study of Occupational Segregation by Gender among Law Professors' (2004) 73 *University of Missouri–Kansas City* 293
Krechel, U, *Landgericht* (Jung und Jung, 2012)
Kuper, R, 'A History of Pluto Press: 50 Years of Radical Publishing' (Pluto Press)
Lacey, N, *A Life of HLA Hart: The Nightmare and the Noble Dream* (OUP, 2006)
Ladwig-Winters, S, *Das Ende eines Aufbruchs – jüdische Juristinnen und Juristinnen jüdischer Herkunft nach 1933: Minderheitenerfahrung und weibliche Diskriminierung* (Verlag Bundesanzeiger, 2016)
Ladwig-Winters, S, 'Verfolgung, Exil und Tod – Die Situation der jüdischen Juristinnen nach 1933' in D Juristinnenbund (ed), *Jüdische Juristinnen* (Beck, 2019) 24–32
Ladwig-Winters, S, 'Lebenswege jüdischer Rechtsanwältinnen nach 1933' (*Anwaltsblatt* online, 2022) anwaltsblatt.anwaltverein.de/de/anwaeltinnen-anwaelte/portraets/lebenswege-juedischer-rechtsanwaeltinnen-nach-1933
Lambeth Community Law Centre, 'Annual Report, 1978–79' (Lambeth Community Law Centre, 1979)
Lammasniemi, L, 'First Woman to Hold Regular Judicial Office in England and Wales, Rose Heilbron, 1964' in E Rackley and R Auchmuty (eds), *Women's Legal Landmarks: Celebrating the History of Women and Law in the UK and Ireland* (Hart, 2018)
Landry, C et al, *What a Way to Run a Railroad: An Analysis of Radical Failure* (Comedia Publishing, 1985)
Langan Teele, D and Thelen, K, 'Gender in the Journals: Publication Patterns in Political Science' (2017) 50 *PS: Political Science and Politics* 433

Lapierre, S and Cote, I, 'Abused Women and the Threat of Parental Alienation: Shelter Workers' Perspectives' (2016) *Children and Youth Services Review* 120
Law Commission, *Family Law. Domestic Violence and Occupation of the Family* Home (Law Com No 207 HMSO 1992)
Law Commission of Canada, *Beyond Conjugality: Recognizing and Supporting Close Personal and Adult Relationships* (Law Commission of Canada, 2001)
Law, S, *Suffrage and Power: The Women's Movement 1918–1928* (IB Taurus, 1997)
Leask, P, 'Law Centres in England and Wales' (1985) 7 *Law and Policy* 61
Lee, BH, *Divorce Law Reform in England* (Peter Owen, 1974)
Lee, L, *Oscar's Ghost: The Battle for Oscar Wilde's Legacy* (Stroud Amberley, 2017)
Lentin, A, 'Isaacs, Rufus Daniel, First Marquess of Reading (1860–1935), Politician and Judge' *Oxford Dictionary of National Biography* (DNB, 2004)
Lentin, A, 'John Andrew, Viscount Sumner (1859–1934), Barrister and Judge' *Oxford Dictionary of National Biography* (DNB, 2004)
Lentin, A, *The Last Political Law Lord, Lord Sumner (1859–1934)* (Cambridge Scholars Publishers, 2008)
Liemer, SP and Temple, HS, 'Did Your Legal Writing Professor Go to Harvard: The Credentials of Legal Writing Faculty at Hiring Time' (2007) 46 *University of Louisville Law Review* 383
Lindsey, K, '"Deliberate Freedom": Using Speculation and Imagination in Historical Biography' (2018) 50 *Text: Special Issue* 'Life Writing in Troubled Times' 1, K Douglas, DL Brian and K Cordell (eds)
Lobban, M and Williams, I (eds), *Networks and Connections in Legal History* (CUP, 2020)
Loney, M, *Community Against Government: The British Community Development Project, 1968–78: A Study of Government Incompetence* (Heinemann Educational Books, 1983)
Long, MT et al, 'Female Authorship in Major Academic Gastroenterology Journals: A Look over 20 Years' (2015) 81 *Gastrointestinal Endoscopy* 1440
Longman, K, 'Perspectives on Women's Higher Education Leadership from around the World' (2018) 35 *Administrative Sciences* 35
Lord Chancellor's Advisory Committee on Legal Education and Conduct *First Report on Legal Education and Training* (ACLEC, 1996)
Loveless, N and Smith, C, 'Attunement in the Cracks: Feminist Collaboration and the University as Broken Machine' (2022) 34(1) *Feminist Formations* 272
Lowenthal, EG, (ed), *Bewährung im Untergang. Ein Gedenkbuch. Im Auftrag des Council of Jews from Germany, London* (DVA, 1965) 103–105
Lysack, K, *Come Buy, Come Buy: Shopping and the Culture of Consumption in Victorian Women's Writing* (Ohio University Press, 2000)
Burton, M and Bettinson, V, 'Domestic Abuse and Child Arrangement Proceedings: Identifying and Assessing the Risk of Harm, Including Coercive and Controlling Behaviour' (2022) *Child and Family Law Quarterly* 3
Mackay, F, 'Dilemmas of an Academic Feminist as Manager in the Neoliberal Academy: Negotiating Institutional Authority, Oppositional Knowledge and Change' (2021) 19 *Political Studies Review* 75
MacKinnon, Catharine A, *Feminism Unmodified: Discourses on Life and Law* (Harvard University Press, 1987)
MacKinnon, Catherine, 'Reflections on Sex Equality under Law' (1991) 100 *Yale Law Journal* 1297
Macneil, I, in F Snyder (ed), 'Relational Contracting in a Digital Age' (2005) 11 *Texas Wesleyan Law Review* 675
Macneil, I, 'A Primer of Contract Planning' (1975) 48 *Southern California Law Review* 627
Macneil, I, 'Contract Adjustments of Long-Term Economic Relations under Classical, Neoclassical and Relational Contract Law' (1978) 72 *Northwestern University Law Review* 584
Macneil, I, 'Contracting Worlds and Essential Contract Theory' (2000) 9 *Social and Legal Studies* 431
Macneil, I, 'Exchange Revisited: Individual Utility and Social Solidarity' (1986) 96 *Ethics* 567
Macneil, I, 'Political Exchange as Relational Contract' in J Martin (ed), *Generalised Political Exchange* (Westview Press, 1990)

Macneil, I, 'Relational Contract Theory as Sociology: A Reply to Professors Lindenberg and de Vos' (1987) 143 *Journal of Institutional and Theoretical Economics* 272
Macneil, I, 'Relational Contract Theory: Challenges and Queries' (2000) 94 *Northwestern University Law Review* 877
Macneil, I, *The New Social Contract: An Enquiry into Modern Contractual Relations* (Yale University Press, 1980)
Macneil, I, 'Values in Contract: Internal and External' (1983) 78 *Northwestern University Law Review* 340
Maharg, P, *Transforming Legal Education: Learning and Teaching the Law and the Early 21st Century* (Ashgate, 2007)
Maine, HS, *Ancient Law* (John Murray, 1861)
Manchester Law Centre, 'Annual Report, 1977–78' (Manchester Law Centre, 1978)
Manchester Law Centre, 'Annual Report, 1978–79' (Manchester Law Centre, 1979)
Manchester Law Centre, 'Annual Report, 1979–80' (Manchester Law Centre, 1980)
Marsh, J, 'Christina Rossetti's Vocation: The Importance of "Goblin Market"' (1994) 32 *Victorian Poetry* 233
Massoud, MF, 'The Price of Positionality: Assessing the Benefits and Burdens of Self-Identification in Research Methods' (2022) 49 (Supp) *Journal of Law and Society* 64
Matthew, HCG, 'Haldane, Richard Burdon, Viscount Haldane (1856–1928)' *Oxford Dictionary of National Biography* (DNB, 2004)
May, L, '"Eat Me, Drink Me, Love Me": Orality, Sexuality, and the Fruits of Sororal Desire in "Gob(b)lin(g) Market" and Beloved' in J Mink and J Ward (eds), *The Significance of Sibling Relationships in Literature* (Bowling Green State University Popular Press, 1993)
McCabe, S, 'Unfinished Business' (1977) *British Journal of Criminology* 280
McGann, J, 'Christina Rossetti's Poems: A New Edition and a Revaluation' (1980) 23 *Victorian Studies* 237
McGinley, AC, 'Reproducing Gender on Law School Faculties' (2009) 2009 *Brigham Young University Law Review* 99
McGlynn, C, 'Strategies for Reforming the English Solicitors' Profession: An Analysis of the Business Case for Sex Equality' in U Schultz and G Shaw (eds), *Women in the World's Legal Professions* (Hart, 2003) 159
McGlynn, C, 'The Status of Women Lawyers in the United Kingdom' in U Schultz and G Shaw (eds), *Women in the World's Legal Professions* (Hart, 2003) 139
McGlynn, C, 'Strategies for Reforming the English Solicitors' Profession: An Analysis of the Business Case for Sex Equality' in U Schultz and G Shaw (eds), *Women in the World's Legal Professions* (Hart, 2003) 159
McGlynn, C, 'The Business of Equality in the Solicitors' Profession' (2000) 63 *Modern Law Review* 42
McGlynn, C, *The Woman Lawyer* (Butterworths, 1998)
McGlynn, C, 'Women, Representation and the Legal Academy' (1999) 19 *Legal Studies* 68
McKenna, M, 'Clark, Charles Manning (1915–1991)' (2019) 19 *Australian Dictionary of National Biography*
Meier, J, *Parental Alienation Syndrome and Parental Alienation: A Research Review* (National Resource Center on Domestic Violence, 2013)
Melville, A and Barrow, A, 'Persistence Despite Change: The Academic Gender Gap in Australian Law Schools' (2022) 47 *Law and Social Inquiry* 607
Mendoza, V, '"Come Buy": The Crossing of Sexual and Consumer Desire in Christina Rossetti's Goblin Market' (2006) 73 *Journal of English Literary History* 913
Menke, R, 'The Political Economy of Fruit' in M Arseneau, A Harrison and L Kooistra (eds), *The Culture of Christina Rossetti* (Ohio University Press, 1999)
Mermin, D, 'Heroic Sisterhood in "Goblin Market"' (1983) 21 *Victorian Poetry* 107
Michl, Fabian, *Wiltraut Rupp-von Brünneck (1912–1977)* (Frankfurt/New York, Campus, 2022).
Mill, JS, *The Subjection of Women* (Longmans et al, 1870)

Ministry of Justice, 'Diversity of the Judiciary: Legal Professions, New Appointments and Current Post-Holders' (MoJ, 2020)

Ministerium der Justiz NRW (ed), *Zwischen Recht und Unrecht. Lebensläufe deutscher Juristen*, 2nd edn (2016)

Ministry of Justice, *Assessing Risk of Harm to Children and Parents in Private Law Children Cases. Implementation Plan* (Ministry of Justice, 2020)

Ministry of Justice, HM Courts and Tribunals Service, Lord Wolfson KC, 'Press Release: Pioneering Approach in Family Courts to Support Domestic Abuse Victims Better' (2022)

Minow, M, 'Forming underneath Everything that Grows: Toward a History of Family Law' (1985) 4 *Wisconsin Law Review* 819

Misselwitz, F, *Marie Luise Hilger. Zum Leben und Wirken einer Arbeitsrechtlerin im 20. Jahrhundert* (Nomos, 2016)

Moran, L, 'Researching the Visual Culture of Law and Legal Institutions: Some Reflections on Methodology' (2022) 48 (Supp) *Journal of Law and Society* 44

Morely, L, 'Troubling Intra-Actions: Gender, Neo-Liberalism and Research in the Global Academy' (2016) 31 *Journal of Education Policy* 28

Morgan, R et al, 'Gendered Geography: An Analysis of Authors in The Lancet Global Health' (2019) 7 *The Lancet Global Health* e1619

Morley, L and Lund, RWB, 'The Affective Economy of Feminist Leadership in Finnish Universities: Class-Based Knowledge for Navigating Neoliberalism and Neuroliberalism' (2021) 42 *Discourse: Studies in the Cultural Politics of Education* 114

Morris, A, 'Sex Discrimination Act 1975' in E Rackley and R Auchmuty (ed), *Women's Legal Landmarks: Celebrating Feminist Legal History* (Hart, 2018)

Morris, Caroline, 'Dr Ivy Williams: Inside yet Outside' (June 2020) 29(4) *Women's History Review* 583–614

Mossman, MJ, 'Feminism and Legal Method: The Difference It Makes' (1987) 3 *Wisconsin Women's Law Journal* 147

Mottershead, T (ed), *The Art and Science of Strategic Talent Management in Law Firms* (Thomson Reuters, 2010)

Mulcahy, L, 'Eyes of the Law: A Visual Turn in Socio-Legal Studies?' (2017) 44 (Supp) *Journal of Law and Society* 111

Mulcahy, L, 'The Limitations of Love and Altruism – Feminist Perspectives on Contract Law' in L Mulcahy and S Wheeler (eds), *Feminist Perspectives on Contract* (Glasshouse Press, 2005)

Müller, I, *Furchtbare Juristen. Die unbewältigte Vergangenheit unserer Justiz* (Kindler, 1987)

MWA Annual General Report, May 1963, 5MWA/3/1, The Women's Library, London

MWA Bulletin, April–May 1981, 5MWA/8/1, The Women's Library, London

MWA Bulletin, January–February 1980, 5MWA/8/1, The Women's Library, London

MWA Bulletin, January–March 1983, 5MWA/8/1, The Women's Library, London

Napier, A and Pottle, M, 'Schuster, Claud, Baron Schuster (1869–1956), Civil Servant' *Oxford Dictionary of National Biography* (DNB, 2004)

Nelken, D, *The Limits of the Legal Process: A Study of Landlords, Law and Crime*, (Academic Press, 1983)

Nicolaysen, R, 'Für Recht und Gerechtigkeit über das couragierte Leben der Juristin Magdalene Schoch (1897–1987)' *Zeitschrift des Vereins für Hamburgische Geschichte, Band 92* (2006) 113–43

Noakes, L, *Chrystal MacMillan and Elsie Bowerman: First Women Barristers' Negotiation of Professional and Political Identities* (The Open University, 2021)

Noakes, Laura, 'Early Women Barristers and the Negotiation of Professional and Political Identity' (2022) *Women's History Review* 8

Norcia, M, '"Come Buy, Come Buy": Christina Rossetti's "Goblin Market" and the Cries of London' (2012) 17 *Journal of Victorian Culture* 24

North Kensington Law Centre, 'The First Ten Years, 1970–1980' (North Kensington Law Centre, 1980)

North Kensington Neighbourhood Law Centre, 'Annual Report, 1971' (North Kensington Neighbourhood Law Centre, 1971)

North Kensington Neighbourhood Law Centre, 'Annual Report, 1972' (North Kensington Neighbourhood Law Centre, 1972)
North Kensington Neighbourhood Law Centre, 'Annual Report, 1974' (North Kensington Neighbourhood Law Centre, 1974)
North Kensington Neighbourhood Law Centre, 'Annual Report, 1978' (North Kensington Neighbourhood Law Centre, 1978)
Norton, A, 'Higher Education Commentary from Carlton'
Norton, C, 'A Letter to the Queen on Lord Chancellor Cranworth's Marriage and Divorce Bill' (1855) in P Hollis (ed), *Women in Public: The Women's Movement 1850–1900* (George Allen & Unwin, 1979)
Nussbaum, M, 'Whether from Reason or Prejudice: Taking Money for Bodily Services' (1998) 27 *Journal of Legal Studies* 693
O'Connor, P, 'Gender Imbalance in Senior Positions in Higher Education: What Is the Problem? What Can Be Done' (2019) 3 *Policy Reviews in Higher Education* 28
Oakley, A, *Housewife: High Value–Low Cost* (Penguin, 1974)
Oleschuk, M, 'Gender Equity Considerations for Tenure and Promotion during COVID-19' (2020) 57 *Canadian Review of Sociology* 502
Oram, A, 'Serving Two Masters? The Introduction of a Marriage Bar in Teaching in the 1920s' in The London Feminist History Group (ed), *The Sexual Dynamics of History: Men's Power, Women's Resistance* (Pluto Press, 1983)
Oram, A, *Women Teachers and Feminist Politics 1900–39* (Manchester University Press, 1996)
Ostler, F, *Die deutschen Rechtsanwälte 1871–1971* (Juristischer Verlag W. Ellinghaus, 1971)
Overall, C, 'What's Wrong with Prostitution?' (1992) 17 *Signs* 705
Overbaugh, J, 'Defining the Barriers to Women Publishing in High-Impact Journals' (2018) 92 *Journal of Virology* e02127
Paddington Advice and Law Centre, 'Annual Report, 1978–80' (Paddington Advice and Law Centre, 1980)
Paddington Neighbourhood Advice Bureau and Law Centre, 'Annual Report, 1973–4' (Paddington Neighbourhood Advice Bureau and Law Centre, 1974)
Parker, M and Jary, D, 'The McUniversity: Organization, Management and Academic Subjectivity' (1995) 2 *Organization* 319
Partington, G, *Women Teachers in the 20th Century in England and Wales* (NFER Publishing Company, 1976)
Pasma, C and Regehr, S, *Basic Income: Some Policy Options for Canada* (report prepared for the Basic Income Canada Network, 2019)
Pate, K, *Why a Guaranteed Livable Income?* (Office of Kim Pate, Independent Senator, 10 May 2020)
Pateman, C, *The Sexual Contract* (Polity Press, 1988)
Peterson, L, 'Restoring the Book: The Typological Hermeneutics of Christina Rossetti and the PRB' (1994) 32 *Victorian Poetry* 209
Pettigrew, R, 'An Untenable Workload: COVID-19 and the Disproportionate Impact on Women's Work–Family Demands' (2021) 113(4) *Journal of Family and Consumer Sciences* 8
Phipps, E, *History of the National Union of Women Teachers* (NUWT, 1928)
Pionke, A, 'The Spiritual Economy of "Goblin Market"' (2012) 52 *Studies in English Literature* 897
Pizzey, E, *Scream Quietly or the Neighbours Will Hear* (Penguin Books, 1974)
Planner, The, Journal of the Royal Town Planning Institute, 'Obituary', Vol 2 (Royal Town Planning Institute, 1916)
Plett, K, 'The Loss of Early Women Lawyers from Collective Memory in Germany: A Memoir of Magdalene Schoch' in S Karstedt (ed), *Legal institutions and collective memories. Criminology and Policing* (Hart, 2009) 353–70
Plum, G, 'Wirtschaft und Erwerbsleben' in Wolfgang Benz (ed), *Die Juden in Deutschland 1933–1945* (Beck, 1988) 288
Polden, P, 'Portia's Progress: Women at the Bar in England, 1919–1939' (2005) *International Journal of the Legal Profession* 293

Polikoff, N, *Beyond (Straight and Gay) Marriage: Valuing All Families under the* Law (Beacon Press, 2008)
Pollard, L, *Margery Spring Rice: Pioneer of Women's Health in the Early Twentieth Century* (Cambridge Open Book Publishers, 2020)
Popple, K, 'Rise and Fall of the National Community Development Projects 1968–1978: Lessons to Learn?' in R Gilchrist et al (eds), *Reflecting on the Past: Essays in the History of Community Youth Work* (Russell House Publishing, 2011)
Popple, K, *Analysing Community Work: Its Theory and Practice* (Open University Press, 1995)
Prescott, M, '50 Years of the NKLC' (2020) *Socialist Lawyer* 48
Pring, R, *Closing the Gap: Liberal Education and Vocational Preparation* (Hodder and Staughton, 1995)
Pritchett, VS, MWA Annual General Meeting, 11 May 1972, Secretary's Report for Year Ended 30 April 1972, 5MWA/3/1, The Women's Library, London
Proskauer, E, *Wege und Umwege. Erinnerungen einer Berliner Rechtsanwältin* (Fischer, 1996)
Prosser, M and Watts, G, *Your Seat is at the End: My Story* (Feather Duster Publications, 2010)
Prothero, A and McDonagh, P, '"It's Hard to Be What You Can't See" – Gender Representation in Marketing's Academic Journals' (2021) 37 *Journal of Marketing Management* 28
Pugh, M, 'Palmer, (Beatrix) Maud [née Lady (Beatrix) Maud Gascoyne-Cecil], countess of Selborne (1858–1950), Suffragist and Political Wife' *Oxford Dictionary of National Biography* (DNB, 2004)
Purvis, J (ed), *Women's History: Britain, 1850–1945: An Introduction* (Routledge, 2008)
Purvis, J, *Emmeline Pankhurst: A Biography* (Routledge, 2003)
Rackley, E and Auchmuty, R, 'The Case for Feminist Legal History' (2020) 40 *Oxford Journal of Legal Studies* 878
Rackley, E and Auchmuty, R, 'Women's Legal Landmarks: An Introduction' in E Rackley and R Auchmuty (eds), *Women's Legal Landmarks* (Hart, 2019)
Rackley, E and Auchmuty, R (eds), *Women's Legal Landmarks: Celebrating the History of Women and Law in the UK and Ireland* (Hart, 2019)
Rappoport, J, *Giving Women* (OUP, 2012)
Rayner, J, 'Class Warrior' *Law Society Gazette* (London, 3 June 2019)
REF2014 (2015) Overview Report by Main Panel C, 2015: 70–75, REF2021 (2022) Overview Report by Main Panel C of Sub-groups 13-23, sub-panel 18: 104–15
Reilly, A, Jones, D, Vasquez, C and Krisjanous, J, 'Confronting Gender Inequality in a Business School' (2016) 35 *Higher Education Research and Development* 1025
Reinicke, P, 'Israel, Clara' in H Maier (ed), *Who is who der Sozialen Arbeit* (Lambertus, 1998) 273
Robinson, C, Chakraborty, T and Dabezies, C, *18 Years: Coming of Age, 1970–1988* (North Kensington Law Centre, 1988)
Ronksley-Pavia, M, Neumann, M, Manakil, J and Pickard-Smith, K (eds), *Academic Women: Voicing Narratives of Gendered Experiences* (Bloomsbury Academic, 2023)
Rosser, E, 'Women and the Legal Profession' *St Hugh's Chronicle* (Oxford, nd)
Rossetti, W, *The Poetical Works of Christina Georgina Rossetti* (Macmillan, 1904)
Röwekamp, M, *Juristinnen – Lexikon zu Leben und Werk* (Nomos, 2005)
Röwekamp, M, *Die ersten deutschen Juristinnen: Eine Geschichte ihrer Professionalisierung und Emanzipation (1900–1945)* (Böhlau, 2011)
Röwekamp, M, *Marie Munk. Rechtsanwältin – Richterin – Rechtsreformerin* (Berlin, Hentrich & Hentrich Verlag, 2014)
Röwekamp, M, 'Margarete Berent (1887–1965) und Marie Munk (1885–1978). Pionierinnen im Kampf um gleiche Rechte für Frauen' in *Kritische Justiz.* Sonderheft Streitbare JuristInnen (2016) 72–107
Röwekamp, M, 'Women's Admission to the Legal Profession in Germany between 1900 and 1933' in E Schandevyl (ed), *Women in Law and Lawmaking in Nineteenth and Twentieth-Century Europe* (Routledge, 2016) 91–116
Rowbotham, S, *A Century of Women: The History of Women in Britain and the United States* (Viking, 1997)
Rowbotham, S, *Hidden From History: 300 Years of Women's Oppression and the Fight* (Pluto Press, 1977)

Rycroft, G, 'A Forgotten Figure in the Garden City Movement' *Lancaster Guardian* (30 August 2015)
Sachs, A and Hoff Wilson, J, *Sexism and the Law: A Study of Male Beliefs and Judicial Bias* (Martin Robertson, 1978)
Samuels, H, 'Education Act 1944' in E Rackley and R Auchmuty (eds), *Women's Legal Landmarks: Celebrating the History of Women and the Law in the UK and Ireland* (Hart, 2018)
Sandberg, R, 'The Time for Legal History: Some Reflections on Maitland and Milsom Fifty Years On' (2018) 180 *Law and Justice* 21
Sandberg, R and Doe, N, 'Textual and Contextual Legal History' in N Doe and R Sandberg (eds), *Law and History, Vol 1: Critical Concepts in Law* (Routledge, 2016)
Sandberg, R, *Subversive Legal History: A Manifesto for the Future of Legal Education* (Routledge, 2021)
Sankey, rev HCG Matthew, 'Duke, Henry Edward, First Baron Merrivale (1855–1939)' *Oxford Dictionary of National Biography* (DNB, 2004)
Sarat, A, 'Off to Meet the Wizard: Beyond Validity and Reliability in the Search for a Post-Empiricist Sociology of Law' (1993) 15 *Law and Social Inquiry* 155
Sawer, M, *Sisters in Suits: Women and Public Policy in Australia* (Allen & Unwin, 1991)
Scanlon, J, 'Challenging the Imbalances of Power in Feminist Oral History: Developing a Take-and-give Methodology' (1993) 16 *Women's Studies International Forum* 639
Scheicher, D, 'From Here All-the Way-Down, or How to Write a Festschrift Piece' (2013) 48 *Tulsa Law Review* 401
Schmerbach, F, *Das 'Gemeinschaftslaget Hans Kerrl' für Referendare in Jüterbog 1933–1939. Beiträge zur Rechtsgeschichte des 20. Jahrhunderts* (Mohr Siebeck, 2008)
Schultz, U, 'Wie männlich ist die Juristenschaft?' in U Battis und U Schultz (eds), *Frauen im Recht* (C.F. Müller, 1990) 319–59
Schultz, U, 'The Status of Women Lawyers in Germany' in U Schultz and G Shaw (eds), *Women in the World's Legal Professions* (Hart, 2003)
Schultz, U, 'Legal Education in Germany – an ever (never?) ending story of resistance to change' *RED, Revista de Educación y Derecho* n. 4 (2011) 1–24 revistes.ub.edu/index.php/RED
Schultz, U, 'Marie Luise Hilgers – Zum Leben und Werk einer Arbeitsrechtlerin im 20. Jahrhundert. Rezension des gleichnamigen Buches von Frederike Misselwitz' (2016) 4 *djbZ*, 185–87
Schultz, U, 'Introduction: Gender and Careers in the Legal Academy: Overview and Synthesis' in U Schultz, G Shaw, M Thornton and R Auchmuty (eds), *Gender and Careers in the Legal Profession* (2021) (Hart, 2021)
Schultz, U, 'Knowledge and Opinion About Law – The importance of Law Related Education' in H Hyden, D Nelken, R Cotterell and U Schultz (eds), *Combining the Legal and the Social in Sociology of Law. Anthology in Memory of Reza Banakar* (Bloomsbury, 2023)
Schultz, U, 'Gender in Socio-Legal Teaching and Research in Germany' (2020) 21 *German Law Journal* 1345–361
Schultz, U, 'Introduction: Gender and Careers in the Legal Academy: Overview and Synthesis' in U Schultz, G Shaw, M Thornton and R Auchmuty (eds), *Gender and Careers in the Legal Academy* (Hart, 2021) 1–36
Schultz, U, Böning, A, Peppmeier, I and Schröder, S, *De jure und de facto: Professorinnen in der Rechtswissenschaft. Geschlecht und Wissenschaftskarriere im Recht* (Nomos, 2018)
Schultz, U, Shaw, G, Thornton, M and Auchmuty, R (eds), *Gender and Careers in the Legal Academy* (Hart, 2021)
Schuyt, K, Groenendijk, K and Sloot, B, 'Access to the Legal System and Legal Services Research' in B Blegvad, C Campbell and C Schuyt (eds), *European Yearbook in Law and Sociology* (Springer, 1977)
Scott, E and Scott, R, 'Marriage as Relational Contract' (1998) 84 *Virginia Law Review* 1225
Scoular, J, 'The "Subject" of Prostitution: Interpreting the Discursive, Symbolic and Material Position of Sex/Work in Feminist Theory' (2004) 5 *Feminist Theory* 343
Setting Standards: The Future Of Legal Services Education And Training Regulation In England And Wales: the Final report of the Legal Education Training Review in England and Wales Independent Research Team (2013)

Seymour, D, 'English Law and the Dilemmas of Assimilation' (2012) 21 *Social and Legal Studies* 567
Sherr, A, 'Legal Education, Legal Competence and Little Bo Peep' (1998) 32 *The Law Teacher* 37
Sherr, A, Moorhead, R and Sommerlad, H (eds), *Legal Education at the Crossroads: Education and the Legal Profession* (Routledge, 2018)
Sherr, A and Sugarman, D, 'Theory in legal education' (2000) 7(3) *International Journal of the Legal Profession* 165
Simon, J, 'With all my Worldly Goods …', Presidential Address (Holdsworth Club, University of Birmingham, 1 January 1964)
Simon, R, *The Touch of the Past: Remembrance, Learning and Ethics* (Palgrave, 2005)
Smart, C, 'Power and the Politics of Child Custody' in C Smart and S Sevenhuijsen (eds), *Child Custody and the Politics of Gender* (Routledge, 1989)
Smart, C, 'Reflection' (2012) 20 *Feminist Legal Studies* 161
Smart, C, *The Ties that Bind: Law, Marriage and the Reproduction of Patriarchal Relations* (Routledge & Kegan Paul, 1984)
Smith, C, 'The Disruptive Power of Legal Biography: The Life of Lord Phillimore – Churchman and Judge' (2020) 41 *Journal of Legal History* 164
Smith, HL, 'British Feminism in the 1920's' in HL Smith (ed), *British Feminism in the Twentieth Century* (Edward Elgar, 1990)
Smith, R, 'Clinics in a Cold Climate: Community Law Centres in England and Wales' (1997) 35 *Osgoode Hall Law Journal* 895
Soble, A, 'Fact and Value: Essays on Ethics and Metaphysics for Judith Jarvis Thomson' (2003) 4(1/Jan) *Essays in Philosophy* 1
Solace Women's Aid and Justice Studio Ltd, *'When I Needed You to Protect Me, You Gave Him More Power Instead': Covid-10 Lockdown and Domestic Abuse* (2021)
Sommerlad, H, Webley, L, Muzio, D, Tomlinson, J and Duff, L, *Diversity in the Legal Profession in England and Wales: A Qualitative Study of Barriers and Individual Choices* (University of Westminster Press and the Legal Services Board, 2013.
Sontag, S, *On Photography* (Penguin, 1977)
Sotiropoulou, P and Cranston, S, 'Critical Friendship: An Alternative, "Care-full" Way to Play the Academic Game' (2022) *Gender, Place and Culture* 5
Sowards, R, '*Goblin Market's* Localism' (2012) *Modern Philology* 114
Spender, D, *There's Always Been a Women's Movement This Century* (Harper Collins, 1983)
Staff, I (ed), *Justiz im Dritten Reich. Eine Dokumentation*, 2nd edn (Fischer Taschenbuch Verlag, 1978)
Stark, E, 'Re-Presenting Battered Women: Coercive Control and the Defense of Liberty', Prepared for Violence Against Women: Complex Realities and Violence in Changing World (LesPresses de l'Université du Québec, 2012)
Stark, E, 'Rethinking Coercive Control' (2012) *Violence Against Women* 1509
Stauffer, A, 'The Goblin Men and the Flower Girl: New Sources for "Goblin Market"' (2018) 56 *Victorian Poetry* 47
Steele, D, 'Palmer, Roundell, First Earl of Selborne (1812–1895), Lord Chancellor' *Oxford Dictionary of National Biography* (DNB, 2004)
Stenton, M and Lees, S, *Who's Who of British Members of Parliament* vol III (Harvester Press, 1979)
Stephens, M, *Community Law Centres: An Appraisal* (Avebury, 1990)
Stetson, D, *A Woman's Issue: The Politics of Family Law Reform in England* (OUP, 1982)
Stevens, Robert, 'Hewart, Gordon, First Viscount Hewart (1870–1943)' *Oxford Dictionary of National Biography* (DNB, 2004)
Stiefel, EC, 'Die deutsche juristische Emigration in den USA' (1988) *Juristenzeitung* 421–26
Stone, OM, '"With all my Worldly Goods …"' (1965) 14 *International and Comparative Law Quarterly* 707
Strachey, R, *The Cause: A Short History of the Women's Movement in Great Britain* (Virago, 1928)
Sturgess, HAC, *Register of Admissions to the Honourable Society of the Middle Temple* (Butterworth & Co, 1949)

Subhedar, O, 'From a Butcher's Shop to the Tory Cuts' (2018) *Socialist Lawyer* 19

Subject Benchmark Statement Law March 2023 5ed (Quality Assurance Agency, 2023)

Sugarman, D, 'Hart Interviewed: HLA Hart in Conversation with David Sugarman' (2005) 32 *Journal of Law and Society* 267

Sutherland, J, 'Ward [née Arnold], Mary Augusta [known as Mrs Humphry Ward] (1851–1920), Novelist, Philanthropist, and Political Lobbyist' *Oxford Dictionary of National Biography* (DNB, 2004)

Symes, P, 'Indissolubility and the Clean Break' (1985) 48 *Modern Law Review* 44

Symonds, R, *Inside the Citadel, Men and the Emancipation of Women 1850–1920* (Palgrave Macmillan, 1999)

Taggart, M, 'Gardens or Graveyards of Scholarship? Festschriften in the Literature of the Common Law' (2002) 22 *Oxford Journal of Legal Studies* 227

Takayanagi, M, 'Sacred Year or Broken Reed? The Sex Disqualification (Removal) Act 1919' (2020) 29 *Women's History Review* 563

Tansley, C, 'What do we mean by the term "talent" in talent management?' (2011) 43 *Industrial and Commercial Training*

Tarr, C, 'Covent Goblin Market' (2012) 50 *Victorian Poetry* 297

Taylor, CA, 'Slow Singularities for Collective Mattering: New Material Feminist Praxis in the Accelerated Academy' (2020) 39 *Irish Educational Studies* 255

Thomas, T and Boisseau, T (eds), *Feminist Legal History: Essays on Women and Law* (NYU Press, 2011)

Thompson, S, 'Against Divorce? Revisiting the Charge of the Casanova's Charter' (2021) *Child and Family Law Quarterly* 193

Thompson, S, 'Feminist Relational Contract Theory: A New Model for Family Property Agreements' (2018) 45 *Journal of Law and Society* 617

Thompson, S, *Quiet Revolutionaries: The Married Women's Association and Family Law* (Hart, 2022)

Thomson, M, 'Femocrats and Babes: Women and Power' (2001) 16(35) *Australian Feminist Studies* 193

Thornton, M, *Dissonance and Distrust: Women in the Legal Profession* (OUP, 1996)

Thornton, M, 'Neo-liberal Melancholia: The Case of Feminist Legal Scholarship' (2004) 20 *Australian Feminist Law Journal* 77

Thornton, M, 'Corrosive Leadership (or Bullying by Another Name): A Corollary of the Corporatised Academy' (2004) 17 *Australian Journal of Labour Law* 161

Thornton, M, *Privatising the Public University: The Case of Law* (Routledge, 2012)

Thornton, M and Roberts, H, 'Women Judges, Private Lives: (In)visibilities in Fact and Fiction' (2017) 40 *University of New South Wales Law Journal* 761

Tosh, J, *The Pursuit of History: Aims, Methods and New Directions in the Study of History*, 7th edn (Routledge, 2022)

Trends in the Solicitors' Profession Annual Statistics Report 2021 (The Law Society of England and Wales, 2022)

Treitschke, H von, *Politik. Vorlesungen*. 1897–1898, 2 volumes (Hirzel, 1911–1913)

Tucker, H, 'Rossetti's Goblin Marketing: Sweet to Tongue and Sound to Eye' (2003) 82 *Representations* 117

Turnadge, I, 'The Merits of the Case' *Time and Tide* (London, 3 December 1926)

Turner, C, González, V and Wong, K, 'Faculty Women of Color: The Critical Nexus of Race and Gender' (2011) *Journal of Diversity in Higher Education* 199

Twining, W, *Blackstone's Tower: The English Law School* (Sweet and Maxwell, 1994)

Tyler, J and Parsons, C, *Madame Clapham: Hull's Celebrated Dressmaker* (Kingston Upon Hull City Museums and Art Galleries, 1999)

van Zwanenberg, Anna, 'Preface', *Megarry's Rent Acts*, 1st Permanent Supplement (Stevens & Sons, 1970)

Vaughan, S, 'The State of the Nation: Diversity and the British Legal Academy' (2016) 50 *The Law Teacher* 255

Vauxhall Community Law Centre, 'Annual Report, 1974–75' (Vauxhall Community Law Centre, 1975)

Vejvoda, K, 'The Fruit of Charity: Comus and Christina Rossetti's *Goblin Market*' (2000) 38 *Victorian Poetry* 555

Vellacot, J, *From Liberal to Labour with Women's Suffrage: The Story of Catherine Marshall*, 2nd edn (McGill-Queen's Press, 2016)

Venn, J (ed), *Alumni Cantabrigienses, A Biographical List of All Known Students, Graduates and Holders of Office at the University of Cambridge, from the Earliest Times to 1900* (CUP, 2011)

Viglione, G, 'Are Women Publishing Less during the Pandemic? Here's What the Data Say' (2020) 581 *Nature* 365

Vinodh, NS, *A Forgotten Ambassador in Cairo: The Life and Times of Syud Hossain* (S & S Publishers, 2020)

Waldman, S, '"O Wanton Eyes Run Over": Repetition and Fantasy in Christina Rossetti' (2000) 38 *Victorian Poetry* 533

Walter, J, 'The Solace of Doubt? Biographical Method after the Short Twentieth Century' in H Renders and B de Haan (eds), *Theoretical Discussions of Biography: Approaches from History, Microhistory and Life Writing* (Brill, 2014)

Ward, L and Branigan, T, 'Level's Best' *The Guardian* (London, 14 November 2007)

Webb, J and Williams, J, 'Canberra: Ideal City, Imagined City' (2015) 29 *Continuum* 490

Webley, L 'Great Debates in Gender and the Legal Profession' in R Auchmuty (ed), *Great Debates in Gender and Law* (Palgrave MacMillan, 2017)

Webley, L, 'Legal Professional De(Re)Regulation, Equality, And Inclusion, And The Contested Space Of Professionalism Within The Legal Market In England And Wales' (2015) 83 *Fordham Law Review* 2349

Webley, L, 'Sociology of the Legal Professions' in J Přibán (ed), *Research Handbook on the Sociology of Law* (Edward Elgar, 2020) 215

Webley, L and Duff, L, 'Women Solicitors as a Barometer for Problems Within the Legal Profession – Time to Put Values before Profits?' (2007) 34 *Journal of Law and Society* 374

Webley, L, Tomlinson, J, Sommerlad, H, Muzio, D and Duff, L, 'Access to a Career in the Legal Profession in England and Wales: Race, Class and the Role of Educational Background' in Nelson, R, Headworth, S, Dinovitzer, R and Wilkins, D (eds) *Diversity in Practice* (CUP, 2016)

Wells, C 'Ladies in Waiting: The Women Law Professors' Story' (2001) 23 *Sydney Law Review* 167

Wells, C 'The Remains of the Day: The Women Law Professors Project' in U Schultz and G Shaw (eds), *Women in the World's Legal Professions* (Hart, 2003) 225

Wells, C, 'Working out Women in Law Schools' (2001) 21 *Legal Studies* 116

West, R, 'Women in the Legal Academy: A Brief History of Feminist Legal Theory' (2018) 87 *Fordham Law Review* 977

Westoby, C et al, 'What Are the Barriers and Facilitators to Success for Female Academics in UK HEIs? A Narrative Review' (2021) 33 *Gender and Education* 1033

Westoby, C, Dyson, J, Cowdell, F and Buescher, T, 'What Are the Barriers and Facilitators to Success for Female Academics in UK HEIs? A Narrative Review' (2021) 33 *Gender in Education* 1033

Wheeler, S, 'Modelling the Contracts of the Future' (2017) 26 *Griffith Law Review* 593

Wheeler, S, 'Visions of Contract' (2017) 44 *Journal of Law and Society* 74

Whittaker, WJ and Maitland, FW (eds), *The Mirror of Justices* (Selden Society, 1893)

Wiener, C, 'Seeing What Is "Invisible in Plain sight": Policing Coercive Control' (2017) *The Howard Journal* 500

Wightman, J, 'Intimate Relationships, Relational Contract Theory and the Reach of Contract' (2000) 8 *Feminist Legal Studies* 93

Wilkinson, G, 'Prepare a Festschrift' (1989) 299 *British Medical Journal* 612

Wilson, J, 'A Survey of Legal Education in the UK' (1966–67) 9 *Journal of the Society of Public Teachers of Law* 1

Wolf, S, *Das Jenaer Studium der Rechte im Dritten Reich. Zwischen Tradition und nationalsozialistischer Ideologie*. Rechtshistorische Reihe 442 (Peter Lang, 2013)

Women's Aid, *The Harm Report – One Year On* (The Transparency Project, 2021)

Women's Aid, *Transforming the Response to Domestic Abuse Consultation: Response from the Women's Aid Federation of England* (Women's Aid, 2018)

Women's Aid, *Two Years, Too Long: Mapping Action on the Harm Panel's Findings* (Women's Aid, 2022)
Women's Aid Federation England 2020, *Joint Recommendations Briefing for the Domestic Abuse Bill* (Women's Aid Federation England, 2020)
Woodcraft, E, 'Greenham Common Women's Peace Camp 1981–2000' in E Rackley and R Auchmuty (eds), *Women's Legal Landmarks: Celebrating Feminist Legal History* (Hart, 2018)
Woolf, V, *Diary of Virginia Woolf*, A Olivier Bell and A McNeillie (eds) (Hogarth Press, 1977–1984)
Workman, J, 'Normanton, Helena Florence (1882–1957), Barrister and Feminist Campaigner' in *Oxford Dictionary of National Biography* (DNB, 2011)
Wrobel, H, 'Otto Palandt zum Gedächtnis 1. 5. 1877–3. 12. 1951' (1982) 15(1) *Kritische Justiz* 1–17
Wrottesley, F, rev Samuels, A, 'Pollock, Ernest Murray, First Viscount Hanworth (1861–1936)' *Oxford Dictionary of National Biography* (DNB, 2004)
Wykes, T and Evans, J, 'Gender Diversity in the Journal of Mental Health – How Are We Doing and What Do We Need to Do?' (2020) 29 *Journal of Mental Health* 493
Yeatman, A, *Bureaucrats, Technocrats, Femocrats: Essays on the Contemporary Australian State* (Allen & Unwin, 1990)
Young, C and Boyd, S, 'Losing the Feminist Voice? Debates on the Legal Recognition of Same Sex Partnerships in Canada' (2006) 14 *Feminist Legal Studies* 213
Young, C, *What's Sex Got To Do With It? Tax and the Family in Canada* (Law Commission of Canada, 2000)
Young, C, 'Beyond Conjugality: Time for the Tax System to Take That Concept Seriously' in K Brooks (ed), *The Quest for Tax Reform Continues: The Royal Commission on Taxation Fifty Years Later* (Carswell, 2013)
Young, CFL, 'Taking Spousal Status into Account for Tax Purposes: The Pitfalls and Penalties' in A Bottomley and S Wong (eds), *Changing Contours of Domestic Life, Family and Law: Caring and Sharing* (Hart, 2009)
Zambrana, R, *Toxic Ivory Towers* (Rutgers University Press, 2018)
Zander, M, *Legal Services for the Community* (Maurice Temple Smith, 1978)
Zemans, FH and Thomas, A, 'Can Community Clinics Survive? A Comparative Study of Law Centres in Australia, Ontario and England' in F Regan et al (eds), *The Transformation of Legal Aid* (OUP, 1999).
Zimmermann, R, 'Was Heimat hieß, nun heißt es Hölle' in J Beatson and R Zimmermann (eds), *Jurists Uprooted. German-speaking Émigré Lawyers in Twentieth-century Britain* (OUP, 2004)

INDEX

www.ingramcontent.com/pod-product-compliance
Ingram Content Group UK Ltd.
Pitfield, Milton Keynes, MK11 3LW, UK
UKHW020242290926
15470UKWH00002B/683